Out of the Sweatshop

Out of the Sweatshop

The Struggle for Industrial Democracy

Edited by Leon Stein

Quadrangle/The New York Times Book Co.

Book design: Beth Tondreau

Library of Congress Cataloging in Publication Data

Main entry under title:

Out of the sweatshop.

Includes index.
1. International Ladies' Garment Workers Union—
History—Addresses, essays, lectures. 2. Clothing
workers—United States—History—Addresses, essays,
lectures. 3. Women—Employment—United States—
History—Addresses, essays, Lectures. I. Stein,
Leon, 1912–
HD6515.C508   331.88′18712   76-50828
ISBN 0-8129-0679-9

**For Rachel
to remember**

Contents

4. THE SHIRTWAIST MAKERS' STRIKE, 1909   59

5. THE CLOAKMAKERS' STRIKE, 1910   87

Contents

Acknowledgments

We would like to thank the copyright owners for permission to reprint the following articles:

"Toilers of the Tenement," by Theodore Dreiser, reprinted from *The Color of the City* by permission of The Dreiser Trust.

"The Italian Seamstress" is excerpted from *Italian Women in Industry* by Louise C. Odencrantz, pages 38–44 and 224–226. © 1919 The Russell Sage Foundation.

"Subcontracting," by Pearl Goodman and Elsa Ueland, and "The Stumbling Block," by J. B. McPherson, reprinted from the *Journal of Political Economy*, by permission of the University of Chicago Press.

"Survival of the Meanest" reprinted by permission of the publisher, The Vanguard Press, Inc., from *An East Side Epic: The Life and Work of Meyer London* by Harry Rogoff. Copyright 1930, 1957 by Harry Rogoff.

"Eyewitness at Triangle," by William G. Shepherd, reprinted by permission of United Press International.

"Safety Laws and Their Enforcement," by Alfred E. Smith, reprinted from *Up to Now: An Autobiography* by permission of The Viking Press. © 1929 by Alfred E. Smith.Copyright renewed by Walter J. Smith.

"The ILGWU Civil War," by Will Herberg, reprinted by permission from the *American Jewish Yearbook*, volume 53, 1952.

"The N.R.A. Codes," "The ILGWU Heads South," by Ed Townsend, and "Made in Japan," by Gordon Walker, reprinted by permission from *The Christian Science Monitor*. © 1933, 1954, 1955 The Christian Science Publishing Society. All rights reserved.

"The 1936 Challenge," by David Scheyer, reprinted by permission from the *Nation*.

"D.D. and the American Dream," by A. H. Raskin, reprinted with permission from *The New Leader*, March 11, 1966. Copyright © the American Labor Conference on International Affairs, Inc.

"The Price Line Shifts," by J. C. Furnas, reprinted from *The Saturday Evening Post*, © 1941 The Curtis Publishing Company. Copyright renewed © 1969 by J. C. Furnas. Reprinted by permission of Brandt & Brandt.

"The Color Line Is Green," copyright 1968 by Newsweek, Inc. All rights reserved. Reprinted by permission.

We would also like to thank *The American Federationist*, *The New Republic*, *Business Week*, *Memphis Press-Scimitar*, *Chicago Sun-Times*, *Women's Wear Daily*, *Atlanta Constitution*, *Southern Economic Journal*, and *The Economist* for permission to quote from their articles.

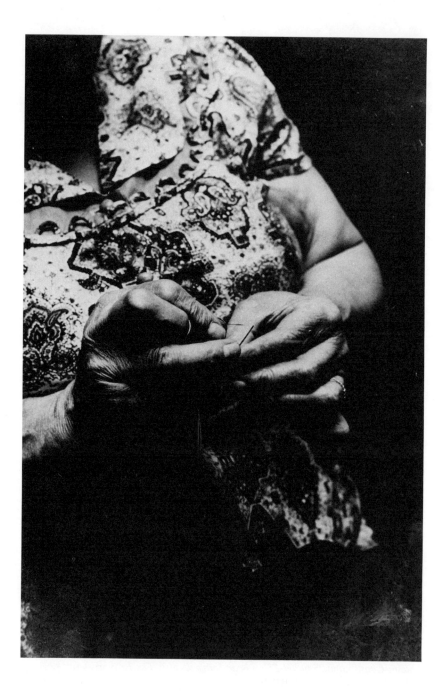

Introduction

The sweatshop is a state of mind as well as a physical fact. Its work day is of no fixed length; it links pace of work to endurance. It demeans the spirit by denying to workers any part in determining the conditions of or the pay for their work.

In the sweatshop, employers may discharge at will workers who protest against conditions or pay. The sweatshop, whether in a modern factory building or a dark slum cellar, exists where the employer controls the working conditions and the worker cannot protest.

During most of the nineteenth century workers were able to stage only occasional resistance to the sweating conditions in their shops. For the most part the campaign to remedy the abuses of the sweating system was conducted from outside the shop—by reformers, clergymen, and other humanitarians.

But with the arrival in the mid-1880s of masses of Jewish immigrants fleeing persecution in Czarist Russia there was a beginning of organized revolt against the sweatshop. Several factors contributed to this historic turn.

First, the newcomers brought with them great expectations, which persisted despite initial disenchantment caused by the realities of the ghetto. Second, many came to the Golden Land with considerable political and trade union experience so that organizing for a common effort was a familiar undertaking. Third, they came as a total community that included intellectuals as well as workmen, poets as well as barbers, and were thus able to achieve readily a formulation of goals.

The challenge for them was an industry that seemed to be impervious to union organizing. Production in the garment industry involved simple technology and handicraft skills. The heaviest equipment in use was the sewing machine. Cutting could be done in one place, sewing in another, and both could be done by small groups of workers. The result was a competitive and chaotic industry with a dispersed labor force always on the edge of hunger.

The product—fashioned women's garments—remains the most unstandardized and unpredictable commodity in the market economy. Its variations in size, price, purpose, and design; the uncertainties of future consumer fashion preferences, and of weather and season, all contribute to the frenetic production race with time and costs.

Finally, as it seemed clear to scholarly observers like John R. Commons at the start of the twentieth century, the people in the sweatshops were not the stuff out of which unions were generally organized. Immigrant men, women, and children, driven by the fear of hunger or the ambition to rise in the new, free homeland, trapped in the ghetto by the strange language and overbearing size of the host city, hidden in the tenement hovels where the sound of the sewing machine could be heard at all hours of the day and night, were improbable future members of a union.

This book tells how the improbabilities were overcome. The culmination of efforts to organize a ladies' garment workers' union came in 1910 when, after a lengthy strike, the cloakmakers of New York negotiated the Protocol of Peace. This collective agreement firmly established the International Ladies' Garment Workers' Union that had been founded in 1900, set the pattern for labor-management relations in the industry, defined the rights and responsibilities of management, labor, and the public, and opened new areas of trade union concern in health, sanitation, education, and political action.

Today, the garment industry remains basically a handicraft industry, but one in which analysis of job and work flow plays an increasingly important role. Production of garments has spread from large city centers to rural areas. More recently, employers, seeking helpless, low-wage workers—as of old—have taken their production overseas and have revived the sweatshop. Now, as in the past, ILGWU members and leaders are involved in the fight to preserve hard-earned standards against the erosion of competing substandard production.

In this book, the story of the garment workers' battle against the sweatshop is told by presidents, professors, and garment pressers; by journalists, scholars, and historians; by participants in and witnesses of the events described. My concern has been with the work as well as the worker, with the union member as well as the union leader. Their narrative styles vary and I have left them that way.

But cut, trimmed, shaped, and joined together with minimum editorial comment, the selections in this book make a unique mosaic depicting an important and inspiring phase of the American struggle for industrial democracy. I have been aided by my colleague Meyer Miller, supported by ILGWU President Sol C. Chaikin and Executive Vice President Wilbur Daniels, encouraged by my wife, Miriam, and my daughter, Barbara, and inspired by the wonderful men and women in the garment shops whose ranks I joined as a member of the ILGWU fifty years ago, whom I served first as union organizer and educator, and then for the past quarter of a century as editor of *Justice*.

Out of the Sweatshop

1. Sweatshop—Native Style

The roots of the sweatshop can be found in the home. At the start of the nineteenth century, a vast, invisible army of women still labored by lamplight at day's end, sewing the family's garments with needle, thread, and thimble. They learned to measure, adjust, and fit the fabric. The latter was not always easy to come by; garments were handed down or taken apart so skillfully that in recutting, usable areas of fabric might be salvaged.

Fashion was beyond the reach of most women. But for those with means it had become a primary symbol of wealth and status. Itinerant tailors and dressmakers regularly visited wealthier rural homesteads and brought costly fabrics and rare sewing skills. In the towns, resident seamstresses were ready with the latest fashion news from Europe. In time, stores in the larger cities displayed bolts of expensive materials from which lengths were sold. Engraved plates of the latest fashions pictured what the sewing girls in the workrooms located at the back of the store were ready to make to measure.

While the custom-made garment continued to be produced for the individual customer of means, the ready-to-wear garment produced at the start of the century introduced the daring idea that apparel could be made in advance of sale to as yet unspecified customers.

Several problems had to be surmounted in order to produce garments for stock, including anticipating the customer's needs and style preferences. Early on in the century, enterprising operators—notably those located in the eastern seaboard cities catering to the supply needs of sailors waiting for their ships to be turned around—discovered that their customers cared little for fit and less for style. Their chief demand was for shirts and pants made of sturdy fabric and ready on demand.

Waterfront slop shops began to stock such items. Agents for these shops in areas around Boston found a labor force desperate for work among the wives and daughters of impoverished farmers and of men off to the sea or venturing westward across the continent. At the start of each week, the agents would ride the usual circuit to distribute the cut parts of the garments, which they would then collect at the end of the week. In order to keep the lid on wage rates, they played off the out-of-town sewers against their impoverished sisters trapped in the furnished rooms of Boston's slums.

The system of farming out work, an American version of the British cottage industries, was well developed by 1846, the year in which Elias Howe produced a practical sewing machine. Apparel producers, who appreciated the difference between fashion and utility garments, had by this time introduced elements of mass production with production by a large group of workers assembled in a single workroom. Workers in charge of making undergarments, hoops, bandeaux, slips, pantaloons, and other nonvisible items worked in large, crowded rooms. They could still put only two pieces of fabric together at one time. However, as a result of subsequent improvements on Howe's contraption by Isaac Singer and others, they could put these two pieces together with greater speed.

The selections in this chapter trace the effects of the production of women's apparel as a salable commodity and foreshadow future developments in the garment industry. For example, Helen L. Sumner cites employers who used learners to keep wages down and records the existence of a true sweating system before mid-century. Mathew Carey rejects the interplay of supply and demand as the means used to determine seamstresses' wage rates and pleads for a moral minimum wage. John B. Andrews cites a machinists' union organizer who called for equal pay for equal work.

James Parton reports that while Howe's machine was at first sold in fashionable Broadway stores as a status symbol meant to be displayed in the parlor alongside the piano, workers soon recognized its potential for exploitation and turned their backs on it.

While Virginia Penny inspected apparel factories, Wirt Sikes, equating city and sin, went below stairs to the grimy, high-fashion sweatshops; both perceived the terrible human cost of the fast pace of production.

The Working Women's Protective Union, motivated by high moral standards and the wish to uplift the disadvantaged, provided practical help by processing individual worker's complaints. Carroll D. Wright, in scholarly fashion, rebutted the popular belief that the working girl easily slipped into the ways of sin.

Generations of theatergoers have thrilled to Francis S. Smith's creation, Bertha, the sewing machine girl, who first appeared in his low-priced story paper in 1871. In an immortal moment of independence, she told her villainous employer what he could do with his charity.

Sumner (1876–1933) was one of the scholars who, under John R. Commons's direction, produced basic studies of American labor history. From "History of Women in Industry in the United States, Report on Conditions of Women and Child Wage-earners in the United States," Volume IX; 61st Congress, 2nd Session, Senate Document No. 645, 1910.

A TRUE SWEATING SYSTEM
by Helen L. Sumner

Mathew Carey asserted in 1829 that a comparison of the prices charged to the public for articles and the wages paid for their manufacture proved that wages might be raised sufficiently to insure comfort. In 1836 the *Philadelphia Public Ledger* stated that "a common stock, the material of which cost about 25 cents, and for making which a female receives about as much more, is sold by a merchant tailor for $3 or 500 percent advance." Those who employed female labor, added the *Ledger,* were "deriving from it immense fortunes."

Orestes Brownson, too, commenting in 1840 upon the insufficient wages of the seamstresses, blamed the employer who, he said, "grows rich on their labor—passes among us as a pattern of morality, and is honored as a worthy Christian." Four years later the *New York Sun* also referred to the merchants as "getting rich from the labor of the poor, because," it said, "as fair prices are paid for clothing, if seamstresses and tailoresses only received sufficient for their work to enable them to live, no complaint would be made."

In 1845, the chairwoman of a meeting of working women in New York said that she knew several employers who paid only from 10 to 18 cents per day, and that one employer, who offered girls 20 cents per day, told them that if they did not take it "he would obtain girls from Connecticut who would work for less even than what he offered."

By 1844, moreover, and probably earlier, there were instances of the true sweating system. In that year it was recorded that a man and two women working together from 12 to 16 hours a day earned a dollar amongst them, and that the women, if they did not belong to the family, received each about $1.25 a week for their work, the man paying out of the remaining $3.50 about $1 a week for rent of his garret, and being obliged to pay this amount whether employed or not.

In 1853, moreover, the investigation of the clothing trade made by the *New York Tribune* disclosed the existence of a "middle system." For example, near one of the streets running from the Bowery to the East River an old Irish woman was found who had four girls at work for her, their compensation consisting solely of food for six days of the week. In another case a woman had hired four "learners," two of whom received only board and lodging, and the other two $1 a week each without food. These were all evidently instances of the true sweating system.

Publisher and pamphleteer Carey (1760–1839) fled to Philadelphia in 1784 to avoid arrest in England. From "Appeal to the Wealthy of the Land, Ladies as Well as Gentlemen, On the Character, Conduct, Situation, and Prospects of Those Whose Sole Dependence for Subsistence Is on the Labor of Their Hands," 1833.

AN APPEAL TO THE WEALTHY OF THE LAND
by Mathew Carey

In discussing the sufferings of the seamstresses, etc., I have been pleading the cause of probably 12,000 women in Boston, New York, Philadelphia, and Baltimore, (with souls as precious in the eye of heaven as the most exalted females that ever trod the earth—as a Maria Theresa, a Princess Victoria, a Mrs. Washington, a Mrs. Madison, or a Mrs. Monroe), who are greviously oppressed and reduced to the utmost penury, in a land literally flowing with milk and honey, while many of those for whom they toil, make immense fortunes, by their labours.

Nine cotton shirts a week are as much as the great mass of seamstresses can make. Those shirts are frequently made for 6, 8, and 10 cents, leaving 54, 72, 90 cents a week for the incessant application of a human being, during thirteen or fourteen hours a day, for the payment of rent, the purchase of food, clothes, drink, soap, candles and fuel! !

It is often triumphantly asked, respecting the case of the women who are so very inadequately remunerated for their labours, What remedy can be applied to such an inveterate evil? Does not the proportion between supply and demand, in this, as in all other cases, regulate prices? And while there is such an over-proportion of labour in the market, must not competition reduce prices, as it has done, to the lowest grade, even below the minimums necessary to support existence?

I contend that every principle of honour, justice, and generosity, forbids the employer to take advantage of the distress and wretchedness of those he employs, and cut down their wages below the minimum necessary to procure a sufficiency of plain food and of clothes to guard against the inclemency of the weather. Whoever passes this line of demarcation, is guilty of the heinous offence of "grinding the faces of the poor." And I am persuaded that there are thousands of honourable men who give inadequate wages to males as well as females, merely because they have never thought sufficiently on the subject; and who, therefore, have no idea of the real state of the case.

They not only enjoy all the comforts and luxuries of life, but many of them make immense fortunes. My object is to induce upright men thus circumstanced, to scrutinize the affair, and obey the dictates of their better feelings as soon as they have ascertained the truth. Of the honourable issue I cannot entertain a doubt.

The ladies will, I hope, pardon me for an observation which applies to some of them, but I hope only a few. I have known a lady expend a hundred dollars on a party; pay thirty or forty dollars on a bonnet, and fifty for a shawl; and yet make a hard bargain with a seamstress or washerwoman, who had to work at her needle or at the washing tub for thirteen or fourteen hours a day, to make a bare livelihood for herself and a numerous family of small children! This is a "sore oppression under the sun," and ought to be eschewed by every honourable mind. "Let it be reformed altogether."

In 1867 the Weed Sewing Machine Company pictured the late-night hand sewing work its machine was designed to abolish.

Andrews (1880–1943) was a member of the Wisconsin-
Commons group of young labor historians. From "History
of Women in Trade Unions, Report on Conditions of
Women and Child Wage-earners in the United States,"
Volume X; 61st Congress, 2nd Session, Senate Document
No. 645, 1911.

HAND-IN-HAND
by John B. Andrews

The condition of the "sewing women" in our large cities has never
been an enviable one, but during the period beginning with the opening of the Civil War their plight was truly distressing. To the familiar
unfortunate circumstance of tenement-house work with low wages
and long hours was added the accidental competition of thousands of
"war-widows."

On January 24, 1865, women held a large mass meeting at Early
Closing Hall, No. 267 Bowery, under the auspices of the Working
Women's Union. Miss M. Trimble, the president, presided, and
another lady officiated as secretary. Several prominent leaders in the
men's trade union movement were among the speakers.

Malcolm Macleod, organizer for the machinists, said: "The proper
way to improve the condition of any class of the laboring community
is to increase its compensation, and until this is done no permanent
improvement may be expected." He would have more faith, he said,
"in the cry to open more avenues to female labor" if the same remu-
neration was given to the females that was previously given to men
performing the same work.

William Harding, president of the New York Trades Assembly,
invited the women to attend a mass meeting at Cooper Institute and
told them their influence was indispensable. He urged the sewing
women to ask their gentlemen friends whether they belonged to any
trade organization, and if not to induce them to join immediately.

"If they do not join," said the speaker, "then have nothing to do
with them, and tell them you do not wish to associate with any gentleman who refuses to aid in a movement calculated to benefit his
fellow-man."

At this meeting, 18 new members were admitted, the regular members forming in a ring to receive them, and singing:

> Welcome, sisters, to our number,
> Welcome to our heart and hand,
> At our post we will not slumber,
> Strong in union we shall stand.

The lady president then addressed the new members as follows:
"Sisters, from a favorable opinion entertained of you by the members of this society, you are admitted as one of our members. It is a

mark of our esteem and confidence that we extend to you a sister's welcome. You will be expected to attend our stated meetings, and are bound to observe our laws by the strongest of human ties—your sacred honor. In the lodge let your conduct exhibit a womanly frankness and sisterly courtesy; above all be careful to cultivate a forgiving spirit; write the errors of your sisters in sand, but engrave their virtues on the tablets of enduring memory, that you may learn to imitate them. Let no consideration of personal regard mislead you in recommending an unsuitable person to become a member of this society.

"This chain which you now behold is a bond of that union that should always exist among working women. Remember that union is power; a good many can help one when one can not help the many. Behold, the chain is now broken that you may be added as another link.

"In conclusion, sisters (taking them by the hand), I congratulate you most cordially on your accession to our society, and with the best wishes for your prosperity I commend you to their friendship. Sing:

No angry passions here should mar
Our peace, or move our social band,
For friendship is our beacon star,
Our motto, union, hand in hand."

Parton (1822–1891) was the most famous biographer of his day and interviewed many of the subjects whose lives he recorded. From "History of the Sewing Machine," *Atlantic Monthly,* May 1867.

CONTEST: HAND VS. MACHINE
by James Parton

Like all the other great inventors, Mr. Howe found that, when he had completed his machine, his difficulties had but begun. After he had brought the machine to the point of making a few stitches he went to Boston one day to get a tailor to come to Cambridge and arrange some cloth for sewing, and give his opinion as to the quality of the work done by the machine. The comrades of the man to whom he first applied dissuaded him from going, alleging that a sewing machine, if it worked well, must necessarily reduce the whole fraternity of tailors to beggary; and this proved to be the unchangeable conviction of the tailors for the next ten years.

It is probable that the machines first made would have been destroyed by violence, but for another fixed opinion of the tailors, which was, that no machine could be made that would really answer the purpose. Mr. Howe, a few weeks after he had finished his first model, gave them an opportunity to see what it could do. He placed his little engine in one of the rooms of the Quincy Hall Clothing Manufactory, and, seating himself before it, offered to sew any seam that might be brought to him.

One unbelieving tailor after another brought a garment, and saw its long seams sewed perfectly, at the rate of two hundred and fifty stitches a minute, which was about seven times as fast as the work could be done by hand. For two weeks he sat there daily, and sewed up seams for all who chose to bring them to him.

At last, he challenged five of the swiftest seamstresses in the establishment to sew a race with the machine. Ten seams of equal length were prepared for sewing, five of which were laid by the machine, and the other five given to the girls. The gentleman who held the watch, and who was to decide the wager, testified, upon oath, that the five girls were the fastest sewers that could be found, and that they "sewed as fast as they could—much faster than they were in the habit of sewing"—faster than they could have kept on for one hour. Nevertheless, Mr. Howe finished his five seams a little sooner than the girls finished their five; and the umpire, who was himself a tailor, has sworn, that "the work done on the machine was the neatest and strongest."

Penny (1826–?) devoted many years of her life and her meager financial resources to compiling a pioneer survey of work opportunities for women. From *How Women Can Make Money, Married or Single,* 1870.

HOOP SKIRTS
by Virginia Penny

There are now hundreds of women employed in the manufacture of hoopskirts, that will, when the fashion ceases, be thrown out of employment. What resource will they have? It may be that some other fashion will spring up requiring their services, but we doubt it.

D. & S., New York, employ from 600 to 1,000, and once had 1,500 girls working for them. They have large well-aired rooms. We passed through and saw their girls at work. They were neat, well-dressed, and cheerful looking. Nine tenths are Americans. Most of the girls have homes.

The trade of D. & S. is Southern. Their girls earn from $4 to $8 per week, and working 9½ hours a day in winter. The girls can change their position frequently. Women are superior to men for this kind of work. While learning, girls receive enough to pay their board. The continuance of this occupation depends entirely on fashion. S. thinks the fashion as likely to last as the wearing of bonnets. Most of the small establishments in this business have been absorbed by the large ones. From December to April are the best seasons for work; from June to September the most slack.

T., a large manufacturer, says the average pay is from $4 to $4.50. His forewoman earns $400 a year. Some girls are dull, and some are smart—so the time of learning depends much on that. They pay the girls something from the time they begin to learn. They work ten hours a day. Some they pay by the piece; some, by the day, and others, by the week, or year. Some seasons they employ about one thousand work people, of whom nine hundred and fifty are women and girls.

I saw, at a factory, some girls covering wire for hoops. The machinery was very ingenious. They are paid $3, and a few $3.50. They have to stand all the time, and watch their work constantly. They work ten hours. Owing to the want of proper management on the part of the proprietor, I found the girls do not have work steadily. Sometimes they get out of clasps, or tape, or hoops, and cannot get them immediately, because of their distance from the stores.

More hoopskirts are manufactured in New York than in any other city. I was in a factory where hoopskirts were woven by hand. The weaver girl we spoke to, said she did not get tired now, but did when she commenced. The girls are paid by the piece, and a good weaver, when industrious, can earn $1 a day.

Those at machines sit, and those at frames stand. Some skirts excel in elegance of shape, some in durability, and some in elasticity. Many improvements have been made since their introduction into this country. The prices paid were better at first than since there has been so much competition.

In New York City there is always a surplus of girls seeking labor; they are daughters of the poorer classes, and live in tenement houses, in close quarters—are shabbily clad, and their wages go to support perhaps a drunken father, or a widowed mother and fatherless children. This class of girls contrast sadly in looks and health with country girls, accustomed to breathe the free air of heaven. Their flattened chests, pale faces, and scanty wardrobe tell too plainly of the competition of labor among girls in the great city.

Representatives of the Working Women's Protective Union hear a complaint against a sewing machine dealer. (R. Lewis in *Harper's Weekly*, February 21, 1874)

> Sikes, a popular social reformer in his day, worked with church groups and supported the efforts of the Working Women's Protective Union. From *Putnam's Magazine*, April 1868.

AMONG THE POOR GIRLS
by Wirt Sikes

There are some roomy and cheerful shops in the city. But there are scores, and hundreds, that are not roomy and cheerful. The worst of these are owned and conducted by women. Look into this establishment, where Madame Fripperie, the fashionable dressmaker, holds her court. It is a handsome building, in one of the streets of the Fifteenth Ward. Hour on hour, throughout the day, the carriages of Fifth-avenue ladies drive up before her door. The liveried driver sits on the box waiting, while his liveried mistress trips up the steps, to consult with Madame on the new silk contemplated, planned, or in progress.

While the momentous question is being discussed, let us slip down these stairs into the basement. This is the workroom. Faugh, how it smells! There is no attempt at ventilation. The room is crowded with girls and women, most of whom are pale and attenuated, and are being robbed of life slowly and surely. The rose which should bloom in their cheeks has vanished long ago. The sparkle has gone out of their eyes. They bend over their work with aching backs and throbbing brows; sharp pains dart through their eyeballs; they breathe an atmosphere of death. Madame pays her girls four dollars a week. She herself lives in as fine a style as the richest lady she serves.

And this is the story—a true one: Susie L____ was a beautiful girl of seventeen, the daughter of a farmer in western New York. Her eyes were black and brilliant; her lips were red with rich life-blood of health; her complexion was pure pink and white, with such a lustrous, blooming freshness as is seldom seen, even among farmers' girls. Susie was a superior seamstress; her fingers were nimble, and her work always beautiful. Especially was she skilful in embroidery work; and in the old farm-house you may still see specimens of her handiwork, the pride of her mother and the wonder of the farmers' wives for miles about.

She came to New York to work, and it was not long before she found employment in the shop last named above. The prices there paid are of the best that are paid in the city; Susie received a dollar a day. That she should get rich very soon, the girl felt sure; and it does not take much money to make a simple farmer's girl feel rich. It was two miles from her boarding-place to the shop; but such was her high health and strength, that she made nothing of walking this distance, morning and night.

Three months had not passed before she found her strength unequal to the task, and thereafter she rode to and fro in the streetcars. Dark lines had come under her eyes; her complexion was losing its color, her form its roundness and its springy life. In a word, the poison had entered her system, and was killing her by degrees. Still, in her pride, her anxiety to make the "old folks" happy—she had sent home to her father more than one welcome bank note—she concealed her sufferings, and struggled on.

One day she dropped from her chair heavily upon the floor of the dark, noisome apartment—was conveyed to her sister's home—and, when she left it again, a hearse stood at the door, and she was borne to her grave. She had not been one year absent from her country home.

"The Industrious Needlewomen" by M. Trayer (1885).

The American Working Women's Protection Union was a social agency for dealing with grievances brought to it by individual workers. From "Fifteenth Annual Report, Working Women's Protective Union," November 19, 1878.

SPECIMEN CASES OF FRAUD

Case 5134. Bangs, Macy & Evans are dealers in dress goods in one of the extreme Western cities. They applied to the Union for a dress trimmer, and Harriet Springer, of Harlem, was recommended, and engaged for one year at a salary of fifteen dollars per week. The engagement was liberal, but Harriet was an expert and could command good pay in any establishment, and she was required in this case to make a new home for herself in a faraway place.

While "the season" lasted—about four and a half months—her employers treated her as they had promised; but when the "busy time" was over they were ready to break the contract. "A new victim for another year" was, apparently, their method of reasoning; and so Harriet was unceremoniously dismissed, without even so much consideration as a passage ticket back to her home. But the four months' earnings had been saved in large part, and soon her story was told at the rooms of the Union.

In due time Bangs, Macy & Evans were called upon to defend a suit for $175, as damages. Somewhat astonished that a poor girl could get judgment against them at a district court, they filed bonds and appealed to a higher and more costly process of litigation. But even there they were followed, and after a sharp contest were again defeated. And now they are debating whether to pay the claim—the amount of which has been nearly doubled by costs incurred—or make a higher appeal. Harriet will get every cent that is due to her. The cost of getting it will be paid by the Union.

Case 6115. Raisebread & Son on Broadway employed Esther Merriman, of East 20th Street, in the making of scarfs at seventy cents per dozen, giving her a sample scarf to show the work they required. Three dozen were made, and the $2.10 payment for the weeks' work was asked for. But the Raisebreads discovered that the work was not well done.

To the Union the case came, and there the gentlemen were requested to point out the inferior workmanship of which they complained. They did this with great alacrity, and when they had found particular fault with one of the scarfs, they were shown that this particular scarf was the one they had given Esther as a sample to work by.

With most men this would have ended the contest, but they persisted in argument and explanation until they found that $2.10, or a suit at law, were the only alternatives. Then, suddenly, they became benevolent and paid the $2.10 "for charity sake."

Wright (1840–1909), head of the Massachusetts Bureau of Statistics of Labor, became the first U.S. Labor Commissioner. From "Fifteenth Annual Report, Massachusetts Bureau of Statistics of Labor," 1884.

THE WORKING GIRLS OF BOSTON
by Carroll D. Wright

In the *Clothing* business, the general testimony is that the work is very hard, and is the cause of a great deal of sickness among the working girls so employed. The tax on the strength is very great, and it would seem that unless a girl is strong and robust, the work soon proves too severe for her, and if followed thereafter results disastrously.

The running of heavy sewing machines by foot power soon breaks down a girl's health, as several girls have testified. One girl says that steam was introduced six months ago to her great satisfaction, as she thinks foot-power machines too severe for female operators. The girls think all the machines should be run by steam. Other girls object to standing so much.

A girl who used to bring her work home, says she overtaxed her strength and is now sick. Others say that overwork, and the desire to do more than strength would allow, has very seriously affected their health. Several girls testify that they work at times when they ought to be in bed, but being obliged to work, cannot take all the rest needed to fully recover strength. One girl in particular (a press girl) says she is now doing work formerly done by a man, is obliged to be on her feet all day, and in the vicinity of two hot fires.

Dressmakers, for themselves, get from $2 to $3 per day, with meals; when on a long job, one reports that she gets $10 a week.

Seamstresses, on dresses are paid 75 cents to $1 per day; in private families, $1 a day and board; and when going out by the day, $1.50 per day. A seamstress on buttons gets 10 cents a set for sewing buttons on wrappers, a set being 18 wrappers.

A *sewing machine operator* on fine "white goods" can make from $11 to $15 a week.

A *buttonhole maker* on ladies' dresses gets 3 cents a piece; a good price, it is said, and good wages can be made.

Cloak and sack makers say they have to work very hard to average $6 a week the year round, prices being low; one girl gives her weekly earnings for the year, as follows: 8 weeks at $9; 8 at $2.50; 13 at $9; 13 at $2.50; 5 at $9; and 5 weeks idle; average $6.09. The prices paid in some places are 15 cents for an entire cloak, raised, however, on protest to 25 cents; and 22 cents for making a short walking coat, running two rows of stitching around the entire edge and sewing on 30 buttons.

It takes 3½ hours to make a cloak for 25 cents. In making Jersey sacks, one girl says she got 90 cents for making a sack by hand, which took three days to finish; she was obliged to take the work home and sit up until 11 at night to make $2.50 a week. Another girl says she has to baste, stitch, and face with crinoline, and finish seven seams, for 25 cents.

Bustle makers used to get 65, 75, and 85 cents a dozen, but the price has been recently cut down 15 cents; the bustles are now made for 50, 60, and 70 cents per dozen. They can do one and one half dozen a day by working from 8:30 A.M. to 6 P.M., with half an hour for dinner. The work is often slack and they are now making a bustle which pays but 25 cents a dozen, and a girl can make a dozen only per day.

The idea that well-dressed girls receiving low wages must live disreputable lives is a very common one, but a large number of these girls live in comfortable homes with parents in comparatively easy circumstances and well able and willing to support their children, who pay little or no board and spend their earnings as they please, chiefly for dress.

Other well-dressed girls, who live at home, turn their earnings into the common family fund and their clothes are provided for by their parents and these are generally made during the evening by themselves, and by skill and ingenuity a good appearance is made at little cost.

It is only the few who are well dressed and helped by their friends, who attract attention, and of these the question is often asked, how can they dress well when they earn so little? Such questions led to the idea that they take up prostitution, but the fact that the girl works hard all day for three or four dollars a week is sufficient proof that she is not living in prostitution; girls cannot work hard all day and be prostitutes too.

The fact that here and there a girl forsakes the path of virtue and lives a sinful life should not be used to the detriment of the class to which she belongs, especially when her life is peculiarly exposed to temptation, as is the case with girls struggling along on five dollars or less per week. It is easy to be good on a sure and generous income; it requires the strongest character to enable one to be good and respectable on an unstable income of five dollars per week.

Early in 1871, the *New-York Weekly,* a popular story paper, began a serial entitled "Bertha, the Sewing Machine Girl, or Death at the Wheel," by Francis S. Smith. The following year it was dramatized by Charles Foster. This excerpt is from act I, scene 3.

BERTHA, THE SEWING MACHINE GIRL
by Francis S. Smith and Charles Foster

CALEB: There, Miss Bascomb, are your wages in full, and it's more than you deserve. It is simply charity on my part. I hope that you will appreciate it.

BERTHA: Charity? Yes, it's very charitable. Very. You are charitable, Mr. Carson. Look around your factory and gaze into the faces of

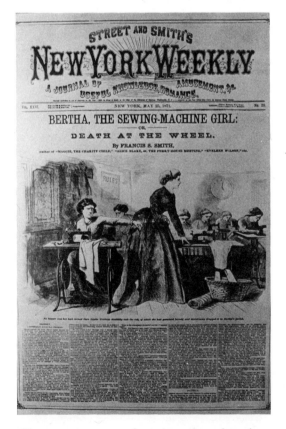

First appearance of an American heroine.

some of the poverty-stricken people in your employ. Contrast your ill-gotten gains with the miserable pittance paid those patient, willing hands already grown feeble with work that fills your coffers and then talk of charity. You do not know the meaning of that sacred word; not that we seek it at your hands, thank Heaven. Poor and underpaid as many of your working girls are, they inherit some of the old spirit of independence that has made our country great. And while they demand fair returns for a fair day's work, they neither ask nor will they accept from you what you call charity.

CALEB: Oho, a firebrand, eh?

BERTHA: No sir, an honest working girl, and I know of no more honorable title. (returns to her work)

CALEB: Curses on her proud spirit. I'll find some way of taming it.

2. Sweatshop—Immigrant Style

The assassination of Czar Alexander II in March 1881 had a direct and profound effect on the garment industry in the United States. This desperate act by a group of young revolutionaries who considered the czar's liberal reforms inadequate merely opened the way for a much more reactionary successor. To hide their own corruption, the sycophants and grafters comprising the newcomer's court entourage encouraged a wave of bloody and diversionary pogroms against the Jewish enclaves in towns and rural areas of Russia.

The exodus thus touched off sent a stream of Jewish refugees westward across Europe, their hearts and hopes fixed on the vision of a better and freer life in the land across the ocean. Emerging from the stifling holds of the ships which transported them to the Golden Land of Opportunity they soon discovered that their new homeland was an urban slum or ghetto in cities whose size and pace first stunned and then puzzled them.

There was a desperate need to find work. As Ray Stannard Baker points out in the first selection of this chapter, everyone could sew. With entire families converted into miniature labor forces, men, women, and children sweated in a confusion of kitchen, workshop, bedroom and nursery, quickly realizing that tyrannies had been exchanged but not escaped.

The hellish homework scene has been described by numerous reformers, each of whom has stressed its destructive effect on human existence. The excerpts by Jacob A. Riis and Edwin Markham represent a sampling of the large body of documentary literature devoted to life in the slums at the turn of the century. Riis's reforming zeal was a precursor of the muckrakers and progressive campaigns to come. In the last year of the century, Markham had stirred the nation with a powerful poem entitled "The Man with the Hoe"; the latter envisioned the degradation of the worker through oppression and endless toil.

Millions of immigrants who had made the traumatic leap from a peasant or medieval town life existence to the streets of the great metropolis turned the ghetto into a fortress. Within its walls newcomers anxiously sought to halt the march of time and the process of change by preserving Old World traits and customs. Inevitably, however, the enticements of the new life seeped through defenses and the need for work and wages penetrated the invisible ghetto walls.

The article from the *Commercial Advertiser* heralds a new breed of child worker. The agonizing fear and trembling of the first job experience is unforgettably pictured by Rose Cohen. In New York, as well as in such distant immigrant enclaves as those located in Chicago, mass revolt simmered. Florence Kelley, first Illinois state factory inspector, penetrated the vast netherworld of the Chicago sweatshops and charted its human geography in her testimony before the U.S. Industrial Commission.

The most significant aspect of the Jewish exodus from Russia was its all-inclusiveness. Other nations sent only select groups of their children to make their fortunes in the New World—those hungry for land, the politically disaffected, even the criminal. But the population streaming out of Russia represented a total community, including scholars as well as shoemakers, journalists as well as lawyers, plus barbers, bakers, and playwrights.

They could thus discover within their own ranks the resources necessary for social self-analysis and action, based on experience in fighting tyranny and prejudice in the Old World.

William M. Leiserson's scholarly pioneer study recounts the first immigrant strike by the newcomers. The selection by Abraham Rosenberg carries the story forward from the days of the Knights of Labor to increasingly daring organizational efforts in what was then considered a distant, out-of-town satellite (Jamaica, Long Island) of the New York garment center. The *New York Times* article describes one of the frequent confrontations between strikers and police.

In terms of lasting results, the strikes and walkouts of the final decade of the last century were not enough. The gains secured at the end of one season disappeared at the beginning of the next. Looking back on these events, Joseph Barondess, the first major labor leader of the garment industry, notes that the strikes drained human energy and resources, often alienated public support, and substituted sound and fury for the evolutionary development which alone could consolidate the scores of battles and skirmishes and mold them into a single, enduring union.

Baker (1870–1946) a member of the World War I Peace
Commission and biographer of Woodrow Wilson, was on
the editorial staff of the leading muckraking publication.
From *McClure's Magazine,* December 1904.

PLIGHT OF THE TAILORS
by Ray Stannard Baker

Each year crowds of foreign immigrants poured into the East Side.
They were poor, ignorant, and they had been oppressed; they knew
nothing of American life, though they expected much; they found at
once that living here—rent, food, fuel—was far more expensive than
in their old homes. The first necessity, therefore, was work, no matter
what, to furnish them with the necessaries of life.

There are not many things that an unskilled foreigner, knowing no
English, can do; but almost any man or woman can sew. And thus
flourished the sweatshop, the home of the "task system," where men,
women and children worked together in unhealthful, often diseased,
and sometimes immoral surroundings. Nowhere in the world at any
time, probably, were men and women worked as they were in the
sweatshop—the lowest paid, most degrading of American employment. The sweatshop employer ground all the work he could from
every man, woman and child under him.

It was no uncommon thing in these sweatshops for men to sit bent
over a sewing machine continuously from eleven to fifteen hours a
day in July weather, operating a sewing machine by foot-power, and
often so driven that they could not stop for lunch. The seasonal
character of the work meant demoralizing toil for a few months in the
year and a not less demoralizing idleness for the remainder of the
time.

A bronzed, wiry young peasant, coming here to the land of freedom and hope from the oppressions of Russia, sat down at a sewing
machine in a hot, dusty, fetid tenement-shop in East Broadway or
Clinton Street; and sometimes he lasted five years, sometimes seven,
rarely ten. Caught in the wheels of a "cold, universal, laissez-faire," he
was wrung dry, worn out in half a dozen years, and flung upon the
human scrap heap. He had merely changed oppressions—from the
political tyranny of Russia to the industrial tyranny of America; and
while the former had robbed him of some of his rights, the latter took
his life.

Riis (1849–1914) was a police reporter, social reformer and friend of Theodore Roosevelt. From *How the Other Half Lives*, 1890.

BUSY SEASON
by Jacob A. Riis

Turning the corner into Hester Street, we stumble upon a nest of cloak-makers in their busy season. Six months of the year the cloak-maker is idle, or nearly so. Now is his harvest. Seventy-five cents a cloak, all complete, is the price in this shop. The cloak is of cheap plush, and might sell for eight or nine dollars over the store counter.

Seven dollars is the weekly wage of this man with wife and two children, and nine dollars and a half rent to pay per month. A boarder pays about a third of it. There was a time when he made ten dollars a week and thought himself rich. But wages have come down fearfully in the last two years. Think of it: "come down" to this.

The other cloak-makers aver that they can make as much as twelve dollars a week, when they are employed, by taking their work home and sewing till midnight. One exhibits his account-book with a Ludlow Street sweater. It shows that he and his partner, working on first-class garments for a Broadway house in the four busiest weeks of the season, made together from $15.15 to $19.20 a week by striving from 6 A.M. to 11 P.M., that is to say, from $7.58 to $9.60 each.

The sweater on this work probably made as much as fifty percent, at least on their labor. Not far away is a factory in a rear yard where the factory inspector reports teams of tailors making men's coats at an average of twenty-seven cents a coat, all complete except buttons and buttonholes.

The Third Annual Report of the Bureau of Statistics of Labor, State of New York (1885) located this sweatshop on the top floor of 12 Hester Street.

In 1899, a poem by Markham (1852–1940) entitled "The Man with the Hoe" stirred the nation with its poetic depiction of brutalized labor. From *Cosmopolitan Magazine,* January 1907.

LABOR FORCE: CHILDREN

by Edwin Markham

And the children are called in from play to drive and drudge beside their elders. The load falls upon the ones least able to bear it—upon the backs of the little children at the base of the labor pyramid.

All the year in New York and in other cities you may watch children radiating to and from such pitiful homes. Nearly any hour on the East Side of New York City you can see them—pallid boy or spindling girl—their faces dulled, their backs bent under a heavy load of garments piled on head and shoulders, the muscles of the whole frame in a long strain. The boy always has bowlegs and walks with feet wide apart and wobbling.

In the rush times of the year, preparing for the changes of seasons or for the great "white sales," there are no idle fingers in the sweatshops. A little child of "seven times one" can be very useful in threading needles, in cutting the loose threads left on, or for any stitch broken by the little bungling fingers. The light is not good, but baby eyes must "look sharp."

In New York City alone, 60,000 children are shut up in the home sweatshops. This is a conservative estimate, based upon a recent investigation of the Lower East Side of Manhattan Island, south of 14th Street and east of the Bowery. Many of this immense host will never sit on a school bench.

Is it not a cruel civilization that allows little hearts and little shoulders to strain under these grown-up responsibilities, while in the same city a pet cur is jeweled and pampered and aired on a fine lady's velvet lap on the beautiful boulevards?

The *Commercial Advertiser* was edited by muckraker Lincoln Steffens. The following unsigned report is from the issue of August 13, 1898.

THE BOY ORGANIZER

The children's jacketmakers' strike is as good as ended. The first settlements were made yesterday, and one of the wits among the strikers entertained a crowd of his fellows by pointing out to them that the first agreement between a boss and the union had been signed at the same hour as the peace protocol was signed by the representatives of the United States and Spain.

The settlement presented the same scenes which attended the conclusion of every tailors' strike, but there was a novel feature in addition, and that was the role played in them by the so-called boy agitator of the East Side.

Harry Gladstone, who is about 15 years old, is a machine tender or "basting puller" in a sweatshop. He has been in this country eight years, only three of which he spent in the Chrystie Street Grammar School. Still he speaks English fluently enough, and prefers that tongue to his native Yiddish in addressing the boys, whom he is fond of referring to as his "fellow workmen."

His prominence in the children's jacketmakers' strike was due to the initiative he took in organizing the boys and girls of the trade. The union he founded is 75 strong, the youngest boy in it being 12 years old. Asked about the age of the biggest girl in his organization, Harry said with a smile which looked 10 years older than himself: "We have very big girls, but they won't tell you their right age."

The average machine tender, or "turner," or "basting puller," gets from $2 to $3 a week, and the strike was for an advance of the scale of wages.

"What we wanted was $1 per machine," said Harry. "While the operators are workin' on them jackets we must keep turnin' the sleeves and the flaps and the collars, and sometimes three or four operators commence to holler at us, so that we get mixed up and nearly go crazy tryin' to attend to them all. But the boss, he don' care; he pays us the same. That won't go. We want a dollar for each machine and no more'n nine hours a day. It's enough, ain't it?"

"Sure!" put in one of the group of boys of Harry's union, who had been following their leader's talk breathlessly.

"Shut up! Let Harry talk to the reporter," whispered the others. "He is pannin' it out nice, ain't he, Mosey?"

The next meeting of the Machine Tenders' Union will take place this afternoon at 78 Essex Street, the headquarters of three of the striking tailor organizations. Young Gladstone will be the principal

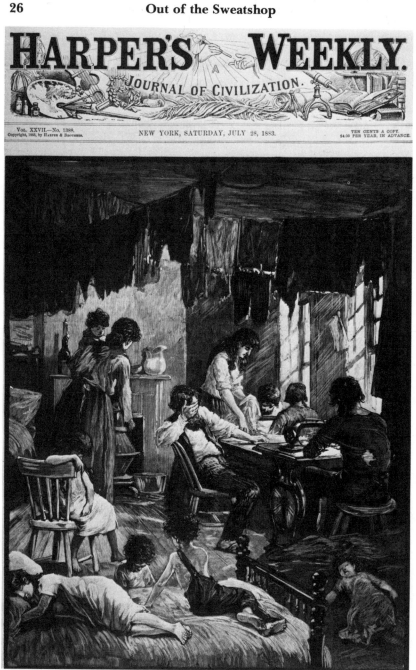

This masterpiece by the great illustrator T. de Thulstrup mocked the subtitle of the magazine—Journal of Civilization.

speaker, and when asked to give an outline of today's address, he said modestly that there was nothing to tell, that he was not much of a speaker, and that his "fellow workmen" were too worried about their bread and butter to have a mind for speeches, anyhow.

"I'll tell them to stick together and to think about their poor fathers and mothers they have got to support. I'll speak to them of the schools and how they can't go there to get their education, but must spend from 14 to 15 hours a day in a pest-hole, pulling bastings, turning collars and sleeves and running around as if they were crazy.

"If you don't look out for yourselves, who will? You have not had time to grow up, to get strength for work, when you must spend your dearest days in the sweatshop. Think of the way your mothers kiss you, how they love you, and how they shed tears over you, because they see their dear boys treated like slaves.

"Try to make a few dollars for them at least. Then you will come home and kiss your mammas and say, 'Don't cry, dear mamma. Here, I've brought you some money for rent, or for a Sabbath meal.' The only way to get the bosses to pay us good wages is to stick together, so let us be true to our union."

As he spoke, his voice now and then trembled with emotion, and his deep, dark eyes shone. He gave the impression of one who meant every word he said. There was not a trace of affectation about his manner, and the expression of his face bore that stamp of melancholy which is characteristic of much older representatives of his race.

From *Out of the Shadow*, 1918.

MY FIRST JOB
by Rose Cohen

About the same time that the bitter cold came father told me one night that he had found work for me in a shop where he knew the presser. I lay awake long that night. I was eager to begin life on my own responsibility but was also afraid. We rose earlier than usual that morning for father had to take me to the shop and not be over late for his own work. I wrapped my thimble and scissors, with a piece of bread for breakfast, in a bit of newspaper, carefully stuck two needles into the lapel of my coat and we started.

The shop was on Pelem Street, a shop district one block long and just wide enough for two ordinary sized wagons to pass each other.

We stopped at a door where I noticed at once a brown shining porcelain knob and a half rubbed off number seven. Father looked at his watch and at me.

"Don't look so frightened," he said. "You need not go in until seven. Perhaps if you start in at this hour he will think you have been in the habit of beginning at seven and will not expect you to come in earlier. Remember, be independent. At seven o'clock rise and go home no matter whether the others go or stay."

He began to tell me something else but broke off suddenly, said "good-bye" over his shoulder and went away quickly. I watched him until he turned into Monroe Street.

Now only I felt frightened, and waiting made me nervous, so I tried the knob. The door yielded heavily and closed slowly. I was half way up when it closed entirely, leaving me in darkness. I groped my way to the top of the stairs and hearing a clattering noise of machines, I felt about, found a door, and pushed it open and went in. A tall, beardless man stood folding coats at a table. I went over and asked him for the name (I don't remember what it was). "Yes," he said crossly. "What do you want?"

I said, "I am the new feller hand." He looked at me from head to foot. My face felt so burning hot that I could scarcely see.

"It is more likely," he said, "that you can pull bastings than fell sleeve lining." Then turning from me he shouted over the noise of the machine: "Presser, is this the girl?" The presser put down the iron and looked at me. "I suppose so," he said, "I only know the father."

The cross man looked at me again and said, "Let's see what you can do." He kicked a chair, from which the back had been broken off, to the finisher's table, threw a coat upon it and said, raising the corner of his mouth: "Make room for the new feller hand."

One girl tittered, two men glanced at me over their shoulders and pushed their chairs apart a little. By this time I scarcely knew what I was about. I laid my coat down somewhere and pushed my bread into the sleeve. Then I stumbled into the bit of space made for me at the table, drew in the chair and sat down. The men were so close to me at each side I felt the heat of their bodies and could not prevent myself from shrinking away. The men noticed and probably felt hurt. One made a joke, the other laughed and the girls bent their heads low over their work. All at once the thought came: "If I don't do this coat quickly and well he will send me away at once." I picked up the coat, threaded my needle, and began hastily, repeating the lesson father impressed upon me. "Be careful not to twist the sleeve lining, take small false stitches."

My hands trembled so that I could not hold the needle properly. It took me a long while to do the coat. But at last it was done. I took it over to the boss and stood at the table waiting while he was examining it. He took long, trying every stitch with his needle. Finally he put it down and without looking at me gave me two other coats. I felt very happy! When I sat down at the table I drew my knees close together and stitched as quickly as I could.

When the pedlar came into the shop everybody bought rolls. I felt hungry but I was ashamed and would not eat the plain, heavy rye bread while the others ate rolls.

All day I took my finished work and laid it on the boss's table. He would glance at the clock and give me other work. Before the day was over I knew that this was a "piece work shop," that there were four machines and sixteen people were working. I also knew that I had done almost as much work as "the grown-up girls" and that they did not like me. I heard Betsy, the head feller hand, talking about "a snip of a girl coming and taking the very bread out of your mouth." The only one who could have been my friend was the presser who knew my father. But him I did not like. The worst I knew about him just now was that he was a soldier because the men called him so. But a soldier, I had learned, was capable of anything. And so, noticing that he looked at me often, I studiously kept my eyes from his corner of the room.

Seven o'clock came and everyone worked on. I wanted to rise as father had told me to do and go home. But I had not the courage to stand up alone. I kept putting off going from minute to minute. My neck felt stiff and my back ached. I wished there were a back to my chair so that I could rest against it a little. When the people began to go home it seemed to me that it had been night a long time.

The next morning when I came into the shop at seven o'clock, I saw at once that all the people were there and working as steadily as if they had been at work a long while. I had just time to put away my coat and go over to the table, when the boss shouted gruffly, "Look here, girl, if you want to work here you better come in early. No office hours in my shop." It seemed very still in the room, even the machines stopped. And his voice sounded dreadfully distinct. I hastened into the bit of space between the two men and sat down. He brought me two coats and snapped, "Hurry with these!"

From this hour a hard life began for me. He refused to employ me except by the week. He paid me three dollars and for this he hurried me from early until late. He gave me only two coats at a time to do. When I took them over and as he handed me the new work he would say quickly and sharply, "Hurry!" And when he did not say it in words he looked at me and I seemed to hear even more plainly, "Hurry!" I hurried but he was never satisfied. By looks and manner he made me feel that I was not doing enough. Late at night when the people would stand up and begin to fold their work away and I too would rise, feeling stiff in every limb and thinking with dread of our cold empty little room and the uncooked rice, he would come over with still another coat.

"The Slaves of the 'Sweaters,'" by W. A. Rogers, appeared in the April 26, 1890, issue of *Harper's Weekly*.

"I need it the first thing in the morning," he would give as an excuse. I understood that he was taking advantage of me because I was a child. And now that it was dark in the shop except for the low single gas jet over my table and the one over his at the other end of the room, and there was no one to see, more tears fell on the sleeve lining as I bent over it than there were stitches in it.

I did not soon complain to father. I had given him an idea of the people and the work during the first days. But when I had been in the shop a few weeks I told him, "The boss is hurrying the life out of me." I know now that if I had put it less strongly he would have paid more attention to it. Father hated to hear things put strongly. Besides he himself worked very hard. He never came home before eleven and he left at five in the morning.

He said to me now, "Work a little longer until you have more experience; then you can be independent."

"But if I did piece work, father, I would not have to hurry so. And I could go home earlier when the other people go."

Father explained further, "It pays him better to employ you by the week. Don't you see if you did piece work he would have to pay you as much as he pays a woman piece worker? But this way he gets almost as much work out of you for half the amount a woman is paid."

I myself did not want to leave the shop for fear of losing a day or even more perhaps in finding other work. To lose half a dollar meant that it would take so much longer before mother and the children would come. And now I wanted them more than ever before. I longed for my mother and a home where it would be light and warm and she would be waiting when we came from work.

Kelley (1859–1932), social reformer and secretary of the National Consumers League, was the first factory inspector for the state of Illinois. She campaigned against child labor and the sweatshop. From testimony before the U.S. Industrial Commission, May 3, 1899.

IN CHICAGO'S SWEATSHOPS
by Florence Kelley

Question.

What was the proportion of native Americans to the whole?

Answer.

We never found any in sweatshops. The native Americans who are working at the garment trades are perhaps the most dangerous of all from the point of view of the purchaser. They are women with young children, who are dependent upon themselves and upon charity, and who work in their own homes, and take the work directly from the factory and make it up, and take it back, and they are so isolated that it is perfectly impossible to keep up any sort of scrutiny as to the sanitary conditions under which they work. We always reported that, so far as we were able to judge, that was the most dangerous of any kind of work.

Q. We want to know what the wages were; if we know that we can readily judge of the social conditions. We want to know what the surroundings of the family are—the school facilities and things of that kind.

A. As to making any general statement of average wages, my knowledge is not on a large enough scale to make such a general statement, except this one; I have never found, in 7 years of living among people who do finishing at home—I never found anyone who worked at home who made a living. There is a very large body of American, German, Jewish, Bohemian, Polish, and Italian women, who take work home.

I have never been able to ascertain through our charity people, or through my own acquaintance, that even one could support herself through that. Invariably, if she is a married woman, her husband keeps the family; or, if she is an unmarried woman, she receives relief from the county charitable agencies or private agencies. The wages of the people who work in the shops vary from those of children, whom I have known to work 6 months for nothing with the understanding that they would later get $1 a week and work up slowly to $4 and $5, up to the Scandinavian custom tailors, who make a relatively good living at it.

Q. Would the average wage of a woman vary much over $5 a week?

A. I do not know a sufficient number of cases to make any average. The people are so unintelligent that it is almost impossible to get any statement of that kind. The State Bureau of Labor Statistics, in 1892, made a special investigation of the wages of the people in the garment trades, and I acted as expert at that time, and I hunted up a very large body of people working in these shops and I found such examples as this—of the extreme difficulty of learning facts: I found a girl who told me she bound seams in ladies' cloaks and made $18 a week.

She was a Russian Jewish girl, who had been there for a number of years. When I questioned her I found her week began Saturday morning and ended a week from the following Monday. She would really work 9 consecutive days, violating her Jewish belief by working on Saturday, and would pay a man to run the machine during the night. They divided the $18 she drew. And still to this day she always speaks of herself as earning $18 a week at binding cloaks. It is quite impossible to form a trustworthy opinion of what they earn.

On the other hand, I tried to find out what the poorest lot earned at sewing cloaks. They always have a little book from the contractor with the prices marked in. I collected a lot of these books and tried to get the cloak makers working at home to reduce the prices to hours and tell me how much they got. Five families agreed to do that, and then it transpired that not one of the five families owned a clock. They go by light and dark. If they are not intelligent enough to tell the time, of course they are not intelligent enough to give any trustworthy statement about the wages per hour, per day or per week.

Those examples represent the two extremes. These last people were of the Sicilian peasantry; they had always told time by the sundial, and I do not suppose they ever saw a clock, and they do not know enough to keep a record. The only people who can give any intelligent statement are the sharpest of the contractors, who keep books, and those are entirely misleading, because they will have a man working in the shop who runs a machine, and pay him a lump sum for working for a given time, and he employs young girls, who work at perhaps one-half a man's pay, and also hires a man to run a machine at night, and you cannot tell how much of the lump sum is peddled out. So finally the statements of the Bureau of Labor Statistics were exceedingly noncommittal. They gave statements made up from the books of the contractors, with the qualifying statement that they never could tell how much of the money stayed with the man to whom it was paid and how much was paid out for subdivisions of labor.

It is perfectly safe to say that the poorest people working in any trade in Chicago are the people who work in the garment trades. There is no other set of people who are both working and also to so great an extent receiving relief from public and private charity. Of course that is not a definite statement about their wages.

Q. (by Mr. Phillips) Have you known of any contagious or cutaneous diseases conveyed through manufacture in sweatshops or private houses; have you traced them definitely?

A. I think that has never been done. We never were able to make the connection between a case of infectious disease and the manufacture of the goods in a house in which there was infectious disease, for this reason: The garments are cut in the cutting room and go to the foreman, and he gives them to the contractor, who takes them to the shop and, after the seams are stitched, gives them to the person who does the handwork at home; then she takes them back to the shop, and either the contractor himself or an expressman takes them back to the foreman, and they go into the stock of goods, then to the retailer, and then to the purchaser.

The nearest I ever came to making a connection did not really connect. I found an overcoat, a good summer overcoat, being made up in a room in which there was a patient dying of smallpox; that was in Twentieth Street, in Chicago; and the hanger on the coat, the little silk strap, was marked with the name of a custom tailor in Helena, Montana. The garment had been ordered there. If we had not caught it, the garment would have gone back. That was an unusually close connection between the custom tailor and the disease. There are usually more people between the two, so that it is impossible to trace it.

Q. (by Mr. Farquhar) Do you think the contagious diseases are spread pretty largely that way?

A. Yes; the longer I worked at it the stronger that conviction grew.

Q. Do you know any way that the employees of the sweatshops could better their condition?

A. No. We have tried for 10 years at Hull House to organize the girls. We have been having trade union meetings for 10 years in the garment trades. It has never been possible to get an organization that amounted to anything at all. There was an organization of the cutters in 1893 and 1894, which was broken up by the combination of 28 manufacturers; and that was the only relatively strong organization in this trade, because there are no women and children in the cutter branch; they were all men. They were the most intelligent people in the trade. They had built up the organization in a year and a half, and the manufacturers broke it up like that (snapping fingers).

Leiserson (1883–1957) was a noted labor economist and mediator who helped develop basic concepts of social unionism. From "History of the Jewish Labor Movement in New York City," 1908.

THE FIRST IMMIGRANT STRIKE
by William M. Leiserson

Of the purely trade union organizations the first that the immigrants of 1882 formed was the Dress and Cloak Makers' Union. It arose out of a strike of about 700 men and women in July 1883. The New York papers made considerable comment on this first "Emigrants' Strike," as they called it.

The strikers wanted a rate of $2.50 per day, hours to be from 8 A.M. to 6 P.M. Piecework was to be arranged so that an operator might earn about $15 a week. Prior to the strike wages had been $5 and $6 a week.

Nearly half of the strikers were women and they met in separate halls from the men. Delegates from unions affiliated with the Knights of Labor encouraged the strikers and promised them financial aid.

The character of the new unionists was thus described in a daily paper:

"The members of the new Cloak and Dress Makers' Union have never before been on a strike, and had never before taken part in labor movements. Nevertheless, the men and women who compose the union have realized all the hopes of the leaders in standing by the association and holding out against the bosses.

"There were fears that the great poverty of many of them and the wealth of the bosses, who at first stoutly declared that they would make no concessions whatever, might induce these poor people to return to their daily toil for the pittance they were receiving, but the weak ones were encouraged and now they all seem determined to stand out until their wages are raised."

The organization was completed during the strike. It became a local assembly of the Knights of Labor and also sent delegates to the Central Labor Union.

During the strike the first Cloak Manufacturers' Association was also formed. The purpose of this association was to fight both the contractors and the workmen. The contractors offered to strike with the cloakmakers if they would refuse to work for certain contractors who were taking out work at rates lower than the rest. No agreement was reached, however, between the strikers and the contractors.

Rosenberg (1870–1935) was president of the ILGWU during the crucial period 1908–1914. From *Memoirs of a Cloakmaker*, 1920.

THE REINGOLD AFFAIR
by Abraham Rosenberg

Only chosen members of the committee knew who the other committeemen were. Even as they set forth, committee members had no exact knowledge of the purpose or place of their assignment. Only their chairman had been given the address and the others followed him blindly until the group arrived at the designated location. This was the best way to avoid leaks to the spies.

During the course of the strike the union succeeded in stopping all shops but one. A certain Greenberg, a former union man, had opened a shop in the woods near Jamaica, Long Island. Approach to the shop was impossible. Greenberg had surrounded his shop with a circle of hungry hounds. These vicious beasts were chained, but every time they caught our scent they raised an unnerving howl which alerted the shop in time to take cover.

It took a few days until our people found a way to get around the dogs. Carrying bags of old meat and bones, members of Picket Committee Number One—bearded and hungry—set out on foot in the dark of the night through the Jamaica woods, encountered and diverted the hounds and pierced the Greenberg defenses. The men arrived shortly before dawn to find the shop going full blast.

Undaunted, Greenberg and his wife battled the invaders. The shop ceased to function. In the confusion, as scabs confronted strikers, the stove used by the pressers to heat their irons was overturned. Hot coals scattered across the floor. Greenberg's small daughter was standing nearby. Her foot was burned.

Having accomplished its mission of stopping the shop, the committee hurriedly left. Its members caught a trolley car heading for East New York. Meanwhile, subcontractor Greenberg ran to the Jamaica City Hall where he telephoned the East New York Police Station and gave the alarm that his shop had been attacked by a band of thieves now making their getaway in a trolley car speeding toward their precinct.

A detachment of East New York policemen was waiting when the trolley arrived. Having spied them, our committee members mingled with the other passengers. All but one eluded the policemen. The police, spotting the rip and the mud on his coat, arrested poor Reingold.

The afternoon New York newspaper "extras" screamed in their headlines: Cloakmakers had burned children with vitriol in Jamaica. Pictures showed two bloodthirsty villains, unkempt and wild-eyed, gripping a small child while a third poured the deadly stuff on the innocent victim.

The manufacturers bought thousands of copies and distributed them free in the streets. In every shop, the bosses read the hair-raising "reports" to their employees. The entire city was in an uproar. Attempts to obtain Reingold's release on bail were turned down by the courts.

From the *New York Times,* October 12, 1894.

POLICE CLUB STRIKERS

The parade of the striking cloakmakers began with something like a riot last night. In the disturbance the police of the Madison Street Station used their clubs freely and with vigor. More than one striker was removed to neighboring drugstores and doctors' offices to have wounds from clubs dressed.

Joseph Barondess, the strikers' leader, was taken to the Elizabeth Street Police Station, but was released.

It had been announced that several thousand strikers, men and women, would form in Rutgers Place last evening and march to Union Square, where a mass meeting was to be held. It was about 6 o'clock when the cloakmakers began to assemble.

At that time a Roundsman and six patrolmen of the Madison Street Station were on hand, and they ordered the gathering to disperse. The strikers refused to do so. The Roundsman ordered his men to draw their clubs and clear the square. Then a scene of confusion followed. The strikers were clubbed. As many as could escape fled, closely followed by the policemen, into Essex and Division Streets, where they ran into hallways and saloons.

Leader Joseph Barondess, who was in the committee room at 412 Grand Street, was summoned. He reached Rutgers Square, where the strikers again endeavored to form a line, just as Captain Grant and a squad of police from the Madison Street Station arrived on the scene. Policemen again drew their clubs when the strikers refused to disperse, and a conflict with the crowd took place. Policeman No. 720 fired his revolver into the air, and several other policemen followed his example.

Barondess forced his way through the crowd and urged the police to cease their clubbing. He says that Policeman No. 2,227, who was whacking a striker, replied, with an oath: "I'll kill them."

The square was nearly cleared for the second time when Joseph Bowlofsky arrived with a permit from Superintendent Byrnes allowing the parade to take place.

Barondess (1867–1928) was the charismatic leader of the
cloakmakers in the last two decades of the nineteenth century. From Souvenir Journal, ILGWU Convention, 1903.

HOW THE NEW YORK CLOAK UNION STARTED

by Joseph Barondess

The first attempt to organize the cloakmakers on a real trade union
basis was made in the year 1889.

I called the first meeting to order, as the secretary of the United
Hebrew Trades, and from that time on remained at the head of the
organization, which assumed the name "Operators and Cloakmakers
Union of New York and Vicinity."

From the first day of its existence the Operators and Cloakmakers
Union was a militant organization, and we achieved one victory after
the other and our power for good grew to immense proportions.

The manufacturers, frightened at our power, organized a manufacturers association, and in the month of October 1889, all of them
locked out all of our members, who then numbered about 10,000.

This lockout lasted for nearly six months, during which time we
succeeded in entering into a treaty with the outside contractors.

Aside from our victory, we also succeeded in compelling the manufacturers to pay to the Cloak and Suit Cutters somewhat near
$20,000 for loss of time.

Strikes followed one after the other on the least provocation. We
did not understand at that time that in the labor movement as well as
in any other branch of activity and reform, things must develop by the
process of evolution, and that reforms and improvements can only
have a lasting influence where they have been achieved gradually.

Our employers saw fit to invoke the aid of the courts and the police
force in order to break up our union. Most of the prominent members of the Executive Board, including myself, were arrested on all
sorts of charges, thereby compelling us to spend all our means and
energies to defend ourselves instead of assuming the aggressive position against the unscrupulous employers as a labor organization.

It was then that we became convinced that no matter how powerful
an individual organization might be, it must have the backing of a
national union which would aid it in its struggles, and also influence
the consuming public to stand by it against the atrocities of mean and
oppressing employers.

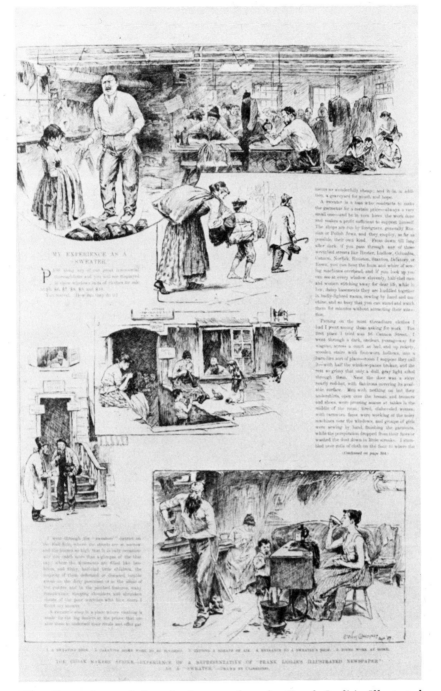

Clinedinst pictured the cloak sweatshop in *Frank Leslie's Illustrated Newspaper* (July 26, 1890).

3. Years of Survival

Surveying the sweating system at the start of the 20th century, John R. Commons concluded that conditions in the garment industry were not ripe for the founding of an enduring union. The labor force consisted of ethnic and national minorities, immigrants who were either too beaten or too ambitious to support a union. They were trapped by a mode of production that camouflaged the employer and defied their efforts to locate the center of industrial responsibility.

The degradation experienced by the garment worker clearly emerges in William M. Leiserson's terse description of the "Pig Market," the informal, open-air labor exchange in the heart of New York's East Side where "hands" offered themselves for hire. Theodore Dreiser toured the tenement warrens and saw men, women and children bent over their work in homes that lacked ventilation as a result of being divided in half to increase landlord income; the air in these homes was loaded with dust and tuberculosis bacilli.

Despite their miserable existence, however, the dream that had drawn them to the new homeland refused to die. Exploited families remembered the promise of free education, political democracy, and a legal trade union movement.

At the start of each season workers banded together to face their employer with consolidated strength. Each strike lost was a rehearsal for the next one. From season to season cloakmakers grew more sophisticated in waging battle—and employers became more skillful in undermining shop unity. The union that was formed on June 3, 1900, in a meeting hall on the East Side was another one of those seasonal unions. Few expected it would survive. The men who gathered together that day, arriving in holiday spirit from Baltimore, Philadelphia, Newark, and New York, repeated a familiar ritual; they formulated rules that provided for union dues, affiliation with the American Federation of Labor, and the issuance of a union label, the minutes of their historic meeting show.

In its first few years of existence the new union often teetered on the edge of failure. One early convention entertained a resolution calling for the disbanding of the ILGWU. The *Daily Forward*, as the sample news notices in this chapter disclose, chronicled the daily battle in the shops—a treadmill of conflict which Benjamin Schlesinger analyzed regularly in his pieces for this newspaper.

But desperation was mounting in the ranks of the cloakmakers. Occasionally, as in Boston and New York in 1907, things came to a boil and the men walked out of the shops. Jacob Heller answered the question raised by Schlesinger—how to fashion a fighting army out of the weak human material in the shops—by describing the battle scenes of the 1907 walkout.

From the vantage point of a later decade, Isaac A. Hourwich stressed the significance of these strikes. He demonstrated their their frequency contrasted sharply with the record of preimmigration decades. So-called native workers, lacking leadership and cohesion, readily yielded to the conditions of their exploitation. Newcomers, however, drawn by great expectations, battled against these conditions and clung to the dream of a better life for their children.

During the first few years in the urban ghetto, many who were trapped by the reality of the sweatshop were often engulfed by despair. From the depths of misery John A. Dyche cries out that his brave colleagues are being overwhelmed by hunger and joblessness and that his dear union is in deep trouble.

From "History of the Jewish Labor Movement in New York City," 1908.

THE "PIG MARKET"
by William M. Leiserson

Except during the crisis of 1893 the Jewish workman of New York had never had such a hard time as that which he experienced during the years 1887 and 1888. His unions were breaking up, and his countrymen were coming in great numbers to compete for his job. His wages have seldom been lower than in those years, and in many Jewish trades the hours reached their highest point just about this time.

A good barometer of labor conditions in the Jewish trades of New York has always been the "Pig Market." This is the name applied to the district about Essex and Hester Streets. Here the Jewish women buy their provisions for the Sabbath and here the workman out of a job stands waiting for an employer. When times are hard the crowd that gathers about this corner becomes so great that special police are detailed to keep order.

Many a newly arrived immigrant has received his first impression of American law from the club of one of these policemen. The "Pig Market" is the Jews' labor exchange. The contractor goes there and shouts for a "hand"—an operator, a baster or a presser. The passerby is stopped there at every step with the question: "Need a hand?" As the crowd increases hands are hired at lower rates, and the reduction is felt throughout the trades. Vice versa as laborers on the "Pig Market" become scarce, wages generally go up.

To do away with this "market" had been an important part of the programs of the first Jewish unions. At the earliest opportunity they established offices and labor bureaus where employer and workman could find each other. They advertised their labor bureaus as an inducement for men to join the union and as long as the bureaus existed the number standing around Hester Street was small.

But when the unions began to weaken in 1887 the "Pig Market" revived. The New York Jewish *Volks-Zeitung*, in an editorial deploring the lack of organization among the Jews, stated that the number of unemployed was constantly increasing. The "Pig Market" was overflowing with men who could not get work; and many were becoming tramps.

The situation of the Jewish workingmen seemed hopeless. Those who had had experience with unions had lost faith in them, while the new immigrants were met by the active anarchist agitation with [its] argument that trade unions were useless, as far as improving the condition of the worker was concerned. The socialists tried to keep up the interest in trade unions, but their influence had waned with the breaking up of the unions.

The beginning of a reaction in favor of organization came early in the fall of 1888. It came in the form of a suggestion from a shirtmaker to the Jewish branch of the Socialist Labor party that a central organization ought to be formed which would carry on the work of organizing the trades and keep them united for mutual aid and support. The suggestion met with immediate approval.

Dreiser (1871–1945), the great American novelist, clearly sensed the tragedy of those trapped in the sweatshops and described it in articles later reprinted in *The Color of the City*, 1923.

TOILERS OF THE TENEMENTS
by Theodore Dreiser

New York City has one hundred thousand people who, under unfavorable conditions, work with their fingers for so little money that they are understood, even by the uninitiated general public, to form a class by themselves. These are by some called sewing-machine workers, by others tenement toilers, and by still others sweatshop employees; but, in a general sense, the term tenement workers includes them all. They form a great section in one place, and in others little patches, ministered to by storekeepers and trade agents who are as much underpaid and nearly as hard-working as they themselves.

Men, women and children are daily making coats, vests, knee-pants and trousers. There are side branches of overalls, cloaks, hats, caps, suspenders, jerseys and blouses. Some make dresses and waists, underwear and neckwear, waistbands, skirts, shirts and purses; still others, fur, or fur trimmings, feathers and artificial flowers, umbrellas, and even collars. It is all a great allied labor of needlework, needlework done by machine and finishing work done by hand. The hundred thousand that follow it are only those who are actually employed as supporters. All those who are supported—the infants, school children, aged parents, and physically disabled relatives—are left out. You may go throughout New York and Brooklyn, and wherever you find a neighborhood poor enough you will find those workers. They occupy the very worst of tumbledown dwellings. Shrewd Italians, and others called padrones, sometimes lease whole blocks from such men as William Waldorf Astor, and divide up each natural apartment into two or three. Then these cubbyholes are leased to the toilers, and the tenement crowding begins.

You will see by peculiar evidences that things have been pretty bad with these tenements in the past. For instance, between every front and back room you will find a small window, and between every back room and the hall, another. The construction of these was compelled by law, because the cutting up of a single apartment into two or three involved the sealing up of the connecting door and the shutting off of natural circulation. Hence the state decided that a window opening into the hall would be some improvement, anyhow, and so this window-cutting began. It has proved of no value, however. Nearly every such window is most certainly sealed up by the tenants themselves.

In regard to some other matters, this cold enforcement of the present law is, in most cases, a blessing, oppressive as it seems at times. Men should not crowd and stifle and die in chambers where seven occupy the natural space of one. Landlords should not compel them to, and poverty ought to be stopped from driving them. Unless the law says that the floor must be clean and the ceiling white, the occupants will never find time to make them so. Unless the beds are removed from the workroom and only one person allowed to work in one room, the struggling "sweater" will never have less than five or six suffering with him. Enforce such a law, and these workers, if they cannot work unless they comply with these conditions, will comply with them, and charge more for their labor, of course. Sweatshop

From Italy's sunny fields to a New York railroad flat sweatshop. (Lewis Hine photo)

manufacturers cannot get even these to work for nothing, and land-lords cannot get tenants to rent their rooms unless they are clean enough for the law to allow them to work in them. Hence the burden falls in a small measure on the landlord, but not always.

The employer or boss of a little shop, who is so nervous in wrong-doing, so anxious to bribe, is but a helpless agent in the hands of a greater boss. He is no foul oppressor of his fellow man. The great clothing concerns in Broadway and elsewhere are his superiors. What they give, he pays, barring a small profit to himself. If these people are compelled by law to work less or under more expensive condi-tions, they must receive more or starve, and the great manufactories cannot let them actually starve. They come as near to it now as ever, but they will pay what is absolutely essential to keep them alive; hence we see the value of the law.

Commons (1862–1945) was a labor historian, founder of institutional economics, and an early formulator of labor legislation. From "Report by the U.S. Industrial Commis-sion," Volume XV, 1901.

THE SWEATING SYSTEM
by John R. Commons

The term "sweating," or "sweating system," originally denoted a sys-tem of subcontract, wherein the work is let out to contractors to be done in small shops or homes. "In practice," says the 1892 report of the Illinois Bureau of Labor Statistics, "sweating consists of the farming out by competing manufacturers as to competing contractors of the material for garments, which in turn is distributed among competing men and women to be made up."

The system to be contrasted with the sweating system is the "factory system," wherein the manufacturer employs his own workmen, under the management of his own foreman or superintendent, in his own building, with steam, electric, or water power. In the sweating system the foreman becomes a contractor, with his own small shop and foot-power machine. In the factory system the workmen are congregated where they can be seen by the factory inspectors and where they can organize or develop a common understanding. In the sweating system they are isolated and unknown.

A manufacturer usually has an "inside shop" and several "outside shops." The inside shop is usually on the manufacturer's own premises, and includes the cutters who cut the cloth for the contractors, the examiners who inspect the garments on their return, and the "bushelmen" who repair and reshape the garments if necessary.

The "outside shops" are the shops of contractors who take the goods out from the manufacturer for stitching and finishing. If the manufacturer does his own work directly under a superintendent or foreman, instead of indirectly through a contractor, this shop also is known as an "inside shop."

The position of the contractor or sweater now in the business in American cities is peculiarly that of an organizer and employer of immigrants. The man best fitted to be a contractor is the man who is well acquainted with his neighbors, who is able to speak the language of several classes of immigrants, who can easily persuade his neighbors or their wives and children to work for him, and who in this way can obtain the cheapest help.

The contractor can increase the number of people employed in the trade at very short notice. During the busy season, when the work doubles, the number of people employed increases in the same proportion. All the contractors are agents and go around among the people. Housewives, who formerly worked at the trade and abandoned it after marriage, are called into service for an increased price of a dollar or two a week. Men who have engaged in other occupations, such as small business and peddling, and are out of the business most of the year, are marshaled into service by the contractor.

The contractor in the clothing trade is largely responsible for the primitive mode of production—for the foot-power sewing machine, for the shops in the alleys, in the attics, on top floors, above stables, and in some cases in the homes of the people. These small shops are able on account of low rent and meager wages to compete successfully, although with foot power, against the large shops and factories with steam or electric power.

The unlimited hours of work, often seven days in the week, is a feature of the contracting system. The contractor himself works unlimited hours. His shop is open most of the time. He deals with people who have no knowledge of regular hours. He keeps them in the dark with regard to the prevailing number of hours that other people work.

The contractor is an irresponsible go-between for the manufacturer, who is the original employer. He has no connection with the business interests of the manufacturer nor is his interest that of his help. His sphere is merely that of a middleman. He holds his own mainly because of his ability to get cheap labor, and is in reality merely the agent of the manufacturer for that purpose.

Usually when work comes to the contractor from the manufacturer and is offered to his employees for a smaller price than has previously been paid, the help will remonstrate and ask to be paid the full price. Then the contractor tells them, "I have nothing to do with the price. The price is made for me by the manufacturer. I have very little to say about the price." That is, he cuts himself completely loose from any responsibility to his employees as to how much they are to get for their labor, throwing the responsibility on the manufacturer who originally gave him the work.

The help do not know the manufacturer. They cannot register their complaint with the man who made the price for their labor. The contractor, who did not make the price for their labor, claims that it is of no use to complain to him. So however much the price for labor goes down there is no one responsible for it.

In case the help form an organization and send a committee to the manufacturer, the manufacturer will invariably say, "I do not employ you and I have nothing to do with you"; and when they go back to the contractor and file their complaint, he will invariably say, "I am not making the price for your labor. I am simply paying you as much as I can out of what I get from the manufacturer."

Eleven delegates answered the call of the United Brotherhood of Cloakmakers to meet in convention on June 3, 1900, to establish a garment workers' union. Following are the minutes of their historic convention.

MINUTES OF THE FOUNDING MEETING

The first national convention of Cloakmakers, called by the United Brotherhood of Cloakmakers, No. 1, of New York and Vicinity, was held on Sunday, June 3, 1900, at Labor Lyceum, 61 East 4th Street,

New York City. At 10 A.M. the meeting was called to order by B. Braff.

After considerable deliberation a motion to form an International Union was unanimously carried. It was moved and seconded, the name of this organization shall be "International Ladies' Garment Workers' Union."

The following temporary officers were elected: B. Braff, of New York, Chairman, and M. Silverman, of Baltimore, Secretary. The temporary chairman in his opening address declared that the Cloakmakers of New York had come to the conclusion that, in order to improve the condition of the working people in the trade, it is imperative that besides having local organizations in their respective cities the Cloakmakers should be united the whole country over. To this end the convention has been called by the New Yorkers.

After the chairman had concluded his remarks, credentials were presented and the following delegates were seated:

Cloakmakers' Protective Union of Philadelphia—Goldberg and Solat.
United Cloak Pressers of Philadelphia—Schwartz and Schweiger.
Cloakmakers' Union of Baltimore—Silverman.
United Brotherhood of Cloakmakers, No. 1, of New York and Vicinity—Braff, Grossman and Lubner.
Newark Cloakmakers' Union—Leibovits (2 delegates absent).
Skirt Makers' Union of New York—Pulman and London.

The meeting then proceeded with the nomination and election of a permanent chairman and secretary of the convention. Brother Goldberg, of Philadelphia, was duly elected chairman and Brother Braff of New York, secretary.

Brother J. Barondess greeted the convention. In his speech he demonstrated the importance of an International Union and declared that at the first convention a cornerstone would be laid for the sacred edifice of unity in the cloakmaking trade, and he expressed hope that this enterprise would bear good fruit in the future. Next after him Mr. Robinson, organizer of the AFL, addressed the convention and gave valuable advice as to the way of forming an International Union.

The first point was next taken up. The delegates of the Philadelphia Protective Union reported that they were instructed in favor of an International Union. United Brotherhood of Cloakmakers of New York reported that they numbered from three to four thousand members in good standing, and that they were instructed in favor of an International Union.

Cloak Pressers of Philadelphia, that they are well organized, have no instructions. Baltimore Cloak Makers Union, instructed in favor of forming an International Union. Skirt Makers of New York and Newark Cloakmakers Union, instructed in favor of an International.

At 12:30 recess was taken. At 2 P.M. the convention reconvened. A credential was presented from Brownsville Cloakmakers for delegate Ginsburg, who was duly admitted.

Moved, seconded, and carried, each local shall be taxed $10 for a preliminary fund. In the future due stamps shall be provided by the Executive Board of the International for all locals, and the locals shall pay the International for the stamps at the rate of one cent apiece. These stamps shall be sold by the locals to their members as weekly due stamps.

Moved, seconded, and carried to issue a label. The Executive Board instructed to attend to this.

Moved, seconded, and carried that all unions in the ladies' garment trade shall be eligible for admission.

Resolved by a unanimous vote to join the American Federation of Labor. The question in regard to an organizer left to the Executive Board.

Moved, seconded, and carried, to call upon the labor periodicals and request them to publish all reports and announcements of the International Union.

Nomination for election of officers was next proceeded with. Elected: H. Grossman, New York, President; B. Braff, New York, Secretary and Treasurer. Brother Braff volunteered to serve his term

In the pit of a basement sweatshop.

without any compensation and promised to furnish the necessary books. A vote of thanks was unanimously carried.

Executive Board: Silverman of Baltimore; Solat, Schweiger, and Schwartz of Philadelphia and Leibovits of Newark. Resolved, that the President be authorized to require security of the Secretary whenever in his judgment it may become necessary.

Moved, seconded, and carried, to request the United Brotherhood of Cloakmakers of New York to permit the Secretary-Treasurer, Braff, to have a desk in their office. Braff, Silverman and London were appointed a committee with power to draw a set of resolutions.

Motion carried, to submit the actions of the convention to a referendum vote of the locals composing the International Union, and to request them to send in their reports of their votes upon all subjects decided by this convention, not later than within fourteen days.

Closing exercises then followed. All delegates expressed great satisfaction with the formation of the International Union and pledged their best efforts to the advancement of the new body.

The United Brotherhood of Cloakmakers of New York tendered to the delegates an invitation to an entertainment. Amid universal enthusiasm the convention adjourned *sine die*.

The *Daily Forward,* a Yiddish newspaper founded by Jewish trade unionists in 1897, chronicled the ordeal of the immigrant garment workers. Following is a sampling of its daily bulletins.

NEWS BULLETINS

August 4, 1904—The seven cloakmakers who work at the Harris and Samuels Company, on the eighth floor of 97 Fifth Avenue, decided last night to stop work early, at 9 P.M.

But when they wanted to get out of the place, they discovered that the boss wasn't back yet to open the locked door. One of them had a key to the shop that would open the door only from the outside. So they waited some time. But the boss forgot to return.

After waiting for an hour and a half, they opened the windows and yelled down their predicament to passers-by who called the firemen who brought a ladder that was just a few inches short of the eighth floor.

Finally, one of the trapped cloakmakers remembered his key. He threw it down and one of the firemen unlocked the door.

December 25, 1904—Benjamin Schlesinger has issued a strong denunciation of the new trick of the cloak bosses who ask "security" from the cloakmakers. In the better shops, a worker must now deposit a $50 cash guaranty that he will neither belong to a union nor try to organize the shop, nor even dare protest against wages or working conditions.

If a cloakmaker does any of the above listed things, he not only loses his job but also forfeits his $50 deposit. In some shops a $25 deposit will do. In the cheaper line a $10 "security" is accepted.

The sad fact about all this is that many cloakmakers are only too willing to deposit "security" in order to get a chance to slave for starvation wages.

May 3, 1905—A new agency at 49 Prince Street hung out a sign yesterday saying cloakmakers are wanted in Astoria, Long Island. Four hundred workers offered their services, but all they got was the address of the place, for which they had to pay 50 cents to the agency, which gave them each a receipt for the money.

When cloakmakers arrived at the place in Astoria, the receipts were taken away from them and they were told: no workers needed. The workers refused to budge without the receipts, which were finally returned after the police intervened. When the cloakmakers got back to the Prince Street outfit, they demanded the return of their money, which was refused. The case is now in court.

April 9, 1905—Until three years ago, even the poorest boss had to supply machines for his workers. But then some cloakmakers began to realize that the new Singer machine works much faster than the household sewing machine that was used in cloak shops. And since the bosses were not interested in spending money for the new machines, the cloakmakers themselves bought the speedier sewing machines in order to produce more work and make more money.

Naturally, the employers did not object. Little by little, the old machines were replaced by new ones. And now if a cloakmaker wants a job, he must bring his own machine. If he happens to be too poor to own one, he may find a generous boss who has new machines, and for a nominal weekly fee he will let the cloakmaker use one.

One result of the faster machine was a continual cut in the piece rate, so that now the cloakmaker with the fast machine actually earns less than he did three years ago with the slow household machine. Another result of machine ownership is the little pushcart the cloakmaker must use to move his machine whenever he changes jobs, which happens frequently in these days of non-union shops and the bosses' right to fire a worker whenever he pleases.

As long as the workers stay out of the Cloakmakers' Union, they will have to pay for their own machines and carry them from shop to shop, or pay the boss for the privilege of being permitted to sweat 12 or 14 hours for a pittance. They must act at once to end this practice by building a strong, permanent union which will fight for them.

February 1, 1906—Although the Philadelphia waistmakers recently won a strike against having to pay for power, there is still one shop in which the workers are forced to pay the boss 50 cents a week for the use of machines and electricity, 5 cents a week for the use of a mirror and a towel and another 5 cents for taking drinking water from the faucet.

Altogether, workers are paying the boss 60 cents a week for these "services." In spite of this outrageous fee, the union has been unable to organize this shop. The workers are afraid to strike. The boss has 11 children and threatens that if the workers walk out he will use all of his children to break the strike.

May 4, 1906—One hundred and fifty children, ranging from 14 to 17 years in age, are striking against the waist contractor Izzi Lock, who never suspected that these girl slaves would be able to stage such a walkout. The strikers are asking for a 10-hour working day instead of 11 and recognition of the Ladies Waistmakers' Union.

Schlesinger (1876–1932) was to serve as ILGWU president three times, returning to his post on the *Daily Forward* staff in the interim. From the *Daily Forward,* December 3, 1906.

WHAT BECAME OF THE OTHER 42,500 CLOAKMAKERS?
by Benjamin Schlesinger

There are 45,000 cloakmakers in New York. But only 2,500 are members of the union. What about the rest of them?

About 5,000 women, widows and wives of husbands who can't provide for the entire family, finish cloaks in their miserable tenement flats where they are compelled also to raise their children. They earn from 80 cents to $2 a week working all hours of the day and night.

Then there are about 2,000 cloakmakers who came to America from the old country just to make money and go back across the seas. Their hearts are not here; they work day and night, eat nickel meals, sleep in the shops, save every penny. They are unorganizable.

Another group of cloak finishers is comprised of about 3,000 girls who consider their stay in the cloak industry as only temporary—to be terminated as soon as they find husbands. Why should they even bother with a union?

Perhaps the most exploited group is the one made up of about 4,000 "green" hands. They would gladly join a union in order to improve their conditions. But they can't move. They are terrorized by fear. One sign of friendliness to the union and out they go, with no job, no money and no opportunity to learn the trade.

Add to these about 2,000 cloakmakers who are 50 years or older. They are devoutly religious and they are getting older and older. They are haunted by the fear of being told to get out.

Nor can the union expect help from the 3,000 hustlers who dream only of the day when they will themselves become bosses. Why expect them to join a union they will shortly be fighting?

We mustn't forget the favorites. Every shop has a few "good boys" who get the breaks from the boss for services rendered. There are about 3,000 of them.

Then there are about 2,000 cloakmakers who manage to get by thanks to the help they get from their children. Why should they spend money for dues?

Next we must take into account the few thousands of seasonal cloakmakers. For most of the year they work in different trades making pants or vests or shirts. But as soon as it gets busy in cloaks they come flocking back and suddenly become cloakmakers. Then they work 15 hours a day, make $20 a week, and as soon as the slack starts again they leave the trade. Would it be fair to ask them to pay dues all year round when they work as cloakmakers for only the best weeks of the season and after that don't care what happens to the trade?

The same answer may be expected from those whose ties with the bosses are thicker than water—the thousands of bosses' relatives and "landsleit" and "paisanos." The union would be going too far if it expected these workers to turn on their own flesh and blood even though they are more mercilessly exploited than they would be if they worked for strangers.

And what about the thousands of oldtimers, the veterans of the general strike of 1894? They bask in the glory of their memories about which they never seem to tire of talking. But ask them to join the union and they raise their hands in horror, cry they are disgusted with present-day cloakmakers and grow nostalgic about the "good old days."

Yet from these elements we must build a union. Each one walks in a different direction, but they must be taught to march together if the garment industry is ever to be organized, if its workers are ever going to be able to make a living, if they are ever going to regain the human dignity which is rightfully theirs.

Heller (1889–1948) became a vice president of the ILGWU in 1920. From Local 17 Souvenir Journals, 1920, 1935.

THE BATTLE OF 1907
by Jacob Heller

Until 1907, the reefer manufacturers still thought that Local 17 was only a temporary phenomenon in the trade, just like the other Jewish unions up to that time, which used to arise during the season and disappear with the slack. In 1905 they eagerly awaited the end of the season to be able to celebrate the end of the union too. . . . However, when the union failed to "accommodate" them, they decided to take active steps to destroy it.

At first, they used a "friendly" approach. They gave beer parties for the workers, organized societies, promised them sick benefits, and even offered to buy cemetery plots for them.

However, all these inducements didn't help. The situation came to a head precisely at one of these parties, which was given by the largest reefer firm at that time, Weinstein Brothers. The event was held in an East Side hall, back of a saloon.

The hall was gaily decorated, the floor covered with sawdust. Long tables were set up in the middle of the room, so that the hungry crowd would surround them from all sides. At "strategic" positions on the tables were heaps of bread, herring, corned beef and other delicacies that would be certain to win the good will of the workers. Beer flowed freely for all these thirsty, lonely Jewish workers who apparently had gathered together on the advice of their boss to organize a society of "hometown" brethren.

But then, in the midst of an impassioned speech by one of the bosses, in marched a union committee, which upset the bosses' happy little plans. For the unfortunate bosses hadn't known that most of those present had informed the union in advance of the event, and were waiting impatiently for the union's "invasion."

Realizing that their "friendly" tactics had failed, the manufacturers turned to their only remaining weapon—the use of force—to destroy Local 17. They organized themselves into an association and decided to remain together until they had accomplished the destruction of the Reefermakers' Union.

As their first step, they decided upon a lockout. Towards the end of March 1907, they hung up signs in their shops reading, "Beginning April 1, this will no longer be a union shop."

These signs only aroused the workers further. They considered each word on the signs to be a challenge to their unity and strength. There was an immediate, spontaneous feeling among the reefermakers that an answer must be given the bosses on the spot—and the answer came swiftly.

Shop after shop quit work. Within a few minutes, the streets in the factory area were filled with reefermakers, streaming by in compact columns, singing the "Marseillaise." That was how the historic battle of the Reefermakers' Union began.

The first thing the union did was to declare an official strike in reply to the lockout. The fight continued for 11 weeks, in a strike which was one of the bloodiest in the history of the Jewish labor movement. The city officials realized that most of the strikers were "greenhorns" and therefore could not produce any votes in the elections. The hired thugs of the bosses realized it also, so both they and the city's law enforcement personnel did their "work" without fear. Not a day passed without numerous strikers being beaten up severely.

Strike headquarters took on the appearance of a hospital. Bandages were evident wherever one turned. The gangsters used two methods of attack: either slashing with knives, or splitting strikers' heads with blackjacks. The reefermakers' blood colored the whole factory district.

On one occasion, it seemed as if Brother Schlesinger would have to deliver a funeral oration over a striker who was beaten up so terribly that he appeared almost lifeless. Schlesinger, who was deeply moved by the scene, delivered one of the most outstanding speeches in his union career. His talk was so effective that it was evidently able to revive the seemingly mortally-wounded striker, for he remained alive, and in a few days he was again active on the picket lines on Lispenard Street.

These acts of brutality did not frighten the reefermakers. They merely adjusted themselves to the developments. Instead of confining themselves to picketing two abreast, marching up and down (as per official instructions in accordance with picketing laws), they began to march around the shops in whole groups, until all the strikers became one huge mass, completely surrounding the reefer shops.

These "mass attacks" served to scare off somewhat the hired thugs of the bosses. And although the brutal attacks against the reefermakers did not cease, the strikers at least were able to defend themselves, and no longer provided the only casualties of the strike.

Neither were the strikers intimidated by threats of hunger. They managed to exist on the free lunches which were served in saloons with the purchase of a glass of beer. Many strikers used to have their "meals" at Edeson's saloon at 88 Monroe Street, where their plates always were heaped high with bread, herring, peas, etc.

Finally, in the 11th week, victory was in sight. The bosses were tired of working themselves and decided to give in. All demands of the union were won.

Hourwich (1860–1924), statistician, lawyer, college lecturer, and government specialist, became the center of controversy in the ILGWU in 1913. From *Immigration and Labor,* 1912.

IMMIGRANT STRIKERS, AMERICAN STANDARDS
by Isaac A. Hourwich

The view that the new immigrants tend to lower the wages of the older immigrants apparently finds support in the statistics of the Immigration Commission, which show for each race at present employed in the clothing industry "a general increase in weekly earnings with the increased period of residence." In other words, the earnings of the recent immigrants are lower than those of the older immigrants, because, it is explained, "the immigrants of long residence have acquired a higher standard of living and consequently demand a higher wage." Quite naturally then, "the older employees are unable to meet the competition of the recent immigrants, whose demands are not great."

The statistics of the Immigration Commission do not disclose any tendency on the part of the new immigrant races to accept lower wages than the immigrants of older races. The percentage of recent German immigrants earning $15 a week or over is much less than the percentage of Hebrews and Russians and about the same as the percentage of Italians with the same average earnings.

On the opposite end, the percentage of Germans earning less than $10 a week within the first five years of their residence in the United States is somewhat greater than that of Hebrews, Russians, Poles, and Bohemians. These figures show that the "new immigration" does not underbid the immigrants of the older races. On the other hand, the variation in the earnings of representatives of each race indicates that the rate of wages is not determined by racial factors, but depends upon the personal qualifications and opportunities of individual workers.

The Immigration Commission speaks in general terms of the "availability of cheap woman and child labor of the immigrant households" for locating "men's and women's clothing manufacturing establishments" in certain districts "developed in connection with some of the principal industries of the country." But the statistics of the Commission show that the earnings of recent immigrant women and children in the clothing industry are higher than those of native

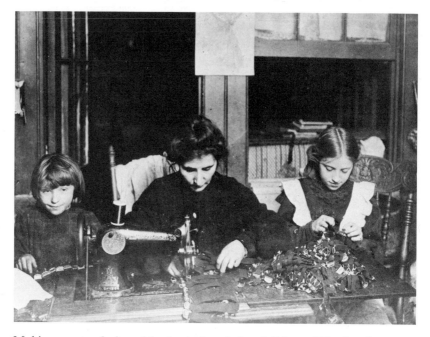

Making garter belts with the help of the children. Window between
rooms compensates for windowless bedroom.

Americans. Thus, adult Russian Hebrew women averaged $8.09 per
week, Polish women, $8.07, North Italian women, $7.54, whereas
native women of native American parentage earned only $7.41 per
week. The majority of Polish women (55.4 percent) earned more than
$7.50 per week, while the majority of American women of native
parentage (57.2 percent) earned less than that amount.

The same is true of girls between the ages of 14 and 18. Russian
Hebrew girls earned on an average $6.13 per week, other Hebrew
girls $6.24, South Italian girls $5.56, Polish girls $5.25, whereas native
American girls of native parentage made only $5.02 per week. Nearly
one half (45.9 percent) of the latter earned less than $5 while only a
little over one fourth (27.4 percent) of the Russian Hebrew girls
earned less than that amount.

Another cause of the "low standard of wages" of native American
country workers is their isolation, in consequence of which "they must
accept his (the contractor's) rate of payment offered through the
driver who delivers the goods." The Southern and Eastern European
clothing workers in the cities, on the contrary, are comparatively well
organized. The percentage of organized workers among them is
above the average for the country. Their capacity for concerted action
finds full expression only in strikes which rally around the unions

many workers not regularly affiliated with them. *The highest percent of employees joining in strikes in 1887–1905 was found among clothing workers.*

The strike statistics published by the United States Bureau of Labor permit of a comparison between the recent period beginning with the fiscal year 1895, when the immigrants from Southern and Eastern Europe for the first time outnumbered all others, and the earlier period from January 1, 1881, to June 30, 1894. During the '80s the principal nationalities employed in the clothing shops were the Germans and the Irish; since 1895 the Jews and the Italians have become the predominating element among the workers. It appears that during the thirteen and a half years previous to the fiscal year 1895 the average annual number of strikers in the clothing industry was 9,094, and during the eleven and a half years following it rose to 38,683.

This is the unbiased testimony of figures in answer to the sweeping generalizations of the Immigration Commission about the reluctance of the Southern and Eastern Europeans "to enter labor disputes involving loss of time," their "ready acceptance of a low wage and existing working conditions" and "willingness seemingly to accept indefinitely without protest certain wages and conditions of employment."

Dyche (1867–1938) was ILGWU General Secretary-Treasurer during the crucial decade 1904–14. From a letter to Charles Jacobson, January 7, 1909.

"THE UNION IS AUF TZORES"
by John A. Dyche

You want to know the latest in New York? Well, things are as bad as they can be. Locals 9 and 23 had no meeting for the last few weeks. Local 17 is "auf tzores." I just received a letter from Philadelphia that Local 15 Waistmakers are organizing or reorganizing and people are coming to the union but they have no one to take care of them. They want that we should send an organizer from New York and here we have no money to pay the rent. The monthly financial report shows a deficit of $92—that means I draw no wages.

The trade is as bad as the union is. The earnings are small. You can get plenty of work but I do not in the least exaggerate when I tell you that you will be lucky if you can get a job to earn a dollar a day. Regen worked in an outside shop and got 15 cents a skirt of fifteen gores first-class work. He made 8 skirts in two days. The next day himself and Rightman went up to Katz & Quint and they worked 4 days and a half and earned both of them $5. Yes, there is plenty of work in this city.

The police are active on 5th Avenue arresting cloakmakers looking for work. Polakoff has just returned from the Police Court. He was arrested with the bunch. This is how things are here. Otherwise we are all O.K. "auf tzores." Rosenger and Grossman are doing nothing. Grossman was a janitor for two months, had to look after a whole block of houses. The work nearly killed him. He dropped it and is starving again. The devil knows what the end of it all will be.

4. The Shirtwaist Makers' Strike, 1909

Charles Dana Gibson, without knowing it, became a most effective organizer of garment workers. The heroine of his popular drawings wore a shirtwaist, an item of apparel which sold in such great quantities that it kept large shops where the garment was cut and sewn busy. In these larger shops young women, many of them teenagers, soon became a self-conscious labor force, increasingly rebelling against a subcontracting system that featured a built-in wage depressor.

Pearl Goodman and Elsa Ueland describe this system in detail and tell how the girls, under a primitive "sectional" basis for assigning the work, labored in "sets." Amidst the din of shop noises they devised plots against the system. Women such as Sadie Frowne and Clara Lemlich describe how it felt as they moved toward action.

Some young girls were daring, while others, such as those portrayed by Louise Odencrantz, were more restrained by Old World customs. A crucial incident, described by Constance Leupp, led to a massive walkout at the Triangle Shirtwaist Company. The women rose from their machines, turned off the motors, and walked out. Soon aided by leaders of the Women's Trade Union League, as reported in *The Survey*, they defied police, thugs, and others who assaulted their picket line.

The grievances at the Triangle Shirtwaist Company paralleled similar complaints in other shirtwaist shops. On November 22, 1909, in a strike-support rally in the Great Hall at Cooper Union (which was reported by the *Call*), where Lincoln had criticized the spread of slavery half a century earlier, Lemlich voiced the prevailing sentiment favoring a general strike. It was an unprecedented call, soon followed by a fateful decision, and affirmed by the packed audience with a sacred oath from the Psalms.

The next morning thousands of youngsters faced the fearful move out of the shops and onto the picket lines, a move described by Sue A. Clark and Edith Wyatt. In the weeks that followed, the city watched in wonder. Dressed in their best clothes—and defying the judgment of the experts—young, inexperienced immigrant women marched on the picket lines, faced arrest, survived the workhouse, and resisted police provocation, all of which was vividly described by the *New York Tribune*.

The unique amalgam of forces on the picket lines placed impoverished young women shoulder to shoulder with socially prominent and wealthy women in the vanguard of the fight for suffrage; these women envisioned the battle for dignity taking place in the shops as merely another facet of their own campaign.

Some women from the shops required help, as Sarah Comstock's report from the strike hall shows; others, as Mailly points out, immediately displayed extraordinary qualities of leadership. The phenomenon described by Allan Benson—the joining of forces irrespective of social class, as in the remarkable tea given at the exclusive Colony Club (reported by the *Call*)—could only happen in America.

In her daily record of the strike, F. E. Sheldon outlines the steps by which various elements in the community were fused into a general movement of support for the walkout.

With the successful termination of the strike in February 1910, contracts had been won and a sense of solidarity had been achieved by workers who had hitherto been divided against themselves, as described by Miriam Finn Scott. In a larger sense, Ida M. Tarbell noted that for the first time garment workers had swayed public opinion to support their cause and had brought working women and immigrants into the mainstream of organized labor in America.

From the *Independent*, September 25, 1902.

DAYS AND DREAMS
by Sadie Frowne

My name is Sadie Frowne. I work in Allen Street (Manhattan) in what they call a sweatshop. I am new at the work and the foreman scolds me a great deal. I get up at half-past five o'clock every morning and make myself a cup of coffee on the oil stove. I eat a bit of bread and perhaps some fruit and then go to work. Often I get there soon after six o'clock so as to be in good time, though the factory does not open till seven.

At seven o'clock we all sit down to our machines and the boss brings to each one the pile of work that he or she is to finish during the day—what they call in English their "stint." This pile is put down beside the machine and as soon as a garment is done it is laid on the other side of the machine. Sometimes the work is not all finished by six o'clock, and then the one who is behind must work overtime.

The machines go like mad all day because the faster you work the more money you get. Sometimes in my haste I get my finger caught and the needle goes right through it. It goes so quick, though, that it does not hurt much. I bind the finger up with a piece of cotton and go on working. We all have accidents like that.

All the time we are working the boss walks around examining the finished garments and making us do them over again if they are not just right. So we have to be careful as well as swift. But I am getting so good at the work that within a year I will be making $7 a week, and then I can save at least $4.50 a week. I have over $200 saved now.

The machines are all run by foot power, and at the end of the day one feels so weak that there is a great temptation to lie right down and sleep. But you must go out and get air, and have some pleasure. So instead of lying down I go out, generally with Henry.

I am very fond of dancing and, in fact, all sorts of pleasure. I go to the theatre quite often, and like those plays that make you cry a great deal. "The Two Orphans" is good. The last time I saw it I cried all night because of the hard times that the children had in the play.

Some of the women blame me very much because I spend so much money on clothes. They say that instead of $1 a week I ought not to spend more than 25 cents a week on clothes, and that I should save the rest. But a girl must have clothes if she is to go into high society at Ulmer Park or Coney Island or the theatre.

Those who blame me are the old country people who have old-fashioned notions, but the people who have been here a long time know better. A girl who does not dress well is stuck in a corner, even if she is pretty and Aunt Fanny says that I do just right to put on plenty of style.

I have many friends and we often have jolly parties. Many of the young men like to talk to me, but I don't go out with any except Henry. Lately he has been urging me more and more to get married—but I think I'll wait.

One of the social studies done under the auspices of the Russell Sage Foundation was by Odencrantz. Excerpted from *Italian Women in Industry*, 1919, pages 38–44 and 224–226.

THE ITALIAN SEAMSTRESS
by Louise C. Odencrantz

The needle trades appeal especially to Italians. Their idea of the woman is primarily as a homemaker. Just as in every home you find a sewing machine in order that the mother can make her children's clothes, so the daughter, when she is ready to go out to work, wants to choose dressmaking. In this way she believes that she will some day be able to sew her own clothes.

Unfortunately they have no realization of the fine subdivisions that exist in the trade today, when such tasks as sewing on buttons on shirtwaists, cutting threads off petticoats, operating a ruffling or buttonhole machine, or setting in sleeves may be the one process that a girl will work at year after year. Even when she has secured a chance to work in a custom dressmaking place she rarely learns how to make a whole garment, but spends the day as a finisher, sleeve draper, waist finisher, repair or alteration hand, or even a presser or stock girl.

Many of the women had learned fine hand sewing in the public or convent schools in Italy; others had worked as apprentices and finishers with the village dressmaker, or had themselves been the dressmaker for the village. One girl, who began to learn dressmaking as soon as she left school, said that nearly all girls in Italy do this so that they will know how to sew. Lola became an apprentice in a shop in Turin at the age of twelve. After she had worked three years without pay, she received *buona paga* (good pay), $5.20 a month. She said that girls trained in Italy as dressmakers were much in demand here, as they knew all the processes and did better work than those who had learned the trade in this country.

Other immigrant women were found in the needle trades besides those who learned to sew in Italy. Many, especially the older ones, who had been farmhands or housewives in Italy and were often illiterate, had turned to the simple work of finishing on both men's and women's tailored garments. Little training is required for this work. Moreover, the organization of the work in the shop requires so little supervision by the employer that ignorance of English forms no bar to these women. As pieceworkers they may be trusted to work at top speed to earn the small wage of $6 or $7 a week.

Through neighbors or relatives who did home work, some newly arrived immigrants had heard of jobs in these shops and, according to the law of least resistance, there they went to work. Often, too, the friendly home worker would show the woman the rudiments of the trade, so that she did not feel as "strange" as if she had been plunged into the midst of work in a noisy candy or paper-box factory. This appealed especially to the older women, who were timid in seeking work.

The extensive advertising in Italian papers by New York firms—American, German and Russian—especially for workers in the clothing trades shows that to them, at least, Italian women are desirable employees. Often advertisements in Italian to attract those who cannot speak English offer special inducements of "*buona paga, lunga stagione,* union shop" (good pay, long season, union shop). Advertisements appear for *"operatrici per vesti di sciffon $15 a $25 per settimana"* (operators on chiffon dresses to earn $15 to $25 a week). *"20 ricamatrici cercansi, laboro a pazzi o a settimana. Si da lavoro a casa"* (20 hand embroiderers wanted, piece or week work. Work given home).

The name of her industry and her particular job are usually the first English words that the immigrant learns. A woman will shrug her shoulders helplessly when you ask her where she lives or how long she has been in this country. Her attempt to answer you with "feenisher," "press," "west," "dress," or "cloding," suggests that her work forms the strongest link with her new world.

In some cases the relatives with whom the women were living admitted that the cost did not cover expenses. For instance, two sisters, living with an aunt who provided them with a sleeping space in a flat already crowded and three meals a day, gave her only $1.50 a week each so that they might send money to Italy. A married brother allowed his two sisters to occupy a folding bed in the kitchen gratis and charged them only for their meals—$1.50 a week—"because they are relatives."

Others of the group were similarly subsidized by relatives, even friends, who undercharged them or kept them without payment

Samuel Gompers, president of the American Federation of Labor, addresses historic November 22, 1909, Cooper Union meeting, which voted for shirtwaist strike.

when they were out of work. Such generosity and kindness often serves to conceal and to relieve the hardships of women who are trying to be self-supporting on a wage that is both insufficient and uncertain. Even with such subsidies many are able to obtain only the barest necessities.

Rarely did a woman enjoy the luxury and privacy of a room to herself. "Room" frequently meant sleeping space, perhaps only in a folding bed or on a cot in a room with two or three other women. Their clothes they stowed away in a chiffonier shared with the family, or in a trunk, box, or valise. If their wardrobes had been more extensive many would have been hard put to it to find a place for them.

The presence of these boarders and lodgers means great overcrowding in the household, especially at night, when every bit of floor space in the small flats is covered with a great variety of sleeping devices. Folding beds are dragged out from corners, and imposing pieces of furniture that by day appear to be chiffoniers or sideboards become beds for two or three lodgers at night.

Even the kitchen, which serves as the common cooking, dining and living room, and in the absence of a bathroom as a washing place where the various members of the household have to perform their morning ablutions at the sink, must do service at night as a bedroom. For 50 cents a week, one woman who earned $3 a week was entitled to share a folding bed in the kitchen.

One of a number of scholarly articles on the garment industry was written by Goodman and Ueland. From *Journal of Political Economy*, December 1910.

SUBCONTRACTING
by Pearl Goodman and Elsa Ueland

The shirtwaist trade is a new one, only fifteen or twenty years old, and is also peculiarly local. The great bulk of our shirtwaist manufacture is done in New York and Philadelphia and their suburbs, and the whole country is the market for the waists and dresses made here. But new and local as it is, this shirtwaist industry—or the waist and dress industry, as we might more properly call it, for dresses are made by the same people and in the same shops as waists—has grown to enormous proportions. It does an amount of business in New York City alone which the president of the Associated Waist and Dress Manufacturers estimates is worth a hundred million dollars a year. There are in this city in the neighborhood of 450 factories, employing about 40,000 workers.

The trade is full of surprising differences and contrasts in shop organization. One manufacturer has little knowledge of the methods of the next. The first will claim that it is an advantage to have a single skilled girl do as much of the waist as possible, the second will put his shop upon as extreme a "sectional" basis as he can, and make one garment go through thirty hands in the making. Again, in one shop the employees work individually, under the direction of a foreman; in another they work in "partnerships"; in a third they are organized in groups of five or six; in a fourth they are under subcontractors, and in a fifth all these methods may be combined.

There is also unusual diversity of work in a single shop. The tasks range from those performed by a skilled operator to the simple cutting of threads, which can be done by an unpracticed girl of fourteen. Adaptability to change is demanded of the worker in a way that is peculiar to his trade. There may be three or four styles made in a single day. There are various materials prevalent in the various seasons and the workers themselves have to shift sometimes from one kind of work to another.

In one other respect the shops differ widely, and that is in their methods of breaking in the "learners." There is no apprentice system, and yet some of the work requires a great deal of dexterity. How do the girls get started? Some get training by working "partners" with a worker who is more experienced. These partnerships are very common. Often two sisters or two friends will be found who have worked together as partners for years.

Only one name or one number is put on the payroll, and the partners divide the wages according to some agreed ratio. A partnership with more than two members is called a "group" or "set." Its members are related to each other or are friends, just as are the members of the typical partnership. One group of eight was found which includes four brothers, a sister, a brother-in-law, and two cousins, all paid under one number on the wage book.

This partnership or group system gives one way of breaking in the "learner"; another way is by subcontracting. The subcontracting system is an admitted evil, a system which has been justly fought by the union. The contractor's interest is to get a quantity of work done by driving employees who have not independence enough to sell their services directly to the boss. The best manufacturers all condemn the system.

Lemlich, executive board member of Local 25, sparked the
1909 walkout of shirtwaist makers with her call for a strike.
From *New York Evening Journal,* November 28, 1909.

LIFE IN THE SHOP
by Clara Lemlich

First let me tell you something about the way we work and what we are
paid. There are two kinds of work—regular, that is salary work, and
piecework. The regular work pays about $6 a week and the girls have
to be at their machines at 7 o'clock in the morning and they stay at
them until 8 o'clock at night, with just one-half hour for lunch in that
time.

The shops. Well, there is just one row of machines that the daylight
ever gets to—that is the front row, nearest the window. The girls at all
the other rows of machines back in the shops have to work by gaslight,
by day as well as by night. Oh, yes, the shops keep the work going at
night, too.

The bosses in the shops are hardly what you would call educated
men, and the girls to them are part of the machines they are running.
They yell at the girls and they "call them down" even worse than I
imagine the Negro slaves were in the South.

There are no dressing rooms for the girls in the shops. They have
to hang up their hats and coats—such as they are—on hooks along the
walls. Sometimes a girl has a new hat. It never is much to look at
because it never costs more than 50 cents, but it's pretty sure to be
spoiled after it's been at the shop.

We're human, all of us girls, and we're young. We like new hats as
well as any other young women. Why shouldn't we? And if one of us
gets a new one, even if it hasn't cost more than 50 cents, that means
that we have gone for weeks on two-cent lunches—dry cake and
nothing else.

The shops are unsanitary—that's the word that is generally used,
but there ought to be a worse one used. Whenever we tear or damage
any of the goods we sew on, or whenever it is found damaged after we
are through with it, whether we have done it or not, we are charged
for the piece and sometimes for a whole yard of the material.

At the beginning of every slow season, $2 is deducted from our
salaries. We have never been able to find out what this is for.

The fuse which set off the general strike of shirtwaist makers was the strike at the Triangle Shirtwaist Company. From *The Survey,* December 18, 1909.

THE FIRST SHIRTWAIST WALKOUT
by Constance D. Leupp

Curiously enough, it was a subcontractor who started the strike. Some 18 months ago at the Triangle shop on Washington Place (Harris and Blanck's) this man because he was "sick of slave-driving" protested to the manager, saying that he wanted to go and take his girls with him.

He was not allowed to speak to the girls after he had expressed himself, but was told to report to the cashier for his pay. Fearful of a slugging on the way up in the elevator, he asked to have someone go with him, and was not only refused, but set upon and dragged out of the shop—the original "assault."

As he was dragged along he shouted, "Will you stay at your machines and see a fellow worker treated this way?" And impulsively 400 operators dropped their work and walked out.

Socially prominent women, battling for the right to vote, recognized a common bond with the immigrant strikers and joined the picket line at Triangle. From *The Survey,* November 3, 1909.

ON THE PICKET LINE

The strike of 200 women employees of the Triangle Waist Company of New York has been going on for several weeks according to the most approved strike methods. The management of the company has tried to "protect its rights" against these girls by calling into commission a regiment of police, plainclothes detectives and other burly men, the girls declare, who are nothing more than neighborhood thugs, sufficient in number to handle a general industrial disturbance, quite willing to strike women and to hustle them off to court on flimsy pretexts.

The strikers declare that the management has brought pressure to bear upon the employees to prevent their forming a union, discriminating against union members by giving them less well-paid positions and dismissing them.

The Triangle Waist Company girls have been entirely orderly, but police interference has made them appear otherwise. The officers break in upon any who are talking together; men loafing about in the employ of the company have insulted the girls; and the least resistance or answering back by the women is made excuse for a prompt arrest. Unfair treatment has not stopped there, for in court the judges have railroaded through a whole batch of girls at a time without so much as a hearing.

A somewhat different aspect was put upon the matter and a vast amount of publicity in behalf of the girls secured by the entrance into the field of the Women's Trade Union League and other interested people, largely women settlement workers, which resulted in the arrest of their president, Miss Mary Dreier of Brooklyn.

These volunteer workers have formed themselves into an organized patrol, six or eight of whom place themselves in front of the shop at opening and closing time, looking after the rights of the girls and going to court as witnesses with strikers who are arrested. Miss Dreier was discharged upon arrival at the nearest station house, and the police attitude toward the women was deliciously revealed when the officer in charge upbraided her for not having told him that she was "the rich working girls' friend," had he known which, of course, he would not have arrested her.

The Triangle walkout, sparked by grievances common throughout the shirtwaist industry, exploded into a general strike. From the *Call*, November 23, 1909.

THE COOPER UNION MEETING

The decision to strike was reached yesterday at the Cooper Union meeting which was addressed by Samuel Gompers, president of the AFL.

Gompers was given an ovation when he was introduced by Chairman Benjamin Feigenbaum. The vast crowd rose to its feet and cheered him very enthusiastically for several minutes.

"A man would be less than human," said Gompers, in opening, "if he were not impressed with your reception. I want you men and women not to give all your enthusiasm for a man, no matter who he may be. I would prefer that you put all of your enthusiasm into your union and your cause."

Continuing, Gompers said: "I have never declared a strike in all my life. I have done my share to prevent strikes, but there comes a time when not to strike is but to rivet the chains of slavery upon our wrists."

Speaking of the possibility of a general strike, Gompers said: "Yes, Mr. Shirtwaist Manufacturer, it may be inconvenient for you if your boys and girls go out on strike, but there are things of more importance than your convenience and your profit. There are the lives of the boys and girls working in your business."

Appealing to the men and women to stand together, he declared: "If you had an organization before this, it would have stood there as a challenge to the employers who sought to impose such conditions as you bear.

"This is the time and the opportunity, and I doubt if you let it pass whether it can be created again in five or ten years or a generation. I

On December 4, 1909, shirtwaist makers, passing Chambers Street on way to City Hall, petitioned the mayor for police protection.

say, friends, do not enter too hastily but when you can't get the manufacturers to give you what you want, then strike. And when you
strike, let the manufacturers know you are on strike!

"I ask you to stand together," said Gompers in conclusion, "to have
faith in yourselves, to be true to your comrades. If you strike, be cool,
calm, collected and determined. Let your watchword be: Union and
progress, and until then no surrender!"

This was greeted with a storm of applause.

Clara Lemlich, who was badly beaten up by thugs during the strike
in the shop of Louis Leiserson, interrupted Jacob Panken just as he
started to speak, saying: "I wanted to say a few words." Cries came
from all parts of the hall, "Get up on the platform!" Willing hands
lifted the frail little girl with flashing black eyes to the stage, and she
said simply: "I have listened to all the speakers. I would not have
further patience for talk, as I am one of those who feels and suffers
from the things pictured. I move that we go on a general strike!"

As the tremulous voice of the girl died away, the audience rose en
masse and cheered her to the echo. A grim sea of faces, with high
purpose and resolve, they shouted and cheered the declaration of war
for living conditions hoarsely.

In a moving historic moment, young women for the first
time made the profound personal decision to act. From
McClures' Magazine, November 1910.

FIRST MORNING OF THE STRIKE
by Sue Ainslee Clark and Edith Wyatt

On the evening of the 22nd of November, Natalya Urisova, and how
many others from the factory she could not tell, attended a mass
meeting at Cooper Union, of which they had been informed by hand-
bills. It was called for the purpose of discussing a general strike of
shirtwaist workers in New York City. The hall was packed. Overflow
meetings were held at Beethoven Hall, Manhattan Lyceum, and Astoria Hall. In the Cooper Union, addresses were delivered by Samuel
Gompers, by Miss Dreier, and by many others. Finally, a girl of eigh-

teen asked the chairman for the privilege of the floor. She said: "I have listened to all the speeches. I am one who thinks and feels from the things they describe. I, too, have worked and suffered. I am tired of the talking. I move that we go on a general strike."

The meeting broke into wild applause. The motion was unanimously endorsed. The chairman, Mr. Feigenbaum, a Union officer, rapped on the table. "Do you mean faith?" he called to the workers. "Will you take the old Jewish oath?" Thousands of right hands were held up and the whole audience repeated in Yiddish: "If I turn traitor to the cause I now pledge, may this hand wither from the arm I now raise."

This was the beginning of the general shirtwaist strike. A committee of fifteen girls and one boy was appointed at the Cooper Union meeting, and went from one to the other of the overflow meetings, where the same motion was offered and unanimously endorsed.

"But I did not know how many workers in my shop had taken that oath at that meeting. I could not tell how many would go on strike in our factory the next day," said Natalya afterward. "When we came back the next morning to the factory, no one went to the dressing room. We all sat at the machines with our hats and coats beside us, ready to leave. The foreman had no work for us when we got there. But, just as always, he did not tell when there would be any, or if there would be any at all that day.

"And there was whispering and talking softly all around the room among the machines: 'Shall we wait like this?' 'There is a general strike.' 'Who will get up first?' 'It would be better to be the last to get up, and then the company might remember it of you afterward, and do well for you.' But I told them," observed Natalya, with a little shrug, "What difference does it make which one is first and which one is last? Well, so we stayed whispering, and no one knowing what the other would do, not making up our minds, for two hours.

"Then I started to get up." Her lips trembled. "And at just the same minute all—we all got up together, in one second. No one after the other; no one before. And when I saw it—that time—oh, it excites me so yet, I can hardly talk about it. So we all stood up, and all walked out together. And already out on the sidewalk in front the policemen stood with the clubs. One of them said, 'If you don't behave, you'll get this on your head.' And he shook his club at me.

"We hardly knew where to go—what to do next. But one of the American girls, who knew how to telephone, called up the Women's Trade Union League, and they told us all to come to a big hall a few blocks away.

"Then a leader spoke to us and told us about picketing quietly, and the law."

The circular of advice issued a little later by the Union reads as follows:

RULES FOR PICKETS

Don't walk in groups of more than two or three.

Don't stand in front of the shop; walk up and down the block.

Don't stop the person you wish to talk to; walk alongside of him.

Don't get excited and shout when you are talking.

Don't put your hand on the person you are speaking to. Don't touch his sleeve or button. This may be construed as a "technical assault."

Don't call anyone "scab" or use abusive language of any kind.

Plead, persuade, appeal, but do not threaten.

If a policeman arrests you and you are sure that you have committed no offense, take down his number and give it to your Union officers.

Mailly pointed out the larger significance of the strike. From the *Independent,* January 1, 1910.

THE LARGEST STRIKE OF WOMEN
by William Mailly

The metropolis is now witnessing a conflict between employer and employees not only unique in its inception and unprecedented in its development, but also the largest strike of women ever known in the United States. Never before have so many working women quit work at one time in one place, and with such spontaneity and unanimity. The occurrence is not alone remarkable in itself—it is still more remarkable for what it signifies, as an illustration of the growing unrest that is permeating the ranks of working women.

This strike which takes on almost the character of a revolt, came practically without intimation, preparation or organization, but it had its beginnings long before when successive efforts to organize a shirtwaist makers' union in various shops and factories proved a failure. The union was growing, but growing slowly, in spite of the reverses which it continually met with. It was out of one of these reverses that the present situation emerged to surprise the union leaders as much as it startled the employers. And it is certain that the conflict would not have assumed the magnitude it has if the police and the police courts had not accelerated its development by their harsh and unwarranted treatment of a group of girls who were locked out by a waist company in September last.

Now, non-union employers are sending work to other cities. A sympathetic strike has occurred in a Newark shop on account of this. In Philadelphia the union shirtwaist makers have decided to have a general strike if necessary to win the strike in New York. The same action is pending in Hartford and other cities. . . . In several instances workers in shops not directly affiliated with the waistmakers "came down" in sympathy but were requested to return to work by the waistmakers officials.

In every shop there are always a few girls in the lead. Some of these have been agitating for a long time; some are new and are having their first experience as leaders. But these leaders are invariably the best paid, the ones who get the most wages, in each shop. They are the ones who have less reason to complain. They have carried their sisters along with them by the very force of their own determination and the spirit of resistance to the general conditions prevailing. One has but to associate with these fine, . . . intelligent and courageous girls to appreciate their moral caliber and their capacity for self-sacrifice and devotion.

In shirtwaist strikers' march to City Hall.

Comstock visited one of the strike halls where upper-class social workers gave guidance to the strikers. From *Colliers Magazine,* December 25, 1909.

IN THE STRIKERS' HALL
by Sarah Comstock

Clinton Hall has been the caldron of the strike from first to last. Here union strikers have poured in to compare grievances and hearten one another; non-union strikers to register and "join." Employers have come here to settle; blackboard bulletins have kept the workers informed of the shops settled, where they might find work again. Through the clamoring, angry, merry, flirting, anxious complaining, hysterical thousands seething there, the old bearded Jews pass constantly with their baskets of pretzels and apples. A penny or two will buy such a lunch, and, munching it, the strikers have stood by their colors.

At the end of a swarming corridor I found fortifications of tables where the Women's Trade Union League was conducting an information bureau. This organization is under the leadership of certain social workers and "organizers," and is a sort of foster-mother to women's unions. At the first news of the strike its officers went to Clinton Hall, and there they have toiled day and night, endeavoring to bring order out of chaos.

A line of girls, thirty or more long, balked my progress.

"What is their goal?" I asked a member of the League.

"Registration. They are girls who have never belonged to a union, but they have caught the striking fever and have gone out—and now they find themselves without work, without a head, confused, frightened, excited."

The girls in this room were in truth "confused, frightened, excited." Yiddish words, Yiddish gestures, here and there Italian chatter made a pandemonium. Flirtations had been left in the entrance hall; here was the real chaos of the strike.

"He gotta raise me. I don't work till he does," one would tell another.

"Them scabs, they make us starve."

"Say, I tell the boss it's good if he go broke after what he done to us."

Vindictiveness, determination, anxiety leaked through the talk even when it was in an unknown tongue. They were mature vindictiveness, determination, anxiety too. And yet few of these girls were over twenty, many as young as twelve. Mrs. Weyl has since said to me that it has been like handling a vast kindergarten to control them.

"Can't you help?" somebody asked me. A minute later I was ensconced at a table taking down addresses. They were of small East Side halls where groups of unorganized striking girls had been gathered so that a speaker from the League might address them and urge them to organize.

"Say, you send a speaker quick—right now. The girls are there and they don't wanta wait."

"Say they're all leavin'. We can't keep 'em. Hurry up a speaker in Italian." Another address.

"Have we an Italian speaker?" I broke away to ask a League officer, while a clamor of "We want a Yiddish . . . Say, they won't wait no longer . . . Say, ain't there nobody to tell 'em not to give in?" dinned in my ears.

"Can't get an Italian today. Hardest thing to find," said Miss Marot.

At my left was the table where money flowed in. For a deposit of twenty-five cents the non-union girls were being admitted to the organization. At my right, queries and complaints in general found refuge.

"There!" said Miss Pike, suddenly turning to me. "Did you hear that? People won't believe it, but we have proved it over and over!"

Two excited young Italians had just appealed to her for help. Their story ran that a group of girls had been sent to a certain Wooster Street shop as pickets, peaceful picketing being legitimate in the State of New York. The employer, annoyed by their attempts to induce scabs to leave him, had engaged a gang of toughs, strikebreakers, to guard his shop by frightening the pickets away, and the intimidated girls were now unable to approach the shop, the policeman on duty being accused of supporting the toughs.

Selling special edition of the *Call* for benefit of the strikers.

Daily incidents on the picket lines provided a quick course
in labor education for the strikers. From the *New York
Tribune*, December 11, 1909.

PROTECTING STRIKEBREAKERS

"We ain't here to protect the strikers nor anybody belongin' to 'em.
We're here to protect the scabs," one of the officers detailed to a shop
in Grand Street said frankly last night to a member of the Women's
Trade Union League who was picketing.

The length of Greene Street and all over the surrounding district
shops could be seen similarly picketed and guarded by policemen and
detectives in plainclothes. At 6 o'clock the first squad of women
strikebreakers was hurried down from the shop.

"Girls, do you know there's a strike on at Abrams's?" called the
pickets as they passed them. That was all, and none of the pickets
stopped walking a minute, but the officer laid his hand on his club
and proceeded to hustle the pickets.

"Move faster!" he admonished them, "an' walk further. You've no
right to keep walkin' in front of this shop. Do you want to get t'rown in
de gutter? Ah!"

But the pickets gave him no opening. The shop "boss" took a
hand.

"Get along and stop obstructin' my sidewalk!" he shouted.

"We are moving, and you're not an officer," retorted the little Barnard graduate who was walking with the trained nurse. She's about
four feet high.

"This is my sidewalk. You move!" he threatened her. She was moving. All the pickets kept moving, only as they moved they kept up
their call to the women who poured out of the shops from time to
time.

"Girls, do you know there's a strike on?"

The magistrates seem to be changing their attitude toward the
strikers. In the Essex Market Court yesterday morning Magistrate
Krotel imposed a fine of $10 each on five girl shirtwaist makers
charged with taking part in a riot on Clinton Street Thursday night,
and told them if they were brought before him again he would send
them to the workhouse. Magistrate Breen, in the Jefferson Market
Court, who heretofore simply lectured the strikers brought before
him, fined several yesterday for "annoying non-union girls going to
work."

Benson reported that class distinctions were ignored in the battle for a common cause. From *Munseys Magazine,* April 1910.

SISTERS UNDER THE SKIN
by Allan L. Benson

All women—being sympathetic creatures—could feel that. Some of the richest women in the country felt it. Mrs. O. H. P. Belmont, mother of the Duchess of Marlborough, felt it. Miss Anne Morgan, daughter of J. Pierpont Morgan, felt it. Mrs. Belmont sat up nearly all night in the night court to save some accused strikers from the necessity of spending Sunday in the Tombs, and, at three o'clock in the morning gave her Madison Avenue mansion as security for the appearance of the strikers in court the following day.

The daughter of another rich woman induced her mother to deed the family mansion to her in order that she might sit in court, day after day, and give bail for arrested girls. Miss Morgan showed her interest by attending a demonstration given in honor of a poor girl returned from the workhouse. Girls from Vassar—Miss Elsie Cole, Miss Elizabeth Dutcher, and Miss Violet Pike—showed their interest by giving up their holiday vacations, going on picket lines and doing everything else that they could to promote the cause of their suffering sisters.

But the spur did more. It caused the women whom it had driven into factories to act like men who work in factories. Men who thus work do not weep or mourn when things in the factories pass beyond what they conceive to be their endurance. They strike. Not only do they strike, but they stick to their colors and battle for their cause as long as they have strength to do so. Yet no man ever gave a greater exhibition of dogged determination to persevere to the end than did these girls not yet out of their teens.

When they "picketed" the factories and tried to prevent other women from taking their places, there was excitement and some disorder in the streets. In the scuffling, some of the girls were grabbed by the hair, and their heads were bumped against the curbstones. Never mind—let the strike go on!

More than six hundred were arrested, and a score were sent to the workhouse. What of it? Merely incidents of industrial warfare—let the strike proceed!

Barriers of class and language were leveled in mid-December when members of high society gave a tea for the shirtwaist strikers in the exclusive Colony Club. From the *Call,* December 16, 1909.

TEA AT THE COLONY CLUB

A remarkable meeting, one that was as peculiar as it was interesting, and as unique as it was pathetic, took place yesterday afternoon for the striking waistmakers at the Colony Club, the most exclusive club in the city, of which Miss Anne Morgan, Miss Elizabeth Marbury, Mrs. Edgerton, Mrs. J. B. Harriman and others of the same financial and social standing are members.

These women, the cream of the "400," had come to listen to the story of the strike from the lips of the strikers, told in simple words by those who had been mistreated, abused, enslaved by capitalism, poverty and police persecution. Four hundred women, representing the richest people of the world, occupied as many gilt chairs in the beautiful gymnasium of the sumptuous club.

In contradistinction to this bejeweled, befurred, belaced, begowned audience, Miss Mary E. Dreier, president of the Women's Trade Union League, brought with her 10 of the girl strikers, 10 wage slaves, some of them mere children, who, as they subsequently told, worked from early morning till late at night for as little as $3 a week; girls on whose meagre earnings depended children still younger, mothers sick and fathers out of work.

And the rich women listened. Seldom, if ever, have they listened with such interest to the tales of the war between capital and labor, to the incidents of pain, of misery, of grief in the great struggle between the classes.

Miss Dreier, introducing the strikers, said that she would not give their names, as some of them had to tell of circumstances too painful to appear in print.

One young girl, who said that she worked at the Triangle Waist Company, told how that firm hired prostitutes to abuse them when they first began to picket. She said, "They hired immoral girls to attack us and they would approach us only to give the policemen the excuse to arrest us. In two weeks 89 arrests were made. I, too, was arrested, and the policeman grabbed me by the hand and said such insulting words that I am ashamed to tell you."

One pretty girl told what happened to her the day before when she was picketing. "I just called to a girl and said that I wanted to talk to her. She then turned on me and smashed me in the face, breaking my glasses and cutting my eye. I began to scream and called on the policeman to protect me. Instead of that he arrested me and dragged me to the station house where I had to spend the entire night."

Another girl said that there are on the books of the manufacturers girls who make as high as $30. But when you come to examine the thing closer you will find that there are four girls working under her, and that the money is to be divided among them.

One girl told how some firms have a systematic way of stealing time from the girls. She said: "I worked for the Bijou Waist Company and they made us work long hours by moving the hands of the clock when we did not see it. Sometimes we found that we got 20 minutes for lunch and that when the clock showed 5 it was really after 6."

After the meeting the girls and the women of the league were taken down to tea.

Sheldon kept a record of events during the strike. Following are sample entries from "A Souvenir History of the Strike of the Ladies Waist Makers' Union," 1910.

DAY TO DAY
by F. E. Sheldon

December 3rd initiated the month's activities with a monster indignation parade to City Hall—ten thousand striking Waistmakers, marching four abreast, in orderly fashion, to call upon the Mayor, their Mayor, to present to him their petition and their protest against the abuse and mistreatment received at the hands of their police force. Inspiring host of class-conscious workers, bent on maintaining their rights, headed by three noble women of the [Women's] Trade Union League and three noble victims of brutal assault, they reached City Hall Park at 2:30 P.M., where their entrance was barred by mounted police and they were obliged to rest arms on both sides of Park Row at the Post Office.

A petition in the name of thirty thousand women, signed by S. Schindler, was handed Mayor McClellan by the spokesman, Miss Marot, who described her experiences when picketing, and also had some of the striking girls tell the Mayor of how they had been handled by the police.

December 5th was one of the red-letter days. The Political Equality Association, with Mrs. O. H. P. Belmont's help, had previously engaged the Hippodrome for the Ladies' Shirtwaist Makers' Union, and

long before the advertised hour every seat was filled, every foot of the
mammoth stage was occupied. It was one of the largest meetings in
the history of organized labor, and thousands were the disappointed
sympathizers turned away by a line of surly police formed to disperse
the overflow crowd.

Baskets were passed and a goodly collection raised to help maintain
those out of work.

A mass meeting was held in Newark to aid the work of organization
in cooperation with the New York movement, and at their request, S.
A. Stodel, Max Danish and Publio Mazella, of New York, made
speeches and secured four hundred new members.

December 9th a mass meeting was held in the Thalia Theatre by
the Socialists of local New York. Such a rousing meeting, with such
general helpings of encouragement, was described by those fortunate enough to be there, to strikers otherwise engaged, and always
first in their report was a pleasant reference to Mother Jones, whose
speech rang true with the words, "This is not play; this is fight," and
was ably followed by Algernon Lee, Edward F. Cassidy and Albert
Abrahams, who were all ably introduced by Carrie W. Allen, who
presided.

Sunday the 12th, Rev. Alexander Irvine preached a noteworthy
sermon at the Church of the Ascension, Fifth Avenue and Tenth
Street, and held an after meeting in the chapel, where the Misses Elsie
Cole, Violet Pike, Jeffries, Mrs. Leroy Scott and Mrs. Rose Pastor
Stokes each presented an interesting side of the strike and helped
make a collection, which amounted to over one hundred and fifty
dollars.

The afternoon of the 13th was alive with interest, as thousands
packed themselves into Grand Central Palace to hear Messrs. John
Mitchell and Morris Hillquit's report of the arbitration conference.
Mr. B. Weinstein opened the meeting, and after making a welcome
report of the conditions of the strike in regard to the number of
manufacturers who had settled, reporting the same to be two
hundred and thirty-six firms to date, and that fifteen thousand good
unionists had returned to work under union conditions, with full
demands granted. Mr. Weinstein then, by request, asked Miss Rose
Schneiderman to preside, who, after a few well-chosen remarks, introduced Brother John Mitchell, who was entirely convincing that the
waistmakers, by rights, should have a union, and he quoted a statement made by no less an authority than President Taft, to support his
contention, that all right-minded men recognized the union as necessary in modern industrialism.

Then Mr. Morris Hillquit was introduced, and, as usual, held his
audience as long as he chose. The writer regrets that limited space
forbids a portrayal of his inimitable description of an alleged deal
between the bosses' association and a fake union leader, who, for a

small favor like two or three thousand dollars, would show them how to break up and sell out the entire Shirtwaist Makers' Union. He also exposed the unrepresentative proportion, the bosses' association held to the number of manufacturers in the trade, showing that not over 10 percent were represented by their decisions.

Miss Mulholland's satisfactory rendition of one or two vocal selections was much appreciated; also her leading in the singing of the "Marseillaise" aroused a mighty chorus. . . .

December 21st an automobile parade with placards as an adjunct to picketing was a novel sight.

December 22nd there occurred in the evening one of the most enjoyable affairs arranged under the auspices of a committee of Socialist women at Arlington Hall, and given in honor of the girls who had been sent to the workhouse. They were introduced from the stage and each presented with a medal. There was a musical program, including elocutionary numbers and a dance afterward. Refreshments were served to the strikers. Speeches were made by Carrie Allen, Leonora O'Reilly, Rose Schneiderman, Mrs. Meta Stern and others.

December 29th was a red-letter day in the strike and an eye-opener to the public. The *Call,* the only New York daily paper printed in English representative of the interests of labor, printed a special edition, telling the true story of the strike and donated it to the union. Imagine the interest caused when girls with six-inch wide white ribbons pinned across from shoulder to hip, appeared in the street, in every section of the city, selling the special *Call* for five cents or more per copy, as was advertised in large black type on the said white ribbons. The committee in charge had a newsgirl in every prominent spot, the papers went quickly and other editions had to be printed. Many a quarter, and a half, and even dollars, were given to the brave girls who stood out in the bitter cold, many with summer clothes on, and sold papers for hours, and in many cases before having had anything to eat.

December 30th, girls still selling special edition of the *Call.* Thirty-five thousand more printed today. Forty-five thousand copies sold so far at an average price of eight cents. Word received that Flora Zabelle, the popular actress, is leading a movement whereby five hundred actresses will boycott non-union-made waists.

January 1st is a peaceable day because the pickets can rest. Luckily, for one day there are no scabs to be watched, no police or thugs to be feared, and each girl wishes her sister an early settlement. Today I observed many a Jewish girl with her arm around an Italian girl's neck, not able to speak, one to the other, but both understanding they are fighting the same fight for each other's interests.

Sunday, January 2nd, was a quiet day, but an active evening—active in more ways than one to many people who thronged Carnegie Hall from the topmost gallery to the farthest seat, waiting to hear the accusation and censure to be heaped upon the heads of the public servants—in fact, their servants.

On the stage, in the front row, beside the speakers, sat 20 girls who had been sent to the workhouse, and behind them the stage was filled with three hundred and fifty girls who had been arrested and fined. Each young lady wore a printed sash, readable from the audience, telling how she had been distinguished by the court, and in six-inch letters labeled "Workhouse Prisoner" and "Arrested." Over their heads were banners bearing inscriptions such as, "The Workhouse is No Answer to a Demand for Justice."

Mr. Morris Hillquit made the speech of the evening. His reasoning, always clear and logical, never for a moment over the heads of his audience, was increasingly appreciated as he made point upon point, plucking the thistles and planting the lilies as he went.

Among other things he observed (in substance) that this effort for industrial organization was only a bromide given to a sick society, a good palliative, but in no wise a cure. That the Union is needful at present, and therefore good, but that after getting the Union, not to forget to work for that state of society, where such strife between two classes of the servants of society would be unknown; to abolish the discontent, so intimately a part of the competitive system, by changing the system.

Miss Leonora O'Reilly, organizer of the Women's Trade Union League, spoke for the girls. She told of their struggle for a Union, and how much more difficult to bear the attitude of police and magistrates had made it; how perplexed they were to be advised that they had a right to a union and a legal right to picket, and then to experience the treatment they had from both judge and police in a country they had not long ago believed to be the free harbor of all the oppressed. She told how costly a daily average of $125 a day in fines was to a Union feeding so many thousands.

She led out little Miss Rose Perr and encouraged her to say a few words regarding her experience. This child, no taller than the average girl of ten years, with her hair in a braid down her back, and her dress but to the top of her shoes, stood before that great audience and with simple faith told that she had been taken to court as a witness because she had asked a police captain to arrest a ruffian that had slapped a girl; how she was confronted there by the hireling of the boss, whom she had never seen; how they had testified that she had assaulted a scab and how she was railroaded to the workhouse for five days without being given an opportunity to be heard.

"So that is why we want to ask whether we are criminals or not," she concluded.

January 5th. Miss Elizabeth Dutcher, of the W.T.U.L., cabled Mr. Bernard Shaw as follows:

SHAW, 10 ADELPHI TERRACE, LONDON:—MAGISTRATE TELLS SHIRTWAIST MAKER HERE SHE IS ON A STRIKE AGAINST GOD, WHOSE PRINCIPAL LAW IS MAN SHOULD EARN BREAD IN SWEAT OF BROW.

PLEASE CHARACTERIZE REPLY, CHARGES PAID.

His reply:

W.T.U.L., N.Y.:—DELIGHTFUL MEDIEVAL AMERICA, ALWAYS IN THE INTIMATE PERSONAL CONFIDENCE OF THE ALMIGHTY.

BERNARD SHAW

The above refers to Magistrate Olmstead, who said to a girl brought before him, among other things: "You are on strike against God and Nature."

When interviewed and shown the above he took the position that it was part of the duty of the Court to be schoolmaster to these working girls and teach them a proper respect for their boss and to find contentment in work.

January 12th. Miss Pauline Newman and Rose Schneiderman start on a visit to other cities to collect funds for the strike, Miss Newman going as far as Buffalo, Miss Schneiderman to Boston. . . .

January 15th. The Vassar College girls in Poughkeepsie collect over $100 at an enthusiastic meeting held in sympathy for their sisters that toil and are forced to strike.

January 17th. The Bijou Waist Company, of 536 Broadway, installed 150 cot beds for their scabs to sleep on in the factory and had Inspector Daly and a large force of police stand guard in front of their shop, not because the little girl pickets were likely to steal the big iron doors, or to break into the factory and kidnap their cherished scabs: no, it was but too plainly evident that all this was but part of the bribery and coercion needed to prevent the voluntary desertion that had been going on among their scabs. However, within a week from the time of this last bluff by the said Company they settled with the union, all demands and closed shop granted.

Thus, after three months of strike the 500 employees rejoice in their victory and congratulate Organizer Joseph Goldstein, who made the settlement, as he had many others, proving himself to be one of the big timbers in this strike.

January 19th. Wellesley College girls send $1,000 to help the strike and an order for 1,000 waists if manufactured by the cooperative company that has been projected. Professor Emily Balch presided; Professor Vida Scudder spoke.

January 22nd. L. Leiserson, the manufacturer whose employees have been on strike the longest, finally settles; Mr. Leiserson's long friendship for Mr. Morris Hillquit helped him to talk with Mr. Hill-

Arrested strikers were taken to the Jefferson Market prison at 6th Avenue and 10th Street.

quit in his office, and come to a satisfactory adjustment of the difficulties involved. This settlement, together with the Bijou Waist Company, which followed, and which were two of the strongholds of the Manufacturers' Association, which had just before been weakened by the settlement of Bloom & Millman (said to be secretary of the Manufacturers' Association) and the Princess Waist Company, all four large concerns, had done much to hasten the end of the strike, which is breaking up like the ice going out of the river in spring, and as I write a number of small firms are hourly coming in under cover with a settlement that still further warms the air so long frigid in the environs of those pinched by want.

January 23rd. In Grand Central Palace, 2,000 merrymaking unionists celebrate, rejoice and contribute money for the final battle, and dance and listen to witty speeches from 9 P.M. to 5 in the morning.

Scott summarized the gains scored by the strikers. From *Outlook Magazine*, July 2, 1910.

WHAT THE WOMEN STRIKERS WON

by Miriam Finn Scott

For fourteen weeks, amid the greatest hardships, they carried on the fight, and at length carried it on to complete victory. At the time the strike was declared off, 354 employers had signed the union's contract, and with a very few exceptions all had agreed to a closed shop, to a fifty-two-hour week, to a raise of wages from twelve to fifteen percent, to do away with the subcontracting system and many other abuses, to limit night work to two hours per day and not more than twice a week, to pay week-workers for legal holidays, and in the slack season to divide the work among all workers, instead of giving it to a favored few.

Important as are the direct economic results of the victory, there is another result of even greater significance, and that is the existence of a real union where before there had been but the shadow of one. Very recently I had the occasion to visit the new headquarters of the union, and the contrast with the headquarters before the fight began was enough in itself to tell what a different thing the Ladies' Waistmakers Union now is from the union of six months ago.

Instead of a corner in one room, the union has a suite of two rooms, which it already finds too small for its purpose; instead of a few hundred scattered members, there are now twenty thousand girls in good standing, with new ones coming in daily; instead of the entire staff of officers being incorporated in one man, the union has two organizers, two recording secretaries, two financial secretaries, nine walking delegates, one bookkeeper, and three stenographers. Besides, each organized shop has a volunteer chairman, and once a week all the chairmen meet with the walking delegates to report the conditions of the shops. In this way the union is kept in constant touch with each individual shop. Instead of an income of but little better than nothing a week, the average weekly income from dues and initiation fees is $2,400. The union has also established an employment bureau in its offices. When any girl is out of work, instead of tramping from shop to shop, she need only come to the bureau at the union's offices.

And, besides, the strike has had another result. There has been a tradition that women cannot strike. These young, inexperienced girls have proved that women can strike, and strike successfully.

Tarbell (1857–1944) was a pioneer muckraker with her exposé of the Standard Oil Company. From the *American Federationist*, March 1910.

THE LARGER ISSUE
by Ida M. Tarbell

I have talked to a number of the girls and heard them speak at meetings and everything corroborates this impression. All of the girls without exception that I have talked with, had worked out practically for themselves the conviction that the only chance for fair treatment in their industry was in standing together. They were so convinced of this that they were willing to go hungry, if necessary, in order to see it established.

This feeling seemed to be quite as strong among the girls who received good wages and fair treatment as among the girls who were underpaid and badly treated. They all argued that while their own condition might be better now, there was no telling when, if they atempted to stand alone, they would lose what they had. And in any case, they all argued that the stronger ought to help the weaker.

The logical way in which these girls argued this proposition has been most impressive to me. It proves conclusively how strong and how general the principle of unionism has grown. There is no escaping the deep seriousness with which this mass of girls were inspired, or the willingness with which they were ready to make sacrifices to establish their belief.

Not less impressive or less important in my judgment is another phase of the strike, and that is the almost general recognition on the part of the New York public that it is a movement which must be respected. From the start the press, if not altogether sympathetic, was respectful; while a large body of people, who had perhaps thought very little on the subject of unionism, and who had little acquaintance with the conditions under which the shirtwaist workers lived, immediately came to their assistance.

They said very rightly that these girls had a right to make an orderly stand to improve their condition. In doing that they are working not merely for themselves, but for a society as a whole. Anything which improves their condition must improve everything in the town. It was a recognition, perhaps in most cases unconscious, that the struggle of one is the struggle of all. The women who in New York went to the aid of these strikers did not as a rule, in my judgment, do so because they were women, but rather out of a new and growing sense of the solidarity of society, and new and growing sense that if anybody was making a fight against a wrong, it was their business to stand by and help. It seems to me the clearest and most interesting example of the growing sense there is on all sides of the relation between classes, of the interdependence, consequently of their mutual responsibility. I do not believe that it will ever be possible again for a group of men or women in any industry to make a fight in New York to improve their condition without their receiving substantial aid and sympathy from all ranks of society.

5. The Cloakmakers' Strike, 1910

Less than half a year after the shirtwaist workers had won their demands and returned to their shops, the cloakmakers were out on thz picket lines in a general industry strike. Their walkout contrasted markedly with the shirtwaist makers' strike.

The women had struck almost spontaneously. Their colorful appearance on the picket lines won the sympathy of community leaders and articulate upper-class women. The walkout dramatized a reprehensible industrial setup and proved that women—even immigrant womzn—could conduct a strike.

On the other hand, many of the men who were encouraged by this victory to go out on strike again were battle-scarred veterans of earlier strikes; being family breadwinners, they had experienced the grim reality of hunger. Many had moved beyond sophistication to bitter cynicism as a result of having seen favoritism triumph in the shops. If they were to move once again into the breach, it would have to be with greater assurance of victory than ever before.

Leiserson cites an example of the kind of experience that, for more than a generation, prepared the cloakmakers for the ultimate test. Abraham Cahan's piece of fiction illustrates the strange ambiguities of the task system, in which units of time were defined by volume of work.

But it is the eyewitness account by Abraham Rosenberg, himself a prime officer of the union during the cloakmakers' strike, that catches the excitement of the days leading up to the decision to act—the skillful technique of tightening organization through smaller strikes; the careful formation of committees and pooling of resources; and the thrilling moment of decision. Meyer London's brief account describes how the men marched into the streets with a deep awareness of the sense of the historic moment.

How the vast strike machinery was mounted and set in motion in July 1910 is explored in detail by Morris Hillquit. In this battle, no well-meaning citizens, no auxiliary of reformers came to the aid of the striking cloakmakers; they had to scrounge for strike relief and food packages for their women and children.

As the knot of hunger tightened—and employers grew desperate in the silent shops—leaders in the Jewish community, apprehensive over growing tensions, attempted to reach a settlement. Louis D. Brandeis presided over a conference unprecedented in American labor-management relations—a face-to-face confrontation between both parties, with the focus on basic issues. This meeting is described in the excerpt from the conference record.

But a stalemate at the negotiation table lowered hopes and increased despair. Leaders called for courage, a move reflected in the strike bulletin and the news items from the *Call*. Meanwhile, as J. B. McPherson reports, the men at the bargaining table sought to formulate definitions and procedures, an effort frustrated by the sudden branding of the strike as an illegal activity, as reported by the *New York Tribune*.

In the steamy days of August, both parties understood that the Goff injunction, reported by the *New York Tribune,* by removing the police surveillance the mayor had ordered, opened the way for bloody warfare in the Jewish enclave. Edith Wyatt describes the anxiety and confusion rampant on the East Side as disbelief and rumors of settlement spread. In the end, Louis Marshall and other leaders of the Jewish community forced a compromise.

The jubilant spirit resulting from the settlement of the walkout clearly emerges in Rosenberg's account of the end of the hostilities. Mary Sumner Brown itemizes the compromises that led to the settlement. B. Hoffman (Zivyon) draws a comparison between the cloakmaker's strike and the shirtwaist walkout of the previous year; whereas the latter had been settled by means of hundreds of shop agreements (as a result of which the gains soon were lost), the former was resolved by a single Protocol of Peace in which workers and employers had, for the first time, bargained collectively.

The ILGWU had survived its severest trial. It had established its permanency and, under the Protocol, had created enduring concepts of collective bargaining: wage scales and minimums; an impartial settlement of disputes; and a tripartite responsibility for the health, safety, and decent living standards of the garment workers. For the first time the public interest and public representatives were actively involved in the relations of labor and management—this in an industry long considered impervious to unionization and industrial statesmanship.

From "History of the Jewish Labor Movement in New York City," 1908.

THE 1890 LOCKOUT
by William M. Leiserson

In February 1890, the cloakmakers began to rebel against the reductions in wages and the bad treatment to which they were subjected at the hands of the contractors. Shop after shop went on strike, and they called upon the United Hebrew Trades to conduct thz strikes for them. That body sent a committee of three, among them Joseph Barondess, a delegate from the Knee Pants Makers, to 92 Hester Street, where most of the strikers were assembled. The committee found the men from each shop conducting separate meetings in different rooms. To each of these meetings they repeated their plan of uniting all the strikers in one strong union. It was hailed with joy, and Barondess was elected to lead the united strikers.

The strike lasted six weeks, and ended with a complete victory for the union. Even Meyer Jonasson, the most prominent cloak manufacturer in New York, was forced to come to the basement at 92 Hester Street, the strikers' headquarters, to sign the union agreement. All together 3,500 cloakmakers had been out, but many went back to work within three weeks when some employers began to concede the demands.

As a result of the victory the Cloakmakers' Union became very strong. Immediately after the settlement it had 2,800 members divided into nine branches, one for each cloak manufacturing house. This form of organization was found unsatisfactory and the executive committee decided to divide the union into branches of 300 members each ... By May 1, 1890, the union had grown to eleven branches with over 3,000 members. It had good control of the trade, and the employers were afraid of it. For a short time there was peace. Toward the end of May, however, ten manufacturers suddenly locked out all their cloakmakers. They refused to employ any more union men.

The struggle was most bitter. At first it seemed as if the union would be defeated, but Barondess got the cutters and the contractors to join the operators against the manufacturers. On June 16, 1890, Operators and Cloakmakers' Union No. 1, Cloak and Suit Cutters' Union and the Contractors' Union, entered into an agreement to combine their strength against the manufacturers' association until the unions were recognized. The united forces held a mass meeting in Cooper Union, where addresses were delivered in Yiddish and in English. Six thousand people were present at this meeting.

The sympathy of the press during this strike was with the strikers. Many New York papers opened subscription lists to help them. The suffering of starving cloakmakers fighting for a chance to live they described in great headlines. When, after striking for two months some of the men became violent and attacked the scabs, the papers said they had been driven to desperation by hunger.

The public helped the strikers in many ways. A Jewish congregation offered dinners at five cents apiece to cloakmakers with union cards. Collections for their benefit were taken up in churches, department stores and bank houses. A certain Professor Garside, of whom very little was known except that he was an eloquent speaker, became prominent in this strike as a friend of the cloakmakers. He brought to the union every day sacks full of money which he had gathered by collections throughout the city.

The lockout had lasted nine weeks when the manufacturers asked the union to send a committee to settle all difficulties. The joy of the strikers was unbounded. A monster mass meeting was held in Cooper Union to celebrate the victory. The large auditorium was packed and many were turned away.

The negotiations of the committee with the manufacturers lasted three days. Then an agreement was brought to the union, signed by the manufacturers. It was written in English. Since few cloakmakers could understand the language, the strike committee decided to take the agreement to Abraham Cahan to find out whether it was a good settlement or not. Cahan read it and was astounded. "It is the worst settlement that could have been made," he declared, and advised them to call a mass meeting immediately, and there read the agreement to the audience in their own language.

That mass meeting will be remembered by those who attended it as long as they live. Cahan read the agreement point by point and there arose cries of "Treachery! Villainy! Let us continue the strike!"

A vote was taken by ballot on the question of remaining on strike. The affirmative received 1,536 votes, while twenty voted against striking. Then came the question of getting funds. All the old sources were exhausted. But hundreds of men and women took off their rings, watches and earrings. With tears in their eyes they took them to the chairman on the platform and told him to sell or pawn their jewelry, only that they may have money to continue the strike. In a quarter of an hour there was thrown on the chairman's table over $10,000 worth of jewelry.

This meeting was fully described in the newspapers the next day. The manufacturers saw that the strikers were bound to hold out for a long time. In two weeks an agreement was signed granting all the demands of the union. The important difference between the agreements was that the first one submitted made no mention of a price list. It left the employers free to lower wages.

Cahan (1860–1951) was the editor of the *Daily Forward,* which served as the chief organ of the Jewish immigrant garment workers. From "A Sweatshop Romance," 1898.

THE TWELVE-DAY WEEK
by Abraham Cahan

Leizer Lipman was one of those contract tailors who are classed by their hands under the head of "cockroaches," which—translating the term into lay English—means that he ran a very small shop, giving employment to a single team of one sewing-machine operator, one baster, one finisher, and one presser.

The shop was one of a suite of three rooms on the third floor of a rickety old tenement house on Essex Street, and did the additional duty of the family's kitchen and dining room. It faced a dingy little courtyard, and was connected by a windowless bedroom with the parlor, which commanded the very heart of the Jewish markets. Bundles of cloth, cut to be made into coats, littered the floor, lay in chaotic piles by one of the walls, cumbered Mrs. Lipman's kitchen table and one or two chairs, and formed, in a corner, an improvised bed upon which a dirty two-year-old boy, Leizer's heir apparent, was enjoying his siesta.

Dangling against the door or scattered among the bundles, there were cooking utensils, dirty linen, Lipman's velvet skullcap, hats, shoes, shears, cotton spools, and whatnot. A red-hot kitchen stove and a blazing grate full of glowing flatirons combined to keep up the overpowering temperature of the room, and helped to justify its nickname of sweatshop in the literal sense of the epithet.

Lipman's was a task shop, and, according to the signification which the term has in the political economy of the sweating world, his operator, baster, and finisher, while nominally engaged at so much a week, were in reality paid by the piece, the economical week being determined by a stipulated quantity of made-up coats rather than by a fixed number of the earth's revolutions around its axis; for the sweatshop day will not coincide with the solar day unless a given amount of work be accomplished in its course. As to the presser, he is invariably a pieceworker, pure and simple.

For a more lucid account of the task system in the tailoring branch, I beg to refer the reader to David, although his exposition happens to be presented rather in the form of a satire on the subject. Indeed, David, while rather inclined to taciturnity, was an inveterate jester, and what few remarks he indulged in during his work would often cause boisterous merriment among his shopmates, although he delivered them with a nonchalant manner and withhthe same look of good-humored irony, mingled in strange harmony with a general expression of gruffness, which his face usually wore.

"My twelve dollars every week?" David echoed. "Oh, I see; you mean a week of twelve days!" And his needle resumed its duck-like sport in the cloth.

"How do you make it out?" Meyer demanded, in order to elicit a joke from the witty young man by his side.

"Of course, *you* don't know how to make that out. But ask Heyman or Beile. The three of us do."

Making cloaks in the Golden Land.

"Tell him, then, and he will know too," Beile urged, laughing in advance at the expected fun.

A request coming from the finisher was—yet unknown to himself—resistless with David, and in the present instance it loosened his tongue.

"Well, I get twelve dollars a week, and Heyman fourteen. Now a working week has six days, but—hem—that 'but' gets stuck in my throat—but a day is neither a Sunday nor a Monday nor anything unless we make twelve coats. The calendars are a lot of liars."

"What do you mean?"

"They say a day has twenty-four hours. That's a bluff. A day has twelve coats."

Biele's rapturous chuckle whetted his appetite for persiflage, and he went on: "They read the Tuesday Psalm in the synagogue this morning, but I should have read the Monday one."

"Why?"

"You see, Meyer's wife will soon come up with his dinner, and here I have still two coats to make of the twelve that I got yesterday. So it's still Monday with me. My Tuesday won't begin before about two o'clock this afternoon."

"How much will you make this week?" Meyer questioned.

"I don't expect to finish more than four days' work by the end of the week, and will only get eight dollars on Friday—that is, provided the Missis has not spent our wages by that time. So when it's Friday I'll call it Wednesday, see."

"When I am married," he added, after a pause, "and the old woman asks me for Sabbath expenses, I'll tell her it is only Wednesday—it isn't yet Friday—and I have no money to give her."

Unlike the spontaneous uprising of the previous year, the 1910 general strike of cloakmakers was carefully planned. From *Memoirs of a Cloakmaker*, 1920.

THE DIE IS CAST
by Abraham Rosenberg

Delegates elected by the cloak and skirt locals were instructed to introduce at the convention the question of a general strike. As soon as the General Strike resolution was approved delegates rose to their feet. Some stood on chairs while others leaped onto the tables and the shouting and cheering continued in the hall for half an hour. Telegrams were sent at once to New York and ILGWU locals throughout the country calling on them to begin immediately preparations for the strike. When news of the convention's decision in Boston spread among the New York cloakmakers, thousands swarmed to the union office.

The press throughout the country carried long articles about the coming strike in New York. Only the New York cloak manufacturers maintained a front of innocent calm. They didn't believe workers would leave the shop for the union.

Our historic Madison Square Garden meeting was set for June 28 at eight in the evening. But by three o'clock in the afternoon streets in the neighborhood of the Garden were flooded with thousands of workers. The committee was compelled to open the Garden doors at five o'clock. In fifteen minutes, the huge hall with its galleries was packed to choking.

The committee stationed eight trucks in the street from which speakers could address the masses. The next day the press reported the streets had been jammed by 40,000 workers unable to get into the hall. New York had never before seen such a demonstration.

The enthusiasm at the meeting defies description. Each one felt this was the start of a new era for the labor movement—of a new life for the cloakmakers. Word had spread that the general strike would be called at this meeting; in many shops cloakmakers had already refused to start new work; others had hurried to finish work in progress so as not to be stuck with it.

However, the chairman opened the meeting with the announcement that the strike call would not be issued at this gathering. First there would have to be a secret vote by the members of all the nine locals.

On Saturday, Sunday and Monday, July 2, 3, and 4, eight polling places were opened in various locations. In each, there was placed a locked ballot box. The paper ballot measuring two by four inches was perforated down the middle for easy separation. One half had the word "Yes" in English, Yiddish, and Italian; the other half had the word "No." The voter needed only to tear along the perforation and insert the half of his choice into the ballot box.

As soon as the results were known, many cloak- and skirtmakers left their shops, thinking once again that the general strike had been declared. But through a *New Post* extra the union warned that no one should dare to leave the shop until the *Red New Post* carried the official call. Our masses obeyed—and waited.

Reporters tried by all means to ferret out the date of the strike call. Manufacturers called our office to ask when was the strike going to be called. They had to know in order to decide if they should continue to cut garments. Only the committee of three knew. But they kept silent. "Cut only singles!" we told the manufacturers.

On Wednesday morning, the sixth of July, the committee of three met. They fixed the time for the General Strike at exactly 2 P.M., Thursday, July 7.

The same day the committee wrote the following strike call in English, Yiddish and Italian. It directed that it be printed on blood-red paper.

GENERAL STRIKE DECLARED TODAY
2:00 P.M.

Today, at 2 P.M.—not earlier, not later—every cloak and skirt worker—operator, tailor, finisher, cutter, skirtmaker, presser, buttonhole maker—must put aside his work and together with all other workers go out on strike. Not one of you must remain in the shops! All out!

In leaving your shops be careful to maintain absolute order. Don't lose your heads; keep cool.

At exactly 2 P.M. each of you must pack your tools. Take them with you. Do not leave shears, shuttles or any other tools in the shops.

Leave quietly. Be orderly.

If your bosses refuse to let you use the elevators do not argue. This time, swallow your pride and descend by the stairs.

March in order from your shops to the indicated meeting halls.

Don't wait for committees to come to take you down. We will positively send no committees. We will not give the police the opportunity of making scores of arrests on this first day so that the newspapers can put out extras screaming with their headlines that our strike started with riots.

Go down yourselves.

REMEMBER: The success of the strike depends first of all on the order and discipline you show.

WE URGE AGAIN: Don't lose your heads. Maintain order and discipline:

> By order of the General Strike Committee of the
> Cloak and Skirtmakers Union of New York
> International Ladies' Garment Workers' Union.

The copy for the strike call was given to the printer who was ordered to run off 75,000 copies. Steps were taken to prevent a leak of the date and to make certain that no one learn that the *Red New Post* was rolling off the press.

But several cloakmakers, coming along Broome Street late that night, peered through the windows of our printer's shop and saw the bright red paper on the press. People began to gather.

We ordered the press stopped, the gas turned off, the windows covered. Only after all had departed did the printing resume.

No one except the committee of three—and a solitary cloakmaker who kept vigil near the print shop through the night—knew until ten o'clock Thursday morning that the fateful *Red New Post* strike call was now ready.

That same Wednesday evening, the General Strike Committee met. After all business had been disposed—it was at about one o'clock in the morning—Brother Rosenberg, chairman of the strike committee, called on everyone present to take a solemn oath of secrecy. Then he told them: All preparations for the strike were completed. The strike would take effect the following afternoon at 2 o'clock. Committee members were not to go to their shops on Thursday.

We did not go to sleep that night. There were still many things to take care of.

Thursday morning, at 10 o'clock, the hall chairmen were dispatched to their posts. At the same time all English and Jewish newspapers were notified that the strike would start that day at 2 o'clock.

A union committee picked up hundreds of bundles of the *Red New Post*. Each member of the committee went to his position in an assigned street. All had been directed not to begin distribution before noon. In this way, simultaneously within a half hour, cloakmakers in New York, Brooklyn and Brownsville cloak districts received the call.

Who can describe the turmoil that followed? The excitement was intense. Manufacturers and workers fought in the street for copies of the *Red New Post*. Some offered a quarter, more, for a copy.

In no time, special extras of the newspapers, headlining the strike, were being hawked in the streets.

But in all the tumult, our workers kept their heads. They stuck faithfully to our plan.

Exactly at one o'clock, all returned to the shops as if nothing extraordinary were about to happen.

Those who had some work to finish sat and sewed. Those who had finished their work coolly, calmly waited for two o'clock.

The bosses could not understand the calm. They were certain that all of the fuss was merely a bluff, that only a few fanatics would heed the call.

But when the face of the clock showed the appointed hour, our people rose in their places, gathered together their tools, carefully folded the finished work, handed it back to the bosses. And whzn they saw all was ready, they formed themselves into ranks and quietly marched out of the shops.

Shortly before 2 o'clock, members of the strike committee, along with many newspapermen, went into the cloak district to see how well the cloak- and skirtmakers would respond to their union's call to strike. Union lawyers were now standing by in the courts should confrontation with the police develop as our people left the shops.

Among those anxious to see the masses walk out were Abraham Cahan, the editor, and Benjamin Schlesinger, the manager of the *Daily Forward.* Our people naturally waited to see the results of their work with their hearts pounding with the excitement. Each minute seemed like a year. When the clock showed ten minutes after two we could still not see a single soul. Cahan turned to one of our men and asked, "Well, so where are your strikers, already?" The other's heart sank.

But in that same minute, a wave of humanity began to form, coming from distances on all the side streets, turning into Fifth Avenue, heading downtown. With every minute, the mass grew larger, coalescing in one direction. By half past two, all the streets in New York from 38th Street down, east and west, were crowded with thousands of workers. In many streets all cars and freight wagons were halted by the crush of the crowd. Every striker carried his small pack of tools; all were following the *Red New Post* instructions.

I do not know if many people have ever before witnessed such a scene. Many of our devoted members wept tears of joy seeing their long years of work and sacrifice crowned with success. To me it seemed that such a spectacle had happened before only when the Jews were led out of Egypt—and now, as then, even their riffraff marched in the exodus.

Thousands of marchers passing the union office on 10th Street shouted slogans and greetings. The city was in turmoil. Workers in other trades left their shops to see the amazing sight. So did businessmen. In a word: the entire population of the city was out in the streets.

Fourth Street, between Second and Third Avenues, was so packed with strikers that it took hours to bring order. Cahan, moved by the sight of such a mass of workers, climbed the fire escape on the front of Manhattan Lyceum Hall and saluted the mass of workers for their courage. He assured them of the full moral and financial support of the *Forward.*

Among the newer leaders of the cloakmakers was London (1871–1926), who came from Poland to the United States in 1891, became a lawyer and a founder of the Socialist Party, and was twice elected to Congress. From *An East Side Epic,* by Harry Rogoff, 1930.

SURVIVAL OF THE MEANEST
by Meyer London

We offer no apology for the general strike. If at all we should apologize to the tens of thousands of the exploited men and women for not having aroused them before.

The cloak trade at present is the trade par excellence in which the "survival of the fittest" has come to mean "the survival of the meanest." Among employers the manufacturer who is merciless in reducing wages and in stretching out the hours of labor, the manufacturer who disregards in dealing with his employees all laws human and divine is most likely to succeed. The employer who neglects all sanitary requirements, who does business with money taken from the workmen under the guise of security and who levies a tax upon the employees for the use of electricity, is a danger not only to the employees but to every reputable employer in the trade.

We charge those employers with ruining the great trade built up by the industrious immigrants. We charge them with having corrupted the morale of thousands employed in the cloak trade.

The man who licks the boots of his employer, the individual who works without regard for time and for conditions is promoted in the factory. Treachery, slavishness and espionage are encouraged by the employers as great virtues of the cloakmakers.

This general strike is greater than any union. It is an irresistible movement of the people. It is a protest against conditions that can no longer be tolerated. This is the first great attempt to regulate conditions in the trade, to do away with that anarchy and chaos which keeps some of the men working 16 hours a day during the hottest months of the year while thousands of others have no employment whatever.

We cannot trust ourselves to the kind mercies of the employers. To our sorrow we have trusted them long enough. We ask for humane treatment; we demand the right to live; we refuse to be annihilated. We realize that we must be united; we know that we have the sympathy of every man that deserves the name. We know that organized labor throughout the country will applaud our efforts. We appeal to the people of America to assist us in our struggle.

The complex structure of the strike was explained several years later by Hillquit (1869–1933), who throughout his life served as ILGWU counsel and mentor to its leaders. From "Opening Address by Counsel for the Defendants," September 23, 1915.

HOW A STRIKE WORKS
by Morris Hillquit

A strike has often been called war, industrial war, but there is a great difference between the so-called war of a strike and ordinary warfare. A strike is passive warfare. It is not a war which has for its aim the destruction of the other side, for if the employers' business were destroyed the industry would be destroyed.

It is a war which has for its aim the holding out to such an extent that the employers would be constrained to consider the requests of the workers, to give in at least to some of their demands, and it is warfare, on the other hand, on the part of the employers to hold out without granting the requests of the employees until they will be forced, perhaps starved, into submission.

Each one of the 1,800 shops on strike was organized separately with its own chairman, its own picket committees, having its own meetings, so as to be able to call the roll from time to time to ascertain whether the men were still standing together in the strike.

In order to enable them to do that, they had to be provided with meeting places. Forty thousand or 45,000 men and women, 1,800 different shop organizations, had to be provided for. And so they hired 58 halls in that section of the city in which the industry is principally located and they assigned rooms in these 58 halls for the various meetings of the men.

The next question was to make sure of these people. These men, going out on strike, had given up the insignificant wages they had been working for theretofore, and they had to subsist. Day after day, week after week, they had to keep constantly before them the great and important cause for which they fought, and so they organized a corps of speakers. They took those among them who were older in experience, who had been longer in the union, who could speak to their fellow men, who knew them and who were more influential perhaps than the others, and these reminded the strikers day after day of the importance of the struggle and of the necessity of keeping it up. That was the business of the Speakers Committee.

But in strikes of every kind, both sides begin to realize that the employers and workers are not the only parties to the dispute, that the public also has certain rights, that the public in this city, for instance, is vitally interested in the questions as to how and under what conditions its clothing is being manufactured. Public favor or disfavor has very often effectively determined the success or failure of a strike. The strikers were concerned in having public sentiment with them. They established a Press Committee to keep the public posted on their conduct, objectives, and aspirations.

And then, in a strike of this kind where picketing was done on the street, where trouble often occurred between 1,800 employers and their workers and where pickets were often apt to be arrested, they had to be instructed as to their rights. Their Law Committee was organized to see to it that the law was complied with by these men, and that they be informed of their rights in the premises.

But the most important work, perhaps, of all was that of the Picket Committee. What is a Picket Committee? When the men went out on strike they took with them practically, but not actually, all of the workers. We may estimate that about 90 percent of all the workers employed in the trade responded to the strike call. Ten percent failed to respond.

In other words, out of the 50,000 men and women engaged in the industry, about 5,000 remained working. Employers, of course, sought to enlist other workers in their employment. Men and women engaged in kindred industries or in the same industry in other places, were obtained, so that during the strike we may well figure about 8,000 men and women had at some time or other remained working.

Now here was the crux of the entire situation: If these persons continued to work, if they increased in numbers, it might easily enable the manufacturers to tide over the season or it might cause a stampede among the strikers to return to work. It was necessary for the union to win over the adherence of these men. They could not win the strike otherwise. And when we say to win over the adherence, we mean by it that it became essential to them to make friends of the strikebreakers.

These men and women whose interest it was to support the strike because their own salvation depended upon it, but who did not see far enough to understand it, had to be made to see. They had to be converted. They had to be made loyal union men and strikers. This work which is called "picketing" and which has a certain odious by-taste in some circles, is a most legitimate work in which all of us are engaged at some time.

In politics, when, say, a Republican candidate knows that his party has insufficient votes for election, and that, in order to be elected, he must get the support of some non-Republicans, some Democrats, some Independents, he does not proceed to club these Democrats over the heads to vote for him, but he tries to persuade them, to show them the advantages of electing him. This is exactly the position the striker takes against the non-striker. It is a matter of demonstrating the reasonableness of the strikers' cause and the advantage to the strikebreaker in joining the ranks of the strikers. And this work has time and again been pronounced by all the courts of this state as perfectly legitimate so long as it is limited to peaceful persuasion.

How was that to be arranged? It was necessary to have at least an average of three men in front of each of the shops. Why? First, some faint-hearted striker might take a notion to return to work. This picket is there to keep him back, if possible, to tell him the impropriety of this contemplated step. There was not always hard feelings about it. The men had sympathy for each other. Each of them knew how much the other was suffering. Each of them knew what that strike meant. They could excuse a weakness but they saw the necessity of restraining it.

There might be also professional strikebreakers brought in. There might be other men, unaware that a strike was going on and intending to take the positions offered by the employers. The picket had to be there to approach the would-be strikebreaker and dissuade him, if possible.

A "modern" shop in one of the new loft buildings in the lower Broadway area.

At least 5,000 pickets were required. Work was often going on day and night and a great many strikebreakers were brought in by preference in the night time. Some of them were kept overnight in the shop. Picketing had to be done day and night, in shifts of about four hours each, and so you can easily figure that from twenty to 30,000 pickets were in front of the shops in the course of a day and night. The vast majority of all strikers had to be enlisted in picket duty, so that when we speak of pickets, we practically mean in this case, the strikers as a mass.

By the end of July, interested third parties had prevailed on Louis Brandeis, distinguished Boston attorney, to attempt a settlement. For three days at the end of July, in the board room of the Metropolitan Life Insurance Building in New York City, he sought common ground on basic issues. From "The Cloakmakers' Strike," the record of the conference issued by the Cloak, Suit and Skirt Manufacturers' Protective Association, 1910.

THE CLOSED SHOP

MR. BRANDEIS: You have the floor.

MR. SCHLESINGER (union): We ask for $24 a week. We have taken the maximum that was paid in the line of sample tailoring, and we wanted to raise $1 on it. You offer us less than the minimum. Don't you consider that ridiculous?

MR. COHEN (employer): There are 14 classifications in your list. Now . . .

MR. SCHLESINGER: I am speaking of the sample tailor. I ask you if it is not ridiculous to offer us $19 a week for such work as we have been getting $23?

MR. BRANDEIS: Let me ask you one question before he answers that. Do you mean to say that there is nobody in the trade who today is paying less than $19?

MR. FISHMAN (employer): May I say, Mr. Chairman, that I pay $15 a week.

MR. POLAKOFF (union): It is a shame, if he pays $15 a week.

MR. SCHLESINGER: Mr. Fishman is perfectly right. I believe he pays $15 a week. I know a cloak factory in New York where 15 cents is paid for two duck jackets. I am sure there is not a man in this room that will pay such a low price. I should say that about 70 percent of the sample makers in New York are getting on an average of $21 a week.

I was glad to hear something about Mr. Fishman. I would rather take you to manufacturers who are in this room that are paying $22 and $23 to sample hands.

A VOICE: Will you take the average of manufacturers in this room?

MR. SCHLESINGER: I don't know.

MR. COHEN: Will you try it?

MR. SCHLESINGER: No, I don't want to. I was requested not to mention names.

MR. COHEN: But they are willing now.

MR. SCHLESINGER: But I am not willing now.

MR. COHEN: Why?

MR. SCHLESINGER: Because I do not want to. I do not consider this a court. . . . I say the only remedy for the manufacturers is to employ none but union men, as long as the union is able to supply you with help. Should it be impossible for the union to supply you with help, then you should have the privilege of employing whomever you please.

MR. LONDON (union): You mean competent men at the work?

MR. SCHLESINGER: Competent men, yes; that is understood.

MR. COHEN: That is the chairman's proposition.

MR. SCHLESINGER: If that is so, all right. I will put it as my proposition. As long as you will agree on prices and on all regulations in the shops, then I really do not see why you should not employ only union men. Now you know, Mr. Lefcourt, that if you will have 60 union men in your shop and 40 non-union men, there will be a continuous quarrel among the people. Either the union men will drive the non-union men out or the non-union men will drive the union men out, but before one party will drive out the other you will not be able to make your work.

The employment of union men only is the only proposition that can be accepted by our organization. Should we accept your proposition, that is, having non-union men working hand-in-hand with us, then we will lose our organization, as every organization was lost that went into deals like you are trying to make us go into.

This minute is a very serious one. If we do not agree now, we will have to keep up the strike, and we cannot tell how long. If our union fails in its present effort, then it would not take very long before a good many of the very small firms will drive you people out of business, as they drove out a good many large manufacturers 16 years ago when we had a strike. At that time a good many were driven out of business. We lost that strike, but the result was nevertheless that the manufacturers had lost.

If we leave this room now, it means that the strike will go on. Mr. Cohen and Mr. London and Mr. Brandeis are attorneys. They all did the best they could in this matter, but it is up to the manufacturers to do the right thing. Mr. Cohen thinks it is possible for union men to work alongside of non-union men, but you know it is impossible. You know you will have fights in your shops.

MR. BRANDEIS: Mr. London, I think you had something to say.

MR. LONDON: I desire to say, Mr. Chairman, that I realize the importance of the question which we have been discussing for the last three days, and I share with Mr. Cohen the sentiments that we have approached a crisis. We are not responsible for the low conditions in which some of the people in the trade are today. We are trying to improve these conditions. Now, if you were to consent to employ union men as long as you can get competent union men, why, then, the question is settled. We have 60,000 men and women on strike. They are on strike because they feel there is something wrong; they want some change. Some of them joined the union two months before the strike was called, some of them three months before the strike was called, some of them were so calculating in their unionism that they paid the initiation fee in order to go on strike and in order to get immediate benefit for the $1 or $3 that they paid in. We have practical people among us. Now you have to take those men and women as they are.

We realize that you should have the right to employ non-union men when it is impossible for you to get competent union help.

MR. BRANDEIS: You mean "equally competent" individuals?

MR. LONDON: I bow with reverence to your great command of the English language, but the difficulty is this: if you will attempt to draw fine distinctions in any paper you will submit to our people, the more refined the distinction is the less they will understand it, and think they will be deceived; therefore, I ask you to strike out the word "equally."

MR. BRANDEIS: No. It is a question of using language which you and I and Mr. Cohen and 20 other gentlemen here who are patiently listening to us can understand. I can perfectly well conceive that you may have 10 or 15 or 20 persons, all of whom are declared competent, and yet if I had to choose a tailor or a lawyer or a physician, I would be able to draw a distinction between the competency of the one and the competency of the other. Now, the variation might not be as great in tailors as it would be in physicians, but there must be the liberty of choice of the men to select the best they can get. Otherwise, the trade cannot advance.

MR. LONDON: I should say in reply that the word "competency" will necessarily mean that. It will mean that the employer is at liberty to employ a non-union man as long as the union is unable to furnish him with a man competent to do the work required. As soon as you put in the word "equally" you introduce two elements: you introduce the non-union man along with the union man. You have to take our people as they are.

Because our people have not been as well organized as they should have been, you should not declare in favor of continuing the strike. It is up to you. You are the strike leaders today. You are the organizers and the agitators. Mr. Jonasson, do you like that? Do you want 60,000 men to stay out for five or six weeks? I know they have been used to starving, but still there is a limit. They have become accustomed to privation and starving. They may not endure very long; they may endure four or five or six weeks. Imagine the results. What will be the effect upon the trade?

We have just now settled with 450 manufacturers—some substantial ones and quite a number of small manufacturers. If the union exists, we will, in these 450 factories in which the conditions have been more or less disgraceful, improve things.

MR. FISHMAN: I want to say this, that those manufacturers, some of those who signed, will not live up to the union agreement.

MR. LONDON: If the union will live, we will make every reasonable effort in the world that the manufacturers with whom we have settled should live up to the standard.

MR. DYCHE (union): I have had experience with union shops and non-union shops for a number of years. I will tell you what I do know, and that is this: that the same as a bad coin drives a good coin out of the market, so non-union men drive union men out of the shop. I have seen it as soon as non-union labor has been introduced in a union shop that a stampede took place.

Actually, the fact is it is not a question of how the arrangement has been drawn, but of the temperament and disposition of the people we have to deal with. No amount of agreements or no document, however finely devised, will change at once—it may be in time, but not now—the nature of the people. I tell you, a stampede took place, and a week or two passed and the shop turned non-union. For the sake of self-protection you would be committing suicide to go into an agreement where such a condition prevailed. Give us a chance for a half year and let us see if we can make good.

MR. LONDON: One of the important reasons for our anxiety to end the conference is that with the continuing of this conference we lose the opportunity of sending daily from 1,500 to 1,200 people back to work. That is why I would ask the gentlemen on the other side of the table to work overtime.

A VOICE: That is against union principles.

Despite Brandeis's best efforts, no agreement could be reached on such fundamental issues as union shop and job security. He returned to Boston. From the *Call,* August 3, 1910.

STALEMATE

It looks as if the cloakmakers' strike will be fought to a finish.

Conferences between the strikers and the manufacturers, which have been carried on for nearly a week, first through committees of 10 from each side, then through attorneys for both sides, were broken off yesterday. Louis D. Brandeis of Boston had been acting as chairman.

Meyer London, attorney for the strikers, withdrew from the conference when it became evident that the manufacturers were trying to dodge the most important demands of the union. At the same time they were trying to give the impression to the public that they are willing to grant all the strikers' demands, that is, all that are "reasonable."

The bosses and their representatives constantly talked of "concessions" to the union, but when each of these concessions was examined by the leaders of the strikers it was found to be full of loopholes and "jokers" which would grant the workers nothing and would leave conditions in the cloak trade just the same as they were before the strike.

Immediately after the union broke off negotiations with the bosses, the spokesmen for the manufacturers issued a statement with a "tentative agreement" attached to it which they said they would submit to the cloakmakers' union, giving them till 10 o'clock this morning either to accept or reject. "Should the tentative agreement be rejected by the strikers," the bosses' statement reads, "the employers will feel that all negotiations with their former employees are at an end, and that it will be hopeless to try to continue them."

The tentative agreement, which the bosses herald as another "concession" to the strikers, practically refuses to adjust any of the most important grievances of the union and offers to submit them to arbitration. It defiantly opposes the closed shop and offers to recognize the union "to the extent of cooperating with it for the general benefit of the trade," and pledges to "give preference to union men in the matter of employment."

A copy of this tentative agreement signed by Julius Henry Cohen, counsel for the manufacturers, and addressed to Meyer London, was shown to London and the other strike leaders by newspaper reporters. After reading it the leaders said they would submit it to the organization, but the sentiment was that it would be unanimously rejected, since it was nothing more than a repetition of all that has been discussed at the conference.

Bulletins kept the cloakmakers informed about the deepening crisis. From Strike Bulletin, General Strike Committee, August 16, 1910.

COURAGE: VICTORY WILL BE OURS!

This is how the strike situation shapes up, in this sixth week:

As you are aware, scores of manufacturers are settling every day. You've seen the long lines of workers returning victoriously to their jobs.

Apparently, things are not going too well with the bosses. They've been holding meetings three or four times a day; the association's lawyer, Julius Henry Cohen, has to speak several times a day, urging them not to "scab," not to desert the manufacturers' association.

Last Friday, the bosses' association appealed to Judge Goff for an injunction dissolving the union. Their lawyer really exerted himself in attempting to prove that the union was only a conspiracy to ruin the manufacturers, and he demanded the injunction be granted then and there.

The next day, the bosses suffered defeat when Acting Mayor John Purroy Mitchel ordered the police to cease dispersing pickets and, above all, not to use their clubs. The Mayor stated that as long as the workers conduct themselves in an orderly manner, they have a right to speak to whomever they wish, without interference from the police.

As if this were not enough, the same day they met with another setback, one which they didn't expect at all. Six members of the Manufacturers' Association settled with the union and deserted the organization. And when bricks start dropping from a building, it isn't long before the whole building collapses!

In the past few days, the bosses have published many "open letters" and "appeals" in the newspapers in which they promise the workers they will receive the best of conditions if only they will become scabs. They refer to themselves as "gentlemen." Gentlemen! You know that whenever you dared protest unjust conditions in the shop, they would call police to throw you out of the shop.

If you ever chanced to earn a bit more than usual one week, these "gentlemen" saw to it that some prices would be "missing" the next week. These "gentlemen" treated you like children whose parents take their entire pay, allowing the children to keep only a few cents spending money.

Now, let's consider just how much the bosses are granting, and, even more important, to what extent we can depend on the bosses' "fairness," especially when they will be free to employ both union and non-union workers, and to what extent they will prefer union members. . . . You know that the bosses will never agree that the work of a union man is as "good" as the non-union worker.

Sisters and brothers! We know that many of you suffer from hunger and poverty. We know that many wives of strikers do not have the means to provide milk for their children, but nevertheless we appeal to you: Be loyal to your union! The bosses will have to give in; it's only a matter of time! The greater our suffering, the greater will be our victory! Have courage, victory will be ours!

Striking cloakmakers parading down Second Avenue. (The Bettmann Archive)

On August 27 the strikers were hard hit by Judge Goff's injunction, which declared that the strike was illegal. From the *New York Tribune,* August 28, 1910.

THE STRIKE IS ILLEGAL

Justice Goff ruled against the striking cloakmakers yesterday, handing down a decision in the Supreme Court which branded as illegal not only a closed shop agreement but any strike having such an agreement for its object. The decision is regarded as one of the broadest of its kind ever issued in this country and a pioneer so far as its application to the closed shop is concerned.

Representatives of the cloakmakers' unions had been hailed to court by the Cloak, Suit and Skirt Manufacturers' Protective Association on an order to show cause why a temporary injunction obtained by the association should not be made permanent, "further restraining them from acts in aid of any conspiracy or combination, alleged to exist, to compel members of plaintiff's association to employ only members of the defendant labor unions."

The court continued the injunction saying: "The primary purpose of this strike is not to better the condition of the workman, but is to deprive other men of the opportunity to exercise their right to work and to drive them from an industry in which, by labor, they may have acquired skill, and which they have a right to pursue to gain a livelihood without being subjected to the doing of things which may be disagreeable or repugnant."

Samuel Gompers, president of the American Federation of Labor, was greatly stirred by the decision of Justice Goff, which in effect declared that efforts to enforce the "closed shop" were in violation of law on the restraint of trade. Gompers said: "Justice Goff quotes an unjust decision in support of his own, and that is supposed to be good law. The unions of labor will live despite injunctions and decisions which invade constitutionally guaranteed rights and human liberty. Without the unions there is no possibility for protection to the workers against the tyranny of the absolute autocratic ways of concentrated capital and greed."

The battle over the definitions continued. From the *Journal of Political Economy,* March 1911.

THE STUMBLING BLOCK
by J. B. McPherson

What was needed was a satisfactory definition of the "union shop." Both sides were practically agreed upon the "preferential union shop," but the difficulty was to draw up an agreement which to the manufacturers did not mean the "closed shop," and to the wage earners did not mean discrimination against union men. The burning question was: Who is to construe the words "a man of equal ability" or decide the matter of competency?

On the one hand, the men felt that if the decision were to rest with the employers, non-union men would always be chosen; on the other hand, if competency was to be decided by the unions, the manufacturers felt that union men would always be deemed competent men. Apparently the strike leaders wished to make sure what the "preferential union shop" meant, and would be construed to mean. Each side was suspicious of the other, and wished the meaning so clearly defined before peace was declared that no question of construction could be raised later.

Many times during August there were expectations of an agreement, but as often as they were raised, they were shattered. Each side was facing more and greater difficulties with each day's postponement. While money was being contributed to the union and its treasury was in fairly good condition, the strain on its resources was tremendous, and it was a question of how much longer the struggle could last.

Winter was approaching; businessmen on the East Side were beginning to discuss the situation; the credit of the wage earners was being curtailed; many strikers were in danger of eviction, and it was felt that if the injunction made permanent by Judge Goff . . . were put into full effect, the strikers could not get as favorable terms later as they could then.

Hungry workers on picket lines were being asked to evaluate unprecedented subtleties of collective bargaining. The turmoil and uncertainties were great. From *McClure's Magazine*, April 1911.

THE PREFERENTIAL SHOP
by Edith Wyatt

The final formulation of the preferential union shop, as presented by Mr. Brandeis, Mr. London, and Mr. Cohen, was this: "The manufacturers can and will declare in appropriate terms their sympathy with the union, their desire to aid and strengthen the union, and their agreement that, as between union and non-union men of equal ability to do the job, the union men shall be given the preference."

The manufacturers were willing to make this agreement. But the representatives of the union received it with a natural suspicion bred by years of oppression. "Can the man who has ground us down year after year suddenly be held by a sentiment for the organization he has fought for a quarter of a century?" they asked. "Between union and non-union men, will he candidly give the preference to union men of equal ability? Will he not rather, since the question of ability is a matter of personal judgment and is left to his judgment, prefer the non-union man, and justify his preference by a pretense, in each case, that he considers the skill of the non-union man superior?"

Nevertheless, a majority of the leaders of the cloakmakers were willing to try the plan. A minority refused. This minority was influenced partly by its certain knowledge that the 40,000 cloakmakers would never accept an agreement based on the idea of the preferential union shop, and partly by its complete distrust of the goodwill of the manufacturers. The minority was trusted and powerful. It won. The (July) conference ended.

The *Forward* printed a statement that the preferential shop was "the open shop with honey." The news of the Brandeis conference reached the cloakmakers through the bulletins of this paper; and, during its progress and after its close, frantic crowds stood before the office on the lower East Side, waiting for these bulletins, eager for the victory of the closed shop, the panacea for all industrial evils.

After the decision of the leaders, after the breaking of the conference, the cloakmakers who had settled gave fifteen percent of their wages to support those standing out for the closed shop, and volunteered to give fifty percent. The *Forward* headed a subscription list with 82,000 for the strikers, and collected $50,000. A furore for the closed shop arose. Young boys and bearded old men and young women came to the office and offered half their wages, three quarters of their wages. One boy offered to give all his wages and sell papers for his living. Every day the office was besieged by committees, appointed by the men and women in the settled shops, asking to contribute to the cause more than the percentage determined by the union. These were men and women accustomed to enduring hardships for a principle, men and women who had fought in Russia, who were revolutionists, willing to make sacrifices, eager to make sacrifices. Their blind faith was the backbone of the strike.

This furore was continuing when, in the third week in August, the loss of contracts by the manufacturers and the general stagnation of business due to the idleness of 40,000 men and women, normally wage earners, induced a number of bankers and merchants of the East Side to bring pressure for a settlement of the strike. Louis Marshall, an attorney well known in Jewish charities in New York, assembled the lawyers on both sides. They drew up an agreement in which the preferential union shop again appeared as the basis of future operations, formulated as at the Brandeis conference.

The *Forward* printed the result of the Marshall conference with deep concern. It maintained a neutral attitude. The editorials urged that the readers consider the whole document soberly, discuss it freely in local meetings, and vote for themselves, on their own full understanding, after mature conviction on each point.

Imagine what these days of doubt, of an attempt to understand, meant to these multitudes, knowing no industrial faith but that of the closed shop which had failed them absolutely, wanderers from a strange country, turning wildly to their leaders, who could only tell them that they must decide their own fates, they must decide for themselves. These leaders have been blamed at once for their autocracy and for not mobilizing and informing and directing these multitudes more clearly and firmly.

Terrible was the position of these men. Well they knew that the winter was approaching; that the closed shop would not win; that the workers could not hear the truth about the preferential union shop, and that the man who stood avowedly for the preferential shop, now the best hope of victory for the union, would be called a traitor to the union.

In great anxiety, the meetings assembled. The workers had all come to the same conclusion. They all rejected the Marshall agreement.

Soon after this, the tide of loyalty to the closed shop was incited to its high-water mark by the action of Judge Goff, who, as a result of a suit of one of the firms of the Manufacturers' Association, issued an injunction against peaceful picketing, on the part of the strikers, on the ground that picketing for the closed shop was an action of conspiracy in constraint of trade, and therefore unlawful.

The manufacturers were now, naturally, more deeply distrusted than ever on the East Side. The doctrine of the closed shop became almost ritualistic. Early in September, one of the Labor Day parades was headed by an aged Jew, white-bearded and fierce-eyed—a cloak-maker who knew no other words in English than those he uttered—who waved a purple banner and shouted at regular intervals: "Closed shop! Closed shop!"

Impossible, indeed, to say anything to unionists whose reply to every just representation is, "Closed shop"; or to the employers whose reply to every just representation is, "We do not wish other people to run our business." This reply the Marshall conference still had to hear for some days. It was now the first week in September. There was great suffering among the cloakmakers. On the manufacturers' side, contracts heretofore always filled by certain New York houses, in this prolonged stoppage of their factories were finally lost to them and placed with establishments in other important cloakmaking centers—Cleveland, Philadelphia, Chicago, and even abroad.

Curiously enough, wages and hours had been left to arbitration, had never been thoroughly considered, in the whole situation before. Neither the workers nor the employers had clearly stated what they really would stand for on these vital points. No one, not even the most wildly partisan figures on either side, supposed that the first demands as to wages and hours represented an ultimatum. The debaters in the Marshall conference now agreed on feasible terms on these points, though, curiously enough, the rates for piecework were left to the arbitration of individual shops. In spite of this fact, the majority of the workers are paid by piecework. The former clauses of the agreement related to the abolition of home work and of subcontracting remained practically as they had stood before. As for the idea of the preferential union shop, it had undoubtedly been gaining ground. Naturally, at first, appearing to the *Forward's* staff and to many ardent unionists as opposed to unionism, it had now assumed a different aspect. This was the final formulation of the preferential union shop in the Marshall agreement:

"Each member of the Manufacturers' Association is to maintain a union shop, a 'union shop' being understood to refer to a shop where union standards as to working conditions prevail, and where, when hiring help, union men are preferred, it being recognized that, since there are differences of skill among those employed in the trade, employers shall have freedom of selection between one union man and another, and shall not be confined to any list nor bound to follow any prescribed order whatsoever.

"It is further understood that all existing agreements and obligations of the employer, including those to present employees, shall be respected. The manufacturers, however, declare their belief in the union, and that all who desire to share in its benefits should share in its burdens."

This formulation signified that the union men available for a special kind of work in a factory must be sought before any other men.

The word "non-union man," the words arousing the antagonism of the East Side, are not mentioned. But whether the preference of union men is or is not insisted on as strongly as in the Brandeis agreement must remain a matter of open opinion.

This formulation was referred to the strike committee. It was accepted by the strike committee, and went into force on September 8.

From *Memoirs of a Cloakmaker,* 1920.

THE DAY THE STRIKE ENDED
by Abraham Rosenberg

About 200 of the chairmen quickly assembled. The strike committee presented the agreement to them. It clarified details, answered questions and opened a discussion that lasted several hours. The chairmen then authorized the strike committee to sign the agreement.

News of the settlement spread quickly. Thousands of cloakmakers and others filled the streets. Slowly in the crush they made their way to the square opposite the *Forward* Building on East Broadway. Here they would certainly get an accurate report of what was happening.

By 7 o'clock the entire square and the park beyond it and the side streets were filled to bursting with strikers. In Orchard Hall, Italian workers lifted their strike leaders to their shoulders, jubilantly carried them through the streets, making their way with the mass toward the *Forward* Building. One of the Italian strikers printed an Italian speech in phonetics and had one of our leaders read it to the crowd.

That night, the entire city remained awake. It is impossible to describe the spirit of that night. Only those who have experienced such excitement can really understand what was happening. Everywhere, men and women, young and old hugged and kissed and congratulated each other on the great victory. Only in the early daylight hours of Saturday did the streets grow empty. The police estimated that at least one million people had filled the streets.

On that Saturday morning, September 3, large wagons, draped with flags, with bands blaring music and packed with jubilant cloakmakers proclaiming the strike settlement to all, made their way through the streets. They sang and they shouted the good news.

The General Strike Committee met later that day and declared that the strike was officially over. Unofficially, however, the strike continued in many shops for another two weeks as the committee faced the difficult task of settling piece rates.

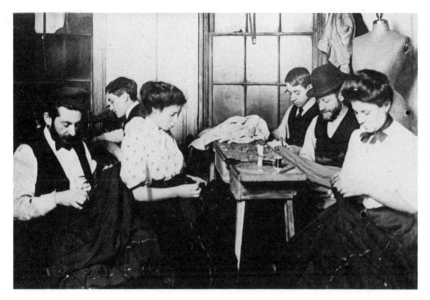

A tenement sweatshop team.

The whole strike was over by September 17th. On Monday, the 19th, the cloak- and skirtmakers of New York were back in their shops, working under union conditions.

Thus, the many years of trials and tribulations of the cloakmakers and their unions came to an end. This great strike of 1910 was the final effort of the New York cloakmakers to build and sustain a union. They had grown weary of always missing the fruits of their efforts. This time they had been determined to establish a strong and permanent union.

The basic provisions of the Protocol of Peace were outlined by Brown. From *The Survey,* September 17, 1910.

WHAT THEY WON
by Mary Sumner Brown

The Protocol of September 2 fixes a definite wage scale and a fixed number of hours per week, the union making concession on its original demands in regard to wages and hours, the employers giving up the right of arbitration in this matter. Even more important the union considers the modifications made in the original preferential union shop idea. The terms of the agreement by omitting the words, "as distinguished from the closed shop," make no such deliberate antagonism between the two forms of union shop; nor do they leave a loophole for the dreaded open shop to mask under the name of preferential union.

The "preference" too is put upon a broader basis. In the first agreement the choice was to be between two men of equal ability, one union and one non-union. By the agreement of September 2, the employer can only choose a non-union man provided he finds no man available in the union of equal ability. He must, that is, exhaust the union resources first. Among union men his choice is unhampered by rules of precedence.

Furthermore, the earlier agreements would not recognize a shop delegate; this provides that the chairman of the price committee shall also act as representative of the employees in a shop. In many of these clauses it is simply greater definiteness of expression that safeguards the union.

The strikers make a decided concession in agreeing to respect existing obligations of their employers towards present employees, a concession which, however, probably can do no harm to the union, as an outside estimate gives 1,000 as the number of strikebreakers in the shops. The first day of settlement saw, in one shop, eighteen strikebreakers apply for union membership—a good augury of what these men will do. Piecework prices, which affect at least half the workers . . . remain to be settled.

Especially noticeable in the agreement is the cordial support given the union idea by the employers. This support by no means existed at the beginning of the conference over which Mr. Brandeis presided, and undoubtedly is due largely to his influence, that of Henry Moskowitz, who had been indefatigable in his efforts to bring about an understanding between the two parties in the dispute, and of A. Lincoln Filene of Boston, who has tactfully brought to bear his large influence as a consumer of the manufacturers' product. It was Mr. Filene who first interested Mr. Brandeis in the strike.

Though there is hardly a clause in the agreement that has not meant some sacrifice by the strikers of their original demands, a comparison with the conditions of work and wages in the trade . . . will show an improvement of the workers' condition which is phenomenal. The wage increase alone, to take one point, is from twenty-five to one hundred percent, according to the grade of shop. And even more important, a "wage standard" for the first time exists in the trade.

Much is expected of the Board of Sanitation, which is to control not only the shops in the Manufacturers' Association but to enforce a standard of sanitation in all union shops, a standard which is sadly needed in the majority of the shops outside of the association. What responsibility that multiform and hitherto inconstant personality known as the public will assume for helping to maintain a high standard of working conditions for the cloakmakers and peace between the two parties, time and experience of the three permanent boards on which the public is represented will show.

The settlement did not come in time to prevent Judge Goff's startling decision enjoining the Cloakmakers' Union from picketing to support the demand for the closed shop, an injunction which, in effect, forbids striking for the closed shop. "This," says the *New York Times,* "is the strongest decision ever handed down against labor," and a correspondent of that paper, though strongly opposed to the closed shop, feels that the injunction cannot hold in law since it interferes with the right of employees to strike "for any reason whatsoever," the curtailing of which right, he holds, would "lead to the grossest industrial slavery."

Until the settlement was ratified the union maintained an attitude of strong resistance to Judge Goff's injunction. The strike was, in the words of that newspaper in English which best expressed the strikers' point of view, the New York *Call,* "lifted from the plane of mere advantage and expediency to that of principle"—the very principle of unionism itself. In one day $18,000 poured into the union treasury from its working members and from other organizations, and in one evening eighty-five pickets allowed themselves to be taken to court.

Hoffman (1874–1954), editor of the Cloakmakers' publication *New Post,* summarized the gains made in the two strikes. From *American Federationist,* December 1929.

BORN AND REARED IN BATTLE
by B. Hoffman (Zivyon)

At the time the ladies' waistmakers went out on strike, the International Ladies' Garment Workers Union actually existed in name only. But when the strike of the cloakmakers was declared, the ILGWU had not only an office, but members. When the strike of the ladies' waistmakers ended, the ILGWU could boast of some twenty thousand members.

But while giving the ladies full credit for having laid the foundation
of the ILGWU, it must be stated that the ILGWU became great and
famous only after it had brought to a close the long and difficult strike
of the cloakmakers in 1910.

The difference between the two strikes, though their causes were
the same, was very great. The strike of the girls in the waist and dress
industry was not regarded by the public as an ordinary conflict between capital and labor. In the strike of the girls a great part was
played by what may be called the social conscience. Ladies of the
highest social circles threw themselves into the strike; the League for
Woman's Suffrage was active in it, and the press, at least a considerable part of it, was outspokenly in sympathy with the girl strikers.
Even newspapers who in case of a strike were wont to be on the side of
capital and against labor, were in the strike of the ladies' waistmakers
not so openly hostile to the strikers.

It was quite otherwise in the case of the cloakmakers' strike. In this
case the conflict took on harsher forms. The "social conscience," apparently, had been appeased by the victory of the striking girls in the
ladies' waist industry and resumed its peaceful slumber. The benevo-
lent and philanthropic ladies of high society, withdrew to their man-
sions during the cloakmakers' strike, while the press abandoned the
friendly tone it had assumed toward the strike of the waistmakers.
The cloakmakers' strike was a pure conflict between capital and labor.
The line was sharply drawn, and the battle was one of considerable
magnitude. Fifty thousand cloakmakers—some say sixty thousand—
went out on strike.

What were the causes of that great revolt of the cloakmakers?
There were causes aplenty. Long hours of work—65, 70, and often
even 80 and 90 hours a week; the cloakmakers would come to the
shops at five o'clock in the morning and work till midnight. A starvation wage of fifteen dollars a week, of ten dollars and even less; twenty
dollars a week was considered a whole lot. Operators had to supply
their own machines, their own cotton, their own needles, and had to
pay various fines. I do not want to paint here a picture of how the
cloakmakers then worked, lived, and were treated by their bosses.
Suffice it to say that the sweatshop in the worst form imaginable
reigned supreme.

And it does not matter whether the shop was located in a small and
rear bedroom or in a large and spacious front room. It is the conditions of work, the enormously long hours, the starvation wages, the
brutal treatment, that mark the sweatshop. A wage worker does not
even need a rich imagination to realize the hell in which the
waistmakers, the cloakmakers, and the other garment workers then
lived. And when they could stand it no longer, they revolted. The only
question is: How were they able to endure it so long? Why did they
not revolt sooner? This question calls for an answer.

The workers of the garment industry at that time were with few exceptions immigrants, most of whom had not been long in this country. A large number of them had not been workmen at all in the old country. They became workmen only after their arrival in America. And even those who had been workers back in the old country, had for the most part been artisans who either worked by themselves or even employed help. Their psychology was not that of a factory worker. It was very easy occasionally to get them to strike for higher wages and shorter hours, but it was impossible to keep them organized in a union. There was not yet developed in them that sense of collective effort which is essential to maintain a union.

But this state of affairs began to change for the better with the great stream of immigration which poured into this country from Russia, Poland, and Lithuania during and following the Russian Revolution of 1905. A great many of these newcomers had already belonged to labor organizations in the old country. These organizations had at first been secret and illegal; afterwards they became public and semilegal.

In this respect the famous Jewish organization known as the "Bund" of Russia, Poland, and Lithuania exerted an enormously great educational influence. A considerable number of the newcomers had received from the "Bund" a certain training, both political and trade-unionist, and all of them were of a revolutionary bent. (At that time every decent person in Russia was more or less in a revolutionary frame of mind.) Now this element constituted excellent material not only for strikes, but also for the organization of unions. It had one great defect, however. In their first years in America these immigrants felt wholly alien and for the most part looked upon themselves as temporary sojourners, as mere visitors.

At this juncture there suddenly broke out the great economic crisis of 1907 with its disastrous consequences. Everything we tried to build up till then was wiped out by the panic. Only after the crisis passed away did it become possible to build anew, and then everything progressed swiftly. In the course of two or three years there arose an excellent fighting army among the waistmakers and cloakmakers and the great revolution in the ladies' garment industry was effected.

6. The Protocol of Peace—Its Rise

The Protocol of Peace won universal acclaim. Scholars, journalists, and government experts cited it as a model worth emulating in a time of rising industrial unrest. Out of the turmoil and chaos of the sweatshop a new concept of industrial democracy had emerged, set down in a document which, Louis D. Brandeis believed, like the Constitution of the United States, rested on universal, timeless principles.

The chief instruments for ensuring peace under the Protocol were its boards of grievances and arbitration. The purpose and operation of these boards are described by Brandeis and Dyche in terms that reflect their confidence that these units would provide justice for the worker, enforce the rights and responsibilities of both employer and employee under the Protocol, and put an end to strikes and lockouts.

The task now became one of spreading the Protocol concept to other garment trades, markets, and regions. In each move forward, as Isaac F. Marcosson reports, union forces once again encountered resistance despite the endorsement of the Protocol by the general public. For some individuals chaos was more profitable than order, industrial dictatorship more welcome than bargaining.

While cloakmakers continued to test and refine the practice of protocolism in their industry, displaying a sophistication gained through decades of union devotion, the uneven development of unionism in other branches soon became painfully evident.

In the dress industry, for example, one more concerted effort proved necessary to firmly establish the new ideas. But in the kimono, white goods, and other shops chiefly employing newly arrived young women, employers generally saw no reason to accept a union where the labor force was still immature and helpless.

Alleyne Ireland noted the various forms of resentment among these young garment workers in the shops; the *New York Times* reported Colonel Roosevelt's reaction after his visit to several kimono shops and subsequently printed his letter describing the conditions he had encountered there. Martha Bensley Bruere captured the pathos of the young workers, strangers in a new and vast land suddenly recruited as warriors in an industrial conflict. Josephine Casey, stationed at an ILGWU frontier quite distant from the big city, defines a cause of battle far more personal than wages. Sonya Levien drew an unforgettable portrait of a youthful veteran of the battle against the sweatshop.

But it was Samuel Gompers, president of the American Federation of Labor, who provided the most convincing summary of the accomplishments achieved during the four years since the shirtwaist workers' strike. Gompers stressed the gains of the Protocol and the manner in which its principles were spread to other branches of the garment industry. He placed special emphasis on the advent of protocolism to the dress industry. He noted that some problems still remained unresolved. In discussing the determination of wages, he voiced his approval of the fact that the new dress Protocol included provisions for future adjustments "on a scientific basis."

Brandeis (1856–1941) served as associate justice of the United States Supreme Court (1916–39). He was one of its most vigorous champions of social justice. Under the Protocol of Peace, he served as chairman of its Board of Arbitration. From a decision handed down by the Board of Arbitration, January 21, 1915.

PURPOSE OF THE PROTOCOL
by Louis D. Brandeis

The Protocol had four definite purposes. In the first place, the Protocol undertook to remove specifically the grievances enumerated. That is, the parties met to decide by agreement upon the specific things that should be done with reference to each of these grounds of complaint: and each matter agreed upon became a specific provision of the Protocol.

The result of that was to raise the industry as a whole, practically each and every part of it, to the standard which it is said was already observed by those shops in the industry which were most advanced. Its effect was to create the uniformly high standing provided by the Protocol—which theretofore had been reached only in individual instances.

The second result which was sought by the Protocol was to create, through the strengthening of the Employers' Association on the one hand, and of the Union on the other, bodies which should be able to enforce compliance with the terms of the agreement which was made. It was recognized that without a strong Union of employees on the one side, and a strong Employers' Association on the other, the agreement could not attain the desired results.

In the third place, it was proposed, in creating the Protocol, to insure to the individual employee not only the compliance with the specific provision named in the Protocol, which involved changes in a large part of the shops, but to secure to the individual employee, through the Protocol, the enforcement of fair, reasonable and just treatment by his employer; such treatment which, independently of the Protocol, could ordinarily have been enforced only through strikes. That is, the Protocol was devised to enforce for the benefit of the employee a right to fair and just treatment; or, to put it another way, to secure, through the instrumentality of the Protocol, the reasonable certainty that the employer would not exercise his legal rights oppressively or unfairly.

In the fourth place, it was the purpose of the Protocol to introduce into the relations of the employer and the employee a whole new element; that is, the element of industrial democracy; that there should be a beginning, at least, of a joint control, and with joint control a joint responsibility for the conduct of the industry: that we should pass from that condition where the employer determined alone what was to be deemed proper, and where the employer alone was held responsible for things that were improper in the trade; and that in place thereof we should impose upon all those in the trade, the employer as well as the employee, the obligation of removing through constructive work, those conditions which properly caused discontent, and which prevented the employer and employee alike from attaining that satisfactory living within the industry which it must be the aim of all effort in business to secure.

It therefore was an essential part of this Protocol that it should look forward to improvement; and that the condition arrived at, although it was very much higher than that which had prevailed before the Protocol was adopted, was merely a stage in that development of the trade which the parties believed to be possible; that the higher steps were to be attained through cooperation, through a removal of that sense of antagonism of interests which had prevailed, and must necessarily prevail under other conditions, and which was believed to be an important cause of the discontent and of the unsatisfactory results hitherto prevailing.

Now, those, as we conceive it, were the purposes sought to be accomplished. It was not intended by the Protocol to change the relation of the employer to the employee, otherwise as I have stated and as is expressly stated in the Protocol. In all other respects the legal rights were to remain what they had been before.

The Union, by signing the Protocol, relinquished its right to secure by strike more than it was getting, and there was substituted for that relinquished power of strike, the powers created under this agreement, which constitutes a government to control the relation between employer and employee. And as this Union and other Unions had frequently exercised their right to enforce the fair, just and reasonable exercise by the employer of his legal rights in regard to the administration of business, and in regard to hiring and discharging, so this instrument involved in its creation the right to secure, through its provisions, the same thing. But it substituted for the strike the machinery of the Protocol as a means of securing the fair and reasonable exercise by the employer of those rights which were, by law, vested in him.

Dyche, a staunch champion of the Protocol, outlined its basic procedure. From "The Protocol of Peace," 1914.

THE BOARD OF GRIEVANCES
by John A. Dyche

In the ordinary union shop or non-union shop the only recourse which the Union or the work people have for the enforcement of any agreement, or reaching any understanding with their employers, or adjusting any dispute, is the method of the Strike, the method of Force, or the method of Compulsion, and of course, in such a case the strongest wins.

In our trade which is subject to seasonal fluctuations, the Union is as a rule the stronger in the beginning of the season, and gets the best of the employer. It often succeeds in unionizing or establishing union conditions if they get hold of the employer when he is rushed with orders. But the tables are generally turned against the Union as soon as the rush is over and then the employer gets the best of the work people.

Under this Protocol the Board of Grievances replaces the strike. In cases of dispute, neither the work people nor the Union issue an order to stop from work. If the work people cannot agree with their employer or if they have a grievance, it is their business to go to the Union, that is to put their case before the Complaint Clerk, who has no other function than to take up and forward complaints of the employees to the Board of Grievances. This body consists of an equal number of representatives of the Union and the Manufacturers' Association.

Each complaint is attended to jointly by a representative of the Union and a representative of the Manufacturers who investigate and adjust the complaint if possible. If both representatives of the Board, or the Deputy Clerks as they are called, agree, whatever their decision may be, either in favor of the employer or employee, such decision must be lived up to. If, however, both deputy clerks do not agree, the case is turned over to the Board of Grievances to decide upon. If the Board of Grievances cannot decide, then it is submitted to the Board of Arbitration, whose decision is final.

Just as in framing a constitution of a state we provide for a police force and courts of justice, so in drawing up the Protocol and laying down the laws which should govern the relations of employers and employees, the framers have taken into consideration the fact that there always will be individual employers who will break the provisions of the Protocol. Just as it is the function of the police courts to enforce the laws, so it is the function of the Board of Grievances and the clerks who are working under the supervision of the Board of Grievances to enforce or stop any attempt on the part of the employers or employees to violate the provisions of the Protocol.

There must, however, be no confusion as to the breaking of the Protocol, and the breaking or violating of the "provisions of the Protocol." No individual employer or employee can break the Protocol. Only the employers or the work people can break or transgress the provisions of the Protocol. For example, if an employer pays below the scale or does not observe the hours stipulated in the Protocol, or practices discrimination, such an employer breaks the provisions of the Protocol. The Protocol is a treaty entered into between the Manufacturers' Association and the Union and not between employer and employee. The Protocol can be broken only by the contracting parties, i.e., the Union or the Association.

The method of adjusting disputes by means of the Board of Grievances is not an ideal one. We may not get absolute justice, but compared with the method of the Strike it is a much superior one. The experience in the Cloak trade has shown that while the method of the Strike has in the past led to demoralization and disorganization, the method of adjusting grievances by means of the Board of Grievances has preserved the organization.

Marcosson (1877–1961) was a popular journalist and author. From *Munseys Magazine*, July 1913.

SPREAD OF THE PROTOCOL
by Isaac F. Marcosson

Closely allied with the cloak, skirt, and suit industry is the making of dresses and shirtwaists, a comparatively new trade which has expanded enormously within the past decade, until it musters seven hundred shops with thirty-six thousand workers and a yearly output valued at fifty million dollars.

Sanitary conditions were not as bad here as in the older trades, because most of the shops were in new loft buildings; but there was the old bickering about wages and union recognition. In 1910 the (dress) employers won a costly victory after a bitter strike. The workers went back sullen and determined to revolt again. Last June the International Union, in convention at Toronto, authorized another strike.

Now the remarkable part of this action was that the parent body urged its New York workers to demand the Protocol. The big dress and waist manufacturers took counsel with their brethren of the cloak trade.

"How is the Protocol working out?" they asked.

"Admirably," was the reply. "We would not change under any circumstance."

The cloak Protocol, together with a board of arbitration and a board of sanitary control, was adopted. But the dress and waist people went their cloak contemporaries one better, for they set about standardizing wages.

In the cloak trade there is still more or less amiable bickering about prices. The question of wages is fixed by the price committees in the various shops. In the making of dresses and waists there is much more fluctuation in style and price, and it has always been difficult to fix a standard wage.

In arriving at this standard, most of the employers showed a woeful ignorance of the very fundamentals of the business. In the main, they knew only the routine and price of their own establishments; yet they were engaged in reorganizing a whole industry.

Out of this idea has developed the wage scale board with N. I. Stone as chief statistician. He had a similar post with the Tariff Board in Washington. Under his direction a trained force is making a searching investigation of the industry. Wages and costs over a long period of years are being summarized and compared. It is a new angle in efficiency engineering and scientific business organization.

On June 6, 1911, workers in Cleveland began a general walkout that ran for 22 weeks and never officially ended. These are some of their wives and children.

From the dress and waist trade the Protocol has now spread to the making of kimonos, wrappers, white goods, and children's dresses. Since the beginning of the year, in New York alone, nearly forty thousand union workers have been added to the army of industrial peace and sanity. In Boston, the Protocol has been adopted in both the cloak and dress and waist industries, while in Chicago the leading manufacturer of ready-made men's clothing has signed it for the benefit of his ten thousand employees.

The Protocol means moral discipline for the employer and the employee, and an awakened public responsibility for labor and its product. In short, it is creating a whole new economic order, and is helping perhaps more than any other agency to realize the long-cherished dream of an industrial democracy.

Ireland, born 1871, was secretary to Joseph Pulitzer. He visited the strike headquarters of the white goods workers and obtained from Rose Schneiderman, the person in charge of the walkout, statements by some of the young strikers. From the *New York World,* March 2, 1913.

HARD TIMES IN THE NEW HOMELAND
by Alleyne Ireland

(P. Y. Russian. Nineteen Years Old): I came to America six years ago with my parents. They wanted to give us all a chance to make a better living.

We did have a better living for a while because everybody, even my little sister, works with my mother at home; but since the last three years there is always somebody sick in our family.

Life isn't worth living in this free country only maybe for those people who live in the fine hotels.

When the boss knew we were going out on strike he wanted to give us what we asked for, but no union. But they can't fool us, we know without the union they will treat us like before.

(K. A.   Russian. Seventeen Years Old): My father saved enough money to bring mother and me to America. He came here first and worked to save the money; but the long hours and poor food made him a nervous wreck, and then mother and me had to support him.

Then mother broke down altogether and I had to support them both. I was so afraid of losing my place I had to work overtime whenever they made me. We worked three nights a week from March until May last year, and for this no extra pay, only wages of $5.50 a week.

I was arrested during the strike and the officer said I had struck a girl. I didn't strike her, but I was fined $5. When he arrested me the officer said I was foolish and I could make an easier living on Fourteenth Street.

(K. G.   Russian): I came over here from Russia in hope that our family of five children would get a better education. I'm getting education all right, but the first school I learned about here was the hunger school.

I had to go to work quick or the whole family would starve. I was young and strong. Tucking is easy to learn. I learned and made good money. The second year and then every year after the price was cut until we couldn't stand it any longer and formed a union.

We had a union shop and all the union conditions ourselves. We went on strike for sympathy. Of course the bosses don't understand the sympathy we have for each other. If they did they wouldn't be bosses.

They would like us to stay in and give five cents a week out of our union wages to support the girls on strike, when maybe we made those wages doing scab work. We used to be that kind of fools, but we ain't any more. One boss for all bosses, one girl for all girls. The union is what will make us strong and nothing else.

(B. A.   Russian. Sixteen Years Old): I came from Russia ten years ago with my mother to get an education in the country of liberty. Mother would not let me work until I graduated. I went right from school to the factory when I was fourteen and a half. I don't tell my mother, but I know it would have been better if I never went to school. School

makes you want things, and there is nothing for us but work in dirty shops, and the policeman's club and the thugs' fists when you won't work. I wish sometimes I was dead.

I think the union is like a mother and father to the children. I'd give my whole life for the union. I want to be with the women suffragists, too. Why shouldn't we have as much rights as men? Oh, it was splendid to feel friends with all those splendid women.

My mother says there is no life comes in the world without bloodshed. Maybe the blood shed by our girls on strike will bring better life to all girls through the union. And for the scabs, too; they must eat. If they could only know how sweet union bread is they would never eat any other kind.

(D. S. Russian. Seventeen Years Old): I was arrested once. It was all right to be arrested, but they treat you so unjust. You might just as well tell lies as the truth. Any lie the police tell or anything the thugs do is all right. You sure get fined, or sent to the workhouse. One of our girls got five days' sentence. We went picketing to help the other girls to do their duty, I wonder what sisters means if it doesn't mean to help each other in all our labor troubles.

The police made fun of us and called us suffragettes. I told him before the strike I was a fool like him, but since the strike and since I was on picket duty I knew why women wanted the vote, and we are going to get it, too.

Why, we were fined for everything damaged or lost. Sometimes they made you pay for the whole garment the price it cost in the store, and they wouldn't even let you finish it. You would have to finish it at home. One dollar and a half for a nightgown. What should I pay a dollar and a half for a nightgown for? What will I have left to eat? They charged us two cents for needles when they only paid one dollar a hundred for them and maybe less.

We want to be treated like ladies. With the union behind us they wouldn't dare use the same language to us. One of our girls gets $4 a week and sends $2 home to Russia.

I eat two meals a day and wear my clothes until they fall off me, but I wouldn't be a scab.

Casey served as an ILGWU organizer for a number of years and was especially effective in the Midwest, where, in the course of the Kalamazoo campaign, she was jailed. From the *Detroit Times,* May 4, 1912.

LETTER FROM PRISON
by Josephine Casey

It is not pleasant to be confined in jail for nearly a week, even if your friends do call on you and bring you flowers and dainty things to eat. But we are determined to win our fight for the principle of a living wage for the girl corset makers of Kalamazoo, and moral conditions in the factory where they work.

I came into this to do the work of a union official. I find now that the work properly belongs to a sociological worker. If the women of Michigan only understood the situation in Kalamazoo, the conditions under which 500 or more girls have been working and what those conditions make for as to their moral status, I am sure they would not blame us for doing as we did, and they would not chide us for disobeying the court's order under the circumstances.

The fight began for higher wages. During the last few weeks the question of wages has been put in the background and we are now fighting to purify the factory, to bring about the dismissal of the foremen and those male employees who have been continuously insulting the girl employees and who have been dragging not a few of them down to ruin. The time has passed when an employer can expect to hold girl employees who are subjected to indignities, no matter how attractive the mingling with men may be to a certain class of girls.

I have held several conferences with Manager Hatfield with reference to the conditions existing in the factory. I told him the conditions were immoral and unsanitary. The state factory inspectors may be ever so conscientious, but there are certain conditions which they may overlook, and these conditions are apparent to the girls who work in the factory. For instance, I told Manager Hatfield that a large number of girls were compelled to use the same towel used by a man with a loathsome disease. After I called his attention to this, the man "resigned."

This is but one instance of the conditions confronting the girls, and if Mr. Hatfield had offered to increase their wages, I do not believe they would have accepted unless there was a guarantee that moral conditions were to be improved. These girls are running terrible risks.

The girls are compelled to pay for their own thread and this is quite an item. It was a common practice for foremen to forget to charge them for the thread for several days and then suggest to them a way which these girls might repay them for their act of "kindness." Many of the girls were working under conditions such as they were ashamed and afraid to describe.

You might ask why the parents of these girls permit them to work in the factory. They are compelled to do so because they are confronted with the old question of living expenses. The families of many of these girls have moved to Kalamazoo because there is an opportunity here for the girls to work in the big corset factory. The company is now advertising throughout the state to bring girls here.

Early in 1911 the girls' wages were reduced 20 percent. The entire shop went out on strike. The company was compelled to give back the old scale of wages and a year's contract was signed. The girls were not organized at that time. Since that strike the girls have organized, and there were comparatively few in the factory who were not members of the union when the strike was called in March of this year.

Before the strike was called I saw Mr. Hatfield and explained to him that the girls were members of an intelligent organization, the Ladies' Garment Workers. I told him what this organization had accomplished in New York and how New York people had cooperated with it.

I told him our object in organizing the girls of Kalamazoo was to insure for them a living wage, a wage which would stand between

During the 1912 strike of Kalamazoo corset workers, Pauline Newman, with the cooperation of the streetcar motormen, organized a picnic for the strikers—and did some of the driving herself.

them and want and possibly a life of shame. Mr. Hatfield was so pleased with the conference that he invited me to come again.

In the meantime, we had several meetings and on February 28 I called the second time on Mr. Hatfield and presented the agreement we wanted him to sign—a demand for more wages. He declared that he wouldn't pay a penny more and that he wouldn't negotiate. The following day 12 active members of our union were dismissed. We held a meeting that evening and in the afternoon 2 prominent clergymen called on us and informed us Mr. Hatfield would again receive us. We went to him the next morning and told him the first thing in order was the reinstatement of the 12 girls dismissed. He said if we would send the girls to him separately he would deal with them as individuals, but we contended that inasmuch as he had dismissed them in a body he should take them back in a body.

The strike was called that afternoon and about 400 girls came out. About 50 men also joined us, they having made a demand for an increase in wages.

We do not expect to return to work until the conditions I have outlined have been remedied.

Wherever the idea of the Protocol spread, it initially encountered resistance by the employer, especially where the labor force largely consisted of young women or even children who, in one case, won the sympathy of an ex-president. From the *New York Times,* January 22, 1913.

COLONEL ROOSEVELT VISITS KIMONO STRIKERS

Colonel Theodore Roosevelt visited the East Side yesterday to study, at firsthand, the conditions surrounding the young women now on strike in the kimono and wrapper industry.

The party went to a hall at 49 Henry Street where between 500 and 600 girl strikers had assembled. When those in the hall saw the Colonel in the taxicab, they ran to the street to greet him.

Shaking hands with them as he walked toward the entrance, and with his hat pressed under his elbow, the Colonel hurried into the hall. Inside there was no attempt at formality. Colonel Roosevelt marched to the front of the room but instead of standing on the platform, he leaned against a desk and waved his hand for silence.

"Now, young ladies," he began, "I want to know all about your lives; how you work, and how you manage to be cheerful. Just gather around me and tell your stories."

When this had been translated into Spanish, Italian, Turkish and Greek, the girls, ranging in age from 18 to 14 years, formed a close circle around their distinguished visitor. He sat on a desk, swinging his feet.

"Now, tell me about yourself," the Colonel said, pointing to a tall and attractive-looking Spanish girl.

Through an interpreter, the girl said she had come to this country when she was 14 years old. She started at once, she asserted, to earn her living as a wrapper maker and she had been employed at that work ever since. Beginning work at 8 o'clock in the morning and finishing at 9 o'clock at night, she earned between $6 and $7 a week. She made 36 kimonos a day at 4 cents each, she said. For the machine on which she did her sewing in the factory and which was owned by the company she had to pay $32, she told the Colonel, the price being taken out of her weekly wages.

The Colonel could hardly wait till the story closed to express anger at such conditions. The smile of greeting which he had worn on entering the hall had by this time completely disappeared, and in its stead was an expression of anger mixed with sympathy. The stories poured in upon the Colonel, girls pressing forward to take the places of those who had finished their recitals. No hesitation was shown, only eagerness to gain the Colonel's attention.

Occasionally the interviewer hastened the proceedings by talking directly to the French girls in their language. Always the story was the same: extreme privations, long working hours and small wages. When the Colonel quit the hall at 6 o'clock, he turned to the leaders and those accompanying him and exclaimed: "This is crushing the future motherhood of the country. It must be stopped. It is too horrible for words."

From the Henry Street hall, and with the girls crowding about and cheering his departure, the Colonel went to Odd Fellows' Hall at 67 St. Marks Place, where another gathering awaited him. The girls here had not been informed that a noted man was to visit them, and they were startled at first when the Colonel pushed his way into the gathering.

At this place most of the girls could speak English and the time needed for translation was saved. Colonel Roosevelt's method of gaining the confidence of the girls was the same. He was quite informal and soon had the young women at their ease.

A story that touched the Colonel deeply was told by a 15-year-old Italian girl. At the end of her narrative she said with a catch in her voice:

"If only they would let us sing while we work."

"The brutes," Mr. Roosevelt muttered under his breath, "to prevent them from singing if they can be cheerful under such conditions."

It was here that one girl, when asked how she used her wages, explained that $2.75 of her $4.50 a week was spent on food and the rest provided all other necessities of life.

"You see," she said, "the boys can go to the saloons and get free lunch with a nickel beer, but we have to buy from a pushcart."

When the Colonel departed for his home he said that he would continue his investigation on Thursday.

Roosevelt (1858–1919) made his investigation and spelled out his findings in a letter to Assemblyman Schaap. From the *New York Times,* January 25, 1913.

LETTER TO ASSEMBLYMAN MICHAEL SCHAAP
by Theodore Roosevelt

No man can inquire in the most cursory manner into the situation as it actually exists among these kimono and white goods workers without realizing that these young girls are absolutely helpless if they are obliged to bargain for their rights individually. They must possess the right of collective bargaining and they must be able to establish for themselves relations with kindred organizations which will support them when they are wrongfully treated.

I visited the girl strikers in Henry Street and St. Marks Place and choosing at random listened to the stories of the different girls. In Henry Street the girls were mostly recent immigrants from southern Spain and the Turkish empire. Those from the Turkish empire could not speak English and although they were of Jewish faith they could not speak Yiddish so that they were peculiarly helpless under our conditions here.

Some of the girls were 14 and 15 years old, others 16, 17 and 18. The wages were in one or two cases as low as $3 a week and up to $5.50 and $6 and $8 a week. I was informed that there were girls who worked for $2.50 a week. One girl of 15 earned $3 a week but had to pay $30 for the machine. Another girl who had to pay for a machine worked from 8 A.M. to 8 P.M. and mentioned that in summer she was charged 10 cents a week for ice water.

Another girl who was earning $5 a week was supporting 2 young children, her brother and sister, in addition to herself. These young girls from Turkey represent the lowest and poorest paid workers that we saw. Their fathers and brothers being ignorant of English find it difficult to get employment and the girls often support the whole family on their scanty sweatshop earnings. Some of the girls, out of the miserable pittance paid them, have themselves to pay for repairs to machines and for thread and needles.

In St. Marks Place the girls looked healthier. They spoke English. Many of these girls did not live at their homes and in such cases the owner of the house in which they lived, whom they generally spoke of as "the missus," charged them $3 a month for lodging, this lodging sometimes consisting of one bed and sometimes of a place in a bed with other girls.

I was informed that often 3 or 4 girls slept in one bed. One such girl was earning $4.50 a week, $18 a month. Out of this she paid $3 a month for lodging, $2 a week or $9.50 a month for breakfast and supper, leaving $6 a month for dinner or the midday meal, for carfare, for clothing, for medicine when sick, for dentist, for oculist as well as for recreation if there was any. We cannot as a community sit in apathy and permit these young girls to fight in the streets for a living wage and for hours and conditions of labor which shall not threaten their very lives.

Time, toil, and the battles in shop and on picket lines produced young/old veterans. Levien became a successful Hollywood scriptwriter. From *Metropolitan Magazine,* March 1913.

VETERAN
by Sonya Levien

She was called the Little Old Girl, they told me, the usual product of long years of sweated labor, starvation wages and radical thought. . . .

"When I came from Russia my cheeks were like this"—she put up her hands to her face, balloon fashion, and puffed her cheeks, "and look at me now!"

"Look at these girls." From the platform where we were standing she pointed to the big Cooper Union auditorium, filled with girls, hundreds and thousands of them, young girls, many mere children, laughing and chatting girls assembled there in answer to the call for a general strike. "That's what I was like eight years ago, young and laughing," she finished.

Except for her eyes and mouth she was ordinary in the sense that there was nothing about her to suggest the so-called "atmosphere of the downtrodden"—the ill-fitting clothes, the worn heels or cadaverous expression. On the contrary, unlike many of the apple-cheeked immigrants in the audience, with half-foreign clothes and shawls on their heads, the Little Old Girl had on a small, becoming hat with a pert feather peeping over its brim, a suit too thin to be comfortable in January, but obviously the best effort of a poor tailor; and at her throat she wore a ribboned flower. The remains of a pretty, childish face were lost in the uncanny precocity of the eyes and the tightly drawn mouth.

The Italian speaker made his parting bow, and now a Yiddish orator was bringing a sober look on the faces before him.

"In this one city tonight," he was saying, "we have two hundred thousand brothers and sisters, the garment makers of the people, appealing unitedly for a chance to live in this golden America, pleading for a chance to be decent citizens in this adopted country of ours. Most of the supplicants are women, because the garment industry offers the largest opportunities for speeding up the human machine and woman and child labor is cheap and unresisting. You women have been forced to work as we do, and now you must learn to fight as we do. You must learn to bargain together for what you want and feel the strength of organization."

The Little Old Girl tugged at my arm. "Come on," she said. She was taking me to another meeting.

On the street she broke the silence. "Did you hear what that man said about organization—unionism? He's got that right. *Unite!* It is the workers' only salvation.

"And it ain't easy to make those kids understand, I tell you. Girls are a shifting lot in trade. You take them young, and all of life is concentrated on the one day—the day they'll marry. 'In a year or two I'll be married and away from this,' they answer when you get them to talk seriously, and you can't make them think of the other fellow's kiddies or even of their own. It is hard to make those young girls and the ignorant immigrants understand the sociology of it, that even now they are lowering the earnings of their future husbands by giving their labor cheaply.

"Did you ever waste time dreaming?" The Little Old Girl talked more to herself than to me. Her eyes were upon me, but she was looking beyond.

"I was that foolish when I was young. I am twenty-two now. I came here from Russia eight years ago to become a great woman. I was going to work and live and love. I was told that in this country I would be as free to live as in Russia I could only dream of. I came here to be—what do you call it—yes, a builder of bridges—and then I was to go back to my people and show them how.

"But my first job in this country was feeding handkerchiefs to the machine. The first English sentence I learned to read was 'Watch your needle—3,000 stitches a minute.'

"I fed handkerchiefs to the machine at the rate of 120 a minute, 7,200 an hour, 86,000 handkerchiefs a day; at the end of the week I got four dollars in my pay envelope—that is, during the busy season, and when that was over, for three long months I'd go around looking for a job. I had hoped to save enough the first few years to send for my little sister. I was so lonely in America.

"It was then I lost my dreams of life and love and cried like the rest of the girls in the shop that I'd marry anybody to get out of it. But I have even stopped saying that. One by one I saw the girls in the shop marry and return to it. There are lots of married women at work in the garment trade. Lots. It was their coming back made me think, and it showed me my future in such white-heat light that no amount of dreams could soften it."

Embarrassed by her confidences, the Little Old Girl took refuge in the giddy vernacular of her mates. "I was some swift kid those days—86,000 handkerchiefs a day, that was my limit."

We hurried on in silence. Turning a corner we were stopped suddenly by a big street gathering. The sidewalks were damp and the air filled with mist and cold, yet hundreds of girls stood listening to the fervored accusations of a woman.

The flickering light of the lamppost cast a ghastly glare on the face of the speaker. It was a worn face, sad in its momentary reposes, but tensely fierce in action. I thought of a caged tiger with the trap door about to open, and I drew nearer the Little Old Girl.

The speaker was wailing her complaints. "In the big department stores," she said, "we are having the January sales of white goods, and grand ladies are buying the lingerie we make. Now is the time for us to tell them that while *their* little girls are reading *Alice in Wonderland* *ours* are sewing buttonholes for the princely wage of one cent for thirty-six holes. Let us tell them that while their little girls are schooling and playing and sleeping, our little sisters are bending over machines fourteen, sixteen and twenty hours a day. Let us tell them that it's the labor of little children in the tenements and the sweatshops that make the bargains, and sells waists at forty-nine cents!"

"There ain't no sale on eggs!" a voice called from the crowd.

"No!" hundreds exclaimed.

"No!" echoed the speaker, "sixty cents a dozen! A waist lasts a year—but we must eat!"

"Girls!" she cried out, and her shrill tones penetrated our very souls, "three years ago I was a scab, and now I am an organizer. I was a greenhorn then, and I had it hard, and my boss promised me eight dollars instead of five. I did not understand unionism. But, girls, if any of you are going to scab, don't scab on the scab job. If you are to be a strikebreaker, don't be a piker! Go to the detective agency and get ten dollars a day as a professional. Be true to the union price of your class!"

The Little Old Girl was maneuvering me out of the crowd. . . . We hastened our steps and soon reached the Labor Temple—the working people's church. The Little Old Girl was recognized, hailed jubilantly and taken from me. I tried to follow the group into the hall; the crowds opened to her and I was left far behind. Finally, my turn came and I was admitted into the hall.

I could not see the speaker, but I heard the voice. I recognized it and pushed my way into a clearing. It was the Little Old Girl. Her wet clothes accentuated her thinness, and the wet feather marked time with her gestures, but her eyes were a living fire that illuminated the pent-up grievances of a people.

"Girls, what have we to lose! We are humble in our demands. In return for our youth and our labor we want a little more leisure so that we may rest for the next day, a little more food so that we may live a few years longer, and a little more joy so that we may keep faith with humanity.

"*You* girls, *you* supposedly ignorant immigrants, untaught, unfed and unloved, *you* are the pioneers that are paving the way for a better race—with your last cent you are purchasing economic freedom for the scabs of our trade, with your lives you are paying for the freedom of those others who are too smug or selfish to know that they, too, are slaves. And it is up to you to have the pride and endurance of pioneers. You, the minute women of this age, unite and stand for a better world for womanhood!"

The Labor Temple was long in clearing. I was cold and wet, my feet were tired and my head confused, but my heart was full and I waited to do homage to the little prophet of the immigrants.

O wasteful America! We boast we are a clever people, yet go on juggling with youth and its dreams.

Bruere, a prominent socialite, an active member of the
Women's Trade Union League of New York, did volunteer
work in the strike halls. From *Life and Labor,* March 1913.

THE WHITE GOODS STRIKERS
by Martha Bensley Bruere

"Cut the bread thick," said the chairman to me. "Oh, thicker than
that, so that two slices will be enough for lunch. Most of these girls
won't have anything to eat today except what we give them."

I had come to help with the lunch in a hall where the shop meetings
of the white goods workers for twenty different firms were held. I was
used to strikes, but not this kind, for when I went into the hall with my
tray of thick sandwiches I had the feeling that school had just been let
out. The hall was full of little girls in short dresses, many of them with
their hair down their backs. They were the youngest, the most ignorant, the poorest and most unskilled group of women workers who
have ever struck in this country.

These white goods workers are already poor; they are striking for
enough to live on. They are mostly Russian and Roumanian Jewesses
sent over as the advance guards of their families in the New World. It
has taken the savings of years to send them, and they are expected to
turn the stream of American gold back towards their families again.
But that stream of American gold must be pretty thin at times for
some of these girls are only getting $2.50 a week, and there can't be
much of that left to send to the little mother in Russia. Of course, the
average wage is more than this; most of the girls get as much as $5 a
week. That was what Sadie Aronovitch got.

My attention was first called to Sadie because she cried when I
passed her the tray of sandwiches. This seemed such an unnatural
thing to do in the presence of food that I persuaded her to come over
and talk with the chairman.

"What is your name?" said the chairman, pulling Sadie down into
the chair beside her.

"Sadie," said the girl, dully.

"You weren't here yesterday, were you, Sadie?"

"No, ma'am."

"Well, how are you getting on?"

The little girl's eyes filled with tears.

"I can't pay my missus," she said. "She puts me out."

"How much do you owe her, Sadie?"

"Two dollars."

The chairman clicked open the clasp of her bag, and then she looked up quickly.

"Have you had your lunch, Sadie?" she asked.

"Yes, ma'am."

"Where did you get your breakfast?"

The girl hung her head and scraped her foot upon the floor.

"Didn't you have any breakfast, Sadie?"

She shook her head.

"Where did you eat yesterday?"

The girl began to cry.

"Didn't you have anything to eat at all?"

"No, ma'am."

"Here's two dollars for your missus, Sadie," said the chairman. "And this other dollar is for you to get breakfast and supper with as long as it lasts. Come here and have your lunch. Do you understand, Sadie?"

"Yes, ma'am," sobbed the child.

I stayed with Sadie Aronovitch long enough to quiet her and she told me that her family were in Russia, all but an uncle who had met her at the boat and bought her an American hat and American dress and shoes—and how can one get a job in this country without them? And then her uncle found her a place to stay "by a missus" and a chance to run pink ribbons in thirty-nine dozen corset covers a day for which she got $5 a week.

Sadie had been running those pink ribbons for two solid years— miles and miles of pink ribbons she had run in the time, and that was practically all besides a little English she had learned in America. Three dollars a month she paid her "missus" for a "sheet," which is the right to half a bed. The "missus" herself might use the other half, or the grandmother, or two or three children might be tucked in.

Her food cost her about twenty-five cents a day—two cents for her "missus" for a cup of coffee in the morning and a penny for a roll; a two-cent sandwich for lunch; a twenty-cent dinner eaten in a basement cafe at night, sometimes an apple or banana between times— about eight dollars a month for food in New York City where the least expenditure for food enough to keep one in health is over nine dollars a month. Sadie must have had always on hand about a dollar's worth of unsatisfiable hunger. Out of the twenty dollars a month she was paid, Sadie had nine with which to buy all her clothes, pay for all her amusements, and contribute to the support of her family at home. Is it any wonder that there are some twelve thousand girls like Sadie on strike here at this moment?

By early 1913, the idea of the Protocol had spread throughout most of the garment industry. More importantly, other industries were studying its possible applications at a time of general industrial unrest. Gompers (1850–1924), president of the American Federation of Labor, best summarized the ILGWU achievement. From *American Federationist,* March 1913.

STRUGGLES IN THE GARMENT TRADES
by Samuel Gompers

Progress in the garment industry during the past three years has taken the form of a fight for the Protocol. Beginning with disorganization, undisciplined workers, spirit-breaking conditions and pernicious practices, these workers have steadily forged upward and onward. Though the struggles have been hard, the sacrifices and suffering severe, not one movement has been made but has counted for humanity and progress. A review of the different stages of the movement brings out the relation and influence of each upon those succeeding it, and reveals an evolutionary and natural development that is stimulating and encouraging to those who have borne the brunt of the struggle, to those who directed the movement and to all the toilers of the world.

The workers in the industry are chiefly natives of other lands who have recently entered our gates, seeking in America the land of freedom, opportunity and hope, and finding—the sweatshop of the East Side of New York. There are many of them who are unacquainted with the customs and standards of American life and work; many speak little or no English and hence are barred from getting into touch with the life and the thought represented in the American ideal—daring hope, constructive imagination, and the will to do things.

The needle industries afford employment which does not require knowledge of English, offer a chance to earn the wherewithal to get shelter at night and food for the morrow. So pressing is the immediate need, the newcomers accept gratefully any work at any price and are caught in the clutches of a struggle for existence so exigent that it leaves neither opportunity nor strength for betterment. Caught and held by industrial and social forces, the workers are victims of the demoralizing effects of long hours, low wages, unsanitary conditions, and brutal treatment.

Because of climatic reasons and social customs, the garment work is largely seasonal—a characteristic which increased the hardships of the workers. Part of the year, except where organization had afforded relief, there was not enough work; part of the time they were driven to the breaking point of human endurance. During part of the year they might come in the morning, be given no work but be expected to wait around until noon when they might be rewarded with a little work or might be told to come again the next morning.

During the rush season they were expected to begin work early in the morning, to take little or no time off for meals, and to work far into the night—and to work under the relentless eye of a superintendent who reminded the worker she was wasting the employer's time did she rest for a second, or make an unnecessary motion to adjust hair or clothing. The system of petty, nagging tyrannies that prevailed before the strike, was either maddening or fatal to self-respect. There were fines and abuses, there were insults and favoritism, with all the subtle influences degrading to womanhood. Under such conditions the human worker sinks into a mere drudge at infinite cost to the human soul.

Nor was the lot of the employers much more satisfactory—they, too, were caught and held by the forces of existing conditions. Higher standards for the individual shop would have resulted in financial ruin. Merciless competition was waged by "pirate" firms which ventured into the contest to make big profits in a short period—these employers cared nothing for the permanent welfare of the industry or the workers, cared only to squeeze out the greatest possible income at the lowest possible cost. Such could easily underbid a factory maintaining decent standards. In order to meet this condition there arose the practice of contracting and subcontracting. Employees were allowed to take day or night work to their homes. They did this work themselves or hired helpers.

Work done through this subcontracting system was under absolutely no control—homes were converted into sweatshops, and made unnecessarily dirty and unsanitary. Little children were utilized as helpers and there was no way to reach the violators of compulsory education or child labor laws. The pay for the work done went to the one contractor who divided it among the helpers, usually adding to his own share the profits of an employer. Another form of subcontracting developed in connection with learners—an expert workman would employ "beginners" or "learners"; this workman controlled the earnings of the group, paying the "learners" as little as possible.

This subcontracting system had advantages for the employers. It relieved them of the necessity of dealing directly with the skilled, unskilled, or foreign work people; it removed much of the work from their own buildings, thereby saving rent; it reduced costs, as the workers must use their own machines, often their own thread. This latter condition, however, prevailed also in some factories where workers had to buy or rent machines and pay for thread that was sewed into the garments from which the employers secured the profits.

The industry was scattered everywhere—in factories, in small shops, in tenement houses, and in single rooms. The system seemed an overpowering octopus whose tentacles were sapping the vitality of a considerable portion of the nation. There seemed to be no vital spot upon which to center attack, for its arms sprawled everywhere.

And the public—that third party interested in every industrial conflict—did the public concern itself about the sanitary conditions under which garments were produced? about the unreasonably low wages meted out to the workers? about the grievously long hours which the toilers were compelled to labor? about the little children deprived of the right to play and grow, and even to live? Did this public busy itself in trying to right these wrongs and accord justice to those misused? On the contrary, this disinterested, "just" public continued its search for bargains, cheap clothing, and gave little thought to the dangers incurred by themselves and others through unsanitary working conditions or the waste and loss of human life. Nor did the public assist these workers when they tried to help themselves.

Those earlier attempts at self-help were sporadic revolts without constructive program or careful thought for the morrow—they represented an uncontrollable desire to get rid of intolerable wrongs. They were impressive, startling manifestations of latent power, entailing tremendous sacrifices and suffering, and frequently wresting concessions from employers. These won, the workers permitted their strike organization to lapse. But the wily employer merely waited for the workers to be lulled into lassitude, then quietly, cautiously, gradually, took away all the newly gained advantages and instituted again all the old, hard conditions.

But the shirtwaist strike of 1909 put new life into the union movement, not only among the New York garment workers but throughout the whole country. The movement started as a spontaneous outbreak in the famous, or otherwise, Triangle Waist Company and spread through the city.

The conditions against which they struck were, as one worker expressed it, uncivilized. For four or five dollars a week the girls worked two days from eight in the morning until five-thirty in the afternoon; on four days from eight in the morning until nine in the evening; and on Sunday from eight in the morning until noon. Those were wages and hours that undermined the health and vitality of the workers; those were conditions that were destructive to minds and morals.

At the beginning of the strike less than 5 percent of the workers were organized. During the strike more than 30,000 were out. The factor which did more than any other to spread the strike spirit was the brutality and violence of the police. Girls who braved the terrors of doing peaceful picketing were assaulted by the police, arrested and imprisoned.

The strike entailed bitter hardship and suffering, but it produced noble, heroic leaders among the strikers and served as an invaluable educational experience. Those girls, cold, hungry, and imprisoned, learned the lesson of collective action and reliance upon constructive programs and trustworthy leaders. They learned that the workers' safety lies in their resourcefulness and mutual association. Having learned that organization must be maintained not only in strike time but also in the time of peace, having learned the value of collective action and collective bargaining with employers' associations, the foundation was laid for future progress in the garment trades.

These strikers who went through the struggle, who fought side by side resisting all attempts to disrupt solidarity, all attempts to foment bad feeling by appeals to social and religious prejudices, learned the heart and soul of unionism. And when "the tumult and the shouting died" and the humdrum of daily toil began, it was seen that unionism would at last abide as a permanent institution in that trade.

This movement was the break in the reign of chaos and injustice in the needle trades. A way which led to better things and decent standards of life had been found. In the summer of 1910 rebellion broke out among the cloakmakers, after vain protests against intolerable conditions and injustice. In May 1910 six thousand workers were members of the union. On the opening day of the strike only twenty thousand workers belonged to the ILGWU; within two weeks practically all of the seventy-five thousand workers joined the union.

The protest was against evils common to the garment trades, and against the following specific conditions:

1. Irregular payment, which entailed hardships and inconveniences to the workers with scanty resources—it was the practice not to pay any workers until the garment was completed, and the payment of wages to operators was deferred until finishers and buttonholers had completed their tasks.

2. The individual contract system which furnished the worker with constant work for the season but required him to furnish security, varying from $25 to $30, for performance of his work. This security was subtracted from his wages and might be declared forfeited in case the worker joined a strike movement.

3. Long, irregular hours due to the seasonal character of the work and absence of effort to equalize work.

4. The subcontracting system which resulted in a chaotic wage scale. The subcontractor was a pieceworker who employed helpers at week pay which varied from $3 to $8. The pieceworker alone had dealings with the employer, and his attitude toward

those under him was usually that of a tyrant overseer. The helpers usually had steady work, sometimes overwork, during six or seven months of the year, and then no work from the middle of November until the middle of January.

But the condition that engineered more bitterness, more antagonism than any other, was the system of "charges." Workers were charged for material or garments spoiled or injured in the process of making regardless of the degree of their responsibility; they were charged for needles, thread, bobbins, shuttles, and for the electric power which operated their sewing machines. It was estimated that charges for electricity consumed 10 percent of the wages paid workers operating machines. Since these operators constituted but 45 percent of the total, it was manifestly unfair that upon them should fall the whole expense when subdivision of labor rendered the method of production collective and interdependent.

One of the most memorable meetings was the one held in Madison Square Garden on June 28, 1910. Inside were gathered 30,000 workers; outside were nearly twice as many. The pulsating, throbbing crowd of human toilers, weary, oppressed, suffering, but courageous and determined to fight for their rights, was charged and vibrating with a spirit that impressed itself upon all who were there, a spirit which we all felt and which I interpreted in my talk to them in these words: "This is not merely the portent of a general strike; it is an industrial revolution." Such it proved, for a new era in the garment trades was dawning.

It was a tremendous epoch-making movement which instilled the spirit of independence, constructive resistance, loyalty into workers who had been badgered, mistreated, swindled by employers and the public. But the strike had many phases that were not so bright and pleasant; the strike meant unspeakable suffering and sacrifices to those who dared rebel that they might secure their rights. It meant days and weeks of dearth of food for themselves and their families, sickness or accident might come to them, and their resources were scarcely adequate for actual physical necessities. Yet these natives of other lands stood shoulder to shoulder, fighting for American ideals and American principles embodied in trade unionism. They felt and knew that the greatest transforming force operating in the melting pot of the nation is the trade union movement.

One sinister influence tried to turn conditions toward reaction, toward old ideals and conditions and things un-American. By right of judicial authority, a judge of the Supreme Court of the City of New York presumed to forbid the strikers to exercise the right of free men—enjoining the cloakmakers from peaceful picketing in support of the demand for the union shop.

The real significance of this injunction was that the strikers were in effect forbidden from striking for the union shop. Such assumption of authority was startling and revolutionary in principle. If a judge could curtail by injunction personal and lawful freedom of action for one purpose, it implied the same right of curtailment for other purposes; if for some personal activities, then for all, and the workers' freedom becomes a farce. However, despite perversion of judicial authority, the movement steadily and surely advanced toward success.

For some time all efforts at negotiations were futile; eventually a committee was selected, composed of five representatives of the unions and five manufacturers, with a chairman representing the public. Demands and counterdemands were presented. The great obstacle to any agreement was the fact that many of the wrongs and abuses grew out of industrial conditions which individual employers were powerless to remedy.

Many desired to grant relief to their employees, but cutthroat competition was a menace to such humane considerations. Then, too, past experience had given them the impression that the cloak workers were unstable, passionate, unreliable—that making a contract with them would be wasted effort. Clearly, what was needed on both sides was organization. Concerted action and agreement upon conditions of work would secure employers self-protection from ruthless com-

Rose Schneiderman (center) at office of Women's Trade Union League during whitegoods workers' walkout.

petition. The workers needed strong organization for self-imposed discipline, to hold them steadily to their word and their agreements and thus increase their bargaining power.

Just such an organization was then controlling the situation for the cloak workers, and its educational force was powerful and vivifying. Strong, resourceful leaders were instilling into these mutinous, undisciplined minds the fundamental theories of unionism. They were held steadily in line, taught to curb their fighting spirit so that terms of agreement might be devised; taught that unreasoning resistance to the finish is vain bravado without profit; taught that negotiation is not a sign of weakness, but is the most potent means by which permanent gains can be secured; taught the lessons of self-restraint; taught that carefully planned policies are of infinitely greater value than irresponsible, revolutionary uprisings—in a word the cloakmakers were taught unionism. And it was the American Federation of Labor, by its consistent and persistent course in its constructive work in the interest of the workers, which taught the lesson.

The most controverted issue perhaps was the union shop. The employers employed all the conventional arguments against it. The workers replied with the unanswerable argument that the union shop was necessary to safeguard union standards and conditions, necessary to the existence of the union itself. The union is the sole guarantee of stability and responsibility on the part of the workers, the sole guarantee that their contracts will be carried out.

Negotiations were broken off and renewed several times, while the strike continued vigorously. Finally, on September 2, the famous "Protocol" was signed by the representatives of the manufacturers' association and the cloakmakers' union. The Protocol was more than a strike settlement; it was a constructive industrial document providing a permanent basis for industrial peace. It instituted machinery by which future difficulties might be adjusted and increasingly advantageous conditions be secured without resort to violent methods or interruption of work. Perhaps the greatest benefits were provisions for fixed hours, a wage scale, abolition of "sweating" or home work, and means for standardizing sanitary conditions.

The signing of the Protocol in 1910 was the result of fully three decades of struggle, pioneering, sacrifice, and growth. In the early days the union of the cloakmakers led a spasmodic sort of existence, dwindling to a mere handful in times of peace, or growing to an unwieldly passionate mass in times of strike. But the years of struggle and disappointment were years of education, teaching them that safety lay in permanent organization. Still more years of education are necessary to instill the habit of self-disciplined, thoughtful action, the weighing of policies, the testing of leaders, and the ability to select those who really have the welfare of the workers at heart and are able to accomplish results.

The Protocol recently ratified by the 20,000 workers of the dress and waist trade is of the same nature as the initial Protocol in the cloak industry. From preamble to closing sentence it is practicable and hopeful. It does not pose as the final solution of details, but makes tentative terms and provides machinery whereby these may be constantly improved and perfected. The Protocol was signed by the officers of the union and the international organization. The representative and the president of the American Federation of Labor also affixed their signatures, pledging that the American Federation of Labor will stand back of the ILGWU in the faithful performance of the Protocol.

The new features of this agreement that mark progress over the gains made by the cloak Protocol are the sanitary label and the tentative character of the wage awards with provisions for future adjustments on a scientific basis. Altogether the Protocol is a constructive solution of some industrial problems, and may be regarded as one of the most hopeful indications of progress toward industrial peace and industrial democracy. It is a permanent basis for future constructive efforts. Or to change the figure, it is the germ from which greater things will be evolved—increasingly better things for each tomorrow, things we can now only dimly discern as we catch glimpses of possibilities down the vistas of time.

The workers, in their organized capacity, through their chosen representatives in whom they have confidence, shall participate in the determination of those things which have to do with their employment, conditions of work and sanitary surroundings. As human beings, men and women, they shall make contracts with their employers and shall be responsible that the contracts are carried out. This means self-discipline and education of the workers. It means they will have a better chance to live decently, humanly, will become better men and women, and increasingly better citizens.

The other organizations also joined in the movement for better conditions. About 15,000 kimono and wrapper makers and 20,000 white goods workers caught the spirit of unrest, ambition, and hope as the stir and inspiration penetrated downward through the ranks of the garment industry. Even the most unskilled, most sorely pressed, caught the inspiring contagion of the struggle for the Protocol with all the advantages which it represented.

February 11 marked the next forward stride for unionism and humanity. On that date the kimono and wrapper workers who had steadily refused partial concessions signed with the New York Association of House Dress and Kimono Association a Protocol, ending the strike which officially began January 8.

While the joy of victory had come to the wrapper and kimono workers who had won their fight, the white goods workers had gritted their teeth in a fight for the union shop. A Protocol had been submitted to them which did not provide for the preferential union shop. The makers of muslin underwear, frail, underdeveloped girls who know already the meaning of cold and hunger, persecution, and mistreatment, involved in the struggle necessary for securing better conditions, refused with one accord to waive the provision they deemed vital to the permanence of advantages gained.

Such a contest developed courage, stability, character, in these girls, many of whom are mere children, but children forced to learn the hard lessons of life and to bear some of its weary burdens, children weighed down by burdens of getting food and clothing and money for rent. The girls have experienced something of the inspiration and exaltation that come from catching a glimpse of the meaning and the future import of the day's work and struggle. They turned from their labor halls, where they refused the compromise, singing the songs of labor that have comforted and heartened the toilers of many ages.

The effort to better themselves will mean progress for the white goods workers whether the goal is now reached or not. An ideal has been established; a way to attain it has been found; realization is a matter of persistent effort and education. Unrest will not cease until all the evils of the garment industry and the sweating system are eliminated. The effect of the victories in some divisions of the trade will be felt in all the others, not only in New York but throughout the country. The gains made for the Protocol policy constitute one of the most helpful, inspiring chapters of industrial history.

Agitation, education, organization, constitute the policy that has brought these tremendous advantages to the garment workers of New York City—advantages whose influence will be felt throughout the length and breadth of the land, spreading through all the industrial centers of the garment industry wherever there are oppression, suffering, and injustice. Everywhere there are indications that the toilers are taking courage and following the guiding precept of the American Federation of Labor to "grit your teeth and organize."

7. The Protocol of Peace—Its Decline

Even as the Protocol of Peace was being widely hailed and its principles extended into other apparel trades, its shortcomings were becoming increasingly clear. Brandeis's heroic vision had suggested a triumph of logic over emotion, of reason over irrational human frailties. Had it taken proper account of profit imperatives, of deeply ingrained workers' fears?

Almost as soon as they were established, the channels for dealing with shop grievances became clogged, perhaps illustrating some perverse principle that the cure first augments the illness. Workers who had for more than a generation learned the lesson that their power lay in a refusal to work were now told that they had signed away the right to refuse to work. Dyche, in a historic session before the Industrial Commission, pointed out that in the ranks of the garment workers were men who had plotted against the Czar and who, ignorant of the system of democatically derived authority, considered all authority violative of freedom.

Called before the commission to spell out the details of the garment industry's unique experiment in industrial peace, Hourwich, Rosenberg, and Dyche instead clearly demonstrated that all was not well under the Protocol. A deep polarization among the garment workers, reflecting personal histories and political preferences, foreshadowed the ILGWU internecine war of the next decade. Dyche, in line with his schooling among the British socialists, held that evolutionary, cumulative gains through contract bargaining would in time bring substantial improvements in the quality of the garment workers' lives. Hourwich, on the other hand, insisted that reform was not enough and that the system was beyond repair, that it quickly exhausted the limits of its generosity in bargaining with workers and then returned to traditional devices of exploitation.

The debate that raged in the pages of the union's *New Post* and *Ladies' Garment Worker* reflected the need for specific definitions under the Protocol and clarification of the ambiguous language of security provisions and workers' rights, both of which were causing continuous conflict between the union and the employers' group.

All of Brandeis's skill as an arbitrator, reflected in the pages of the *New Republic,* could not avert the growing conflict. Even as the magazine praised his industrial statesmanship, stoppages kept shops in a continuous state of turmoil. Employers insisted that in the inter-season reshuffling they had the right to choose their own workers, thus conveniently eliminating staunch unionists.

Once again Hillquit formulated the issues: job security; equal division of work among all the workers of the shop; a more effective procedure for rate determination. As the confrontation between employers and workers grew increasingly bitter, the committee headed by Felix Adler tried to preserve the Protocol.

But in April 1916 the Protocol was abrogated by the employers in the form of a lockout; the latter was soon countered by a strike. Helen Keller, a national figure, spoke for a large segment of the public, which looked upon the employers' action as injurious to the public interest. Mary Dewhurst notes that public support included statements by the Women's Civic Club and the political science faculty of Columbia University.

The present chapter contains a roundup of bulletins from the *New York Press* that marked the end of the Protocol and a return to the use of strikes and lockouts. It concludes with excerpts from Walter Lippmann's seminal essay, a piece of writing that went right to the heart of the issue that strained labor relations of his day: the new and insistent challenge of a minimum wage and a decent standard of living.

Seeking causes of unrest and new techniques for maintaining industrial peace, the U.S. Commission on Industrial Relations conducted hearings in mid-January 1914 in New York City during which garment union leaders were questioned on the Protocol. The resulting testimony disclosed the existence of persistent problems. From "Report of Hearings, U.S. Commission on Industrial Relations," January 15, 1914.

THE STRATTON CASE

ISAAC HOURWICH: There was a stoppage of work—or, let us be plain about it, there was a strike—in the factory of J. C. Stratton Company for the following reasons: There was a foreman there who was rather abusive toward all the employees, and then one day he insulted a 17-year-old girl, and insulted her in the grossest way. The girl became hysterical. The men in the shop were all Italians and became excited and quit work immediately and demanded the removal of the foreman. The association, of course, insisted upon its right; that they had no right to strike; that if a foreman abuses an innocent girl by insulting remarks, why, you have to sit at your machine and file a complaint, and the clerk for the union and the clerk for the association will come, and they will probably render justice; but men with red human blood may not be able to reason that way under sudden provocation.

When Mr. Dyche, who was at that time clerk, came to the factory to tell the men that they had to sit down to work, because the Protocol would not permit them to stop work, that was a strike, and he took out his watch, and he told them, "I give you five minutes to sit down to work. If you do not sit down to work you will be discharged"; and he held his watch in his hand, and when the five minutes were up he told the employer, "Discharge those men," and 500 men were discharged. Later on some were reengaged.

That created a commotion in the union. It was law, of course, it was the Protocol. It was trade-union discipline. It was all of that. He wanted to show that the union was faithful in the performance of its agreement with the association.

JOHN DYCHE: I want to say that in the course of my argument, in trying to persuade the people to go back to work, I took out from my pocket the constitution of the international union, where it reads as follows (this is on the first page of the constitution, in capital letters):

"No member is allowed to stop from work, or come out on strike, without the order of the union, for such illegal strike is a violation of the union rules, and such member will be fined or expelled."

The answer to me by these people was that they had not participated in the making of this constitution, and the framing of its laws, and they would not obey it. I told them, in that case, "Then you are outside the pale of the union," and they said, "Just exactly, we will settle the trouble ourselves the same as we did in this firm prior to your coming." I want to ask you, Dr. Hourwich, are you positive of your assertion that during the recent trouble I pulled out my watch and gave the workers five minutes to return to work; that I went to Stratton's and gave them five minutes' time to return to work. Are you positive about that statement?

DR. HOURWICH: I have read that statement in an official statement of Local No. 1 of the ILGWU. That statement was made by me on the official authority of one of the officials of the union.

MR. DYCHE: Will you apologize if I show you your statement is false, Dr. Hourwich?

DR. HOURWICH: If that statement is not correct, I am not responsible for it.

MR. DYCHE: Is it not correct that I wrote the following day to the newspaper and denied it in toto?

DR. HOURWICH: I regret to say that I have not read it.

MR. DYCHE: Will you apologize to me if that is incorrect?

DR. HOURWICH: I have nothing to apologize for. If the statement is wrong, I am not responsible for it. If I am told that statement is incorrect, I shall not repeat it any more, of course.

MR. DYCHE: It is absolutely false.

DR. HOURWICH: I have said before, Madam President, that I have quoted from an official statement; relying on the authority of that Local, I made the statement; if it is incorrect, it is incorrect. I can't say I have any personal knowledge of the fact.

THE CHAIRMAN: Dr. Hourwich, I would like to ask you, are you opposed to the Protocol as a whole?

DR. HOURWICH: I am not opposed to the Protocol.

THE CHAIRMAN: Do you think the machinery of the Protocol is defective?

DR. HOURWICH: I do.

THE CHAIRMAN: Entirely defective?

DR. HOURWICH: Well, not entirely defective. It has one serious defect that ought to be corrected.

THE CHAIRMAN: In what respect do you think it is defective?

DR. HOURWICH: I think the most important defect is that there is no real board of arbitration. We want a board of arbitration that will arbitrate, and I believe the only way to do business in peace is to have a salaried board of arbitration. Moreover, in my own opinion, it would be a good idea, I think, to have a chairman for the board of grievances, what we call technically an impartial chairman or umpire.

ABRAHAM ROSENBERG: When the board of arbitration decided to establish a system of clerks . . . it was understood that whenever the two clerks, one clerk representing the association and the other clerk representing the union, go upon a case and make an investigation, if those two clerks agreed how this case should be disposed of, it is final, and each side must obey the order of the clerks—the manufacturer as well as the union must obey the order of the clerks.

But whenever those two deputy clerks disagreed and could not come to a conclusion, then it was submitted to chief clerks on each side; each side has a so-called chief clerk . . . and those two chief clerks got together and tried to make a disposition of the case. But whenever those two chief clerks disagreed on a case, then it was brought before the board of grievances, and the board of grievances, sitting as a court, used to hear the case; and whenever necessary they called witnesses to testify, and it was the custom that each side had an equal number of members on that grievance committee, so it required one of each side to decide the case one way or the other; for instance, if the union had a complaint against a certain manufacturer, it required one manufacturer to vote with us; and, on the other hand, whenever the manufacturers brought up one of our people to vote with them, they won the case.

It always required six, or a majority, to dispose of a case, and we got along the best way we could, the best way we knew how; and we used to have these agreements, and we used to have a tie vote, where both sides could not agree even on the grievance board. . . . But, in a general way, I believe that the board of grievances, with the system of clerks, has made adjustment in almost, I should say, 75 percent of the cases brought to the attention of the association and the union.

COMMISSIONER O'CONNELL: Go along and tell us how long it will take to get the case off their hands?

CHARLES W. WINSLOW: The usual machinery is that the complaint is registered in the morning at the office of the manufacturer and the clerks are designated to take up that case immediately, and they go out to the scene of action and endeavor to settle the case. If they fail, the case then goes to the chief clerks of the board of grievances and they endeavor to settle the case. That might take another day. If they fail to settle the case, the case goes to the board of grievances itself. Now, the machinery there means that they might designate two of either side to reinvestigate the case. If they reinvestigate the case and disagree, it could go to the board of arbitration, and then it is a matter of some days before the board of arbitration can be gotten together; in general, that is the machinery.

COMMISSIONER O'CONNELL: It is a matter of some days; how many days can they hold off there without getting the case through?

MR. WINSLOW: Going clear to the board of arbitration?

COMMISSIONER O'CONNELL: The whole machinery. I wanted to see whether the hobble skirt has gone out of existence while we were getting through all this machinery. (Laughter)

MR. WINSLOW: I should say four or five days, Mr. Chairman, going up to the board of arbitration.

COMMISSIONER O'CONNELL: Going up to the board of arbitration and getting through would take two weeks; if they were waiting to kill everybody, it would take a couple of weeks to get up there. That is the general complaint of the men, that there is no action on their cases; and the men get discouraged and they are afraid to bring up their cases because of delay, and so on, and would rather forget about it and go off and get another job. What I want to get at is, is their complaint real? If it is, the Protocol ought to be so arranged, or the machinery ought to be got closer together or new cogs put in the wheel, or make it move faster—another gear put in or one taken out, if there are too many.

MR. WINSLOW: There have been 7,556 cases adjusted from April 15, 1911, to October 13, 1913. Of that number 179 cases have been before the board of grievances. The number referred to the board of arbitration was 20.

The classification of grievances on the part of the union that have been considered by the board of grievances were: discrimination against individuals, 27; alleged wrongful discharge, 21; nonpayment for legal charges, 13; paying under agreed scale of wages, 13; non-protocol conditions in shops, 9; claim for wages due, 8; dispute in price making, 6; inside subcontracting, 3; duplicates made by the week, 3; irregular price settlement, 3; shop lockout, 2; nonpayment for the Jewish holidays, 2; changing piece prices during the season, 2; non-compliance with the terms of the adjustment, 2; cutters working by the hour, 2; ill treatment of employees, 2; unequal distribution of work, 1; week worker discharged in the middle of the week, 1; samples made by piece, 1; unregistered contract shop, 1.

MR. DYCHE: The large influx of immigrants makes the problem of the union so much larger to absorb them and to train them to American methods. The great majority of them come from Russia; a large number of them have been engaged at home in fighting autocracy, in fighting ukases of the Czar, and to a great many of them even obeying an order, even though the order comes from the union, is repugnant. Some of them make no distinction between an order of a business agent and the order of a gendarme; people engaged in fighting obedience to the Czar are not ready to adjust themselves to have to obey a union law, because to them all laws—at least, they have been at home engaged in fighting laws and all of a sudden they must obey union laws.

I say this complicates the problem. . . . Of course, difficulties are not insurmountable, because most of the people are amenable to reason and they are ready to listen to the advice of the leaders, provided they have faith in the leaders. Of course, if a situation arises where the honesty and good faith of the leaders is attacked, naturally the opportunity of getting discipline at all is almost impossible.

I think one of the weaknesses of the Protocol is that it is indefinite. I believe the union should enter into an agreement with the manufacturers for a specified date—two or three years. Under the present existing conditions it is indefinite; any person or officer who is engaged in performing his functions under the Protocol, or who is qualifying for the job, all he has to do is to raise a rumpus and tell them, "You are the slaves of the Protocol." There is no stability to the Protocol. If we had an agreement which has a specified time, say three years, then we would know there could be no agitation for a general strike.

That is to say, during three years we would have a rest and the trade would not go to other cities, as there is always a danger when there is an agitation against the Protocol, to carry the spasmodic agitation among our members, and the trade of New York City is injured by it. Buyers are pledged to supply orders, but if it specified for three years and the giving the parties three months' notice if they want to change, to negotiate different terms, then at least we would be free from this constant agitation among our people by certain disgruntled parties in any organization of 50,000 or 60,000 people, against this organization.

MR. ROSENBERG: Each operator had a machine of his own, and whenever he lost one job and was compelled to go and look for another job he had to pay 50 cents or $1 for the expressman to move his machine for him from one shop to another, and the conditions were such in many instances where the operators used to move their machines two or three times a day; for instance, they came up in the morning at a certain shop and the expressman moved his machine to that shop, and he would put up the machine and make a garment, and perhaps the garment was not satisfactory to the employer or the job was not satisfactory to the employee, and he wanted to get his machine out, and he had to go into the street, and he went to the corner and got another job and then brought the expressman again and he moved his machine to the other job; and in many instances, as

Garment workers attend meeting at Women's Trade Union League headquarters.

I have said, the operator used to pay the expressman $1 and $1.50 a day for moving his machine, when he might possibly only make $1 by turning out two or three garments.

As soon as the strike was settled, as soon as the Protocol was signed, of course every employer must furnish his people with machines. In many shops, also, the operators had to buy their own needles, too; operators had to buy their own oil to oil their machines, and even in some places there were instances where employers had machines of their own and supplied the machines to the operators, and the operators had to pay for the alterations in the machines when necessary. Whenever the machine got out of order, he could never get the employer to pay for the machinist to do the work of repairing it, because the employer, when he was very busy, did not care whether one or two operators worked or not.

Also, the employer would say: "We will have time next week to fix your machine; we will fix your machine next week," and the operator wanted to earn a livelihood, so he had to get a machinist himself and pay for the repairs out of his own pocket; and since the agreements have been signed and the union became a factor in the trade this has all been abolished. The employers are supposed to furnish machinery to the operators in good order free of charge.

Spurred by Hourwich, dissent spread among local cloak unions. While the *New Post* argued that power was more than a paper promise, the dressmakers insisted, in the pages of the *Ladies Garment Worker,* that preference for the union worker was a year-round obligation for employers. From the *New Post,* February 13, 1914.

PROTOCOL AND POWER

Regardless of how good provisions of the Protocol may be, the compact is not self-enforceable. The Protocol itself is but a piece of paper, containing certain points of agreement between the union and the manufacturers' association. The paper does not possess any power which the parties to it do not possess themselves. The paper becomes valuable only when the forces behind it are powerful enough to compel compliance with its provisions.

The Protocol is not a document of justice, because justice does not mean the same thing to all men, and absolute justice simply does not exist, in any case. The workers' idea of justice is quite different from that of the manufacturers.

'The Protocol really is a power document, reflecting the power relationships of the union and the manufacturers at the time it was signed. Had the union been stronger than it was, the pact's provisions would have been more favorable to it, and had the manufacturers felt in a stronger position to resist, the provisions would have been worse for us than they are.

The Protocol can be considered an instrument to measure the strength of the union and the manufacturers. The relative power of the two forces can best be measured in examining the manner in which the Protocol is administered. If it is being strictly enforced, that is a sign that the power equilibrium has not been disturbed. On the other hand, if it is not being obeyed, then that is an indication that one side or the other has been weakened.

The first condition for effective implementation of the Protocol is a balance of power among the parties. However, the way things are, the manufacturers usually are in a better position than the union; the fact that most cases are brought in by the union makes the situation unequal. The position of the accuser is always weaker, because the burden of proof rests with him that an attack against his rights has been made. Meantime, the attacker enjoys the benefits of his action.

The situation cannot be remedied through appealing to the employers for justice; the only remedy is to restore, more or less, the equality of power between the parties, and the only way to do so is to strengthen the union.

And the best way to strengthen the union is to educate the members, inform them of all that takes place, make them feel the organization is theirs, involve them in union activity.

And as the union grows stronger, we can be certain that the Protocol not only will be enforced, but will be continually improved.

From the *Ladies' Garment Worker,* December 1914.

PREFERENCE AND STRIKES

As soon as the first summer season after the strike had slackened, and the employers began to lay off help, they retained the non-union workers, and so deprived the members of the Union of the preference to which they were entitled. That was the first rude shock to the members of Local No. 25. In their view the obligations as to preferring union workers were not carried out in the letter and spirit of the Protocol.

The retention of union help during the slow season is really the crux of the question. In the busy season the employer might claim inability to procure all the union help he needs; thus he is compelled to hire non-union workers. But even in this case the workers must, according to Bulletin No. 98, "join the Union if they desire to secure for themselves the same rights under the Protocol as the union men in the shop. . . . Even the representative of the Association impresses upon them the fact that payment of dues to their organization is a responsibility which they must meet, and for the shirking of which the employer will not protect them, since the Protocol states that all who desire the benefits of the Union should share its burdens."

In the slow season, however, no such claim can be made; and where an employer persists in retaining any non-union workers after they have neglected the opportunity to join the Union, it cannot be otherwise interpreted than that he is deliberately evading his obligation.

Preference is the mainstay of the Union, *because it carries with it the Union shop and Union standards.* It insures a disciplined rank and file. It has made possible organized sanitary supervision. It is the pivot of the entire machinery. Remove it, and the machinery must, sooner or later, break down. Evade it and the control point of the Protocol disappears. What then remains but what the workers could not enforce by the fight to a finish?

We should be a spectacle for gods and men if the very thing that was designed to prevent strikes should have to become the cause or pretext for a strike.

Preference is not only a vital necessity to the Union as an organized body, it is a question of life and death to every member thereof. In the words of the Protocol, the member in good standing with the Union "shares its burdens." If those who shirk the burdens are given equal chances, or are encouraged in their shirking, the loyal member is deprived of the most substantial benefit guaranteed him by the Protocol. He pays to the Union for the protection of his rights, and one of these rights is that the employer shall prefer him at hiring and retaining. When this hoped-for protection proves a delusion, the loyal member conceives a wholesome contempt for the Protocol and similar "scraps of paper" that are duly signed and sealed but not respected.

Let us for a moment compare the case of the Manufacturers' Association with that of the Union. The Association is just as anxious to continue its existence and extend its membership as the Union. One of the motives actuating an employer in joining the Association, is the immunity from strikes. This is the sort of protection that the Association affords him. If, however, rightly or wrongly, shop strikes were to be of frequent occurrence, would not the hoped-for protection of the individual employer prove a delusion? Would not—and does not—

the Association in such instances charge the Union with violation of the Protocol? Indeed, it has happened that employers have claimed protection and immunity from strikes, even though not one of the employees who went on strike was a member of the Union; and the Dress and Waist Manufacturers' Association has filed protests and complaints against the Union in such cases, regardless of the fact that the Union can only assume responsibility for its members in good standing.

It seems to us that preference to union workers and immunity from strikes have such close connection that one without the other is not even thinkable. It is manifestly unfair on the part of the Union to insist on the right of preference without guaranteeing the employer immunity from strikes; but then, it is preposterous to assure any employer immunity from strikes unless he strictly complies with the preference provision of the Protocol.

Protocolism continued to be extolled as a model for labor-management relations, even when the Protocol in the cloak industry was already in jeopardy. From the *New Republic*, February 6, 1915.

INDUSTRIAL STATESMANSHIP

No one could have attended the recent gathering of the manufacturers and labor representatives in the cloak, suit and skirt industry of New York without realizing that here was one of these highly significant experiments. The feeling was tense, for an award was to be made by the Board of Arbitration, the supreme court of the industry, upon a matter of the gravest concern to both parties. But the meeting was friendly. The friendliness was due to four years of negotiation between the two parties.

As the members of the board, headed by the chairman, Louis D. Brandeis, entered the room the suspense reached its highest point. One could read the strain in the sensitive face of the chairman, as in low tones he began to give the award. He went back to the early history of the Protocol; he traced its origin and showed how, as a result of this instrument, the workmen temporarily gave up their right to strike in return for the right to representation in the industry. He appealed to the loyalty of both employers and employees to this great constitution of a trade in which two thousand employers and fifty thousand employees earned their living.

As he continued in his grave discourse, weighing each word thoughtfully, one felt that this realistic leader of the board was reaching out far beyond the immediate problem to some ultimate solution. Naturally he emphasized those interests which are common to both groups, as he also emphasized the necessity of each side taking a long view of the problem.

But the immediate issue, the right of discharge, was not lost from view. The Protocol, he said, did not change the legal relations between the parties, and the employer in the first instance retained the right to discharge. In view of the fact, however, that the union relinquished its right to strike, it should be protected by the Protocol from abuses which a strike might remedy. Discharge should only be upon "reasonable grounds," and where in any case whatsoever a workman felt that he was discharged without good cause he should have the right of appeal to the Board of Immediate Action, a regularly constituted board of employers and employees with an impartial chairman, and in all such complaints no burden of proof should rest upon the aggrieved wage earner.

The meaning of the award was clear. It sought to prevent discrimination and favoritism on the part of the employer while giving to him a certain measure of choice. It aimed at establishing a civil service in the industry, a greater security and continuity of labor, a fairer distribution of work, and the avoidance of unnecessary fluctuations in employment.

It did not define what "reasonable" meant, for the factors which affect reasonableness are too innumerable and diverse. There should be no rigid code of what was reasonable, but the two parties should agree among themselves upon what was fair in certain groups of cases.

Had this been a mere judicial award, the arbitrator might here have ceased. But it is of the essence of economic statesmanship that one go beneath the immediate problem to the underlying conditions which give rise to disputes. What is important is not whether John Doe did or did not commit a crime, but how far crime can be averted in the future.

The arbitrator therefore urged upon the immediate consideration of both parties the problems of price standardization, regulation of employment, control of the labor supply, apprenticeship, and the Protocol label. It was clear that he was studying causes and not mere symptoms, and was working out plans for the future development of the trade. He regarded the industry as dynamic, as a living and growing thing. The time would come, said the arbitrator, when labor must employ capital instead of capital employing labor, when our whole industrial system will have been revolutionized from the bottom, and it is in the light of this vast gradual transition that immediate problems must be considered.

In these days, when striking workmen are assassinated by opéra-bouffe sheriffs, and great metropolitan journals warn us against the sinfulness of trade unionism, this experiment in the cloak, suit and skirt industry is worth bearing in mind. For the need of the age is economic statesmanship. We have our political statesmen, who lead us more or less wisely in the direction in which we push them, and we have worked out certain rules of that game so that we now live in a tolerable political accord and have made some approach to a rule of the majority. But we still find only the rudest beginnings of statesmanship in that powerful state that we call industry.

Under the Protocol, the workers' wish for security on the job clashed with the employers' insistence on the right to discharge workers. As the crisis over the Protocol deepened, Hillquit defined the dilemma. From "Argument Before the Council of Conciliation in the Cloak and Suit Industry Appointed by Hon. John Purroy Mitchel, Mayor of the City of New York," July 13, 1915.

THE RIGHT TO FIRE
by Morris Hillquit

The "average worker" is, of course, a pure abstraction, arrived at by an imaginary equal division of work and wages among all employees in the industry. In actual fact, however, each worker must figure with his individual work time and is dependent upon his individual earnings. The man who has only nine weeks' work during the year derives scant consolation from the fact that his neighbor has employment all year round, and the man who earns $250 per year cannot pay his food, rent and clothing from the pay envelope of his fellow worker who earns $1,000 a year.

The inequality of the worker's opportunity to earn a living is, of course, most glaring in the seasonal industries, and it is particularly iniquitous and ruinous in the cloakmaking industry.

In view of this situation a custom has sprung up in the industry many years ago by which all workers always shared, more or less equally, all available work and wages. In other words, "superfluous workers" were rarely laid off at the end of the season, and when the work was not enough to go around, it was distributed as equally and equitably as possible among all of them, so that no worker would remain absolutely destitute between seasons.

This custom was tacitly recognized by employers and workers in the industry even prior to the adoption of the Protocol. It was continued while the Protocol was in force.

A dispute having arisen between employers and workers in the industry as to the exact extent and application of the custom, the Union submitted to the Board of Arbitration a request to construe the rights of the parties with reference to discharges and equal distribution of work.

The Union argued that immunity from wholesale or arbitrary discharges and a provision for equal distribution of work in slow seasons were necessary for the workers in the industry for the following reasons:

1. Aside from a small number of workers who come into the industry during the height of the season only, and may be designated as casual workers, the cloakmakers depend entirely and exclusively on their earnings in the cloakmaking industry. As a rule they are unfit for any but tailoring work, and as the seasons in all tailoring industries correspond to each other pretty closely, and all are overcrowded, there is rarely a chance for a cloakmaker to find employment in any other branch of the needle industry during off seasons.

If then the employers are to be permitted to discharge all "superfluous workers" at the end of each short season, the result would be that the favored few would enjoy a full year's work and a decent income, while the bulk of the workers in the industry would be left without any income or resources whatsoever during the long periods between seasons. The wages earned by the cloakmakers during the seasons are far from sufficient to support them all year round; consequently the workers discharged at the end of the seasons would be thrown upon charity for relief. The Union contended and contends that the industry itself is primarily charged with the support of the workers in it.

2. If all "surplus workers" would be thrown out of employment at the end of the busy season they would of necessity endeavor to secure some work and would underbid their more fortunate fellow workers who retained their jobs, and the result would be an unhealthy and ruinous competition between the workers in the industry, a cutting of wages and a demolition of all standards.

3. In view of the fact that the bulk of the employees are pieceworkers and that their wages are fixed for each separate style of garment, the men acting on the "Price Committee" could hardly be expected to have the courage of holding out for a decent wage, if they knew that their jobs were entirely at the mercy of their employers. Again, standards would inevitably be lowered

under a system of free and arbitrary discharges on the part of
the employers.

In this connection it must be remembered that the system of tolera-
bly permanent tenure of employment and equal distribution of work
does not impose any additional expense or appreciable inconvenience
on the employer. As stated above, the vast majority of workers are
paid by the piece. The week workers are also not paid by the week, but
by the hour. In other words, if a so-called "week worker" should work
only three hours during any week, he would be paid for three hours
and not for a full week.

Thus the aggregate wages paid by the employer is always measured
by the quantity of work produced in his shop and not by the number
of his employees. An employer who gives a full day's work to 10
persons would pay no less for his work than the one who gives half-
time employment to 20 men. The employer may make some
economies in overhead charges by employing a smaller number of
men at full time than a larger number of men at part time, but these
economies are so paltry that they are not entitled to be considered as
an offset to vital ethical and economic considerations which support
the worker's demands.

The Board of Arbitration did not agree with the construction
sought for by the Union, but instead of that set up the principle that
the right to discharge workers rests with the employer, but that such
right should not be discharged unfairly and without reasonable
grounds. That when a worker claims to have been discharged unfairly, unjustly or unreasonably, his complaint must be heard, and if
found justified, the worker must be reinstated; and also that equal
division of work in slow seasons is desirable and necessary in the
industry.

Or to state the proposal in still different language, the board recognized the right of the employer to discharge his worker, but it also
affirmed the right of the worker so discharged to a review of the
causes of the discharge.

The Union has accepted the decision of the board, and its present
request is formulated in the spirit and practically in the language of
that decision.

The employers now take the position that their right to discharge is
a sacred right, not subject to arbitration. To this we reply that we
grant without hesitancy the employer's legal right to hire and fire as
he wishes. But it must also be borne in mind that the worker has the
similar legal right to work or to refuse to work as he pleases, and that
the strike in the hands of the Union is a legal, legitimate and effective
weapon to correct the abuses of power on the part of the employer.
This right of the worker is as sacred for him as the employer's right to
discharge, and this right he had surrendered under the Protocol in

consideration of the employer's surrender of his right to deal with his hands arbitrarily. The present proposal then is not to deprive the employers of any of their legal rights but one of a voluntary arrangement by which both parties are to limit their legal rights in the interests of peace in the industry.

Adler (1851–1933), founder of the Society for Ethical Culture, served as chairman of the mayor's Council of Conciliation, which sought to save the Protocol and avoid a clash. From "Report to the Mayor, Council of Conciliation," April 26, 1916.

FAIR PLAY
by Felix Adler

We were asked to interpret the words which provide that in the hiring of help, a member of the union is to be preferred. The union claimed that the word "hiring" should be so understood that the employer prefer a union man not only in the moment of hiring him but also later on.

We decided, however, that though the spirit of the agreement really implied what the union claimed, we could not stretch the word "hiring" so as to extend it beyond the very moment in which the contract was made. That was a signal defeat for the union.

At our next meeting, the union presented the following request: "Since you cannot interpret the word 'hiring' in what you yourself admit to be the spirit of the agreement, at least give us the assurance that the man who is hired, in the moment in which he is hired, is a bona fide union man in good standing."

When we gave the first decision, the Manufacturers' Association was entirely satisfied with it. When we defined the word "unionist" to mean a "unionist in good standing," they threw our decision in our faces, and declined to abide by it, despite the fact that they had agreed to abide by the agreement for two years, and despite the fact that when after 23 sessions in the hot month of July 1915 we finally obtained the consent of both sides to the agreement, it was understood that the council itself should be the interpreter of this agreement.

We were acting strictly in accordance with this understanding, and we were interpreting to the best of our ability and good faith the language of this agreement. And then we had the mortification of finding that one side refused to abide by our decision.

The union then declared that the manufacturers, by refusing to abide by the decision of the council, had thrown up the arrangement, and declined to have any further official arrangements with the Manufacturers' Association.

A lockout was declared by the employers on April 28, 1916. The union retaliated with a strike. Public and press support of the cloakmakers was overwhelming. Keller (1880–1968), heroine to millions of Americans, expressed prevalent public opinion in her appeal. From the *New York Times,* July 8, 1916.

WHY I SUPPORT THE CLOAKMAKERS
by Helen Keller

I am with the cloak strikers, heart and soul, in their heroic struggle. If it were possible, I should come to New York to help them with my voice, too. I enclose a check for $200—my earnings—to be used for the strikers in the fight for better wages and a more human life.

May you remain strong and united until your battle is won. Whatever may happen, yours is the strength of a just cause. You are fighting for the right to a life better than the soul-quenching struggle for daily bread, the happiness of your children. Your courage, your enthusiasm, your perseverance are the hope of fellow workers, who bear grievous burdens. Your solidarity will help them win their battles. Let the result of this strike be what it may, the daring fight you have made will be a proud memory, an inspiration, a challenge to all who toil.

The cloakmakers are not asking for charity. They ask for a chance to live. Every dollar you contribute today will count as much as two dollars tomorrow. It will relieve want, and it will help prove to the employers that they cannot defy public sentiment. Show them that the day of cave-man ethics is past.

The following lead paragraphs from accounts that appeared in the New York press during the strike trace the direction it took.

THE 1916 LOCKOUT

MAY 8—Although 8,000 of the 60,000 striking garment makers in this city are to return to work today in 73 independent shops, little progress had been made toward settlement of the dispute between the union and the Cloak, Suit and Skirt Manufacturers' Association.

There are indications that the strike may be extended into Bridgeport, Connecticut, and towns in New Jersey. Officials of the union are investigating reports that contracts have been sublet and women's suits and skirts are being manufactured for New York shops in nearby cities.

—EVENING TELEGRAM

MAY 10—The clothing strike may extend to the fashionable shops on Fifth Avenue, according to a statement issued yesterday by Benjamin Schlesinger, president of the ILGWU. Mr. Schlesinger said that he had information that many of the fashionable Fifth Avenue shops were making models for the Manufacturers' Association, which this union is fighting. If proof is received, the president of the union said that he would call a strike of the union employees in the shops.

—NEW YORK HERALD

MAY 10—"This is not a arbitrable matter," was the response received today by Michael H. Reagan, industrial mediator of the State Bureau of Mediation and Arbitration, when he urged the Manufacturers' Protective Association to take the initiative in restoring peace with the garment makers, 60,000 of whom are out of work through lockout and strike.

Mr. Reagan was informed by the organization that "this is a fight to the finish. The manufacturers don't want any arbitration. They're not seeking peace. They want this fight to go on until the union recognizes the right of an employer to run his own shop."

—EVENING SUN

MAY 25—Collection of an $800,000 fund to fight the Cloakmakers' Union was begun yesterday by the Cloak, Suit and Skirt Manufacturers' Protective Association. An assessment of 1 percent of the business done by the members during the last year has been levied by the executive committee of the association. This will be devoted to hiring 500 strong-arm men to guard the 400 association shops. The guards will be recruited from local "detective" agencies which make a specialty of furnishing thugs for strike duty.

—*THE CALL*

MAY 30—Organization of the greatest cooperative enterprise ever launched in New York is perfected and within a few days the ILGWU will put into operation eight commissary centers which will furnish food to 100,000 men, women and children affected by the cloakmakers' general strike. Prominent men and women have volunteered to aid the strikers in their gigantic enterprise. The ILGWU will spend $250,000 on supplies for the stores and when this sum is exhausted it is believed wealthy sympathizers will provide funds to keep the workers and their families from starving.

—*THE CALL*

JUNE 2—E. J. Wile, president of the Cloak and Suit Manufacturers' Association, last night said his organization is "through with the union" in referring to the 50,000 locked out and on strike.

To 400 members of the Garment Salesmen's Association, gathered at the Hotel Martinique last night, he declared, for the first time since the trouble began, that the struggle with the workers' organization would be war to the death.

"We are through with the union forever," he cried. "We have been preparing for this struggle for several years, just as the union has been doing."

—*NEW YORK AMERICAN*

JUNE 2—The lifting of the lockout yesterday in the cloak and suit industry produced no apparent result beyond the tightening of the lines around the union camps.

"It is simply Hester Street strategy upon the part of the manufacturers," said Benjamin Schlesinger, president of the union.

—*NEW YORK HERALD*

JUNE 14—Members of the Cloak, Suit and Skirt Association flatly refused yesterday to attend a conference arranged by the Citizens' Committee, a neutral body composed of wealthy and influential New Yorkers who have been trying to settle the differences through arbitration. The manufacturers also sent to the strikers an official notice, written in three languages, saying in substance that it was their plan to hire an army of strikebreakers if they were forced to. The statement informs the strikers that they will get "a reasonable time to return to the shops, but that if they do not do so soon, steps will be taken to fill their places."

—THE SUN

JUNE 24—Several thousand tailors and sympathizers—among whom were many anarchists, according to the police, assembled on Fifth Avenue yesterday without notifying the police. The parade came to a halt in front of the Union Club at 51st Street.

"Go back to work," cried a member of the club, sticking his head out of a window and commanding the mob to disperse. He was jeered and quickly pulled in his head to avoid a derby hat hurled his way.

"Go back to work yourself!" many in the crowd shouted at him.

Meantime, a riot call had been sent in by a patrolman, and while the club members were peeping out the sides of their windows, expecting an attack in force, the police reserves dashed into sight from the East 51st Street station.

—THE WORLD

JULY 13—Although for a time yesterday afternoon the conferences between representatives of the Cloak, Suit and Skirt Manufacturers' Protective Association and the ILGWU threatened to end in a hopeless break, a conciliation was effected. When the sessions adjourned until this afternoon, both parties were more optimistic than at any time since the meetings started. It was intimated that Samuel Gompers might be present this afternoon to act as presiding officer at the conference.

—NEW YORK HERALD

JULY 17—While 15,000 pickets patrolled the cloak and suit manufacturing districts today, representatives of the strikers and employers, in conference in the Metropolitan Tower, battled on the preferential union shop issue.

Samuel Gompers, president of the American Federation of Labor, presided at the conference. He made it plain that he had at his back the united strength of 2,000,000 members of his organization who would fight to uphold the dignity of the union.

—EVENING MAIL

JULY 19—With charges and countercharges of bad faith and unfair aggression flying back and forth, the striking garment workers and the employers yesterday broke off their conferences working toward a settlement of the strike and lockout.

The seventh meeting between representatives of the association and of the union in the Metropolitan Building proved to be the last. Samuel Gompers, president of the AFL, who had been attending the peace meetings, abandoned hope of a settlement and left for Washington.

—THE SUN

JULY 20—Following the announcement in Washington today that President Wilson had called for an immediate federal investigation into the cloakmakers' strike here, representatives of the Cloak, Suit and Skirt Manufacturers' Protective Association and officials of the union went into secret session at the Hotel Knickerbocker this afternoon, with the intention, if possible, of agreeing upon tentative terms of a settlement. It was predicted on both sides that the conference would lead to a final settlement.

—EVENING POST

JULY 26—Shortly before midnight last night the General Strike Committee of the 60,000 striking cloakmakers, by a divided vote, decided to accept in its entirety the tentative agreement reached between representatives of the union and the cloak manufacturers Monday night at their conference, and to submit it to the strikers today for ratification. The action followed a session at the Broadway Central that had lasted throughout the day and far into the night.

—THE CALL

This shop worked ten hours a day; lighting was by flickering gas-mantle; top floor roof lacked insulation against summer heat, winter cold.

Never before had the public intervened so directly in a labor/management dispute. From the *Outlook Magazine,* July 12, 1916.

POWER OF PUBLIC OPINION
by Mary Dewhurst

In 1915 a change came over the personnel of the Executive Committee of the Association. The more liberal element lost control to a group of an opposite understanding. A narrow determination to accept no restrictions dominated the committee. They announced that they would tolerate no "sentimental interference" by the public in their affairs. They sought to do away with arbitration as a stabilizer of the industry, smash the union, and go back to individual in the place of collective bargaining. All efforts at mediation were rejected, the Protocol was abrogated, and a lockout declared in the four hundred shops owned by the Manufacturers' Association, thereby forcing the union to call a strike in the remaining shops of the subcontractors.

The lockout came on April 28, 1916, and for two months sixty thousand workers, with their two hundred thousand dependents, have been debarred from earning their living.

During these two months the solidest array of public opinion ever ranged upon one side in a labor struggle has supported the locked-out workers. At the outset not a voice was raised for the manufacturers, not even their own. Except for an angry retort or two they at first doggedly maintained silence and insisted that they were the only ones concerned in the fight and that the public had no interest in the controversy.

First to resent this attitude was the mayor of New York. Mr. Mitchel's request to the members of the Association to continue discussion with the union had met with a curt refusal. Here is a part of his comment on their action:

"I have taken this step of asking for this conference . . . not only because a strike is always injurious to the city as a whole, but because at the present time New York cannot and will not tolerate anything in the nature of disturbance of the peace. . . . Accordingly, I have issued the invitation to the Council of Conciliation, to the representatives of the union, who I understand are here this morning, and to the Cloak and Suit Manufacturers' Association. From them I have received what is tantamount to a refusal either to meet the mayor for the purpose of a conference or to meet the representatives of the union to secure adjustment."

This meant that whatever pressure the mayor felt that he could justly exert to force the controversy to arbitration he would continue to use.

This meant too that police protection for the strikers was readily obtained. *Agents provocateurs,* masquerading as armed guards and deputies, would not be allowed to make picketing unhealthy.

So much for the city authorities. Next to beat against the rocky stronghold of the manufacturers was a group of political scientists and economists at Columbia [University] to whom this industrial situation in their own city seemed highly important. They got together and agreed to study the causes. Both the Manufacturers' Association and the Garment Workers were invited to send representatives to them to explain their contentions. Again the union came. Again the manufacturers refused.

After listening to representatives of the workers, the professors drew up a statement in which they placed the responsibility for the lockout squarely on the manufacturers, to whom they first submitted it for correction and then gave it out for publication. It was signed by men like John Dewey, Charles A. Beard, Franklin Giddings, James Harvey Robinson, E. R. A. Seligman, and James T. Shotwell, and voices the conclusion that "the real reason for the action of the Manufacturers' Association is that its officers were unwilling to accept the consequences of their agreement, and, as their president has stated, they wished to take advantage of the opportunity to return to conditions existing prior to 1910. We regard this as little less than a public calamity and urge that every effort be made to restore the agreement."

When the mayor and the political economists had met with shipwreck the ministers ventured in. A committee of twenty-two addressed a letter to their twelve hundred fellow clergymen of the city which took the form of an industrial credo. "We believe," they began, "that the issue here involved is clearly one between brute force upon the one side and arbitration and conciliation upon the other . . . An enlightened public sentiment must be aroused against the Manufacturers' Association, which has defied the public interest. . . . We believe that the clergy of this city should address their congregations on this subject."

As a direct result of this appeal ministers of varying faiths have organized and sent their names in to the union to act as pickets in case the situation demands more than spiritual support.

About this time the National Consumers' League joined the tide. They came out in hearty endorsement of the union's position and circularized their members with a statement of the facts, which carried the greater authority because the local league had lately conducted an investigation into the physical conditions of the industry.

Finally, the women discovered themselves to be the sole consumers in the industry, and entitled to know the facts. The Women's City Club of New York invited the manufacturers and the union to state their grievances to them and their guests, the members of all the women's clubs and organizations of the city.

A mass meeting was held, but only representatives of the union came to the hearing. The Manufacturers' Association, by its president, E. J. Wile, returned the soft answer that "we do not believe in outside bodies interfering in our affairs. We are tired of the interference we have had for the past six years and of the efforts of men who do not know anything about our business. For this reason we shall return the same answer to the Women's City Club that we sent to the mayor and shall send to others who try to interfere."

The women didn't relish their treatment, and said so in a letter to the sixteen hundred members of the [Women's] City Club. "It is of the utmost importance," they declared, "that public opinion should function definitely and at once in this lockout which involves nearly two hundred and fifty thousand people."

The manufacturers by this time had unlocked their shops and invited their men to return on terms which each employer set for himself. To prevent this the union knew that the workers must be fed and clothed and munitioned for the picketline.

This crisis moved Isaac N. Seligman, R. Fulton Cutting, Mrs. Willard Straight, Miss Ruth Morgan, E. H. Outerbridge, Mrs. Ogden Mills Rein, Sam Lewisohn, Mrs. Gifford Pinchot, Mrs. Benjamin Guggenheim, Allan Robinson, and others prominent in civic and social lines, to organize a citizens' committee to ask for immediate funds. This committee spoke their minds in a statement the like of which has never before been found necessary to meet conditions in a strike in New York. "The inevitable conclusion," they say, "is that they (the manufacturers) rely upon the lash of starvation to force their workers into unconditional surrender. . . . The attempt to starve the workers and those dependent on them, numbering in all over two hundred thousand human beings, is a matter which vitally concerns the people of this American community."

This struggle is unique in the history of organized labor in New York because immediately and continuously the full power of the newspapers has been on the side of the workers since the lockout was declared. Full justice to the strikers has been given in a surprising number of news stories, editorials, and special articles in every paper in the city. A rough count of the space given the strike in its first seven weeks disclosed that two hundred and sixty-two feet of printed words, a column wide, have appeared in the English-speaking press; what the German and Yiddish papers printed has not been counted.

The manufacturers repeated their refusal to arbitrate the right "to hire and fire" in a pamphlet which was sent to every magazine and newspaper editor in the city. On July 3 the same group of Columbia professors who a month before had rallied to the defense of the strikers came out with an answering statement. "The right to discharge, on which the manufacturers lay stress," say the Columbia men, "is not in controversy, as it is the agreement of August 1915, which gives the manufacturer the right to discharge for incompetence, insubordination, or inefficiency those unsuited to the shop or unfaithful to their obligations that the workers are fighting to restore."

Unbought publicity, such as the union has been able to command, is very significant. Public service corporations, long since convinced of the futility of their former policy of silence, now employ experts to secure for them public sympathy. Campaign managers no longer act upon the Boss Tweed principle of "what are you going to do about it," but stay awake at nights planning how to arouse public attention. Not so with the Cloak, Suit, and Skirt Manufacturers' Protective Association. They at first determined to prove that public sympathy which expresses itself in words does not win strikes. Although later dislodged from this position, they dug themselves into their legal entrenchments and snapped their fingers at all attempts to force or coax them into arbitration. They have counted on watchful waiting, backed by determination, to win their fight. They have counted on public indifference.

Have we, under our democracy, any machinery through which public opinion can function directly and with celerity?

Women's Trade Union League contingent included number of garment workers in 1913 Labor Day parade down Fifth Avenue, shown passing at 23rd Street.

Lippmann (1889–1975) identified the ultimate cause for
which the union had gone into battle. From the *New Republic,* March 27, 1915.

TO MAKE A LIVING
by Walter Lippmann

It is all very well to say of a woman that "she is working for her living,"
but suppose she is working and not making her living. What are you
to say then? You can remark that you are indeed very sorry, and leave
the matter there. Or you can say with more piety than wisdom that
wages are determined by natural laws which man must let alone. Or
you can insist that she is being sweated; that a business which does not
pay a living wage is not paying its labor costs; that such businesses are
humanly insolvent, for in paying less than a living wage they are guilty
of as bad business practice and far worse moral practice than if they
were paying dividends out of assets.

Everyone knows what to think of a get-rich-quick concern which
asks people to subscribe to its capital stock, and then uses the money
invested to pay profits. We call it a fraud. When a railroad goes on
paying dividends without charging up deterioration, people speak of
it not as a fraud but as bad business.

But when a mercantile establishment pays its labor less than labor
can live on, it is combining the evils of the mismanaged railroad and
the get-rich-quick concern. It is showing a profit it has not honorably
earned, it is paying a dividend out of its vital assets, that is, out of the
lives, the health, and the happiness of its employees. A business that
exists on labor paid less than a living wage is not a business at all, for it
is not paying its fixed charges. They are being paid either by the
family or the woman worker, or by her friends, or by private charities,
or by the girl herself in slow starvation.

It would be absurd to assume the minimum-wage legislation is a
kind of omnibus for paradise. To fix a "living standard" would be a
great advance over what we have, but by every civilized criterion it is a
grudging and miserable thing. In those moments of lucidity when we
forget our hesitancy before brute obstruction, it seems like a kind of
madness that we should have to argue and scrape in order that we
may secure to millions of women enough income to "live." If we had
not witnessed whole nations glowering at each other all winter from
holes in the mud, it would be hard to believe that America with all its
riches could still be primitive enough to grunt and protest at a living
wage—a living wage, mind you; not a wage so its women can live well,

not enough to make life a rich and welcome experience, but just enough to secure existence and drudgery in grey boardinghouses and cheap restaurants.

We may fail to secure that. So far as the press is concerned, the issue hardly exists. It lies at the moment stifled in platitudes and half truths about "not hurting business." From the little comment there is, we might think that a business was sound if it rested on the degradation of its labor; might think that businessmen were a lot of jumpy neurotics ready to shrivel up and burst into tears at a proposal to increase their wages bill a penny or two on the dollar; might think, from the exclamations of Mr. Brown and his friend John Smith, that a campaign against sweating would do no less than ruin the country.

But you cannot ruin a country by conserving its life. You can ruin a country only by stupidity, waste and greed.

8. Life and Death

During the heated discussions between union leaders and employers at the end of July 1910, Julius Henry Cohen, acting in behalf of the association, initiated a move which eventually led to a precedent-making provision in the Protocol. This provision called for the creation of a Joint Board of Sanitary Control—with a public representative as one of its members—to launch a campaign aimed at improving the work environment of the garment industry.

For generations, wherever apparel was produced, workers had sacrificed their health, indeed, life itself, for a week's pay. Low pay, long hours, poor diet and posture, a "stint" system that lumped the days together, the dust- and moisture-laden air of the shop—all combined to hasten the worker's sad fate.

But beyond wages and hours, the shop itself was an enemy to survival. The homework shop eliminated the distinction between family life and working life and brought the threat of tuberculosis into the home. Ernest Poole and Dr. Antonio Stella utilized their expertise as writer and physician, respectively, to combat the scourge of tuberculosis among the men and women in the ghetto homework sweatshops.

As the chief technician of the Joint Board of Sanitary Control, Dr. George Price launched pioneer studies of conditions in the workrooms. His annual reports surveyed lighting, ventilation, toilet facilities, safety measures, and cleanliness in the shops. Two years after the signing of the Protocol, at about the same time reforms described by Gertrude Barnum were being made, Dr. Price directed the first studies ever of workers' health, followed in 1915 by Dr. J. W. Schereschewsky's classic study of garment workers' illnesses.

Their work, coupled with the union's concern, laid the basis for a continuing battle to make the workrooms safe and healthy. Out of that concern grew a network of health centers, plus sickness, retirement, and vacation benefits that, starting in the mid-1940s, became an integral part of the garment worker's life and, as President Lyndon B. Johnson testified, a part of American life in general.

The battle was also spurred on by the tragic occurrence at the Triangle Shirtwaist Company, where, on March 25, 1911, 146 lives were lost in a disastrous fire. Personal reactions to this event are

176

expressed by William G. Shepherd and Leon Stein. The public's outrage is voiced by Bruere and Stephen Wise.

However, it is Rose Schneiderman who points the accusing finger at the law itself and at a public policy that placed the protection of property above the sanctity of life. Max D. Steuer interprets the law, explaining how the men who had locked the Triangle workers in the shop were acquitted. The weaknesses of the law, the failures in enforcing the latter, and the means of remedying a situation that callously shortened and destroyed life are spelled out by Alfred E. Smith.

The solution lay beyond the power of either union or management. Almost immediately, the tragedy at Triangle dramatized to the nation the plight of its workers, the insignificance of their lives when measured against profit imperatives. But, as Frances Perkins points out, it also brought the realization that government shared in the responsibility for the workers' safety and welfare. Where collective bargaining ended, lobbying and legislation had to begin.

The Triangle tragedy, more than any other single event, demonstrated to American workers the need for political action and the importance of legislation. As the plaque on the site of the fire states: "Out of their martyrdom came new concepts of social responsibility and labor legislation that have helped make American working conditions the finest in the world."

Poole (1880–1950), a settlement house worker, won the first Pulitzer Prize in fiction. From *The Plague in Its Stronghold,* issued by the Committee on the Prevention of Tuberculosis of the New York Charity Organization Society, 1903.

"GIVE ME BREATH!"
by Ernest Poole

"Breath—breath—give me breath." A Yiddish whisper, on a night in April 1903, from the heart of the New York ghetto.

At 18 Clinton Street, back in the rear tenement, a young Roumanian Jew lay dying of consumption. I had come in with a Jewish doctor. With every breath I felt the heavy, foul odor from poverty, ignorance, filth, disease. In this room ten feet square six people lay on the floor packed close, rubbing the heavy sleep from tired eyes, and

staring at us dumbly. Two small windows gave them air from a noisome court—a pit twenty feet across and five floors deep. The other
room was only a closet six feet by seven, with a grated window high up
opening on a air shaft eighteen inches wide. And in that closet four
more were sleeping, three on a bed, one in a cradle.

"Breath—breath—give me breath." The man's disease was infectious; and yet for two long weeks he had lain here dying. From his
soiled bed he could touch the one table, where the two families ate;
the cooking stove was but six feet from him; the cupboard, over his
pillow; he could even reach one of the cradles, where his baby girl lay
staring frightened at his strange position. For his wasted body was too
feeble to rise; too choked, too tortured to lie down. His young wife
held him up while the sleepers stared silently on, and that Yiddish
whisper came over and over again, but now with a new and more
fearful meaning. "Breath—breath—breath. Or kill me. O, kill me."

Two years ago this man had come to America—one of the four
hundred and eighty-eight thousand in 1901. He came young and well
and hopeful, with his wife and their baby son.

Two more had been born since then. It was to be a new country, a
new home, a fresh start, a land to breathe in. "Breath—breath—give
me breath." He had breathed no air here but the close, heavy air of
the sweatshop from six in the morning until ten at night.
Sometimes—he whispered—he worked until eleven. He was not
alone. In New York today and tonight are over fifty thousand like him
working. And late in the night when he left the feverish labor, at the
hour when other homes are sleeping, he had come in through the
foul court and had sunk into restless sleep in the dark closet six feet by
seven. There are three hundred and sixty-one thousand such closets
in the city. And this is home.

"Luft—giebt mir luft." He spoke only Yiddish. The new country
had given the Plague before the language. For the sweatshop and the
closet had made him weak; his weakened body could make no fight;
the Plague came in and fed swiftly. Still on through the winter he had
worked over the machine in the sweatshop, infecting the garments he
sewed—feverish, tired, fearful—to buy food and coal, to keep his
"home" alive. And now, on this last day of life, ten times he had
whispered to his brother, begging him to care for the wife and the
three little children.

The struggle now is ended. The home is scattered. The smothered
whisper is forever hushed. "Breath—breath—give me breath." It
speaks the appeal of thousands.

Dr. Stella (1868–1927) worked chiefly among New York's Italian poor. He was active in medical and civic affairs and was a specialist in pulmonary ailments. From *The Survey*, May 7, 1904.

FROM ITALY'S FIELDS TO MANHATTAN'S SWEATSHOPS
by Dr. Antonio Stella

To have an idea of the alarming frequency of consumption among Italians, especially in the large cities, one must follow the Italian population as it moves in the tenement districts; study them closely in their daily struggle for air and space; see them in the daytime crowded in sweatshops and factories; at night heaped together in dark, windowless rooms.

From some tenements in Elizabeth and Mulberry Streets there have been as many as 12 and 15 cases of consumption reported to the Board of Health since 1894. But how many were never reported? How many went back to Italy? How many moved away to other districts?

In many tenements, on account of the overcrowding, the quantity of air left for each person is reduced to three or four cubic meters, and the expired air in the sleeping rooms represents one-half or one-sixth of all the air available.

Among those—and they are the large majority—who seek work in factories and shops, instead of pursuing their natural occupations in the open air, the stigmata of progressive physiological deterioration and general low vitality are most apparent.

Six months of life in the tenements are sufficient to turn the sturdy youth from Calabria, the brawny fisherman of Sicily, the robust women from Abruzzi and Basilicata, into the pale, flabby undersized creatures we see, dragging along the streets of New York and Chicago, such a painful contrast to the native population! Six months more of this gradual deterioration, and the soil for the bacillus tuberculosis is amply prepared.

In many of those occupations, besides the direct irritation to the bronchial mucous membrane from the inhalation of dust, the work itself requires a sitting position in which the chest is bent forward, and thus prevents the expansion of the lungs, and directly interferes with the proper aeration of the pulmonary apices.

Still worse is the condition where the sweatshop system flourishes at home, either as extra work, done late in the night, by young men and women already exhausted by ten hours of work in a crowded factory, or as a regular practice, by poor housewives, desirous of adding to their husbands' earnings.

Words can hardly describe the pathetic misery of these Italian women, compelled to sew, using up their last spark of energy to make life better, when in fact they only accomplish their self-destruction. For their health is usually already drained by a too productive maternity and periods of prolonged lactation; they live on a deficient, if not actually insufficient, diet; they sleep in dark, damp holes, without sunshine and light, and have already had enough to exhaust them, with the raising of a large family and the strain of hard housework.

This high susceptibility is not due to any inherent lack of vitality in the race. The Italians otherwise show the most wonderful elements of resistance and recuperation, as may be seen in the favorable manner they react to surgical operations, extreme temperatures, and all sorts of trials. Nor is it dependent upon any individual hereditary predisposition, for while the younger generation, emigrated to America, die rapidly, their parents at home live to a surprisingly old age. Their rapid fall is due solely to an ensemble of deleterious causes, acting simultaneously, steadily and forcibly on their constitution, and in a manner so complete, that the fertilization of the ubiquitous Koch bacillus must result of necessity. . . .

The statistics show that the higher we move up in the social scale, the lower the mortality from consumption; or as Gebhard puts it, "the death rate from tuberculosis among the various classes, in large cities, is in inverse ratio to their individual income." This inequality of fortune in our modern society plays really the most important role in the spread of tuberculosis, and as long as present conditions prevail, we shall always find tuberculosis to be "the disease of the masses" par excellence, and the inseparable ally of poverty.

Cohen (1873–1950) served as legal counsel for the employers' representatives throughout the 1910 strike and ensuing period of negotiations. He was the first to suggest that a joint sanitary board be created. From *The Cloakmakers' Strike,* issued by the Cloak, Suit and Skirt Manufacturers' Protective Association, 1910.

WE ARE CONCERNED
by Julius Henry Cohen

May I say this, that in the published discussion of this strike emphasis seems to have been laid upon the unsanitary conditions in the industry, and the better class of manufacturers were very sensitive about that, because of the fact that they had been making earnest efforts to create sanitary conditions and had met considerable difficulties on the part of their employees.

Now, undoubtedly in some of the shops of the cloak manufacturers unsanitary conditions exist. . . . But in the statement of grievances there was nothing said about sanitary conditions.

I was very glad, therefore, when Mr. London, in making up the [agenda], included it for discussion here. Now, we are very much concerned about this question, because we have some pride in our industry, and we know that it is exceedingly difficult to observe sanitary conditions. I am frank to confess that I do not see that it will make very much progress here to go into the specific details of unsanitary conditions. I will suggest to my learned brother that he take under advisement with his people the proposition that both parties establish as the result of this conference a board of sanitary supervision, on which there shall be people representing the public who shall endeavor to establish a standard to which factories in this industry shall conform. And when that board of sanitary control makes its recommendations, we will legislate for our members on our side, so that no worker will work where these conditions do not exist, and no honorable cloak manufacturer will remain a member of our association if he does not observe these conditions.

We realize that the suggestion that I made requires a great deal of efficient work to carry it into effect. We are prepared on our part, if the suggestion is adopted, to establish a corps of paid inspectors. If your organization cannot afford to pay the whole expense, we will bear the larger burden of it. We are perfectly willing that you shall bear half of the expense, if you can do it out of your organization funds. But we want this general board of control to be effective, to have reliable people, people whom your committee selects, whose business it will be to visit, not only the shops of our own members, but as far as possible, the shops of non-members of our association, and let their reports be the reports on which the General Board of Sanitary Supervision will act.

That is going to require efficient management . . . skill, good inspection, and we expect to get out of it, by way of return, the knowledge on our part that no loose criticism can hereafter be made. We will be able to make practical the pride that we have in our industry at the present time. Now, we do not pretend to be white-robed angels on our side; we do not pretend that every man in our association has reached the highest stage of human development, but we are going to do our level best to raise him to that standard if we can.

We are going to do our level best to make the standard clear, and we are going to do our best to make it enforceable. We also want you to feel that all of your people are not white-robed angels, to see that you have your fair share of the job, and you must be willing to undertake it with us. We will join hands, and we will get out of this strike ... something that will lift the entire standard of civilization in our city.

Dr. Price (1866–1942) was one of the first tenement inspectors. Under the Protocol, he became director of the Joint Board of Sanitary Control and then first director of the ILGWU's Union Health Center. From *First Annual Report, Joint Board of Sanitary Control,* 1911.

THE SWEATSHOP
by Dr. George Price

The advance from the East Side one-room shop in a converted tenement house to the big Fifth Avenue loft establishment marks great progress in sanitary conditions; but between these two extremes lies the bulk of the shops of the industry. All of them from poorest to the richest and biggest, suffer from various sanitary defects peculiar to this industry and to this city.

In justice to the industry, it must be stated that the shops in the cloak trade are not only not the worst in the city, but are actually better than those of a large number of similar industries in this city, and it is only because the cloak industry is the first to make a general survey of its shops, that conditions have been discovered as they are; but if a comparative survey should be made of other industries, it would surely be shown that the shops in the cloak industry are by far superior to the shops of kindred occupations.

As the cloak workers are mostly men and women between twenty and forty-five years of age, the general health of the trade should be above the average of workers of other industries.

There are no vital statistics to show the rate of mortality and morbidity among cloak workers. The general impression, however, which the bulk of the workers made upon the writer, who had ample opportunity within the last year to see the majority of the workers in the trade, is that they are not of a robust type, that they largely suffer from anemia, possess a more or less stooping gait, and are not, as a rule a very healthy lot of men and women.

There are no definite figures as to the extent of tuberculosis among cloak workers, but it is well known among the physicians of the East

Side that tuberculosis is a very frequent disease among this class of workers.

The real menace to the health of the workers and the real dangers in their lives, lie not in the nature of the industry itself, but in the defective sanitary conditions of the shops; not in the peculiar character of the work but in the inadequate provisions for fire protection, in the insufficient light and illumination, in the overcrowded and unventilated shops, in the lack of cleanliness, and in the absence of needed comforts and conveniences.

In the past, the shops in the cloakmaking industry were the most overcrowded industrial establishments in the city. There were a number of reasons for this overcrowding, the chief one being the fact that the cloakmaking seasons lasted generally thirty weeks out of the fifty-two. In leasing his shop, the employer usually calculated the space, not according to the needs of the short season, but according to the longer between-season period, so that during the height of the season the shops were taxed to the maximum of their capacity, machines being placed almost in solid rows with little or no elbow room and breathing space for the abnormally large number of employees working during day, and sometimes night.

At present conditions are very different. The larger percentage of the trade is in the hands of large firms, who find it to the benefit of their employees as well as to their own, to lease large modern lofts for their business. In the smaller houses, the intelligent efforts of the leaders and the rank and file of the labor organizations composing the employees of the industry, have improved conditions.

In many of the shops, the walls and ceilings were found decorated with paper. This is the worst dressing of a wall or surface, as it catches and holds dust, and is generally not clean. The best means of dressing surfaces within shops is probably light colored oil paint. In 144 shops the walls and ceilings were found dirty, in some very dirty. The floors were found dirty in many shops.

The Labor Law provides that the employer furnish receptacles for rubbish and garbage, but these were found in only 267 of the shops. The legal requirement for the provision of cuspidors is a dead letter. In only 16 of the shops were such cuspidors found. While the class of operators in the cloak trades are not addicted to tobacco chewing, the danger from spitting of the tubercular operatives is great.

The separation of the toilet accommodations for males and females leaves much to be desired. In some of the shops (44) the water closets are located in the yards, and in many more (240) in the halls, and these are, as a rule, common to both males and females. Many of the water closets which are within the shop are not properly separated, or if so separated, the separation is not adequate.

The worst conditions are found in converted buildings and the small lofts where the water-closet accommodations have been put in, not originally when the building was put up, but as an afterthought to suit the tenant. This results in inadequate accommodations, which are a menace to health and morals.

The legal limit of one watercloset for every 25 persons working is exceeded in many shops, in some of which a ratio of 1 to 85 had been found by our inspectors.

There are but 378 shops which have been provided with separate washrooms, and in most of the shops the only places available for the operatives to wash themselves, are cast-iron sinks, one, or at the most two, in some corner of the shop. Such an inadequacy of necessary fixtures for washing and cleaning naturally discourages cleanliness on the part of the employees, and is probably also unprofitable to the employers because the operatives soil delicate garments.

In only 25 shops was hot water supplied for the washbasins, and in but 171 shops were towels furnished, and in only 85 shops were receptacles placed for dirty towels. . . .

Special emergency rooms were found in only 57 shops. All other shops were defective in this important provision for employees when taken ill. Such a room is especially necessary where a number of females are employed.

Barnum (1866–1948) was the first national secretary of the Women's Trade Union League and served as an ILGWU organizer from 1911 through 1916. She made a serious effort to spread the Protocol idea. From the *Independent,* October 3, 1912.

FIRST FRUITS OF THE PROTOCOL
by Gertrude Barnum

At the end of the first year every basement shop had been abolished, and before receiving a "sanitary certificate" from the board, factories must comply with the following, among many other sanitary and fire protection conditions:

- No shop to be allowed in a cellar
- No shop to be allowed in rear houses or attic floors without special permission of the board

- At least 400 cubic feet of space, exclusive of bulky furniture and materials, should be provided for every person within the shop
- The shop should be thoroughly aired before and after work hours, and during lunch hour, by opening windows and doors
- Floors of shops and of water-closet [compartments] to be scrubbed weekly, swept daily, and kept free of refuse
- A separate water-closet [compartment] shall be provided for each sex, with solid partitions to extend from floor to ceiling, and with separate vestibules and doors
- A sufficient number of water-supplied wash basins to be provided, in convenient and light locations within the shop
- Suitable hangers should be provided for the street clothes of the employees, and separate dressing rooms to be provided wherever women are working
- All seats to have backs

Now to those who have realized the significance of this well worked out plan for a just industrial peace and sanitary standards, in a hitherto utterly anarchical trade, the question naturally arises, will the New York plan be extended without delay to other city centers of the cloak and suit industry? Or must history repeat itself? Must each separate city learn by painful experience what it has taken years to teach employers and employees of New York, that strikes and lock-outs, broken contracts, blacklists and boycotts, with their attendant waste and suffering and bitterness may be abolished forever in the trade by the substitution of the rulings of industrial courts, where disputes may be adjudicated?

On the 1st of November, 1911, the International Ladies' Garment Workers' Union appointed a committee of union representatives to carry on a campaign in the middle western states and Canada to arouse the public to a realization of their power and responsibility as consumers. By means of circular letters and public addresses, church audiences, women's clubs, suffrage and teachers' associations, benefit societies, trade unions and socialist organizations have been interested to form local communities to insist that merchants shall supply their patrons with "Protocol" garments.

Dr. Schereschewsky's (1873–1940) study, carried out with
the cooperation of Dr. Price and the staff of the Union
Health Center, was one of the first of its kind, focusing on
the health of a particular industrial group. From *U.S. Public Health Service Bulletin No. 71*, 1915.

STRESS AND STRAIN
by Dr. J. W. Schereschewsky

One interesting point brought out by the investigation was the fact
that while in the case of females, occupation in the garment trades was
apparently provisional, with the prospect of marriage and homemak-
ing in the background, among males the industry was entered as a
permanent means of livelihood. This is shown by the low average age
of the women (22 years, as compared to 32 years for males), their
shorter average time in the industry (4.6 years, as compared to 9.25
years for males), the low percentage of married females (7 percent, as
compared to 75 percent for males), and other evidence tending to
show that the large majority of females were members of families in
which they were not the chief breadwinners.

The sense of personal responsibility arising from the knowledge of
others dependent upon them was, therefore, very much greater in the
case of males. This relative lack of responsibility tended to cause a
much greater degree of vivacity and cheerfulness among women.

Tuberculosis was undoubtedly the most important disease among
garment workers. Three and eleven hundredths percent of the males
examined and nine-tenths of one percent of the females were found
to be tuberculous. This is a rate of prevalence for females of nearly
three times and among males nearly ten times that of this disease
among soldiers in the United States Army, for instance. It is thought,
however, that the rate of prevalence may have been artificially raised
from the circumstance that garment workers who suspected their
condition upon hearing of the examination presented themselves for
the purpose of ascertaining whether they were suffering from tuberculosis. On the other hand, in many instances the subject was unaware
of his condition, having been conscious only of general impairment of
health.

Be this as it may, tuberculosis is unduly prevalent among garment
workers, especially among males. Factors influencing the great prevalence in males are apparently their greater average age, long average
time in the industry, the high percentage of males with families dependent upon them, thus leading to self-denial on the part of the
breadwinner in the matter of adequate food and clothing, responsibil-

ity and worry as to future prospects, and finally, the added element of overspeeding in the busy season in the endeavor to earn high wages for themselves and their families in order to take over the slack season.

Tuberculosis was most prevalent among the poorest paid of the workers (pressers and finishers). It is also significant that these two groups occupied domiciles with the fewest average number of rooms among garment workers. As their families contained on the average the greatest number of individuals, the average number of persons to the room was also higher.

A faulty posture was extremely common among garment workers, especially males. Among females the use of the corset and the greater consciousness of the personal appearance had an effect in diminishing the percentage of faulty postures. The bad effects upon health of faulty postures are well known, as they predispose to pulmonary afflictions, including tuberculosis, hernia, displacement of the abdominal organs, digestive troubles, weak and flat feet, habitual constipation.

That the industry per se need not be responsible for faulty posture was shown by the good effects upon the individual of previous military training in European armies or of physical exercise. In many such instances the posture remained excellent, and the influence of the previous training was prolonged.

Fifty years after the founding of the ILGWU Union Health Center in New York, President Kennedy, in one of his last acts, authorized the striking of a commemorative medal. President Johnson made a special trip to New York in order to participate in the anniversary ceremonies. From remarks by President Lyndon B. Johnson, 50th Anniversary Celebration, ILGWU Union Health Center, New York City, June 6, 1964. From *Justice,* June 15, 1964.

THE FIRST OF ITS KIND
by Lyndon B. Johnson

I have come here today to salute the vision and valor of men who founded your union and built this center. They were immigrants to the land and strangers to the language; men and women of Italy, Russia, Poland, Puerto Rico and of the Americas.

But they were not newcomers to courage and they understood the vocabulary of compassion. Against the bitter obstinacy of entrenched interests they battled, first to free workers from the slavery of sweatshops, then to free them from sickness and disease. This health center is a testimony of their success and a memorial to their spirit.

On this occasion, we meet to honor 50 years of responsible and progressive leadership by one of this country's most responsible and most progressive labor organizations—the International Ladies' Garment Workers' Union.

Fifty years ago, this health center stood alone, the first of its kind to be established in our country by a trade union for working men and working women. Your union stood resolute in the thin ranks of those who carried on the struggle for security for the helpless, who fought the battle for a better life for every citizen.

That great cause of compassion suffered many setbacks. But like an irresistible ocean tide, each time it returned with greater force and further reach than before. And that concern of your union, 50 years ago, is today embedded in the conscience of our country, the laws of our land, and the highest hopes of our people.

The nation learned of the horrible fire at the Triangle Shirtwaist Company through the eyewitness account of a United Press reporter who happened to be in Washington Square on March 25, 1911. He phoned in details while watching the tragedy unfold. At the other end of the telephone, young Roy Howard telegraphed Shepherd's story to the nation's newspapers. From the *Milwaukee Journal*, March 27, 1911.

EYEWITNESS AT TRIANGLE
by William G. Shepherd

I was walking through Washington Square when a puff of smoke issuing from the factory building caught my eye. I reached the building before the alarm was turned in. I saw every feature of the tragedy visible from outside the building. I learned a new sound—a more horrible sound than description can picture. It was the thud of a speeding, living body on a stone sidewalk.

Thud—dead, thud—dead, thud—dead, thud—dead. Sixty-two thud—deads. I call them that, because the sound and the thought of death came to me each time, at the same instant. There was plenty of chance to watch them as they came down. The height was eighty feet.

The first ten thud—deads shocked me. I looked up—saw that there were scores of girls at the windows. The flames from the floor below were beating in their faces. Somehow I knew that they, too, must come down, and something within me—something that I didn't know was there—steeled me.

I even watched one girl falling. Waving her arms, trying to keep her body upright until the very instant she struck the sidewalk, she was trying to balance herself. Then came the thud—then a silent, unmoving pile of clothing and twisted, broken limbs.

As I reached the scene of the fire, a cloud of smoke hung over the building. . . . I looked up to the seventh floor. There was a living picture in each window—four screaming heads of girls waving their arms.

"Call the firemen," they screamed—scores of them. "Get a ladder," cried others. They were all as alive and whole and sound as were we who stood on the sidewalk. I couldn't help thinking of that. We cried to them not to jump. We heard the siren of a fire engine in the distance. The other sirens sounded from several directions.

"Here they come," we yelled. "Don't jump; stay there."

One girl climbed onto the window sash. Those behind her tried to hold her back. Then she dropped into space. I didn't notice whether those above watched her drop because I had turned away. Then came that first thud. I looked up, another girl was climbing onto the window sill; others were crowding behind her. She dropped. I watched her fall, and again the dreadful sound. Two windows away two girls were climbing onto the sill; they were fighting each other and crowding for air. Behind them I saw many screaming heads. They fell almost together, but I heard two distinct thuds. Then the flames burst out through the windows on the floor below them, and curled up into their faces.

The firemen began to raise a ladder. Others took out a life net and, while they were rushing to the sidewalk with it, two more girls shot down. The firemen held it under them; the bodies broke it; the grotesque simile of a dog jumping through a hoop struck me. Before they could move the net another girl's body flashed through it. The thuds were just as loud, it seemed, as if there had been no net there. It seemed to me that the thuds were so loud that they might have been heard all over the city.

I had counted ten. Then my dulled senses began to work automatically. I noticed things that it had not occurred to me before to notice. Little details that the first shock had blinded me to. I looked up to see whether those above watched those who fell. I noticed that they did; they watched them every inch of the way down and probably heard the roaring thuds that we heard.

Center above John Sloan's vision of the Triangle fire hell.

Burned, smashed, soaked bodies on the Greene Street sidewalk.

In the mass funeral parade on April 5.

Center below The funeral cortege of a teenage victim of the Triangle fire.

Lining up for mass funeral parade in front of the *Daily Forward* building on East Broadway.

Leaving the morgue after identifying their dead.

As I looked up I saw a love affair in the midst of all the horror. A young man helped a girl to the window sill. Then he held her out, deliberately away from the building and let her drop. He seemed cool and calculating. He held out a second girl the same way and let her drop. Then he held out a third girl who did not resist. I noticed that. They were as unresisting as if he were helping them onto a streetcar instead of into eternity. Undoubtedly he saw that a terrible death awaited them in the flames, and his was only a terrible chivalry.

Then came the love amid the flames. He brought another girl to the window. Those of us who were looking saw her put her arms about him and kiss him. Then he held her out into space and dropped her. But quick as a flash he was on the window sill himself. His coat fluttered upward—the air filled his trouser legs. I could see that he wore tan shoes and hose. His hat remained on his head.

Thud—dead, thud—dead—together they went into eternity. I saw his face before they covered it. You could see in it that he was a real man. He had done his best.

We found out later that, in the room in which he stood, many girls were being burned to death by the flames and were screaming in an inferno of flame and heat. He chose the easiest way and was brave enough to even help the girl he loved to a quicker death, after she had given him a goodbye kiss. He leaped with an energy as if to arrive first in that mysterious land of eternity, but her thud—dead came first.

The firemen raised the longest ladder. It reached only to the sixth floor. I saw the last girl jump at it and miss it. And then the faces disappeared from the window. But now the crowd was enormous, though all this had occurred in less than seven minutes, the start of the fire and the thuds and deaths.

I heard screams around the corner and hurried there. What I had seen before was not so terrible as what had followed. Up on the [ninth] floor girls were burning to death before our very eyes. They were jammed in the windows. No one was lucky enough to be able to jump, it seemed. But, one by one, the jams broke. Down came the bodies in a shower, burning, smoking—flaming bodies, with disheveled hair trailing upward. They had fought each other to die by jumping instead of by fire.

The whole, sound, unharmed girls who had jumped on the other side of the building had tried to fall feet down. But these fire torches, suffering ones, fell inertly, only intent that death should come to them on the sidewalk instead of in the furnace behind them.

On the sidewalk lay heaps of broken bodies. A policeman later went about with tags, which he fastened with wires to the wrists of the dead girls, numbering each with a lead pencil, and I saw him fasten tag no. 54 to the wrist of a girl who wore an engagement ring. A fireman who came downstairs from the building told me that there were at least fifty bodies in the big room on the seventh floor. Another fireman told me that more girls had jumped down an air shaft in the rear of the building. I went back there, into the narrow court, and saw a heap of dead girls. . . .

The floods of water from the firemen's hose that ran into the gutter were actually stained red with blood. I looked upon the heap of dead bodies and I remembered these girls were the shirtwaist makers. I remembered their great strike of last year in which these same girls had demanded more sanitary conditions and more safety precautions in the shops. These dead bodies were the answer.

The immediate impact of the tragedy was felt in East Side homes. The following, based on personal interviews, is taken from *The Triangle Fire,* by the editor emeritus of *Justice*, 1962.

NIGHTMARE OF SURVIVAL
by Leon Stein

Rose Cohen [having escaped the fire and made her way home] sobbed herself to sleep on her bed in the dark bedroom of a long railroad flat on Lewis Street. No one was home when she arrived.

In her sleep she heard shouting and opened her eyes to the darkness. Down the long line of rooms, in the kitchen, her cousin Harry was shouting and crying. He had made the rounds, looking for Rose and had been unable to find her. He feared the worst had happened.

"My mother asked him what had happened. He began to tell her about the fire. I got up from the bed and began the long walk to the kitchen, passing through one room after another as in a dream. Finally, I stood in the kitchen doorway, supporting myself by holding onto the door frame. Then everything broke apart. My mother took one look at me and collapsed to the floor. I began to cry and scream hysterically.

"I couldn't stop crying for hours, for days," says Rose. "Afterwards, I used to dream I was falling from a window, screaming. I remember I would holler to my mother in the dark, waking everybody up, 'Mama! I just jumped out of a window!' Then I would start crying and I couldn't stop."

Isidore Wegodner escaped down the Greene Street stairs from the ninth floor, where he and his father had come to work four months earlier as sleeve setters. He was near that exit when he heard the first cry of fire and had no difficulty reaching the street.

But unaware of the extent of the disaster, he had left his father behind. Only when he emerged into the body-littered street did he realize what was happening. The firemen stopped him when he tried to rush back into the building.

They wouldn't even let him cross the street to look among the dead, and he began to cry softly, certain his father lay among them. He moved away, looking into other faces and asking for his father. He spoke only Yiddish, therefore only dimly perceived that there was something called a morgue to which the dead were to be taken.

Suddenly his young heart was lifted by the thought that perhaps his father was seeking him even as he was searching for the old man and that not having found him he had gone home in the expectation of finding him there.

Isidore ran to the Third Avenue elevated, then ran all the way from the 116th Street station to his sixth-floor home on 119th Street. His father was not there, and when he turned to go down to the street, he lied to his unknowing mother, telling her he had forgotten to buy the old man his newspaper.

In the street, he ran again, determined to return to Washington Place and to find out where this thing called a morgue was located. He missed a train by seconds and stood on the platform breathing hard, watching another pull in on the opposite platform.

"I saw him come out of the train, my dear father who was a quiet man, a dignified man. He looked battered. His pants were torn and in places his flesh showed through. His hat was gone, his face was dirty and bloody. On top of it all he wore a fancy, clean jacket that someone had thrown around his shoulders because his shirt had been ripped off. He stood on the platform dazed and the people walked around him.

"I remember," says Isidore Wegodner, "how with my last strength I shouted to him, how I went tearing over the little bridge that connected the two platforms, how we fell into each other's arms and how the people stopped to look while sobbing he embraced me and kissed me."

> While the city mourned and searched for causes of the tragedy, garment workers buried their dead. From *Life and Labor*, May 1911.

WHAT IS TO BE DONE?
by Martha Bensley Bruere

Well, the fire is over, the girls are dead, and as I write, the procession in honor of the unidentified dead is moving by under my windows. Now what is going to be done about it?

Harris and Blank, the Triangle Company, have offered to pay one week's wages to the families of the dead girls—as though it were summer and they are giving them a vacation! Three days after the fire they inserted in the trade papers this notice:

NOTICE, THE TRIANGLE WAIST CO. beg to notify their
    customers that they are in good working order.
HEADQUARTERS now at 9–11 University Place

The day after they were installed in their new quarters, the Building Department of New York City discovered that 9–11 University Place was not even fireproof, and that the firm had already blocked the exit to the one fire escape by two rows of sewing machines.

And still as I write the mourning procession moves past in the rain. For two hours they have been going steadily by and the end is not yet in sight. There have been no carriages, no imposing marshals on horseback; just thousands and thousands of working men and women carrying the banners of their trades through the long three-mile tramp in the rain. Never have I seen a military pageant or triumphant ovation so impressive; for it is not because 146 workers were killed in the Triangle shop—not altogether. It is because every year there are 50,000 working men and women killed in the United States—136 a day; almost as many as happened to be killed together on the 25th of March; and because slowly, very slowly, it is dawning on these thousands on thousands that such things do not have to be!

It is four hours later and the last of the procession has just passed.

At a memorial meeting held in the Metropolitan Opera House on April 2, 1911, Wise (1874–1949), a noted rabbi, put a moral question to the audience. From the *Reform Advocate,* April 22, 1911.

IN LETTERS OF FIRE
by Rabbi Stephen S. Wise

This was not an inevitable disaster which man could neither foresee nor control. We might have foreseen it, and some of us did; we might have controlled it, but we chose not to do so. The things that are inevitable we can do no more than vainly regret, but the things that are avoidable we can effectively forestall and prevent.

It is not a question of enforcement of law nor of inadequacy of law. We have the wrong kind of laws and the wrong kind of enforcement. Before insisting upon inspection and enforcement, let us lift up the industrial standards so as to make conditions worth inspecting, and, if inspected, certain to afford security to the workers. Instead of unanimity in the shirking of responsibility, we demand that departments shall cooperate in planning ahead and working for the future, with some measure of prevision and wisdom. And when we go before the legislature of the state, and demand increased appropriations in order to ensure the possibility of a sufficient number of inspectors, we will not forever be put off with the answer: We have no money.

The lesson of the hour is that while property is good, life is better, that while possessions are valuable, life is priceless. The meaning of the hour is that the life of the lowliest worker in the nation is sacred and inviolable, and, if that sacred human right be violated, we shall stand adjudged and condemned before the tribunal of God and of history.

Addressing the same audience, Schneiderman (1866–1972), organizer for the ILGWU and the Women's Trade Union League read the handwriting on the wall. From *The Survey,* April 8, 1911.

WE HAVE FOUND YOU WANTING
by Rose Schneiderman

I would be a traitor to these poor burned bodies if I came here to talk good fellowship. We have tried you good people of the public and we have found you wanting. The old Inquisition had its rack and its thumbscrews and its instruments of torture with iron teeth. We know what these things are today; the iron teeth are our necessities, the thumbscrews are the high-powered and swift machinery close to which we must work, and the rack is here in the firetrap structures that will destroy us the minute they catch on fire.

This is not the first time girls have been burned alive in the city. Every week I must learn of the untimely death of one of my sister workers. Every year thousands of us are maimed. The life of men and women is so cheap and property is so sacred. There are so many of us for one job it matters little if 146 of us are burned to death.

We have tried you citizens; we are trying you now, and you have a couple of dollars for the sorrowing mothers, brothers and sisters by way of a charity gift. But every time the workers come out in the only way they know to protest against conditions which are unbearable the strong hand of the law is allowed to press down heavily upon us.

Public officials have only words of warning to us—warning that we must be intensely peaceable, and they have the workhouse just back of all their warnings. The strong hand of the law beats us back, when we rise, into the conditions that make life unbearable.

I can't talk fellowship to you who are gathered here. Too much blood has been spilled. I know from my experience it is up to the working people to save themselves. The only way they can save themselves is by a strong working-class movement.

Harris and Blank, owners of Triangle, were acquitted after trial by jury on December 27, 1911. Noted lawyer Max D. Steuer (1871–1940) explained how he won his case. From his address before the 43rd Annual Meeting, Missouri Bar Association, in *America Speaks*, edited by B. G. Byron and F. R. Condert, 1928.

NOT GUILTY!
by Max D. Steuer

There are many times, many times when a witness has given evidence very hurtful to your cause and you say, "No questions," and dismiss him or her in the hope that the jury will dismiss the evidence too. (*Laughter*) But can you do that when the jury is weeping, and the little girl witness is weeping too? (*Laughter*) That is the question. While there is no rule of conduct which tells you what to do, there is one that commands what not to do. Do not attack the witness. Suavely, politely, genially, toy with the story.

In the instant case, about a half an hour was consumed by the examiner in finding out whom this little girl had seen, where she had lived, how she had been maintained, and where she had been during all the interval since the fire up to the time she was brought to the witness stand; very little progress was made; but the tears had stopped. And then she was asked, "Now, Rose, in your own words and in your own way will you tell the jury everything that you did, everything that you said and everything that you saw from the moment you first saw flames."

The question was put in precisely the same words that the District Attorney had put it; and little Rose started her answer with exactly the same word that she had started it to the District Attorney and she finished it with precisely the same word that she had finished it to the District Attorney; and the only change in her recital was that Rose left out one word. And then Rose was asked, "Didn't you, in answering this question now, leave out a word that you put in when you answered it before?" And she said, "Did I?" and the examiner said, "I think you did."

So Rose started to repeat to herself the answer (*laughter*), and as she came to the missing word she said, "Oh, yes!" and supplied it; and thereupon the examiner went to an entirely different subject and spent about thirty minutes more on that, when again he said, "Now, Rose, would you in your own way and in your own words just tell the jury everything that you saw, and everything that you said and everything that you did after you first saw flames?" And Rose started with the same word and finished with the same word, her recital being identical with her first reply to the same question.

The jurymen were not weeping. Rose had not hurt the case, and the defendants were acquitted; there was not a word of reflection at any time during that trial upon poor little Rose.

A sense of indignation led public-spirited citizens to form a Committee on Safety. With the aid of Smith (1873–1944), then in the State legislature and later to become a four-term governor of New York State and Democratic candidate for president of the United States in 1928, a state commission was created. It included, among its members and aides, Smith, Robert F. Wagner, Sr., Samuel Gompers, Frances Perkins, and Dr. Price. From *Up to Now: An Autobiography*, 1929.

SAFETY LAWS AND THEIR ENFORCEMENT
by Alfred E. Smith

A Committee on Safety was immediately formed to meet the public protest.

John Kingsbury, who represented the Association for Improvement for the Condition of the Poor, and Henry Moskowitz for the Committee on Safety, carried the story to Albany. They sought me out and asked for help in the formulation of remedies to prevent future disasters. Conferences with them and with Senator Wagner, then leader of the state senate, developed the necessity of a thorough study. A commission was suggested.

As outlined in the act creating the commission, the scope of the investigation was very broad. Though it is true that the waist factory fire led immediately to the creation of the commission, such fires are a rare occurrence, while industrial accidents, poisoning, and diseases will maim or disable thousands of people every year.

Considering insufficient ventilation, bad sanitation, and long hours of labor as menaces to the safety and health of industrial workers, the commission did not limit itself merely to the study of the fire hazard in factory buildings but extended its activities to the conditions of employment of women and children, sanitation, accident prevention and industrial poisoning and diseases. In brief, it was the aim of the commission to devote itself to a consideration of measures that had for their purpose the conservation of human life.

So lax had the state been prior to 1911, that the commission hardly began its labors when it was discovered that there was no way for the state even to know when a factory was started. A man could hire a floor in a loft building, put in his machinery and start his factory. There was no provision of law that required him to notify the state that he was engaging in a business which came under the supervision of a department of the state government.

Factory-inspection forces were so small that the inspections in some cities were made only once in two years and in others once a year. Factory managers knew just about when to expect an inspection, and consequently, during the day of the inspector's visit everything was in shipshape. The rest of the year it was allowed to run haphazard, there being no fear of detection by the authorities in charge of the Department of Labor.

A competent staff of experts was organized by the commission, including Dr. George M. Price, who set up the standards of sanitation and safety, and a group of investigators and advisory members representing every phase of the industrial life of the state. I became convinced that a majority of manufacturers were in favor of the reforms suggested by the commission and many of them would undoubtedly have been installed without law had the heads of the concerns themselves been a little more familiar with what was going on in their factory buildings. One prominent businessman in an upstate city was present at a hearing before the commission when a report was being made upon his own factory, and he publicly rebuked his superintendent for permitting such things to exist. He admitted frankly before the commission that he never went through the factory himself.

In the first year of its existence the commission proposed and passed laws controlling the sanitary conditions of factories, regulating the labor of women and children, and providing fire-prevention measures and regular fire drills. One of the important statutes resulting from our investigation was the prohibition of night work for women in factory buildings.

Perkins (1882–1965), who served on the Factory Investigating Commission, later became Secretary of Labor during the entire administration of Franklin D. Roosevelt. She had been an eyewitness at the Triangle fire. From "Address, 50th Anniversary Memorial Meeting, March 25, 1961," in *The Triangle Fire,* by Leon Stein.

NOT IN VAIN
by Frances Perkins

It was a fine, bright spring afternoon. We heard the fire engines and rushed into the square to see what was going on. We saw the smoke pouring out of the building. We got there just as they started to jump. I shall never forget the frozen horror which came over us as we stood with our hands on our throats watching that horrible sight, knowing that there was no help. They came down in twos and threes, jumping together in a kind of desperate hope.

The life nets were broken. The firemen kept shouting for them not to jump. But they had no choice; the flames were right behind them for by this time the fire was far gone.

Out of that terrible episode came a self-examination of stricken conscience in which the people of this state saw for the first time the individual worth and value of each of those 146 people who fell or were burned in that great fire. And we saw, too, the great human value of every individual who was injured in an accident by a machine.

There was a stricken conscience of public guilt and we all felt that we had been wrong, that something was wrong with that building which we had accepted or the tragedy never would have happened. Moved by this sense of stricken guilt, we banded ourselves together to find a way by law to prevent this kind of disaster.

And so it was that the Factory Commission that sprang out of the ashes of the tragedy made an investigation that took four years of searching, of public hearings, of legislative formulations, of pressuring through the legislature the greatest battery of bills to prevent disasters and hardships affecting working people, of passing laws the likes of which have never been seen in any four sessions of any state legislature.

It was the beginning of a new and important drive to bring the humanities to the life of the brothers and sisters we all had in the working groups of these United States. The stirring up of the public conscience and the act of the people in penitence brought about not only these laws which make New York State to this day the best state in relation to factory laws; it was also that stirring of conscience which brought about in 1932 the introduction of a new element into the life of the whole United States.

We had in the election of Franklin Roosevelt the beginning of what has come to be called a New Deal for the United States. But it was based really upon the experiences that we had had in New York State and upon the sacrifices of those who, we faithfully remember with affection and respect, died in that terrible fire on March 25, 1911. They did not die in vain and we will never forget them.

9. Rebirth of the Union

In the 1920s, Communists saw the ILGWU as an ideal beachhead from which to launch an assault against the American trade union movement.

The end of World War I brought an open-shop movement that eliminated wartime gains in wages and working conditions. Apparel sales, boosted by wartime wages and shortages in other consumer areas, slipped back to lower peacetime levels.

The tension resulting from these changes, in turn, intensified the continuing difficulties in the industry: pincer movements by fabric suppliers, on the one hand, and retailers, on the other, to beat down wholesale apparel prices; the evasion of ultimate responsibility for work and wage conditions made possible by the jobber-contractor mode of production; the proliferation of contractors under the easy-entry circumstances of the industry; the reverse auction block system by which jobbers apportioned their work to the lowest bidding contractors.

From its inception, the ILGWU had been an arena in which the forces of reform contended with the forces of revolution. The success of the Bolsheviks in Russia raised a red glare that flushed the faces of those who had consistently deprecated contractual gains indicating a slow yet steady advance toward labor-management peace. For them, the Russian experience bolstered faith in revolutionary laissez-faire; they believed that the worse things got, the better the prospects for revolution.

As George Soule and the *New Republic* pointed out, the Communists held that the reasonable reform approach betrayed workers by forcing them to adopt a system of class collaboration, one which must be countered by militancy in the ranks and at meetings. Just as Governor Smith's special commission had completed its work—it had made innovative recommendations for bringing about industrial peace by setting a limit on contracting—the Communists made their first move to take over the ILGWU at the union's 1925 convention, an event described by James Oneal.

The following year, after the governor's recommendations had been rejected, the Communists launched a strike—without taking a strike vote—that was to last twenty-six weeks. While others loyally rallied in support of the walkout in an effort to preserve the ILGWU, Communist leaders depleted resources, compromised issues, denounced administration leaders with a rhetoric of abuse, and led the union to the edge of disaster. The settlement of the strike, according to Edward Levinson, left the union a shambles.

The General Executive Board warned that the disaster was, in effect, a rehearsal for the whole labor movement, a warning that was fulfilled a decade later. Morris Sigman, who had guided the ILGWU through the perilous period in an effort to preserve enough of the union to make a new beginning, rallied the existing forces in support of the organization. Will Herberg skillfully recounts the course and significance of the internecine battle.

Meanwhile, the garment industry, a key to New York's economy, continued to operate. Eventually discredited, the Communists had departed from the ranks of leadership. In 1938, Schlesinger had returned to the helm of the ILGWU. Franklin Roosevelt, then governor of New York, appealed to Schlesinger to take the lead in stabilizing the industry. Louis Stark reported how a short cloak strike achieved this end.

But it was Schlesinger and David Dubinsky, his young aide, who undertook the task of rebuilding the ILGWU. As the 1920s drew to a close, both labored to bring work into the shops, lift wage standards, build resources, win public opinion, enforce contract terms, and restore the faith of the garment workers in their union.

The first selection, by Soule, is excerpted from the *Nation,* July 23, 1924. The second selection, unsigned, is from the *New Republic,* July 1, 1925.

MILITANCY IS NOT ENOUGH
by George Soule

It is a dogma of the extreme left that the only proper course for labor is amalgamation of the unions and a "militant" spirit leading to strikes on an ever larger scale. At every point the workers must refuse to cooperate with employers. Anything of that sort is damned as "class collaboration."

The lefts in the heat of their dogmas apparently have failed to make a realistic examination of the clothing industries of New York. Here the development has been precisely opposite to that which they say is inevitable.

Units of production have been growing smaller. The amount of capital necessary to start a shop is so small that the industry has become overcrowded and competition has been intensified beyond endurance. The comparatively large "inside shops" which make entire garments under one roof have been gradually giving way.

The result is manufacture in wastefully small shops, overequipment of machinery and personnel among the contractors, heavy seasonal unemployment, a dragging down of labor standards, deterioration of quality of the product.

The International Ladies' Garment Workers' Union had a difficult situation. For months before the expiration of their agreement on May 1, they had been endeavoring to bring about a scientific investigation and a remedy for the ills of their industry through cooperation of the big manufacturers, the jobbers, the contractors and the union.

A joint committee formed for this purpose failed to elicit the necessary detailed information on account of the reluctance of the jobbers to cooperate. The jobbers, though ultimately involved in the disintegration of the industry, were temporarily profiting from the surplus of contractors and were not prepared to cooperate in good faith.

When the agreement expired the union presented demands embodying the best remedies it could devise, and threatened to force cohesion in the industry through a strike.

This threat led to the appointment of a competent investigating committee by Governor Smith, which heard all sides at length and eventually handed down recommendations embodying much of what the union wanted. The jobbers at first refused to accept the verdict, but another strike threat at the beginning of the busy season, which was now at hand, brought them to terms.

The remedies offered by the commission include a stipulation that jobbers shall order goods only from contractors having agreements with the union, that such union contractors' shops shall have at least 14 machine operators and a corresponding number of employees in other branches of the work, that a sanitary label shall be used in products of union shops which shall be subject to the Joint Board of Sanitary Control, that jobbers shall be responsible for the payment of wages by the contractors.

No amount of union amalgamation or "militancy" would help a situation such as this. The need is not for a simple test of power. It is a problem in industrial engineering.

REASON OR FORCE

Damaging to union prestige and destructive of moral unity as is the quarrel between the New York Joint Board and the Communist officers of certain locals, there seems to be no honest way of avoiding it. Friends of labor are inclined to advise factions separated by social theory to agree to disagree in philosophy and unite in practice on the best interests of the union in the existing situation.

In the case of the Communists, however, the conflict of philosophies necessarily leads to a crucial disagreement about policy. The Communists violently oppose constructive measures recently adopted in this and other unions, such as unemployment insurance and regularization of the industry by agreement. They agitate by fair means and foul against any who favor such measures.

However much the tactic recently developed by the more progressive unions may appeal to an open mind, there is no way to recommend them to the closed mind of the Communist, which judges everything by the accepted dogma of class warfare and an approach of catastrophic revolution. Everything which does not obviously point in that direction is condemned as "class collaboration" and is outlawed by the economic-religious authorities of Moscow.

Controversy about policy with the Communists therefore is difficult to carry out in terms of reason, but tends to descend to a brute struggle for control. Like all bigoted believers in a system of absolutes, the Communists will sacrifice any interest for the sake of their ultimate end, believing that the end justifies the means, and are willing to ruin it if they cannot rule. They expect to be vindicated by the "inevitable" denouement—a sort of industrial judgment day, in which they will be found sitting on the right hand of an economically deterministic God.

The unfortunate result is that their opponents are thus tempted into abandoning discussion and turning to methods distasteful to any liberal mind. One does not like to read that the superior officers of a great and progressive union are holding "trials" of duly elected inferiors, or that they have called in police protection.

Thus is illustrated a dilemma which faces liberals today in many fundamental controversies. It is easy to appeal to reason and to trust in the ultimate beneficence of democracy so long as one's opponents accept reasonable criteria of judgment. But when their actions and conclusions rest on some sacred principle outside the universe of discourse, what is to be done? To appeal to force is to accept the standards of the antiliberal measurers. In such a situation the only ultimate hope appears to rest in conversion of the absolutists to a more fruitful state of mind. Perhaps experience in power will prove to be their sole teacher.

Oneal (1875–1962) was a noted Socialist journalist and historian. This selection is from his *The History of Local 10*, 1927.

THE 1925 CONVENTION
by James Oneal

The 1925 Philadelphia convention proceeded with its work in an atmosphere of tense feeling, much of its time being wasted by demonstrations of the "lefts" and by the cheering of a claque which packed the gallery. It was the first national convention of a trade union to meet in this country, where partisans of a political movement flocked into the hall and endeavored to influence decisions of the delegates. Because of the long debates, frequent interruptions and demonstrations, the convention was in session 18 days.

The most determined struggle came on the report of the Appeal Committee, which approved the action of the General Executive Board in the matter of the New York suspensions. It declared that suspended members "have indulged in the practice of breaking up meetings, distributing literature of a slanderous nature against the elected administration of the International Ladies' Garment Workers' Union, obstructing the normal activity of the locals of which they were members, and otherwise acting to the detriment of the union as a whole. . . ."

An amusing *volte-face* occurred on the resolution condemning "class collaboration," i.e., arbitration, and outlining the program of the antiadministration forces. Its main feature was a declaration against submitting union demands to anybody for arbitration, singling out the Governor's Commission for special mention.

The "lefts" became doubtful of their own proposal as it was subjected to criticism, yet it was the gist of their opposition to what they called "class collaboration." Doubt gave way to the fear that they had placed themselves in an untenable position. If they forced the issue and obtained a decision against arbitration under any circumstances, the union would be compelled to strike no matter how favorable an aspect a given union demand might have before an arbitration body.

The "lefts," however, were forced into a position where they eventually abandoned their repudiation of arbitration and were recorded in favor of it "only after a strike has been first called." When the absurdity of their original proposal was shown to the delegates, they modified their original proposal with the explanation that they were not against arbitration in principle but were against resorting to it before the masses have been called on strike. When they have been called out and the union finds itself in a weakened condition, "then and only then," according to their theory, "is it permissible for a union to resort to arbitration."

Strikes are called to improve conditions, and a situation might arise where a strike could be avoided by receiving a favorable decision through arbitration. The Communists and "lefts" had presented an absurd theory which even they were compelled to modify.

On the morning of the 15th day's session, the Communist bloc "bolted" the convention on the issue of proportional representation in conventions, taking 109 delegates with them.

President Morris Sigman observed that the absent delegates had chosen the wrong time to desert. Dubinsky declared that a caucus of "rank and filers" had been held in New York where preparations had been made for the "bolt."

Sigman added that he had received information that a mass meeting had been arranged in New York at 1 o'clock in anticipation of the "bolt" and to receive the deserting delegates. With 159 delegates present the recommendation of the committee was adopted unanimously at the evening session.

By their rash action in leaving the convention the "lefts" had taken a course which they had always claimed to oppose. If they remained away their action meant dual unionism; if they returned it would be an admission that they had made a mistake. Moreover, no action had been taken by the convention to justify the "bolt."

At the evening session the deserting delegates returned. On the basis of what "seemed" to them a forecast of an "intention" of the administration to do something, the "bolt" had occurred!

The convention was the most tempestuous one ever held by a trade union in this country, and it represented the high tide of influence of William Z. Foster's Trade Union Educational League. The proceedings of the convention itself showed that the logical culmination of the league's activities was secession and rival unionism.

Levinson (1902–1945) was labor editor of the *New York Post* and editor of the *United Automobile Worker*. This selection is from the *American Federationist,* January 1927.

THE 1926 STRIKE

by Edward Levinson

The Communists have led 35,000 ladies' garment workers in New York City through a six-month strike. The results are now on record. The Communists have painted their own full-length portrait. It is on exhibition for all to view.

In 1924 ILGWU President Morris Sigman formulated a program conceived to make the jobbers, organized in the Merchants' Ladies' Garment Association, shoulder responsibility commensurate with their position in the industry.

President Sigman demanded that submanufacturers whose shops were so small as to use less than 14 machines be eliminated as a menace to the well-being of the industry and the workers. A second point in his program was that the jobbers be made to designate a minimum number of submanufacturers and assume the obligation of furnishing them with enough work to give their workers a minimum period of employment.

Through the intercession of a commission, appointed by the governor of New York, President Sigman had succeeded in winning much sympathy for his program. Side by side with his education of public opinion on the need for such regulation as he proposed, President Sigman was strengthening his union. He was approaching important initial gains, when the Communist phobia rendered his work useless.

In open espousal of William Z. Foster's Trade Union Educational League, the Communists raised their banner in the New York locals of the ILGWU. They were impatient. "Public opinion" was a capitalistic fetish to be scorned by all true revolutionary unionists; arbitration and mediation were merely schemes of the capitalists to keep the workers in subjection; the Governor's Commission was a symbol of "class collaboration," which had been denounced in Moscow and accepted by American neophytes as tantamount to a "betrayal of the entire working-class movement." Straight-from-the-shoulder "mass action" would do the trick. All who stood in the way of these men of action were termed "klansmen," "gangsters," "Fascisti," "fakers," "capitalist lackeys," "traitors," etc., etc., and worst of all, "class collaborationists."

By a combination of demagogy, intrigue and character assassination, the Communists finally succeeded, in 1925, in winning enough locals to control the New York Joint Board of the ILGWU.

The final report of the Governor's Commission was made public in May 1926. Though the commission had not granted all the demands of the union, it substantially recognized the union's proposal for the placing of greater responsibility on the jobbers. If accepted as a basis of negotiation, it would have led to further concessions over the conference table.

The evident willingness of the commission to go a long way in the direction of the union aroused no feeling of joy in the hearts of the Communists. Acceptance of the report by the union would have won it the support of the public and the press. But the Communists would have none of such reactionary tactics. They would have nothing to do with "class collaboration." It must be "mass action."

A peculiarity of the "mass action" that followed was that the masses had nothing to do with it. The strike was called by the Communist leaders of the joint board in a meeting behind closed doors. No referendum vote of the membership was taken. In vain did President Sigman urge the joint board to place the question of a strike to a referendum vote. Other suggestions he made for the conduct of the strike were ruled aside.

On July 1, the 35,000 men and women employed in the industry struck. The walkout was inspiring. The rank and file had begun its task in an earnest and determined fashion.

As much could not be said for their Communist leaders. From a fight against the jobbers, the Communists immediately turned the strike into one against the Industrial Council. The shops of the members of the Industrial Council are by far superior in point of wages, length of employment and general working conditions to the shops of the submanufacturers. The limitation of contractors, the cardinal demand of the union, was forgotten.

Testimony to the Communists' strike-leading abilities was the manner of settling independent shops in the course of the strike. In settling with these shops caution should have been exercised, as it had been in previous strikes, to see that work produced by them did not find its way to strikebound firms. So rash were the Communists in their settlements with individual shops, that they accorded recognition to a number which were known before the strike to have been producing work in large quantities for jobbers.

The lax method of dealing with the independent shops broke the strike. The Communists, long before the settlement with the Industrial Council had been made, had sent about 16,000 strikers back to work. The result was a foregone conclusion. The jobbers had their work performed, much as though no strike was in force. The shops that had been accorded individual agreements laid off their workers earlier than usual because of overproduction in the market.

The Communist strike leaders had at their disposal the unequaled sum of $3,000,000. A preliminary investigation has revealed the foundation on which the Communists built up the machine which sustained them in office.

A fluid army of 2,000, ostensibly Communist "idealists," was always on hand to do the bidding of the Communist leaders whenever and wherever they were needed—to shout down opposition, to silence insistent askers of embarrassing questions, and to impersonate the "rank and file" whenever the respective commissars appeared on the scene. A glance at the strike expenditures reveals the sinews on which this army fought.

The Hall Committee, which employed 500 people, had spent a total of $200,000 up to November 15, when these figures were tabulated.

The members of this committee were to have received from $10 to $15 a week as compensation. The remainder of the expenditure is put down to "expense."

The Organization Committee, which had charge of investigating prospective signers of individual agreements, spent $100,000 on its 500 employees. Then there was the Law Committee. Here also the Communist faithfuls found posts while the beloved rank and file languished in gloomy rooms in dreary strike halls. This committee had 200 men at work under it. Its expenditure, in addition to legal fees ($62,000), court expenses ($17,000) and bail bonds ($52,000), was $172,000.

The Picket Committee offers an even more interesting case. Up to November 18, it had spent $200,000. It employed 500 people at from $15 to $20 per week per worker. On this committee the "expenses" item was double the amount paid out as "salaries." In connection with the work and expenditures of the Picket Committee, it must be remembered that it did not pay the mass of the workers who were sent to the picket lines by the different shops and paid for by the shops. The Out-of-Town Committee found it necessary to spend $476,000 on its work.

All of these committees were loaded down with Communists. Not only did they dominate the committees by sheer number, but they placed their own people at the helms of committees for which jobs they were pitifully unfit. The leader of the ill-fated strike admitted that the Communists would not permit capable union men who were non-Communists to hold positions for which they were best fitted.

Then came the settlement with the Industrial Council—a settlement which acts as a basis for the agreement with the other employing interests in the industry. And with the settlement, the storm of revolt broke around the heads of the Communists.

More than 15,000 workers had been on strike for 20 weeks. Another 15,000 had lost some part of the season before they were returned to independent shops. Over $3,000,000 had been expended. The full wisdom of Moscow-inspired oracles had been drained. What was there to show for it? Not even the Communists attempted to hide the fact that their agreement had brought upon the union the most severe defeat in its history. A better agreement could have been obtained without a strike.

As recommended by the Governor's Commission, a joint committee was to check sending of goods through unauthorized and substandard channels. The Communists' demand for the right to examine the employers' books was lost. Their oft-repeated demand for the right to strike at any time was not even mentioned. Limitation of the number of submanufacturers to be used by a jobber was agreed upon, but inasmuch as the jobbers are not affected by the agreement this item is virtually meaningless.

The masterstrokes of the Communists were two clauses, in one of which they agreed to place the employment bureau under joint direction of employers and union, and in the other, accorded the manufacturers the right to reorganize the personnel of their shops once in 1927 and twice again in 1928.

Thus the Communists had surrendered the most precious asset of the union—the worker's right to the job. The employment bureau, hitherto under the exclusive control of the union, is now to be administered with the kind assistance of the employer. Not only is the employer to have the right to pick the man he wants for the job, but he may also discharge him on any of a score of pretexts at the end of each season. The three reorganization periods will enable him to discharge 30 percent of his employees. The right to do this will give the employer a club with which he will rush his employees at the old sweatshop pace. The commission had recommended one reorganization a year.

The reaction against the Communists has been swift. A spontaneous gathering of thousands of cloakmakers demanded that the Communists resign and President Sigman take over the remains of the strike. At meetings called by the Communists and packed by the Communists there has nevertheless been sharp and unsuppressible rebellion.

The cloakmakers are up in arms against the Communists. The latter hope to maintain their grip on the union by holding elections in the approved Moscow fashion. The responsible elements in the union retort they will have no confidence in any Communist-run election. In the crisis that now confronts the union, the rank and file is again turning to the ILGWU to free it forever from the clutches of the Communists.

Before admission to December 18, 1926, communist-led rally at Madison Square Garden, pro and con grapple for sign.

On December 3, 1926, the ILGWU General Executive Board summed up the union's position in the following statement.

WARNING TO AMERICAN LABOR

The chief issues for the achievement of which the cloakmakers of New York were called out on strike five months ago have been cast overboard and abandoned. They were abandoned solely through the incompetence of the Communist leadership of the strike.

For the first time in the history of the Cloakmakers' Union a general strike was called without the vote of the membership. It was the workers in the shops who had to bear all the hardships and privations of a general strike. It was they who were called upon to make heavy sacrifices—and yet they were not even given a chance to state in a referendum whether they cared to undertake the fight.

The strike had been on for about three months before it ever occurred to the leadership that a strike is not an end in itself and that efforts should be made to bring about a settlement. It is a matter of general knowledge that we could have settled this strike more than once during these five months on terms more advantageous than those secured now, but the leadership of the strike, who shaped strike policy to suit the wishes of the Communist politicians, sidetracked all these opportunities and kept on groping blindly with the fight.

Throughout this heartbreaking procedure the officers of the International Ladies' Garment Workers' Union did not utter a word of public criticism of the ruinous tactics of the left-wing leadership, though we constantly pointed out to them their blunders and mismanagement. We felt that any dissension in the ranks of the cloakmakers while the active fight was on would aggravate the situation still more.

We cooperated with the strike leadership faithfully and steadily to the extent that we were permitted to cooperate. Time and again we endeavored to bring some measure of system and reason into the conduct of the strike, but our advice and admonitions were rejected by the left-wing leaders who got their orders from the Communist party.

We cannot stop the Communists and their party from blackguarding and besmirching the characters of trade unionists and of leaders in the trade union movement. Character assassination and mudslinging are the Communist stock-in-trade.

But our ILGWU and the American trade union movement must not and shall not permit Communist blackmail chiefs, or such as serve their nefarious schemes and purposes, to assume positions of leadership in the trade union movement. It is the sacred duty of the labor movement to rid itself of this pestilence.

The Communist leadership of the Cloakmakers' Union has all but ruined the organization. The great task before the cloakmakers of New York at this time is to rid themselves of that irresponsible and ruinous leadership and to concentrate their whole strength and energy in the effort to rebuild the union under sane and sensible leadership and to regain its former power and standing for the true benefit of men and women who work in the trade.

On December 17, 1926, ILGWU President Sigman (1880–1931) issued a call to garment workers to save their union.

RESTORE OUR UNION!
by Morris Sigman

The leaders of our ill-fated strike have brought your organization, which was never defeated in all its history, to the brink of destruction. They have dragged you, on the orders of their Communist chiefs, into a disastrous strike which after 25 weeks resulted in the loss of an entire season and in hunger and starvation for yourselves and your families. They have lied to you and deceived you at every step and turn of this tragedy and have abandoned every vital issue of the strike.

They have conducted the strike not for you but for the Communist party, not to win concessions and better conditions for you, but to please the Communist politicians under whose heel they have been all the time. And now, after they had made you lose one season, they have brought upon you this lockout that threatens to bring more hunger, more misery and the loss of another season to you.

Sisters and Brothers: This is a great day for our union, a day of united action, when every loyal member of the organization who wishes to see it saved from the clutches of Communism should rally to the call of the International Ladies' Garment Workers' Union and do everything in his power to help rebuild our union on a basis of tolerance, orderliness and true usefulness to our workers.

Cloakmakers: Remember, we must save our union and our future. Let us set aside our individual and personal dislikes, and let us bear in mind that we must preserve the organization for the upbuilding of which we have toiled, bled and sacrificed tens of years.

Keep yourselves ready and in orderly fashion in the halls, awaiting the orders of the General Executive Board, and let us together restore our great union to its former strength and to its proud position as one of the best organized trade unions in America.

Will Herberg, a noted scholar, was educational director of Dressmakers' Local 22 in the 1940s. He reviewed the ILGWU "civil war" in the *American Jewish Yearbook*, 1952.

THE ILGWU CIVIL WAR
by Will Herberg

The main battleground in the conflict with the Communists was the International Ladies' Garment Workers' Union. Several factors made the ILGWU the chief theater in the civil war. Economic conditions, resulting from the decline of the cloak trade and the demoralizing effects of the jobber-contractor system, were particularly difficult during the first postwar decade, and naturally gave rise to serious grievances among the membership which the Communists were quick to exploit. Equally valuable from the Communist standpoint was the background of hostility between the ILGWU international office and the larger locals in New York. Opposition movements, too, had a long tradition among the New York women's garment workers, a tradition which the Communists knew how to exploit. For these and other reasons, the ILGWU became the primary target in the Communist offensive.

By the end of 1921, the Trade Union Educational League (TUEL) was already established in New York and other centers of the ILGWU, and soon the "left-wing" scored important election victories in New York, Philadelphia, and Chicago. By 1923 this conflict was raging throughout the union. In that year, Local 22 (a newly chartered offshoot of Local 25, consisting of dressmakers) was captured by the Communists; however, the "left-wing" members of the administration were removed from office by the General Executive Board (GEB). Similar action was taken against "left wingers" in Chicago and Philadelphia. In August 1923, the GEB illegalized the TUEL and other intraunion groups. Despite the fact that all candidates were required to disavow membership in the outlawed groups, the chief cloakmakers' and dressmakers' locals in New York were captured by the "left-wing" in 1924–25. The Communist officers were removed and suspended. Thereupon they formed an independent union, issuing membership cards, collecting dues, and controlling shops by their own authority. Yet a final split was, for the moment, averted through a compromise that constituted a substantial victory for the "left-wing." The "left-wing" officers were reinstated, new elections were held, and the Communists and their allies returned to power.

The "peace" did not last long. The eighteen-day convention held in Philadelphia during November and December 1925 was a continuous battle between the two factions. The "left-wing" probably represented a majority of the membership; the ILGWU administration, however, controlled a majority of the convention votes. This convention, at which the "left-wing" was defeated by a vote of approximately three to two, was the prelude to the most violent and, as it turned out, decisive battle in the long-drawn-out conflict. This was the Communist-conducted general strike in the New York cloak industry in 1926.

The strike broke out when the "left-wing" leaders, under direct instructions of the Communist party, rejected proposals of the Governor's Advisory Commission, despite the fact that the ILGWU leadership urged their acceptance. The "left-wing" took over complete and exclusive control of the general strike machinery. The strike was bitterly fought from the beginning, but there were several moments when it might have been settled to some advantage. Indeed, there is good evidence that the leading Communist trade unionists, had they been left to themselves, would have settled much sooner and under better conditions; they were, however, forced to protract the strike by peremptory orders from party headquarters. Finally, after the situation had become utterly chaotic and it was disclosed that the "left-wing" leadership had misused $800,000 of employers' securities deposited with the union, the ILGWU's General Executive Board took over the strike and brought it to a quick conclusion. . . .

The ILGWU was done with compromises. The "left-wing" organizations were dissolved and a new registration of all workers was ordered; locals were reorganized with new charters. The Communist leaders refused to recognize the measure and called upon their sympathizers not to register, but the great mass of the workers went back to the ILGWU. In Chicago and other out-of-town centers, the struggle took a very similar course, though one by no means so acute. All in all, it may be said that by the end of 1926 the Communist bid for power had been defeated. But the union was shattered; the membership was depleted; the treasury empty; huge debts overwhelmed the organization; control over industrial conditions was virtually gone. There were many who despaired of the union.

Even as the ILGWU sought to lift itself out of the ruins, it
faced a strike in the cloak industry. The governor of New
York, seeking to avert a walkout, wrote the following letter,
dated July 2, 1929, to the president of the ILGWU.

LETTER TO BENJAMIN SCHLESINGER
by Franklin D. Roosevelt

The making of cloaks and suits constitutes one of the greatest industries in this state, producing each year for use throughout the country
merchandise valued at hundreds of millions of dollars. Naturally, the
prosperity of this industry and the welfare of those engaged in it are
of concern to the entire state.

Of many accomplishments in your industry you can justly be proud.
These are due to the enterprise of employers, the taste of designers,
and the skill of the craft workers.

In your industrial relations you have developed along the most
progressive and enlightened lines the principle of collective bargaining. I am told that while collective agreements are in force thousands
of minor shop disputes are settled amicably without even the necessity
of final resort to the judgment of the impartial chairman, whom you
have jointly chosen.

Of course, I understand that all parties reserve full liberty of action
upon the expiration of the collective agreements. Such a time has now
arisen, and thus far you have not been able to agree upon the terms of
new contracts. Naturally you have some divergent interests and points
of view. That is characteristic of all human affairs. I am impressed,
however, with the fact that you have worked together in many situations and that you must at least understand each other's purposes and
problems.

My wish is to remind you that you have great common interests to
preserve and to advance. Surely none of you wishes a repetition of the
long and disastrous strike of three years ago, in which an entire season
was lost and from which ever since you have all been suffering.

The usual shortness of your seasons is a handicap which is always a
burden to all factors. You are all far too intelligent to wish to further
shorten a season's work by any prolonged stoppage which can be
fairly avoided.

In an industry broken up into so many relatively small producing
units, strong and comprehensive organizations both of employers and
of workers are of highest importance. Surely, you should be able to

work together heartily to spread such enlightened industrial standards as you can agree upon into the less fair and progressive portions of the industry.

More complete organization and stabilization is the great need. Unfair competition and the depression of standards in unregulated shops undermine the honest efforts both of workers and of employers.

The following account of the strike written by Stark (1889–1954), the labor reporter for the *New York Times*. It appeared on July 21, 1929.

THE SHORTEST STRIKE
by Louis Stark

To many of those present at City Hall several days ago when formal peace terms were signed, ending a fortnight's strike of 30,000 cloakmakers (the shortest in the industry's troubled career), the occasion has something of the miraculous about it. Six months ago when the same men met to write a new agreement they lined up in bitterly hostile camps, ranged on opposite sides of an abyss into which nearly all felt they would inevitably plunge and drag their industry.

Last December the morale of the cloak industry appeared to be at its lowest ebb since the 1910 strike, when the agreement known as the Protocol of Peace brought a large measure of hope out of the chaos and confusion of the industry.

Despite the Protocol, for nearly 20 years the industry has been buffeted by the adverse winds of strikes and lockouts. More recently it has also been affected by the rise of style as a factor in production, the growth of hand-to-mouth buying and the rapid development of chain store and group purchasing on a scale so vast that it could not be conceived of 20 years ago.

Now, with the signing of the new three-year agreement, the industry, in the opinion of its leaders, enters upon a new era, a period which it is hoped will be marked by cooperative endeavor, and that will mean the rehabilitation of one of New York's foremost industries.

Having reassumed the office of president, Schlesinger undertook the task of rebuilding the ILGWU. He was aided
by David Dubinsky, the youthful manager of Cutters' Local
10. Both reported on the rescue operation in the *American
Federationist,* December 1929.

STABILIZING AN INDUSTRY
by Benjamin Schlesinger

When last year I again assumed the office of general president after
an absence of five years, I found the following situation: the agreements which the International Ladies' Garment Workers' Union had
with the employers were no better than scraps of paper.

There was a large membership on our books but comparatively few
members paid their dues or took an interest in the work of the organization. The pernicious propaganda of the Communists and the loss of
the 26-week strike, which was conducted by them, had destroyed the
spirit of our members. Among the leaders themselves I found apathy
and even a great deal of pessimism.

My task, as I saw it, was simple, very simple. The leadership had to
be solidified, enthusiasm aroused in the active members and an appeal made to the workers to get back their union. But when I wrote
my first appeal to be distributed I found that the treasury of the "rich
ILGWU" did not have the wherewithal to pay for the printing. I also
learned that the office employees of the ILGWU did not always receive their salaries and that the union officers had not been paid for
some time. Then, bills were coming in, notes were due, the debts
incurred by the Communists were heavy. All this greatly complicated
matters.

Well, we had to go out and borrow money. We did, and the campaign to rebuild the union started. When, as a result of our campaign,
the ILGWU began to look like a union again and the time of the
expiration of the agreements in the industry was approaching, we
entered into negotiations with the employers with a program designed primarily to stabilize the industry. We realized that the work of
stabilizing the industry is not the union's job alone. True, chaos in the
industry, demoralization, affects the workers the most, but it also
affects the manufacturers, the jobbers and the submanufacturers.

Our suggestion to all three groups of employers was a joint responsibility for the conditions in the industry, a joint control of the industry, a joint effort to stabilize the industry. How? By making each party
to the agreement the only controlling factor in its respective field.

The association of submanufacturers is to be the only group in its field, and the employers are to deal with no other submanufacturers. The association of jobbers is to be recognized as the group of jobbers to which preference is to be given by the submanufacturers. The association of inside manufacturers is to be recognized as the controlling factor of inside manufacturing. And the union is to be given every opportunity to control and guard the conditions of all the workers in all the shops.

The associations of employers accepted our proposition. They realized the necessity of a strong union for the purpose of reviving the industry just as we realized that only the strong and responsible associations of employers can be of assistance in stabilizing the industry.

At our suggestion it was also agreed that a permanent joint commission be organized, of representatives of all parties to the agreement, for the purpose of joint control of the conditions in the industry. More than that, in view of the entry into the market of chain stores, mail-order houses, group buyers, etc., this commission jointly as well as the union individually, will endeavor to enlist the cooperation of the reputable retailers in the effort to eliminate substandard shops which are detrimental to the industry.

And we went a step further. We suggested, and it was agreed, that the public be represented on the joint commission. We thought and think that the public is entitled to know under what conditions garments are made so that it may discriminate against sweatshop products.

One of the most important improvements is the modification of the so-called "reorganization" rights of the employers. Our new agreement provides for only two reorganizations in the course of four years. Furthermore, according to the old agreement each reorganization was spread through an entire month whereas in our new agreement each of the reorganizations is to take place within one week only. Provision is made for the protection of the wages of the worker where reorganization takes place and that no discharge is made because of a worker's "performance of his duties in behalf of the union or of the workers in the shop."

I do not want anybody, however, to be under the illusion that this program was embodied into the agreement without a struggle. True, the employers were sympathetic to it, but they were in doubt as to the ability of the union to carry it out, to enforce it. It required a general strike of the 30,000 cloakmakers of New York to convince the employers that we are alive again. The workers responded splendidly. Their interest was aroused by our systematic agitation, and their enthusiasm by the call to strike. It was a short strike, two weeks only, but it was productive of results. The agreement placed us on the road to order in the industry and we reestablished the union in the cloak and suit industry of New York.

Trouble at June 23, 1927, demonstration to proclaim, "We have swept them out."

Now we are preparing for the performance of a similar operation in the dress industry of New York, which needs it probably more than the cloak and suit industry.

After that—to other markets!

REBUILDING THE UNION
by David Dubinsky

In May 1928, President Benjamin Schlesinger came back into office. His first task was to obtain funds to finance the union program of rehabilitation. In the midst of apathy and pessimism he succeeded in obtaining loans from outside sources. But the agreements were expiring in the summer of 1929, preparations had to be made for a possible strike and the loans were not sufficient.

At the recommendation of President Schlesinger, the General Executive Board decided to issue bonds, which brought in a considerable amount of money. Our International Ladies' Garment Workers' Union began to look like a union again.

The obtaining of funds, however, was only part of the task. The union had to be rebuilt, the spirit and morale of the members revived, and agreements had to be negotiated with the employers.

We started a feverish campaign of organization. In this campaign, as well as in our previous fight against the Communists, we were assisted by the American Federation of Labor, especially by President Green and Vice-President Woll, who took a personal interest in the revival of our union. We appealed to the workers in the shops and at mass meetings, through the press and through our own literature.

The agreements were expiring. We entered into negotiations with the employers, and our members were aroused. They knew that the conditions must be changed, that they were intolerable. They were hoping that the negotiations with the employers would bring a better living for them. And they came back to us; they were again true and loyal union men and women.

Thousands were coming to the ILGWU offering assistance and demanding that the experienced leaders and trained strategists of our ILGWU regain for them the conditions lost under the rule of the Communists. They were clamoring for a union to protect them from the chaos and demoralization in the industry, in the shops. And our negotiations with the employers convinced us they too would prefer to enter into a contract with a strong and responsible union.

The test soon came. We called a meeting at the 71st Regiment Armory which was addressed by President Green and Vice-President Woll, in addition to President Schlesinger and others of our ILGWU. The meeting was called to report the progress of our negotiations with the employers. That meeting was a huge success. For the first time in several years the workers came in thousands at the call of the leaders of the ILGWU. At the same time the Communists called a meeting at the Manhattan Opera House which showed their complete collapse.

We called our strike on July 2. The workers responded, the industry was stopped, and again we had the cooperation of the AFL. President Green even assigned to us a special organizer, Edward F. McGrady, one of the legislative representatives of the AFL, whose assistance during the strike was of inestimable value.

Within two weeks the strike was over. Conferences with the three employers' associations for the final settlement of the strike were attended by Lieutenant Governor Lehman and by President Green, whose counsel and advice was accepted by all the participants in these conferences.

And when the strike was settled, the agreements now in operation were signed by all the parties at the City Hall and attested to by Lehman and Mayor James J. Walker.

It was the shortest general strike in the history of our union. It brought back the power of the ILGWU. It revived the spirit of the workers. The union is now reestablished.

10. The New Deal

By the time Franklin D. Roosevelt began his first term as president of the United States, the ILGWU had launched (in Philadelphia) its first major organizational drive under its new president, David Dubinsky. The New Deal years became a time of turmoil and progress not only for the garment union but also for organized labor throughout the nation.

For most workers the new spirit in the land meant an increase in union activities and battles on the picket lines and around the bargaining table. It also meant the enactment of public policies that gave them the right to organize into unions of their own choice, established pay floors and hourly ceilings, stressed the right of every able-bodied worker to a job and, for the first time, clearly placed responsibility for the well-being—housing, health, employment—of the worker in the lap of the government.

The depression had decimated unions, beaten down the workers' spirit, and set off bitter competition for jobs and food. In the garment industry the clock had been turned back so that while a few hardy ILGers continued to hold the fort in the big cities, the industry itself continued to leak out of the central markets to distant hideaways beyond the reach of the reviving ILGWU.

Conditions in the runaway shops are described in the selections by Perkins and W. G. Shepherd. Rose C. Feld reports the devastating revival of the homework evil; once again garments were being made from sunup to sundown, with women and children laboring alongside men. Whether the mode of payment was by time or by the piece, wages were still sweatshop wages and, more often than not, below the basic subsistence level.

In an effort to break the vicious cycle, the new administration in Washington launched a recovery program that included the creation of industry codes. These were formulated through the tripartite involvement of government, industry, and labor. They provided for basic wage schedules, details of which were reported by the *Christian Science Monitor*. When the National Industrial Recovery Act was declared unconstitutional, the Coat and Suit Industry created its own agency for self-regulation on all but wage matters; this event was described in *Business Week*.

ILGWU–garment center rally for Franklin D. Roosevelt showing corner of 38th Street and 7th Avenue (1940).

The basic task of reinstating decent work and wage standards was to be accomplished by the unions themselves, strengthened by right-to-organize legislation. In the larger cities bitter battles were fought to reestablish the hegemony of the ILGWU in the garment industry; a series of these conflicts in the New York dress industry was described in an article published in the *New Republic,* in a statement by the New York Dress Joint Board, and in the selection by David Scheyer.

As the ILGWU rapidly built up its membership and its resources, new frontiers were opened and the old machinery was revived. Three reports duly reported in hometown newspapers deal with incidents in Boston, Memphis, and St. Louis, where garment workers were stirred into battle for a better life. Workers were often pitted against each other in confrontations involving union spirit versus the lingering fear of joblessness and hunger.

That fear continued to flourish in the backward regions where the union had not yet penetrated. Life in these vestigial pockets of industrial darkness is dramatically described in the Pennsylvania state report by Myrl Cowdrick, who presents a gallery of portraits of the disinherited—many of whom earned little more than three cents an hour.

From the *Survey Graphic,* February 1933.

THE COST OF A FIVE-DOLLAR DRESS
by Frances Perkins

It hangs in the window of one of the little cash-and-carry stores that now line a street where fashionable New Yorkers used to drive out in their carriages to shop at Tiffany's and Constable's. It is a "supper dress" of silk crepe in "the new red," with medieval sleeves and graceful skirt. A cardboard tag on the shoulder reads: "Special $4.95." Bargain basements and little ready-to-wear shops are filled with similar "specials."

But the manufacturer who pays a living wage for a reasonable week's work under decent conditions cannot turn out attractive silk frocks to retail at $5 or less. The real cost is borne by the workers in the sweatshops that are springing up in hard-pressed communities. Under today's desperate need for work and wages, girls and women are found toiling overtime at power machines and worktables, some of them for paychecks that represent a wage of less than 10 cents a day.

The sweatshop employer is offending against industry's standards, as well as against the standards of the community. The employer who, in order to pay fair wages for reasonable hours of work, produces dresses in his shop to retail at $9.50, finds himself in competition with the less conscientious manufacturer whose "sweated" garments are offered at $4.95.

As we have come to know him in New York, this sweatshop proprietor is a "little fellow," doing business on a shoestring. He must make a quick turnover or go under. Since he cannot hope to meet union conditions or the requirements of the labor law, he goes to some outlying suburb where garment factories are not a feature of the local picture and where state inspectors are not on the lookout for him. Or perhaps he goes to a nearby state—New Jersey, Connecticut, Pennsylvania, Massachusetts—where he believes labor laws are less stringent or that he will escape attention.

The goods he makes up are probably cut in a city shop and "bootlegged" to him by truck. His operations are minutely subdivided so that they can be quickly learned and require little skill. His work force is made up of wives and daughters of local wage earners who have been out of work for months or even years and whose family situation is desperate. The boss sets the wage rates, figures the pay slips, determines the hours of work. His reply to any complaint is, "Quit if you don't like it."

The Massachusetts Commissioner of Labor and Industries, in a survey of wages paid in Fall River, reports the earnings of more than 50 percent of the women and girls employed on piecework were as follows in one plant:

One employee at 5 cents an hour; one employee at 6 cents an hour; three employees at 7 cents an hour; two employees at 8 cents; ten employees at 9 cents; nine employees at 10 cents; twelve employees at 12½ cents; thirteen employees at 13⅓ cents; eighteen employees at 14 cents; thirteen employees at 15 cents.

The report adds: "Assuming constant activity by those workers during the 48 hours of the plant's operation, the weekly earnings of the highest paid workers in the group just cited, namely, those earning 15 cents an hour, would have been $7.20."

The factories whose payrolls were studied in this survey had come to Fall River from New York and elsewhere, Commissioner Smith points out, "under the double lure of cheap rentals to be found in the discontinued textile mills and a surplus of unemployed female labor, mostly young, unskilled girls."

And he comments, "These plants are for the most part in the charge of men of inferior business caliber, who probably could not survive at all if it were not for their willingness to be entirely ruthless in exploiting labor."

Working conditions, including safety provisions, sanitation, rest room facilities and so on, are, like standards of wages and hours, holding up well in responsible concerns. In the runaway shop conditions are usually far below standard and the picture of such a plant is a look back to the sweatshops that horrified caseworkers and visiting nurses at the turn of the century.

What is the way out for the conscientious consumer who does not want to buy garments, even at a bargain, made by exploited labor? Common sense will tell the purchaser that someone must pay the price of the well-cut silk dress offered at $4.95. The manufacturer is not producing these frocks for pleasure or for charity. If the purchaser does not pay a price that allows for a subsistence wage and reasonable hours and working conditions, then the cost of the "bargain" must be sweated out of the workers.

The red silk bargain dress in the shop window is a danger signal. It is a warning of the return of the sweatshop, a challenge to us all to reinforce the gains we have made in our long and difficult progress toward a civilized industrial order.

An early New Deal strike in Easton, Pennsylvania.

With much of the garment industry moving out of the big cities into the country, investigative reporters, in the spirit of earlier muckrakers, reported their findings. The first of two accounts, by one who a generation earlier had reported the Triangle fire, is taken from *Collier's Magazine,* November 12, 1932.

SHOPS WITHOUT CLOCKS
by William G. Shepherd

In Middletown a company was making women's coats which retailed at about $35. A girl would come to this plant and ask for a job—and get it, instantly. Payday in this place came for a girl when, finally, in desperation, she made bold to tell her employer that she must have some money. The employer would reach into his trousers pocket and pull out a handful of change. He might ask a girl how long she had worked or how many cloaks she had sewn, or he might not. It all seemed to depend on his mood.

He would hand out the cash, according to his whim. Many such employers paid in cash in this way. The girl took what the boss gave her—and shut up. One defenseless woman with two children received $1.40 for two weeks' work in such a place. Fifty cents, 75 cents, 69 cents for the work of from four to ten days were payments that were uncovered.

One girl on the witness stand in a sweatshop case declared: "Why, I get more money for testifying one day than I got for a whole week's work in the factory. Here I have a chair to sit on, but the girls had to bring their own chairs to the factory where I worked, or stand all day at their machines." She was referring to the fact that the "fly-by-nighters" do not move bulky chairs in their gypsy-industry trucks.

They have no clocks to move, either. Most of the girls in these sweatshops testify that they are even asked not to wear wristwatches. In some places the girls are not allowed to talk to each other. No one ever seems to know what time it is, unless some street clock can be seen through a window or the town-clock chimes tell the secret.

The noon hour? Well, that comes when the boss shuts off the power and the machines stop. Lunch is over as soon as the boss starts the motor again and yells to the backward ones to "get to work."

From *Forum Magazine,* March 1935.

HOMEWORK
by Rose C. Feld

Where the sweatshop involved hundreds of workers, and those concentrated in industrial centers, the homework industries involve thousands, and these are scattered from Maine to California, with a vast number in outlying rural districts.

Ten cents an hour is considered a high wage in the up-to-date homework industry. Three cents an hour is not uncommon. One firm of children's knitted garments has 10,000 homeworkers "on call," employs 3,000 regularly, pays from 4 to 6 cents an hour (which is considered high), and has an annual payroll of $125,000. The pleating, stitching, Bonnaz and hand embroidery industry has 45,000 homeworkers scattered from New York to the Pacific coast.

For bringing this subject of homework out into the open, the writing of the NRA codes has been responsible. Over 600 of them have been drawn since July 1933.

Each industry went to Washington as an independent group, wrangled for a while, and wrote its own code. Where the mass of workers in the industry was factory-employed, the regulation of homework was strict, if the practice was not abolished altogether; where the industry was already preponderantly organized on a homework basis, the regulation was perfunctory. Outstanding in the fight for complete abolition of homework are the garment industries. Their strong labor organizations, determined to avoid the destruction of wage scales brought about by the free employment of homeworkers, have been the chief instruments in this success.

Each industry has four separate provisions in its code for conditions of labor. These are: (1) the limitation of labor to 40 hours a week; (2) a minimum wage somewhere between 30 and 35 cents an hour; (3) the prohibition of child labor; and (4) the right to collective bargaining. The fact remains that they have been widely violated. And one of the most prevalent forms of violation has been through the use of homeworkers.

American manufacturers in many industries have cut their factory personnel to a minimum and have turned to homework as the major source of their labor supply. Today, in tens of thousands of homes, the hours of labor run to 60 and 70 a week, wages range between 3 and 10 cents an hour, and the laborers may be immature children or feeble oldsters who would not be allowed inside a factory gate.

Price competition tempted marginal garment industry employers to evade the codes. When the National Industrial Recovery Act was declared unconstitutional in 1936, the New York cloak industry launched a unique effort at self-regulation. The first selection is from the *Christian Science Monitor,* July 6, 1933.

THE N.R.A. CODES

The sweatshop has returned to American industry in its worst form, and groups combatting the exploitation of workers are following with intense concern Washington proceedings on the fair practices code to be drawn up under provisions of the National Industrial Recovery Act, hoping that this code will make the present $4-a-week wage for 70 hours' work impossible.

Proof of the situation in the garment industry may be seen on every hand in fly-by-night stores of the bargain or receiver's sale variety throughout the United States.

While the jobber is the key to the era of cutthroat competition, the contractor alone knows the hardships endured by the workers, who have practically no escape from his decisions. Such a situation not only oppresses the workers, but exerts a powerful influence to depress the general conditions of the industry. And in the wake of the sweatshop, with its mismanagement of the common welfare and ignorant wastage of human effort, is an inevitable train of child dependence and delinquency and old age for which, on debased wages, no provision can be made.

According to David Dubinsky, president of the International Ladies' Garment Workers' Union, representing the workers of an industry which employs 182,000 women throughout the nation, "it is all due to the mad scramble for cheaper dresses forced on us by the jobbers.

"In 1930, dresses averaged $9 retail; in 1931 and 1932, $6; and in 1933, the price dropped to $3," he said. "Now we have $1.75, $1 and 50-cent dresses. There seems to be no bottom.

"Even at the low prices prevailing for dresses, I believe a better wage could be paid the workers if it were not for the mad desire of jobbers to make speculative profits."

The merchant demands rush delivery. Plenty of workers are to be had, and the manufacturer mans his plant for night and day work. The huge machines roar endlessly; the workers are pressed to the limit of their endurance, and in a week it is all over. The whole force is laid off and the factory shut down until the wasteful process begins again with another rush order.

On terms, then, of racketeering, cutthroat competition and sweated labor, Seventh Avenue, main stem of New York's biggest industry—garment making—has been able to remain a teeming thoroughfare throughout the slump. With prices the lowest in memory, this industry has stayed at the top of the city's production list.

The gypsy contractor does business on a shoestring, choosing for his location places outside the inspection rounds or in a state where labor laws are laxly enforced. In New York State he prefers Long Island, Staten Island and Westchester County, or he goes to Pennsylvania, Massachusetts, Connecticut, New Jersey, trucking his stuff into the retail center at night. . . .

In their desperate need for work and wages, girls and women jump at the invitation to "sit down right now at a machine and go to work"; they do not venture to inquire about wages and, indeed, some are told they must work a week, or even two, as learners. Even experienced workers are having to accept this invitation. At the end of the "learning period" they are told their work won't do and they are dimissed for a new group. By this trick a contractor can get several thousands of dresses sewn for almost nothing.

Thus is the plight of the women and girls of the needle trades being added to the saga of the southern textile operatives, the Kentucky miners and the jobless wanderers.

South River, New Jersey, garment workers made their own signs for August 30, 1932, walkout.

From *Business Week,* June 27, 1936.

THE CLOAK RECOVERY BOARD

On June 16, just one year after the expiration of the National Industrial Recovery Act, whose main provisions had previously been knocked out by the Supreme Court, the National Coat and Suit Industry Recovery Board held its first annual meeting in Washington. It celebrated as the "only functioning voluntary code organization in the United States." Employer associations and the unions performed the feat together.

Climax of the meeting was the announcement that management and labor had agreed to a program of jointly stimulating the industry's market. A council of business development will be created. Besides industry representatives, its labor members will be David Dubinsky, president of the International Ladies' Garment Workers' Union, and Isidore Nagler, general manager of the Joint Board of the Cloakmakers' Union, New York.

The move marks a revolution in the industry. The ILGWU is a mighty and shrewdly managed institution. Of its 200,000 members, some 45,000 are in the cloak and suit trade. Most powerful is the ILGWU's grip on the coat and suit trade. Labor requirements here are exacting. Men form 88 percent of the members in this group. They are craftsmen, old hands at the business, and they are not under pressure from new workmen since few youngsters want to be tailors. Further, shops are concentrated in large towns, under the strictest supervision for style and appearance. Hence, this industry has escaped competition from "runaway shops" which go outside the cities to draw labor from among farm and small-town girls.

But Dubinsky wanted to cut the high mortality rate of garment companies. During the precode powwows, they heard shop owners describe malpractices of trade which made stabilization impossible. Barring the usual frictions, the industry liked the code. Employers were appalled at the possible return of cat-and-dog competition when all NRA codes were killed on May 27, 1935. In desperation they retained a skeleton code organization, finally deciding to change the name of the authority and continue as a voluntary group.

Expiration date of NIRA was June 16. By July 15 the National Coat and Suit Industry Recovery Board had replaced the Blue Eagle with the "consumers' protection label."

At the Washington gathering, Alexander Printz, chairman of this "little NRA," announced that 91 percent of the industry's 1,800 employers were affiliated, that its standards of trade practices and employment had been maintained nationally. Seventeen million of the labels have been used on coats and suits. Women's clubs and consumer organizations that claim a membership of 5,000,000 have aided in promoting the label as a symbol of good working conditions.

A major effort was made to organize the main centers of the industry in the big cities. The following three selections record the different stages of that effort in New York's dress industry. The first is taken from the *New Republic,* March 9, 1932.

THE 1932 DRESS STRIKE

The dressmakers' strike in New York has just ended. The settlement is a reasonable compromise, whose exact terms are not important. What is important, from the public's point of view, is to know that almost certainly the settlement is only a temporary one. Sooner or later—and probably sooner—the workers will again be obliged to resort to strike tactics.

This strike was, of course, only the latest in a long series of revolts against conditions in this branch of the needle industry. Beginning with the great strike in 1909, when the first effective union was established among the dressmakers, the demoralization produced in the industry by the uncontrolled forces of competition has been reduced to some semblance of order and decency only by periodic uprisings of the workers.

Working conditions, bad enough before 1929, have, during our latest depression, fallen to the standards prevailing in the prewar sweatshops. Few who have not had the occasion to observe at firsthand the devastating effects of bad business can realize how completely the thousands who work for a living in the needle and textile industries have borne the full brunt of this depression in savage slashes of wages and in the total loss of the industrial rights for which they fought so courageously in the past. Nor was there any sign, before the strike was called on February 16, that the industry itself could be expected to take any measures to arrest the decline.

For the present state of affairs the manner in which the trade is organized is as responsible as the depression itself. Always an industry of small, changing and irresponsible employers, it reverted, under the stress of unfavorable postwar conditions, to the uncivilized methods of doing business which had prevailed before the union was first organized. Seeking the easiest way out of a difficult situation, many established manufacturers and more new ones succumbed to the methods of cutthroat competition. They abandoned their own shops; farmed out their patterns and work to contractors employing on the average hardly more than ten persons in a shop; reduced costs of production ruthlessly by playing off one contractor against another. Through it all they refused to regard themselves as manufacturers and, consequently, to accept any responsibility for working conditions in shops which in reality manufacture their own product.

With these problems the union has struggled for more than ten years. The control it managed from time to time to establish has again been dissipated by the depression. From the beginning of 1930, the non-union area has spread; wages and prices have been further reduced; and all pretense at effective regulation has been virtually abandoned. After two years of depression some 26,000 workers, 70 percent of them women, were employed on miserable terms in more than 2,500 shops.

When the agreement between the union and the employers in the industry terminated at the end of last year, the latter entered the new negotiations with demands calculated to aggravate conditions already intolerable. They insisted upon additional wage cuts. They sought to increase the excessive unemployment of the waistmakers by demanding unlimited overtime without extra pay and unlimited work on Saturday, thus rejecting the practice of the equal division of work, which, in this depression more than in any other, has been so universally urged upon American industry.

Finally, they undertook to destroy the remnants of union control by asking for the continuous right of free discharge and, what is worse, the right to discharge once a year 10 percent of the work force of each employer. With the employers holding such an attitude toward the problems of both the industry and the union, a strike designed to force fundamental reform was inevitable. In its counterdemands the union proposed measures not alone essential to the barest requirements of labor but to minimum standards of prosperity for the industry.

It is a high tribute to the courage and foresight of the dressmakers that, after years of starvation wages and the sufferings of unemployment, they were willing to face the added hardships of a strike for the purpose of reviving the power of their union and improving ever so little the conditions of themselves and their fellow workers, and that they have won even a partial victory, in these terms, is an equal tribute to their solidarity and spirit.

Text of New York Dress Joint Board general strike leaflet,
August 16, 1933.

DRESSMAKERS' GENERAL STRIKE DECLARED TODAY

The strike will remain in force until the Manufacturers, the
Jobbers and the Contractors will concede the just demands
of our Union, and until the Dress Industry is purged of
sweatshops.

ALL DRESSMAKERS OF THE UNION AND
NON-UNION SHOPS, CUTTERS, OPERATORS,
FINISHERS, PRESSERS, EXAMINERS, DRAPERS,
SAMPLEMAKERS, CLEANERS, ETC., ARE OR-
DERED TO LEAVE THEIR SHOPS PROMPTLY
AT 10 O'CLOCK THIS MORNING AND PRO-
CEED IN ORDERLY MANNER TO THE STRIKE
HALLS ASSIGNED TO THEM.

SISTERS AND BROTHERS! DRESSMAKERS! The International Ladies' Garment Workers' Union, under whose
banner you fought successfully your greatest battles, is calling you again to a **GENERAL STRIKE.** We are calling
this **STRIKE** for the purpose of establishing humane and
orderly working conditions in our great industry, and each
of you is expected to contribute his or her utmost to help
make this strike a complete **SUCCESS.**

**THE PRESENT SITUATION OF THE DRESSMAK-
ERS IS UNBEARABLE.** Never has it been so difficult for a
worker to earn his bread in a dress shop as it is today. The
general depression on the one hand, and the sweatshops
on the other, have made it possible for the employers to
break down the work standards in the shops which you,
dressmakers, have fought so hard to establish.

**WE MUST INTRODUCE A SHORTER WORK WEEK
IN ORDER THAT EVERY DRESSMAKER SHALL
HAVE EMPLOYMENT.** We must improve our living
standards by increasing our earnings. We must establish a
guaranteed minimum scale for every worker in the industry to assure us a living wage. We must eliminate the use by
the jobber of one shop against another and one worker
against the other for the purpose of lowering labor costs.
We must place upon the jobber responsibility for condi-

tions in contracting shops. We must establish our right to the job. We must have a strong and powerful union to enforce union standards and union conditions for us in every dress shop every day of the year.

> THIS GENERAL STRIKE IS BEING CALLED TO MAKE AN END TO THE MISERY AND CHAOS IN THE DRESS SHOPS, TO INTRODUCE UNION CONDITIONS IN THE ENTIRE INDUSTRY, AND TO ENABLE THE DRESSMAKERS TO WORK LIKE HUMAN BEINGS AND TO LIVE LIKE HUMAN BEINGS.

ON WITH THE STRIKE!   ON TO VICTORY!

A heated exchange outside dress shop in Newark (1933).

From the *Nation,* February 19, 1936.

THE 1936 CHALLENGE
by David Scheyer

For three months the jobbers' organization, the National Association of Dress Manufacturers, the United Manufacturers to which the contractors belonged, and the Affiliated, the association of "inside manufacturers" (who make dresses complete on their own premises)—all refused to meet with the union. So the International Ladies' Garment Workers' Union went ahead with its strike preparations, secure in the knowledge that it had a defense fund of $1.5 million and the unswerving loyalty of 100,000 dressmakers.

With the expiration of the agreement at hand the union was ready to act. The jobbers and contractors suddenly began screaming in anguish as they saw a stoppage coming just at the peak of the season. They ran to Mayor La Guardia. They ran to the newspapers. And finally they ran to the union to find out just how little they could give.

Meanwhile the three employers' associations have become five. The jobbers of cheap dresses left the National to form the Popular Price Association. Similarly, the contractors in the low-priced line organized the Interstate Association. The old contractors' group, the United, is on its way out. . . .

For two weeks now the weary-eyed, tired-voiced committee of the union—Dubinsky, Hochman, Zimmerman, Antonini and others—have been sitting through endless nights of conferences trying to discover some responsible group to bargain with. The disintegration, the clash of interests . . . of the employers have made an agreement almost impossible—impossible, that is, without the purgative of a general strike.

The Joint Board of the ILGWU alone has shown a sense of responsibility in this maelstrom. It has sought every possible means to avoid a strike that would be tremendously costly not only to the workers but to New York's economic life as well. One thing it has not done and will not do—abate demands for bringing a decent life to the dressmakers and order to the industry.

On February 3, when Dubinsky and Hochman reported to a meeting of 5,000 shop chairmen at Manhattan Opera House, it seemed that some agreement might be reached, but negotiations broke down. The union then acted. On February 7, 20,000 dressmakers in Madison Square Garden gave their mandate in the ceaseless chant, "We want a strike!" Hurriedly the employers renewed negotiations. It would be a good thing if the union demands could be won in conference, but if they cannot, the whir of 50,000 sewing machines will be stilled in the greatest strike New York has ever known.

In other cities ILGWU drives paralleled the New York effort, as the following three reports demonstrate. The first is taken from the *Boston Herald*, March 4, 1936.

CONFRONTATION ON KNEELAND STREET

Catching the police off guard because of a misunderstanding, 2,000 striking garment workers swept into Kneeland Street shortly before 6 o'clock last night, tried to drag 6 women from a motorcar and rioted for 20 minutes in the heavy homeward-bound traffic before reserves from all sections of the city could restore order.

It was the most serious outbreak of violence thus far in the nearly week-old strike of 4,500 men and women workers in the garment industry.

Between 25 and 30 men were injured and the police last night were trying to get the names of the women in the car which was rushed, in the event that any were seriously injured. Three arrests were made, including the leader of the strike, Philip Kramer, vice president of the International Ladies' Garment Workers' Union.

A total of 7 were arrested during the day, all for assault and battery. Until the Kneeland Street rioting last night, most of the violence during the day was outside a large non-union shop on Shawmut Avenue.

To protect his workers, the owner of the Shawmut Avenue shop started equity proceedings in Suffolk Superior Court yesterday and succeeded in drawing from the union an agreement not to resort to violence or threats pending a hearing on a temporary injunction tomorrow. The stipulation, however, does not exclude "peaceful" picketing, and applies only to the Shawmut Avenue establishment.

Inspectors Benjamin Goodman and William Goulston of the radical squad, and Lieutenant Harold Mitten were assured at about 5:30 o'clock last night by manufacturers that all workers in the non-union shops in the large garment building at 75 Kneeland Street had been dismissed for the day, including the force of mounted police, which has been very effective in keeping the crowds in the strike area scattered.

When there was hardly a handful of patrolmen left in the district, strikers stormed into Kneeland Street from Harrison Avenue and Tyler, Hudson and Harvard Streets. The police were not immediately alarmed, as they had been convinced all strikebreakers and other workers were out of the area.

At about the same time a car drew up to the building at 75 Kneeland Street. A few seconds later 6 women, alleged by the union to be strikebreakers, hurried out of the building and jumped into the car.

Before the door of the machine had closed, a score of strikers, all men, charged across Kneeland Street and surrounded the car.

Severe rioting then followed for the length of Kneeland Street, from Harrison Avenue to beyond Hudson Street, two blocks away. The riot call was sounded from the patrol box at Tyler Street and Harrison Avenue, and reserves were rushed in patrol wagons and cruising cars into the area. At the height of the battle, Sergeant Henry Bailey, who then had only a few patrolmen at his command, ordered clubs drawn.

Later police bitterly criticized the manufacturers for giving them erroneous information that all strikebreakers had left the shops. Throughout the day the police, by frequent conferences with other manufacturers, had got all workers out of the Kneeland Street district unharmed and with only mild demonstrations.

From the *Memphis Press Scimitar,* March 24, 1937.

CLOTHES FLY

Feminine clothing flew in disorders which this morning marked the opening of a strike against the Nona-Lee Dress Company. The disorders, in which 11 were arrested, occurred as non-union workers attempted to enter the plant.

All 11 union members arrested were released on $15 bond each during the noon hour. Charges of threatened breach of the peace were lifted.

Several women were disrobed in the all-feminine affrays, which proved too much for a force of 15 policemen on the scene. The major clashes occurred at 8:30 A.M. when a battalion of girl workers attempted to march through the picket lines maintained by nearly 100 union members. About 40 girls finally got into the factory. The firm normally employs more than 100 operators.

As the workers moved from Adams to Jefferson Street, union workers rushed to Jefferson to meet the girls at the intersection. Girls rolled on the pavement among hats, blouses, skirts and undergarments.

As police quelled the disorder, the workers moved on around the Crane Company to the front door of the factory. There a reserve squadron of unionists, apparently left to prevent girls from moving into the plant from an opposite direction while attention was diverted to the Jefferson corner, rushed the group from across the street.

For two or three minutes clothing flew again. Workers tugged them away from the door, and police tugged to maintain order.

Both the firm and the union claimed that a majority of the workers were with them.

Things got a little out of hand at St. Louis, Missouri, dress picket line in September 1933.

From the *St. Louis Star-Times,* March 24, 1937.

LOCKOUT INTO STRIKE

The number of major strikes and lockouts current in St. Louis reached eight today when the International Ladies' Garment Workers' Union told its members not to report for work at the Solomon Manufacturing Co.

Union officials, who threw a heavy picket line about the plant at the opening hour today, said about 125 workers answered the strike call. Company officers said the picket line was made up of outsiders and maintained that only a few of the firm's employees were participating in the strike.

Several arguments and face slappings occurred when girls, confused by the heavy picketing, appeared to be hesitating between entering the plant to work and joining the strikers.

After several hours of such conduct, a police detail led by Assistant Chief John H. Glasscoe arrested 13 women pickets and ordered the line reduced in size.

Nonstriking workers who attempted to enter the plant found the doorway blocked by pickets. About 6 girls pushed their way through, aided by the police, while a group of about 50 women waited across the street, apparently unable to decide whether to attempt to push their way in or to join the strike forces.

During the scuffle when the 6 girls entered, several striking women were pushed to the floor of the doorway, where 3 of them continued to lie prone in an effort to block entrance. After a few minutes patrolmen lifted the women to their feet, the nonstriking workers entered and the brief scuffle was ended.

The union's main organizing task lay in the out-of-town areas. Hunger, unemployment, fear, antiunion local governments, runaway firms—all combined to keep low-paid workers out of reach of the union. The following excerpt is taken from the bulletin published in 1936 by the Commonwealth of Pennsylvania, Department of Labor and Industry, Bureau of Women and Children.

THREE CENTS AN HOUR
by Myrl Cowdrick

Would it astonish you to know that in thousands of pitiful workshops-within-the-home in Pennsylvania there exists a shameless exploitation of the labor of women and children?

As a member of the consuming public, would it interest you to know that in a considerable number of industries women toil long hours, illegal hours, for as low as one cent an hour to produce articles which you use in everyday life?

Would it horrify you to know that more than 600 firms, taking advantage of the desperate need of these workers, pay wages too low to support life, and are dipping into the community welfare chest, the state emergency relief, and also federal government grants, to meet their payroll? When welfare funds must be used to help the sweatshop operator, it is small wonder that workers are willing to accept the dole rather than accept a below-subsistence wage.

In small-town and rural newspapers throughout the state there are constantly appearing advertisements seeking to recruit the large army of women knitting baby sacques, caps, booties, and embroidering fine dresses at incredibly low wages. Employers maintain no factories; the plants are the humble homes, and the usual costs of production, light, heat and rent, are borne by the women workers. Herein, also, lies an interstate industrial problem.

The enactment of a stringent homework law in New York State has resulted in a migration of homework into Pennsylvania to escape rigid regulation. Parcel post makes it easy to deliver materials to these humblest of all workers who labor long hours silently, in isolation, having no contacts with fellow workers and no voice in rates of re-muneration.

> Mrs. K has worked ten years for one firm, earning 2⅔ cents per hour, knitting baby sacques at $1 per dozen, for which she was formerly paid $1.50 per dozen. The retail price of the sacque is 59 cents but the employer answered the protest against the low wage by saying that he "could not make much on the deal."
>
> Mrs. G says she is "knitting the sacques because she is desperately in need of the money, but too many women do it for pastime and so will work for nothing, which spoils it for those who really need the work." She thinks "something should be done to make the employer pay better wages." She earns 3 cents per hour, or about 9.5 cents per sacque.
>
> Mrs. S needs the work badly because her husband has little employment and they have six little children to feed and clothe. She is so tired at night when she begins to knit and it makes her nerves very bad.
>
> Mrs. M's husband is 84 and she is 72. She knits to supplement his pension of $12 per month and says she earns about $4 per month.
>
> Miss K is a spinster living with her aged father. In addition to taking in washing and sewing, she crochets baby booties earning 3 cents per hour. Her last weekly pay was about 50 cents.

Another widely scattered form of industrial homework is the handwork on infants' and children's dresses. Even machine-made dresses require some handwork, such as smocking, fagoting, embroidering and turning of collars and cuffs. Some manufacturers find it more profitable to send the work to Puerto Rico. Then there are the dainty all handmade dresses which are sold in the finest shops in America. The home worker pays the price for the fortunate mother who insists upon exquisite handwork for her baby's things. Each dress sells for more than the price paid to the worker for a dozen.

> Mrs. M, whose husband is an unemployed miner, embroiders collars at $1.88 per dozen. To earn 13 cents per hour, she must work from 6 A.M. to 10 P.M. She says "her back is so tired at the end of the day she can hardly straighten up." She must go to a neighboring town by bus for the work.
>
> When Mrs. P protested to her employer that his rate of 25 cents per dozen dresses meant 25 cents per day for her, his reply was that if she was not satisfied he could find many other women to do the work. There is no other employment to

Madison Square Garden II on 8th Avenue was frequent rallying place of garment workers preparing to strike if contract-renewal negotiations broke off.

which she can turn to supplement her husband's part-time wage of $9 per week for work in a foundry. Four children must be fed.

The widow S receives a Mothers' Assistance stipend of $50 per month because she has nine children, three of whom work at the mill. When she is not cooking meals, washing clothes, cleaning house, or looking after her children, she knits sweaters for which she is paid $3 and $4. She cannot accomplish as much as her neighbors, who do not have her responsibilities, so she is not given work as frequently. Her employer charges her 30 cents to deliver the work to her. She often works by the light of the radio with blinds drawn so her neighbors will not tell the inspectors she is breaking the law. Her eyes are becoming steadily weaker.

11. Way of Life

The Protocol of Peace, negotiated in 1910, marked the point at which the ILGWU for the first time had moved beyond the question of wages and hours in its fight to improve the lives of garment workers. Drawing strength not only from its own ranks but also from favorable public opinion, the union opened new areas of concern: health, education, political action.

The selection by Charles P. Sweeney, taken from a rare government report, belongs to the pre-radio, pre-television era when hundreds of workers learned to turn to their union for instruction in citizenship education, literature and music appreciation, English, and to take a more active part in union and community life. The pioneer effort described in Sweeney's report was soon followed by similar programs in other garment centers throughout the country.

In the first major increase in union membership during the New Deal years, educational programs became an important adjunct of the union's organizing efforts. Leaflets, pamphlets, and dramatizations supplemented union meetings in the general effort to explain organizational issues to workers.

The most brilliant and memorable production of the period was the ebullient and witty topical revue staged by the union, with a cast drawn directly from the shops, that made "Pins and Needles" a byword of the American theater. Heywood Broun's article reflects the general acclaim that cut across class distinctions.

As the nation moved into the shadow of war in Europe, ILGers began a number of aid and preparedness activities. They organized overseas programs for servicemen and engaged in child rescue efforts. At home the ILGWU sponsored bond sales, civilian defense aid, conservation programs, etc. These activities are discussed in the selections from the *Chicago Sun, Women's Wear Daily,* and the excerpts by Eric Hawkins and by Eleanor Roosevelt describing her wartime visit to Unity House, the ILGWU summer resort in Pennsylvania.

At about this time the pace of work in the shops intensified. Economic pressure mounted as hard goods became scarce, soft goods sales rose, and wages were frozen. The ILGWU was partially able to relieve this pressure by channeling it into new negotiated benefits, most notably in the areas of retirement and health care. These efforts are described in the reports from the *New York Times* and the analysis by Eleanor Herrick.

The union continued its political and legislative activities up to the end of the war. FDR's last campaign (1944) took him to New York City, which once again demonstrated its enthusiastic support; the event is described by the *New York Times*. The ILGWU had consolidated its position—on the picket line, at the bargaining table, and in the polling booth.

At the half-century mark, the union confronted new problems. The ILGWU celebrated its anniversary with a film, *With These Hands*, which chronicled the history of free-trade unionism. In two decades the ILGWU had developed from a union with few members and fewer resources to one of the most prestigious in the family of unions. Ironically, one of the problems created as a result of its success was the growing reluctance of workers—most of whom were now earning fairly good salaries—to move out of the shop and onto the union staff rolls for work in the ILGWU's far-flung frontiers. To meet this need, the union created its own school for the training of organizers, thus providing yet another instance of its pioneer spirit.

During these years the ILGWU bore the strong impress of one man, David Dubinsky, whose name became synonymous with the union throughout the world. Linking the Old World to the New, bridging socialist reform and American pragmatism, voicing the hopes and aspirations of all garment workers for a better life, Dubinsky proved himself a mover in the trade union arena, in American politics and, during World War II, throughout the free world.

A. H. Raskin and Ralph McGill assessed his union contributions at the time of his retirement in March 1966. Five short selections reflect David Dubinsky's enduring idealism and practical dedication.

The rapid turnover in union membership added special significance to the ILGWU's pioneer educational program. From *Bulletin 271*, U.S. Bureau of Labor Statistics, August 1920.

THE ILGWU WORKERS' UNIVERSITY
by Charles P. Sweeney

The first systematic scheme of education undertaken by organized workmen in the United States was put in practice in 1916 by the International Ladies' Garment Workers' Union. So responsive have the members of this union been to the opportunity for continued education that up to the spring of 1919 eight hundred of them had either completed one or more courses or were engaged in the study of the various subjects included in the curriculum of the Workers' University, as this effort in working-class education is called.

Probably the measure of the success attained by the Workers' University in so short a period would not have been so great were it not for the fact that the majority of the membership of the ILGWU is concentrated in one community—New York City. What would be for other unions a great problem—that of bridging the distance between groups of workers—is for the ILGWU, therefore, no problem at all. To achieve the degree of enthusiasm over the subject of education that has been created by the Workers' University movement, it would probably be necessary, in any American community except New York or Chicago, to make the appeal to all workers, as such, and not to the members of a specific craft group.

For the payment of the current expenses of the university and for the purpose of stimulating greater desire for education on the part of its members the ILGWU makes an annual appropriation of $10,000. Inasmuch as it is from the union dues that this appropriation is made the classes and all other activities are free to members.

At the time the report was made the university was conducting regular and systematic work by means of unity centers in Public School 40, 314 East Twentieth Street; Public School 63, First Avenue and Fourth Street; Public School 84, at Glenmore and Stone Avenues, Brownsville. Central classes were conducted in the Washington Irving High School, Sixteenth Street and Irving Place, and in one branch of the New York Public Library. Through such a distribution of centers for its work the university aims to afford educational opportunities to the union members in the sections nearest their homes. This use of public school buildings in convenient locations might be adopted by any other community in the country interested in the provision of education of this character.

The following is a statement regarding the classes carried on, 1918–1919, in the unity centers:

Classes		Activities per week
19	classes in English; three times a week	57
4	health lectures (these lectures are given by prominent physicians and attended by audiences of from 200 to 500)	4
3	classes in literature or reading circles	3
3	classes in gymnastics	3
1	moving-picture center	1
3	public speaking classes	3
1	special class for business agents where public speaking and economics are taught	1
		72

In the central classes at the Washington Irving High School courses were offered in social interpretation of literature, evolution and the labor movement, problems of reconstruction, sociology and civilization, labor legislation, social problems, trade unionism, cooperation, etc. With the exception of a few that consist of from 3 to 6 lectures, each of the above-mentioned courses comprised from 10 to 20 lectures, given weekly.

An examination of the syllabus of the university discloses quite as comprehensive and attractive a program as possible after a short period of development. Use of a section of the New York Public Library, Epiphany Branch, on East Twenty-third Street, has been obtained for Friday, between 3 and 6 P.M., for classes for business agents of the union. The subjects taught are advanced English, public speaking, and economics. It is the purpose in this particular work to develop the leadership of each business agent to the highest possible degree.

In all classes and branches of the work English is taught by school-teachers regularly employed by the Board of Education and paid extra for night work. The Educational Department has stressed the importance of students being able to read, write, and speak English before any other study is undertaken, with the result that the English classes register a larger attendance than any other except those in health and hygiene. And this number will undoubtedly be greatly augmented, since by a recent ruling of the Board of Education only English may be spoken in the schools.

The teaching of English is not confined to members of the union. Day classes have been formed in order that the wives of members may also have the opportunity of acquiring familiarity with the language. These classes are held in schools, union headquarters, and wherever a building can be obtained for them. Much attention is also paid to the [health] care, and gymnasium classes are an important feature of the work at the various centers.

The teachers, with the exception of those furnished by the Board of Education, are associated as professors or instructors with the universities and colleges in and about New York City, and several of them are men of national reputation in educational and labor matters.

In a variety of ways the Educational Department is pressing for increased attendance [in] present classes and for membership for new ones. Speakers visit meetings of local branches of the union to arouse interest in the movement. Circular letters go frequently to individual members urging them to investigate for themselves the advantages of attendance at classes. Posters are placed in branch headquarters and in other places frequented by workers announcing particular features of the university work, and the labor and the foreign-language press are also employed in the general effort to stimulate to the point of activity a desire for knowledge by the workers.

Through arrangements with managers of leading local theaters the Educational Department issues passes to the members of the union, thus enabling them to see good plays at a minimum price, which is sometimes as low as 20 cents for a dollar ticket. Discussions and lectures on the plays are arranged either before or after their presentation. The reduction in price, the department believes, is of minor importance compared with the opportunity for discussion of the relative merits of the different plays afforded the various groups who are able to attend them.

An extension educational service is maintained through which any local may secure the introduction of desired educational activities. These usually take the form of lectures on topics of special interest to

Garment workers mixed learning with play at ILGWU summer resort in Pennsylvania, Unity House. On afternoon of July 8, 1925, Theresa Wolfson lectured on women in the trade union movement at meeting directed by Fannia M. Cohn (right), union's educational director.

Gymnastics class, ILGWU Workers University, February 1926. (Photo by Jessie Tarbox Beals)

the workers, such as trade unionism, history of the labor movement, industrial democracy, political action, piece and time work, shorter workday, etc. The lectures, which, with a short musical program, are usually given at the regular business meetings, help "to increase the attendance at the meetings, stimulate interest among the members, establish a friendly spirit, and strengthen the organization."

There were connected with the educational work of the university, for the season ending April 1919, 44 lecturers, 19 teachers, 88 entertainers, 10 volunteers, 10 members of the staff (supervisors of unity centers), and 4 office workers, making a total of 175.

In addition to the local work which the union does to stimulate educational activity, letters, circulars, and literature in connection with the New York movement are sent to each local of the ILGWU in the United States and Canada urging the introduction of educational activities and offering such services as the New York organization can render. In Philadelphia a beginning has been made with eight classes in English of two periods each, conducted by four teachers; a class in literature and one in economics; a chorus and an orchestra.

A generation later, the New Deal upsurge in ILGWU membership spread a sense of zeal and confidence throughout the union's ranks. In New York, a musical revue produced by the ILGWU's Labor Stage made theatrical history. The following report by Broun (1888–1939), a noted newspaper columnist and founder of the Newspaper Guild, is taken from *Pic Magazine,* August 9, 1938.

"PINS AND NEEDLES"
by Heywood Broun

The drama critics of New York got the surprise of their lives at the first night of "Pins and Needles." Indeed, some of the first-string men had to wait to be surprised because they didn't attend until after the opening.

The general lack of preliminary enthusiasm did not rest on any snobbish feeling. It was built on experience rather than economic theory. In New York, at any rate, the labor stage began in somewhat feeble fashion. And when it did break through with something interesting the theme was nearly always of a serious nature.

The thing which seemed so forbidding about "Pins and Needles," before the event, was the announcement that here would be a revue put on entirely by members of the ILGWU, and those initials stand for International Ladies' Garment Workers' Union. The men and women of the organization make many clothes which first nighters wear, but a young lady may be highly competent in the sewing of a gown and yet not precisely the type to wear it to best advantage.

To put it bluntly, the reviewers believed that the girls who came from the machines might be less pulchritudinous than those whom Ziegfeld chose or even the dancers now selected by the Shuberts. In a sense the critics were right. Mr. Dubinsky and the men he nominated to put on the show were not wholly intent upon glorifying the American girl and finding the particular misses who would go on to a career of marrying rich men or advertising toothpaste, or both.

The chorus girls in "Pins and Needles" came from the workbenches and have every intention of going back to the job. Each person in the cast, whether cutter, stitcher, finisher or machine operator received precisely the same pay in the theatre as in the garment factories. But each and every one brought an enormous zest and enthusiasm and spirit of fun. This is truly a cooperative show. The actors have a good time, and so it has turned out to be the most amusing revue of this or any other season within the recent memory of men.

Some of the performers are highly talented, but in the judgment of this critic there is not a real star in the crowd. Teamwork has been the motto. Although the various numbers depend upon no central plot, there is a coherent idea which holds the entertainment together. The object is mockery. The smug and conservative are held up to ridicule as persons blind to the nature of the world in which they live.

Although the raillery is sharp and pointed, the wounds inflicted are not painful since the weapons are anaesthetized with humor. Indeed, much of the patronage of "Pins and Needles" has been of the carriage trade variety. This is a virtue or a vice, as you choose to look at it. The piece is not revolutionary in its temper, and while stout ladies in ermine must realize that they are being kidded, few if any have rushed screaming into the night. No dowager has been observed standing on a street corner waiting for a tumbril.

"Pins and Needles" was not a show created overnight. Under the leadership of David Dubinsky, the ILGWU, in addition to its trade union functions concerning hours and wages, has conducted throughout the years all kinds of cultural activities, and it would not surprise me at all to learn that the union now stands as a finer educational institution than Yale or Harvard, Vassar or Barnard.

At any rate its students have learned to perfection the useful art of jabbing, and naturally I refer to the left jab.

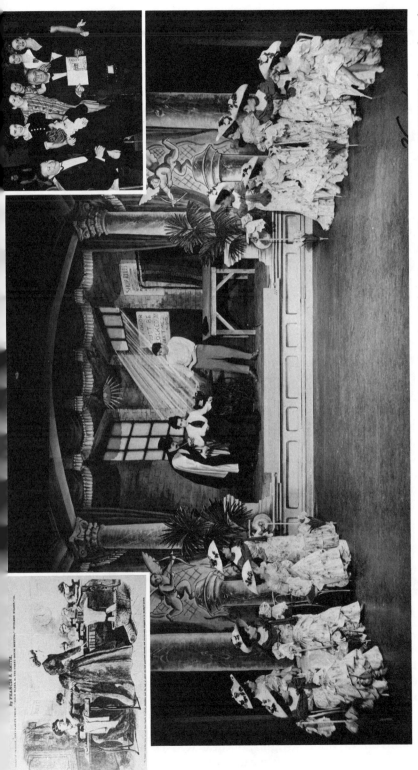

Some six decades later, Bertha lives again in ILGWU's famed early New Deal revue, *Pins and Needles*. Insets show original Bertha and ILGWU members of the cast with union president David Dubinsky and President Franklin D. Roosevelt at 1939 "command performance" at the White House.

Union educational and aid efforts were stepped up as a result of World War II. The following four excerpts indicate these new directions. The first account is from the *New York Herald Tribune,* July 23, 1942.

THE ILGWU MERCHANT NAVY CLUB IN LONDON

by Eric Hawkins

The Merchant Navy Club of London, which was founded on a gift of $75,000 by the International Ladies' Garment Workers' Union, was opened in the West End today by Ernest Bevin, British Minister of Labor and National Service, and John G. Winant, American Ambassador to the Court of St. James.

A. V. Alexander, First Lord of the Admiralty, and Sir Arthur Salter, Parliamentary Secretary to the Ministry of War Transport, attended the dedication. David Dubinsky, ILGWU president, broadcast from New York a message of greeting which was heard by a large gathering of officials and mercantile marine men.

Bevin said the institution, which will be open to officers and men of the British Merchant Marine, originated as a spontaneous gesture by American workers "to pay tribute to the courage and sacrifice of our seamen at war." The donation of $75,000, which was made before the United States entered the war, was transmitted by Mr. Dubinsky to found the club "as a permanent monument to symbolize the labor movement's support and sympathy for Britain."

Ambassador Winant, praising the donors of the gift, said: "I wish some of those great-hearted workers could see these handsome premises in the heart of London and the delight and comfort they will provide for merchant navy men on leave.

"This club is a striking manifestation of the eagerness we all feel to care for seamen ashore, and no seaman coming here can have any doubt that his service in the war ranks among the highest in the hearts of the people."

Dubinsky in his broadcast expressed the spirit of the garment workers' gesture and raised a round of applause when he referred to the Merchant Navy Club as "another symbol of the unity of the United States and Great Britain." This was reiterated by Alexander, who praised the heroism of the merchant seamen.

The club, which is situated in Rupert Street, a block from Piccadilly Circus, was formerly a fashionable Florence restaurant. It has spacious rooms on two floors. Brightly decorated, it has been arranged so as to provide all home comforts to its visitors. It will be run as a company, controlled by a council, the chairman of which will be Ambassador Winant. Members of the council will include parliamentary and shipping officials.

From the *Chicago Sun,* August 12, 1942.

FIRST AID FIRST

In the performance of some 400 Chicago women and girls of the International Ladies' Garment Workers' Union there is a challenge for all of us who say we want to do all we can in the war effort.

These women, after a day's exacting and tiring work from 8:30 to 4:30 in the clothing factories, hurry to the union's Educational Department at 222 West Monroe Street to attend Red Cross classes in first aid, food nutrition and home nursing. It is not easy for them to sit down for two hours of hard study up to 7 P.M., after a confining day at a sewing machine, and, except for a snack, to postpone supper until they reach home after Red Cross classes. But these women are determined to do their part for the preservation of a system that makes possible garment workers' unions.

The Chicago chapter of the American Red Cross properly honored these women at a ceremony last week when certificates were presented to 60 of them who have completed at least one of the three required courses.

These Italian dressmakers won a league championship in 1942.

We might all honor them by asking ourselves, as we sit in the darkness of tonight's blackout, with its reminder that what couldn't but did happen in many parts of the world might also happen here, "Am I doing all that I can for my country and my liberty?"

From *Women's Wear Daily,* January 25, 1944.

ILGWU LAUNCHES LIBERTY SHIPS

BALTIMORE—Two Liberty Ships named in memory of two former leaders of the ILGWU were launched here this afternoon from the Bethlehem-Fairfield shipyards while several hundred spectators looked on.

The *Benjamin Schlesinger* and the *Meyer London* slid off the rails following a brief ceremony that saw the new ships christened by daughters of the former labor leaders. The ship donor is the New York Dress Joint Board, ILGWU, whose members purchased over $8,000,000 in war bonds during the last drive.

Two more ship launchings are scheduled for a later date. These will be named in memory of the late Morris Sigman and Morris Hillquit, who served the ILGWU as president and counsel, respectively, in the sweatshop era of the needle industries in New York City.

From the *New York World Telegram,* June 21, 1945.

AT UNITY HOUSE
by Eleanor Roosevelt

I want to speak of two things today which especially impressed me at the International Ladies' Garment Workers' Union's vacation resort. It seemed to me worthy of comment that the bond drive rally was started by calling for contributions from individuals. As I sat there and saw young women and young men, fathers of families, older men and women, all get up one after the other and pledge to buy anything from a $100 bond up to a $1,000 bond, I could not help thinking, "Thank God for the United States."

The membership of this union is 75 percent women, and therefore many of those at the rally had their interests centered in the fighting forces. By this contribution they could share, not only through their daily work but through their savings, in the daily lives of their men fighting in distant lands. Their ability to make this investment must have been a great satisfaction to them.

The second thing which I thought worthy of note was the number of children getting their chance at country life. Provision is made for them at Unity House. They have a playground of their own and trained people to guide them in work and in play. No matter how much of this world's goods you have, you could not put children in a more favorable environment; and that is something for us as a nation to be proud of.

The war years were prosperous years for garment workers. A growing consumer demand for hard goods, which were in short supply, was channeled to soft goods. With wages under control, unions won many social benefits. From the *New York Times*, May 28, 1943.

FIRST ILGWU RETIREMENT FUND

The first industry-wide agreement under which industry as such assumes responsibility for old-age pensions for its employees was announced yesterday by Israel Feinberg, general manager of the Cloakmakers' Union, an affiliate of the International Ladies' Garment Workers' Union. Thirty-five thousand workers are affected.

The agreement, which extends for five years the industry contract which expires May 31, was signed with the Industrial Council of Cloak and Suit Manufacturers, the Merchants Ladies' Garment Association and the Infants' and Children's Coat Association. It was ratified yesterday by the union.

Under the old-age retirement plan, the manufacturers will contribute 3 percent of their weekly payrolls to a fund to provide pensions for workers who have reached the age of 65 or over and want to retire. The total annual amount to be contributed by the employers will be about $2,000,000. Mr. Feinberg explained that approximately 5,000 workers would be eligible for retirement within the next few years. Each will receive $600 a year.

The retirement fund will be administered by a commission to consist of an equal number of representatives of employers and employees, with three additional members representing the public, to be chosen by the employer associations and by the union.

The employers' contributions will begin on January 1, 1944. The fund will begin functioning within three years, as soon as a specified reserve is accumulated.

Creation of the retirement fund marks the only major addition to the old agreement for the industry, which is to be renewed after May 31, with a clause providing for readjustment of wages in the event of further rises in the cost of living or a change in the War Labor Board's Little Steel wage ceiling formula.

From the *New York Times*, March 23, 1944.

FIRST ILGWU HEALTH FUND

New three-year agreements providing for health insurance financed by the employers were signed yesterday by the Dressmakers' Union, an affiliate of the International Ladies' Garment Workers' Union, and four of the five employer associations in the industry.

The agreements covered 554 shops with 57,000 workers. While the union agreed to hold in abeyance its demand for a general wage increase, it obtained rises in the old minimum rates, paid vacations and establishment of a health insurance fund to be financed by the employers through contributions of 3.5 percent of weekly payrolls, beginning on May 1.

This marked the first adoption of such a plan through collective agreements in any major industry. Contributions to the health insurance fund will amount to $3,500,000 annually.

Regarding general wage increases, it was agreed by the union and the four signatory employer associations that the question might be reopened if the government modified its wage stabilization policy or the War Labor Board altered the Little Steel wage ceiling formula. In such event the question of wages would be brought before the impartial chairman of the industry.

The increases on minimum rates included in the new agreements, Julius Hochman explained, did not require approval of the War Labor Board, since most of the workers earned more than the new minimums. Nor would the new minimums add to the prices being paid by consumers, Mr. Hochman said.

"With the New York dress industry increasing its volume from $344,505,000 in 1940 to $527,000,000 in 1943, the union felt that its proposal for a general wage increase was moderate and entirely justified," Mr. Hochman commented. "In deference to national policy and desiring to maintain uninterrupted production in the New York market, the union made the concession of delaying its wage increase proposal."

From the *New York Herald Tribune,* August 19, 1948.

ILGWU WELFARE FUNDS
by Eleanor M. Herrick

The International Ladies' Garment Workers' Union is self-insured and administers its welfare funds through union channels. However, their funds are controlled jointly by representatives of employers and workers, though actual operation of the funds is in the hands of workers exclusively. It is understood in the agreement that the day-to-day operation of the fund is in the hands of the unions, subject to review, subject to criticism and subject to change.

Adolph Held, manager of the ILGWU welfare and health benefits program, says: "This is very essential. It took a good deal of argument to bring it about. But the relations with our employers have been so good for the last 10 years that we were finally able to convince them that this was the best way to administer the plan. And now, after two years of successful operation, they are very happy that we did take the job of running it."

The General Executive Board of the ILGWU has set up the basic policies for protection of the welfare funds. Within each local union a workers' health committee operates as a court of appeals for any claim that may be made by a worker who thinks himself mistreated in regard to benefit payments.

The ILGWU has pioneered in prepaid medical care, operating its own diagnostic clinics, notably in New York City, Philadelphia and Fall River. The clinical aspect of the program is being rapidly expanded. In localities where there are an insufficient number of members for a health center, the union organizes and trains teams of technicians who work under the direction of a local physician visiting factories to give examinations. Reports are sent to the individual's personal physician.

No other union has followed this pattern, but anyone visiting the six floors occupied by the New York Union Health Center will be impressed by the modern equipment, the thoroughness of the service rendered and its value to the community as a whole because of the care it gives to the 165,000 who used it in a single year.   •

In the ILGWU program it seems to me one finds the essence of sound welfare planning, safeguarded by employer participation in the trusteeship of the funds to which they contribute, but with a wise and mature union leadership doing the actual administration. It must be recognized that not all unions or employers are ready to assume such responsibilities, but the arguments against union administration must be viewed in the light of what some unions have achieved and the soundness of the policies they have developed.

> With renewed enthusiasm the ILGWU, now in the vanguard of organized labor, urged its members to increase their participation in political activities. From the *New York Times,* October 22, 1944.

ROSES FOR FDR

New York's garment district reached record-breaking heights yesterday in its reception for President Roosevelt.

From the moment the president's car reached 41st [Street] and Seventh Avenue until it paused briefly on 23rd Street and Fifth Avenue, where the president was presented with three dozen American beauty roses, the acclaim was of the ear-splitting variety—cheers, piercing whistles, a shower of tons of multicolored confetti.

Above the din was the frequent cry: "We need you." The membership of the International Ladies' Garment Workers' Union, headed by President David Dubinsky, was out in full force. The cold, driving rain was of small consequence. Veteran police estimated the crowds at 3,500 to each block stretching from 42nd Street to 34th Street.

Several thousand signs, held aloft by the rain-swept spectators, and thousands of signs in windows stood out in bold relief, all calling for the reelection of Mr. Roosevelt. The captions included: "Hail to Our Commander-in-Chief," "First in Our Hearts, Roosevelt," "It's a Date Till '48 with Roosevelt."

The ILGWU headquarters at 1710 Broadway was completely blanketed with American flags and pictures of the president, and stretched 100 feet across the face of the building was the sign: "Welcome FDR, the Hope of America."

Mr. Dubinsky and three members of his union carrying three dozen roses preceded the presidential car by ten minutes to 23rd Street and Fifth Avenue.

On this particular corner Mr. Dubinsky and the pretty girls alighted and awaited the presidential car. The moment Mr. Roosevelt reached the corner the three girls and Mr. Dubinsky stepped forward and presented the president with the flowers, remarking:

"We wish you the best of luck and we all hope you are elected; we're all working for you very hard."

President Roosevelt replied: "Thank you, thank you. Glad to see you."

Mayor LaGuardia then added: "Dave, it was a swell, wonderful job." Mrs. Roosevelt remarked: "ILGWU as usual."

The ceremony was brief, lasting about four minutes. Mr. Dubinsky himself was the recipient of a rousing ovation when his automobile passed down Seventh Avenue.

The three girls were "particularly proud" of their assignment.

For its Fiftieth Anniversary the ILGWU produced a memorable film that was eventually dubbed in eleven major languages and was shown outside the United States as visual evidence of the achievements of free trade unions in a democratic country. The film was banned in India in 1956. From the *Congressional Record,* June 18, 1956.

"WITH THESE HANDS" AND INDIA
by Irwin D. Davidson

Mr. Speaker, I should like to direct the attention of this House to an incident that, I believe, sheds considerable light on the problem of our relationships with some nations that claim a neutral status in the present world situation.

This incident involves a movie, *With These Hands,* produced by the International Ladies' Garment Workers' Union, depicting in semi-documentary form the history and purposes of that union. This movie, translated into 11 languages, has been shown to millions of working people around the world, introducing them to the functioning of an American trade union.

Among the other nations in which this movie was shown was the vast and great country of India, whose prime minister, Jawaharlal

Nehru, will shortly be visiting our country. Recently, this movie came up for regular review by the censors in India. When it did, the Indian censors insisted that the United States agency showing the film remove a sequence describing the fight of the ILGWU against Communist attempts to dominate that union in the 1920s. The United States Government refused to conform with this request for censorship.

The executive council of the American Federation of Labor–Congress of Industrial Organizations has called upon the Indian government to act like a free democracy instead of a satellite nation and has called upon the United States State Department to intervene actively to lift the censorship on the ILGWU film.

I wish to go on record as praising our government for its forthright resistance to censorship in this matter. I also wish to insert in the [*Congressional*] *Record* the comments of Mr. David Dubinsky, president of the ILGWU, and several newspaper editorials on this matter, with the express hope that the sentiments of our people may be brought to the attention of Mr. Nehru, so he may understand our shock and protest against these attempts to suppress the truth about the history of an American union simply because it may injure the sensitivities of the rulers of the Soviet Union.

The people of India are entitled to know the truth about the way American trade unions view Communists. The government of India should not conceal this truth because the Communist leaders do not like it.

By mid-century the nature of trade union leadership requirements had changed. As a result of improved conditions, its sources in the shop had grown scarce. The ILGWU founded a training school and reached out for new, youthful leaders. From *New York State Industrial Bulletin,* January 1960.

SCHOOL FOR ORGANIZERS
by Thomas R. Brooks

Where are tomorrow's labor leaders coming from? What will the next generation of union men be like?

These questions are worrying a good many people on both sides of the nation's collective-bargaining tables. Free collective bargaining today turns on too many imponderables—a spider's web of laws and contracts and a radarlike feel for the give-and-take essential to the health of a modern industrial society—to risk the future by placing industrial democracy in the hands of incompetents. Management realizes this: It places a hefty investment in the training and skills of those executives assigned to carry out management's collective-bargaining strategy. The unions also realize that the nature of union leadership has changed. This can be witnessed in the expanded hiring of technicians—the research Ph.D's, the lawyers, trained pension experts recruited to the union staff.

The rise of union leadership nonetheless differs essentially from that of management. Most union officials are "politicians," chosen by the rank-and-file to lead the union. They do not come often from the ranks of the technical staff. However, the world has grown complex for union leaders too. "Thirty years ago," says David Dubinsky, president of the International Ladies' Garment Workers' Union, "the important thing for a union leader was to know how to organize economic strength. Organize! Strike! Settle! That was labor-management relations. But today, with laws and labor boards, almost all of our problems are settled at the conference table through negotiations. This requires new skills, a different kind of intelligence. Now it is diplomacy instead of the big stick."

Today's union leadership has learned that diplomacy pays off in higher wages and better working conditions for its membership. But diplomacy is an art composed of many skills; skills that shift rapidly with the changing times. The unanswered question remains: How is the next generation going to learn the new skills required for the bargaining of the future?

"The present bunch," a top management negotiator said recently, "came up the hard way; they learned through experience as we did. But bargaining is getting more intricate each year. And we go out and hire the best people money can buy to handle these problems. Behind them are many years of training at considerable expense. The unions still must take their new people out of the ranks and I'm not so sure that the College of Hard Knocks can teach all the skills they'll need nowadays."

Many labor leaders share these doubts. Labor leadership, as Mr. Dubinsky points out, "is no longer a hit-or-miss avocation." For this reason, union leaders—and many in management—have been watching with growing interest a ten-year-old experiment—the ILGWU's attempt to build "a workers' West Point." The experience of this unique educational institution, the first and only full-time school for the training of union personnel, indicates that union leaders are made as well as born. Skills can be learned at considerable saving of the waste motion inherent in any knockabout schooling.

The students go out into the field as organizers for two periods of three months each. Here they work under the supervision of the union's field officers. The institute staff keeps a close eye on each student's performance under fire as they pass out leaflets, talk to workers, march on picket lines—in short, perform the routine work of union organizing.

A. H. Raskin was a *New York Times* labor reporter during much of Dubinsky's presidency. More recently, he has served as assistant editor of that paper's editorial page. The present article was written shortly after President Dubinsky's retirement. From the *New Leader,* April 11, 1966.

D. D. AND THE AMERICAN DREAM
by A. H. Raskin

He could still weep. Of all the qualities of heart and mind that carried David Dubinsky to greatness, that distinguished him from the other strong men of labor.

He led a union of immigrant tailors and seamstresses out of the sweatshop; he brought civilization to an industrial jungle; he shifted the mainstream of American labor into a new riverbed of probity and social responsibility; he contributed mightily to checking Communism and building democratic labor organizations in the far places of the world. Honors and monuments have piled up around the irrepressible little refugee from the Tsar's jails. Presidents, governors and mayors have credited him with their election. Towering cooperative apartments for workers rose under his auspices where once had been slums. The treasury of the International Ladies' Garment Workers' Union (ILGWU), choked with debt when he came to top office in 1932, now bulges with a half billion dollars in union, pension and welfare funds.

But none of these badges of accomplishment, none of the trappings of power has stripped him of the compassion and the loneliness that stem from a recognition of the enormity of human misery and social neglect. He could be cruel and overbearing, even autocratic; his rages were fearsome. But overriding this imperiousness is the radiance of spirit, the zest for life and, above all, the intimate concern for people that made him that rarest of leaders, a man who cared. His decision to quit the ILGWU's presidency, at the age of 74, is a loss to the nation and not merely to labor.

Historians will recall his monumental contributions to fashioning the ethical practices code that became the spiritual armor of the merged labor movement. He planted the seeds fully a quarter century ago, and got mauled a bit by extortionist Joey Fay in the process. The merger itself undoubtedly would have taken much longer to achieve without Dubinsky's talents. The map of western Europe might well be different today if it were not for the secret benefactions he dispatched from the ILGWU treasury during World War II and just after it. . . .

Certainly, a major chapter in history will deal with his unification of international labor along progressive, anti-totalitarian lines after V-J Day. He proposed in 1948 that the old American Federation of Labor take a leading part in calling an international labor conference in London to mobilize support for the Marshall Plan. Out of that conference, which Dubinsky and George M. Harrison of the Brotherhood of Railway Clerks attended, came the following year the International Confederation of Free Trade Unions. The Congress of Industrial Organizations pulled out of the Communist-dominated World Federation of Trade Unions to become a cofounder of this new force for democratic unionism in every corner of the globe.

The list of good works could be stretched on for many pages, and the list is not ended. He will serve out a two-year term to which he was elected last December as a vice-president of the AFL-CIO. That means something more than that George Meany will be assured of the company of his favorite gin rummy partner; Dubinsky probably ranks second only to Meany as a force for creativity and action inside the Executive Council. Within the ILGWU he will be more than an elder statesman. Louis Stulberg, his successor and a man long schooled in the ILGWU tradition of community service, has asked Dubinsky to continue as a special steward in directing the union's contributions to labor and liberal causes.

He moves off center stage content that the program of the ILGWU, once a voice in the wilderness, has now become the program of all labor on social advance and responsibility. "A revolution has taken place in the American labor movement," Dubinsky says. "In the old days it used to be 'we' and 'they.' Now it is all 'we'." But the warmest memories for those who were privileged to see him at close range will not be of these historic transformations but of a man so consumed with the pure joy of living that he would often kick off his shoes in exuberance and do a little twirling dance with a shuffling step of his own invention. He made everything around him exciting; there will never be another in the same mold.

McGill (1898–1969) was the influential editor of the *At-lanta Constitution,* where this article first appeared on March 26, 1966.

THE CZAR'S PRISONER
by Ralph McGill

David Dubinsky, who at 74 looks like an Irish leprechaun, has retired as president of the International Ladies' Garment Workers' Union after 34 years in office. One of the assets of this reporter's experiences has been to sit on various committees with Dubinsky and to have had an opportunity to know him. He is a part of American industrial labor and union history. He himself is one of the products of the American dream.

When Dubinsky was 15 years old he was one of the Czar's prisoners—being sent with other "politicals" to Siberian prisons to work in isolated villages under prison guards. His crime was that he, an accomplished baker despite his years, had helped organize a union of bakers in the Polish town of Lodz, then Poland's most indus-trialized and slum-ridden city. His parents had migrated there from Brest Litovsk, where young David had been born.

Young David was arrested in 1908 for having helped organize the General Jewish Workers Union in Lodz. It was a twilight time for imperial Russia. Japan had defeated the Czar's forces in 1904–5. Uprisings in Russia in late 1905 had been put down bloodily. Fear began to grow in the palaces. Secret police became more active, more cruel.

For a year and a half young Dubinsky was shuttled about Siberian villages, always under police supervision. Then, without explanation, he and other prisoners were gathered and put in a train. After a long ride they began a march of several days to their next work assign-ment. Young Dubinsky escaped, aided by a friendly guard who liked the youngster's quick wit and leprechaun charm. He made his way back to Lodz. At last he was smuggled across the border into Ger-many. From there he set his sights for the United States.

On January 1, 1911, a freighter carrying 700 steerage passengers anchored off Ellis Island. Most of them were from eastern Europe. There were Hungarians destined for the steel mills and coal mines in Pennsylvania. There were Polish, Ukrainian and Romanian Jews who would seek work in New York. The next morning Dubinsky landed. He was taken in by a brother who had immigrated earlier. He became a part of the thousands of immigrants who made the East Side a legend of transition into American life.

Within six months the energetic young Dubinsky had qualified for the cutters union. He was 19. The thousands of garment workers had won a strike the year before. But the intolerable working and living conditions which had produced the strike still prevailed.

Work in that period went on seven days per week. Signs in the sweatshop lofts read: "If you can't come Sunday don't come Monday." Wages averaged about 10 cents an hour.

This was the background. When Dubinsky retired the other day his union had made history. It had pioneered with recreation centers, health programs, housing, pensions, and union investments. The union had also created stability in an industry notoriously chaotic.

For one who had been a prisoner of the Czar at 15, Dave Dubinsky has come a long way. So has his adopted country. When we think of a symbol of the "American Dream" Dave Dubinsky will do until a better one can be found.

A good unionist must also be a good citizen, the ILGWU has urged every newcomer group to the industry.

The following are excerpts from five typical addresses by Dubinsky in which his staunch faith in American freedom and tolerance found expression. The first is from the record of the ILGWU's 1934 convention in Chicago.

A BETTER CHOICE

I suppose the delegates are not surprised that we are having our session this morning in the Morrison Hotel instead of the place which was originally arranged for the convention. When the Medinah Club was rented about two months ago, we were promised all reasonable accommodations. The management was anxious to have our convention in that place. We did not solicit the place. They solicited our patronage.

We advised them that we had representatives of all nationalities at our convention, and that we were a labor union and did not share in the racial prejudice that exists in some of the hotels in Chicago and that we wanted all our delegates to be treated on an equal basis. (Applause) They promised us there would be no discrimination.

From the first moment we stepped into that hotel, however, it appeared that it was one thing for the management to promise us accommodations and service, and quite another thing to keep the promise. We were able to endure that they did not live up to their promises so far as accommodations for housing all our delegates and giving us proper service were concerned, but there was one thing we could not swallow, and that was discrimination against some of our delegates. (Applause)

Their discrimination was reported to us on several occasions during the convention. We took the matter up with the management and received assurances that they would be corrected. We gave them a chance to correct them, but soon we saw that even their final assurances were not being lived up to and last Sunday, before adjourning the session, I asked the General Executive Board to meet with me Sunday morning. We invited a representative of Local 22 to be present, and the General Executive Board decided that although it might involve additional expense, our organization, which is committed to equality, justice and resistance to oppression, should actively resist this discrimination and we decided to move our convention out of that hotel. (Applause)

This should serve as evidence to those who suffer from race persecution everywhere that it is the labor movement that is ready to act in their behalf, not merely with words but by deed.

I am glad we did it, and I hope the delegates, although they had a lot of trouble and inconvenience yesterday and this morning because of moving, will realize that we acted in the spirit and tradition of our ILGWU. Fortunately, I think we made a better choice. We have a better place, a more comfortable one, and I think we shall find it a better place for conducting our business and that we shall have better accommodations for the delegates and for the staff—and they, too, need accommodations at a convention.

On November 21, 1953, ground-breaking ceremonies marked the start of the ILGWU housing project on New York's East Side. The following is taken from Dubinsky's remarks on this occasion. From *Justice*, December 1, 1953.

OUT OF THESE SLUMS

We are gathered here to break ground for a housing development that will provide homes for more than 1,600 families. Only a few of the old structures remain standing on this site. When their walls come tumbling down the last sign of the slum and the sweatshop will disappear forever from this corner of Manhattan.

Many of us are here today as natives returning to the scenes of our childhood. We are the sons and daughters of this East Side, the children of immigrants, who dared the terrors of the sea and a strange land to search for freedom. To the miserable hovels on these streets our parents came from the old country with nothing more than their household belongings and with hearts filled with hope.

There were rooms in these houses where the sun never shone. There were rooms in which children slaved over bundles of garment work, breathing in the foul air that made them tubercular before they were grown up. There were rooms in these houses in which, in a not too distant past, men and women worked to the point where they dropped.

Here, on the streets whose outlines are now disappearing, men and women spoke in a multitude of tongues. But all of them spoke of the same dream. The dream of an end to poverty. The dream of enough to eat. The dream of trees in the street and homes filled with fresh air and sunshine.

Now we stand in the midst of this rubble. It is frightening in its similarity to the bombed areas in some European city. But with us this destruction is the beginning of progress. Soon the first of the four new houses will rise from these ashes. Many persons have contributed foresight, skill, know-how, planning to make this development possible. But not present are those who lived out their wretched lives in the slum jungle at the foot of Grand Street. This is the fulfillment of their most daring dream that some day the slum would be ripped down. They held fast to that hope through many years when the sacred right of private property was invoked to justify their misery.

Fifty-three years ago, the International Ladies' Garment Workers' Union was officially organized to war against the sweatshop. This war, that has continued for more than two full generations, has been more than a simple effort to raise wage standards. This has been a war of liberation to free people from endless hours of work in cellars, in stables, in dark hallways, in bedrooms where the garments of 50 years ago were made.

Now 50 years later, the garment workers return to their place of origin. We have wiped out the sweatshop. Now we return to wipe out the slum.

The following is taken from Dubinsky's remarks at the housing dedication ceremony, October 22, 1955. In *Justice*, November 1, 1955.

Two years ago, on this same spot, we turned the first shovelful of earth that started this cooperative venture toward reality. Now we are gathered here, among these magnificent buildings, proud of what we have accomplished and even boastful of the part played by our union in building this ILGWU Cooperative Village.

Why has a union of garment workers turned to building homes? Why have we invaded the jurisdiction of the real estate speculator and the landlord?

The answer lies in the slums. Many of us, of different religious and national origins, are the children of immigrants for whom the Golden Land turned out to be the miserable tenements on the East Side. Our first playgrounds were the streets of these slums. We cannot forget the poverty, the sickness, the homework shops, the child laborers of this neighborhood.

In these slums men and women who had fought oppression in the Old World turned to fighting poverty in the new one. They joined together in unions. They pooled their courage and their strength.

They made their idealism a constructive force for good in the life of America.

It has taken not two years but more than half a century to rip out the slums on this corner of Manhattan and to replace them with the kind of homes human beings deserve. We can stand here now and point with pride to these buildings. We can boast that they are the tallest, the largest, the finest, the most beautiful buildings of their kind.

But the true glory of these wonderful structures lies in the power of the dream that made them come true—the faith that life in this nation can be something better than a slum. We have worked here as we work in our union—together, in cooperation, accomplishing through joint effort what we could never achieve as single workers—or as single tenants.

In what we have done here we have kept human considerations first. We parted company with bankers who put higher mortgage interest rates above these considerations. We turned our backs on a government agency that took its cue from building contractors and politicians seeking windfalls.

The result is here before you: not new tenements for old, not crowded structures that squeeze out the last drop of rent from every square foot of space. No, not these but a beautiful new design for living in comfort, in good health, in fine community surroundings, in a truly American way.

These four structures are the social dividend of our faith in unionism. They are the "profit" of our great strikes. They are monuments to men and women who believed strongly in freedom.

On January 29, 1959, Local 122 of Atlanta, Georgia, saluted its first retirees. The following is an excerpt from Dubinsky's speech on this occasion. In *Justice*, February 15, 1959.

WHAT HAVE WE ACCOMPLISHED HERE?

What is it that we have accomplished here in these 25 years? I remember our first meeting in Atlanta in a Baptist church. I remember the attitude of the employers and the city authorities.

Today, we got a taste of real Southern hospitality. We had a police escort from the airport to this hall. Instead of the police chasing us, we went behind them. This is one of the small accomplishments.

But a far more important measure of our accomplishment is the fact that we are gathered here to honor 13 members who have toiled their lives away in this industry. This is what we have accomplished: Now that they have reached the time to cease from toil, the union is with them, the union is able to sweeten a little these later years of their lives.

Our union has been a constructive influence in the industry. We have won improvements to the maximum ability of the industry to provide them. We have not asked for the sky even when, through our strength, we could have gotten it. But if we had exacted what the industry could not give, we would have hurt both the industry and ourselves.

Twenty-five years ago, we couldn't get a loan from a bank because they told us the scraps of office furniture we had wasn't enough collateral. Tonight, as we retire each one of these ladies, we shall set aside, from the resources of the Eastern Region Retirement Fund, $7,000 for each one of them to insure their retirement benefit. That's a total of $91,000.

The Atlanta garment industry couldn't meet that bill by itself. Altogether, in two years, it contributes about $60,000 to retirement funds. But we are a union. And the spirit of union is not to live only for yourself. This retirement benefit comes from one of the many welfare funds of our union, in which there are more than $200,000,000 in reserves.

The pioneers of our union who gave their lives to build it never dreamed we could achieve this. These 13 retirees were among our pioneers in the South. They built well. They built for a better life.

We have fought for a better life without regard to the creed or the color or the religion or the national origin of the workers who belong to the International Ladies' Garment Workers' Union. We have fought for all, because to undermine any group of workers is to threaten the welfare of every worker.

That is the constructive role of the labor movement. That is the cause it serves. That is how it enriches American life. That is why it does not merit the kind of punitive legislation that has been asked for by the president. Our cause needs constructive reform, not crippling constriction.

The following is excerpted from a message by Dubinsky on the 25th anniversary of the Montreal Dressmakers' Union, November 1962. From *Justice,* December 1, 1962.

NO FOREIGNERS IN THE UNION

Only those who were there 25 years ago will remember that we opened our 23rd ILGWU convention in Atlantic City, New Jersey, with some of the delegates from Montreal absent. They were Montreal dressmakers who, as I told the delegates in my opening remarks, were at that moment "waging an historic battle."

In the crucial struggle of our union in Montreal that year, employers utilized every means in an effort to block the establishment of the ILGWU on a permanent basis, especially in the dress industry.

The workers in the dress shops were told over and over again that they didn't belong in the ILGWU because of their national origin as French Canadians; that they didn't belong in the ILGWU because they were Catholics; that the ILGWU was no good for them because it was made up of foreigners butting into their affairs.

But with all of their threats, the bosses forgot one thing: that in a union, all are equal and that national origin or religious faith makes no difference and that no one is a foreigner in the union. In the mistaken belief that they had aroused the Montreal dressmakers with appeals to prejudice, the employers founded a substitute organization with which they then signed an agreement—without the knowledge of the workers, without the consent of the workers, without improvements and without genuine recognition of unionism.

The result of these tactics was that when the ILGWU issued its call for a walkout, the response was virtually 100 percent effective. And nothing the employers could do after that could break the ranks of the strikers. They enlisted the aid of the provincial government to fight the strikers. They threatened to have the strike leaders thrown into jail. But the more they threatened, the stronger grew the solidarity on the picket line where Jew and Catholic, Canadian and United States citizens marched side by side.

That is the meaning of our union, whether in Canada or the United States or in Puerto Rico. We work together, we fight together on the picket line and, as we move forward, we celebrate together regardless of race, color or creed. That is the way it was 25 years ago and that is the way it is today when we celebrate a quarter of a century of progress of the ILGWU in Montreal.

I remember how at three o'clock in the morning of the fourth day of that convention 25 years ago, I was awakened by a long-distance

President John F. Kennedy dedicates ILGWU-financed houses in midtown Chelsea area on May 19, 1962.

telephone call from Bernard Shane. There was no more sleeping that night because that was the call to tell us that our French-Canadian brothers and sisters had won their gallant fight and that the strike had been settled.

I salute the officers and members of our Montreal union as they celebrate the progress made during the years since then. That progress is the finest result of devoted officers and members, under the leadership of Brother Shane, who have never faltered in their support of the ILGWU and unionism. But it is, above all else, an expression of the faith that wherever in this world men and women join together to improve their lot as workers, differences of language, race, color or belief must not be allowed to slow their progress.

12. Pay and Production

The development of a method to determine a standard wage rate continues to challenge labor-management relations in the garment industry. The problem was central to the opening of negotiations for the renewal of the New York Metropolitan Dress Contracts on November 13, 1975, by ILGWU President Sol C. Chaikin.

From almost every angle, the nature of the garment industry seems to defy any attempt to develop a method of standard rate determination. The industry's product is the most variable one offered to the consumer. It is graded by size, price, silhouette, and use. The high labor-intensity of production stresses the individual worker's skill and stamina. The production volume of any single shop is directly affected by the level of managerial efficiency, the quality of the equipment, and the pattern of work routing in the shop. Under one mode of production a single worker will make the entire garment, whereas under another system that worker may only be responsible for one part of a garment.

Yet if workers are not to degenerate into savage competitors for work and food, a standard rate must be attained despite all variables. Dyche and N. I. Stone explore the time-piece rate equation, pointing out that the rate per piece must be set so as to yield for the worker a stipulated monetary sum per hour worked. Cohen adds that determining the average hourly yield will, in turn, dictate how many pieces the worker must make in that hour. To test the merits and the validity of this relationship, he describes how test shops should be set up by the manufacturers and the union to monitor production. Robert G. Valentine, a professional production engineer, turns directly to the sewing machine in order to define the common denominators in garment making and to assign a time factor to each.

Writing a generation after Valentine, Julius Hochman revised rate settlement concepts into a system of component parts common to all garments and devised a schedule for variations and additions governing the settlement procedure. The latter is described by Nan Robertson.

The enforcement of a standard rate, however, was still conditioned by the jobber-contractor relationship. At the start of the century Commons had pointed out the difficulty of establishing the locus of responsibility for wages and working conditions in the garment industry. In the mid-twenties Governor Smith's special commission had emphasized that only some restraint on the unlimited proliferation of contractors could bring stability to the garment industry, a point also stressed by Sigman.

In the 1940s Wendell Willkie had argued that even with such self-restraint the garment industry would still remain fiercely competitive and differentiated. Senator Robert A. Taft, promulgator of legislation (bearing his name) restraining unions, agreed in the Senate that the jobber-contractor relationship was based on integrated functions.

Changes in the wage-determination procedure have resulted from changes in the mode of production. But these have come about slowly, not as a consequence of technological innovations in machinery but by way of the gradual infiltration of production engineering and planning in work and work flow. Helen E. Meiklejohn describes the unchanging technology of the industry. Sumner H. Slichter recounts the first marketwide effort to introduce production engineering.

The one factor oblivious to change was the handicraft skill of the individual worker, a skill which defied mechanization. However, with the increasing scarcity in the shops of the "whole garment, tailor-seamstress" type of worker—caused by a cutoff in immigration—inroads by engineers increased. Skills were soon broken down by specialists in the front office. Production, as Nathan Belfer reported, was divided into separate operations. New fibers and fabrics, described by J. C. Furnas, led to increased production of styled garments in medium and low price ranges.

By the start of the 1960s, as the *Economist* noted, the industry continued to dress the majority of American women in garments of high quality and styling. But in the shops a major change was underway: the spread of engineered production was challenging shops in older garment centers still using traditional production and pricing techniques and was shifting wage-determination techniques away from the traditional concepts of garment, body, unit, section, or element times and toward the ultimate unit of the stitch.

One major problem outlasted the Protocol of Peace: the determination of a proper method of setting wage rates for an unstandardized product made under the jobber-contractor arrangement. The four selections which follow explore various aspects of the rate-setting problem. The first is taken from *Protocol of Peace in the Dress and Waist Industry* (1913), by the general secretary-treasurer of the ILGWU during the period of its great strikes.

MANY SHOPS, ONE STANDARD
by John A. Dyche

In the ladies' garment industry, where the styles keep changing and where operators are paid by the piece, the question of fixing prices is always a difficult and complicated one. But in all cases, even in non-union shops where only the employer fixes prices, there are two elements taken into consideration when piece rates are fixed. The first is the rate of earnings per hour or per day of the employee, the second is how many garments or how many parts of a garment can an employee make or operate in a specific time, or how long does it take to make a particular part or a whole garment.

Previous to the strike each shop had its own standard; in some shops the average earnings of the girls, or the standard, were as low as 15 cents per hour, some 18, 20, 25, 28 and 30 cents, reaching as high as 40 cents per hour for a girl with average skill.

In this Protocol a standard of 30 cents is set for all shops where the rate has previously been less than that rate. In shops where the standard has been above that previous to the strike, there can be no reduction.

And now that we know what the rate per hour is, it remains for each shop to find out the value of the labor of each particular garment or part of a garment. This could be done by ascertaining how long it takes to make the garment or part of the garment in question. If we know that a particular garment takes three hours to operate then the price is 90 cents, and the employer can pay no less and the employee can demand no more.

Stone (1873–1966) was the chief statistician of the Wage
Scale Board of the New York Dress Industry. From *The
Message,* August 7, 1914.

WORK ENVIRONMENT
by N. I. Stone

The sanitary conditions in one shop do not affect the manufacturer or
owner of another shop in the slightest way. Your neighbor in one
building may have a very unsanitary shop and your shop in the ad-
joining building need not be affected at all. But wages certainly
change every day and conditions change almost every day, so wages
are subject to frequent change and frequent fluctuations.

What is more important, from the viewpoint of the manufacturer,
is that "I am my brother's keeper" especially applies to wages. I should
say, if I may put it in a paradoxical form, that it is more important to
the manufacturer to know what wages his neighbor pays than what he
pays himself. A manufacturer can afford to pay $25 a week to his
cleaners if his competitors are paying $25, but he cannot afford to pay
them $10 if others are paying $15. So what his competitor pays is of
greater importance to him than what he pays.

Therefore, if you find it necessary to control sanitary conditions in
the industry—which is probably more a matter of pride with the
manufacturers though a matter of necessity with the union—when it
comes to wages, they are of very vital interest to the manufactuter and
to the union.

Starting thus I take another step and say it is of vital importance to
the manufacturer as well as to the union to control all the rates, and
not only the apprentices' rates. The Wage Scale Board should become
a Board of Wage Control as much as the Joint Sanitary Board has
been made a Board of Sanitary Control.

From *Annals of the American Academy of Political and Social Science,* January 1917.

TOWARD A STANDARD RATE
by Julius Henry Cohen

Piece prices in the dress and waist, as well as the cloak and suit industry are settled by the process of haggling, the workers in the shop represented by their price committee, the employer acting either personally or through the foreman or superintendent. There are no fixed standards of prices to govern, and delay in the settlement of prices makes not only for friction, but for great waste.

The Protocol of 1913 in the dress and waist industry took a step forward. While in the cloak industry the process of not working upon "unsettled garments" continues to this day, in the 1913 dress and waist Protocol it was provided that work *should not be stopped,* but garments should be made with the provision that when the prices were settled, they operated retroactively. In the cloak and suit industry, until the award of the Council of Conciliation in July of 1915, there was *no base rate* upon which the piece rate might be estimated.

In the 1913 dress and waist Protocol a base rate was fixed; that is to say, thirty cents an hour was fixed as the base, which, multiplied by the estimate of the number of hours it would take an average skilled operator to make the garment, would make the piece price on the garment. This base rate was determined upon the theory of the average skilled operator, and covered a continuous hour of work. In other words, it was assumed that an average skilled operator should make thirty cents for each continuous hour of work; that, therefore, the more skilled operator would earn more than thirty cents an hour, and the less skilled would earn less. Assuming that a garment would take five hours to make, the piece rate would be $1.50. The worker who could make it in four hours would get $1.50 for four hours' work, and the worker who took six hours would get $1.50 for six hours' work.

But how were you to determine in advance how many hours it would take the average skilled worker to make the garment? There was the rub. It presented and still presents a most difficult technical problem to solve. In 1913 the solution accepted was the *shop test.* Employer and worker each selected one person of average skill to test out the garment, and upon the basis of such a test the number of hours was fixed, multiplied by thirty cents, and thus established the piece rate. Actual experience demonstrated that the *shop test* was not a practicable or fair test; it produced conflict and friction, and both sides sought a new and better method. The revision of the dress and waist Protocol presents now the plan or scheme of the *test shop*.

The *test shop* is a place where tests are to be made under impartial supervision, the shop being managed by representatives of both the association and the union. *The controversy is thus taken away from the shop, where it causes friction, to a place where it is to be settled impartially by people not connected with or interested in the shop.* It is too early yet to report upon this experiment.

Valentine (1872–1916) was the first industrial engineer to suggest that organized labor as well as management could benefit from time study and work analysis. He undertook the first such study in the women's garment industry. From the *Survey,* September 9, 1916.

ALPHABET OF THE GARMENT
by Robert G. Valentine

No approach to work analysis can be fundamental which is not based on time study. Let me illustrate my meaning from its application to the dress and waist industry in New York City. The 800 shops of that industry are making thousands of styles of waists and dresses. Numerous as these styles are and much as they differ from each other in completed appearance, this vast riot of variables is nevertheless made up of a comparatively few simple operations. The analogy is the thousands of words built from the twenty-six letters of the alphabet. Similarly, too, the letters of the alphabet are not only combined but combined under varying conditions. These varying conditions in the dress and waist industry arise from three sources:

1. The nature of the product. It may be called shortly, product conditions. They are (a) the material on which the operation is performed and (b) the quality of work required.
2. The second source of varying conditions is the skill of the operators. Here all the immediate human variables arise amid the competence or incompetence of the social organization.

3. The conditions of manufacture. In this field lie all the variables that come from different methods or lack of methods of planning the work and of routing it through the shop and of administering it at the work places. Here, too, impinge the competence or incompetence of the sales and financial policies.

Thus are the comparatively few elementary operations of waist and dressmaking beset on all sides by a host of variables. An alphabet under such conditions would be sufficiently unfortunate. But imagine trying either to create a language without an alphabet at all or to get even some sort of control over the variables of industry without any accurate knowledge of the simple elementary operations. Yet this last is the situation in nine-tenths of all industrial processes in the nation today.

We must no longer fail to build the alphabets of the industrial process so that we may at last create a language in which worker, manufacturer and the state may begin to talk intelligibly to each other. The method of building this language is to determine the (time) required to perform these elementary operations under varying conditions through time study.

A few simple beginnings go very far. A single sewing machine, an operator of any degree of skill, the dozen or so main materials of which waists are made and half a dozen styles, good light, good air, good seating, the material ready cut and sample waists of each style, together with a few dozen time studies made under actual conditions in a number of shops—these furnish in a few weeks along the lines so time-studied more basic elementary knowledge of waistmaking than all the manufacturers and all the workers have ever possessed.

Of course the relating of this knowledge to all the variables, while the variables themselves are being reduced through the slow standardization of manufacturing conditions and slow growth of industrial education, is a long and intricate task in any precisely exact sense; but here, too, the problem is not so difficult as theoretically appears.

Certain approximations here also go far. The fact to note in both cases is that scientific method resting on bedrock is at once conquering with elementary facts large areas of ground hitherto contested by irresponsible and undisciplined opinion and that the remaining areas are steadily and persistently reduced.

The potential consequences of this method on the standard of living of the workers, the costs to the manufacturers, and the prices the consumer pays, as well as on the relation to the social and political structure of the 35,000 workers and the thousand and more members of the employing group are so great that the fact is of the utmost consequence that the particular work I have described is being done at the joint board on which are representatives of the public.

Beyond the problem of labor pricing a garment lay the challenge of establishing responsibility for such pricing, e.g., between the jobber and the submanufacturer or contractor. On the eve of the 1926 cloakmakers' strike in New York, the Governor's Special Advisory Commission, appointed by Governor Smith and comprised of George Gordon Battle, Bernard L. Shientag, Herbert H. Lehman, Arthur D. Wolf, and Lindsay Rogers, made a number of recommendations on May 20. The following is a major recommendation excerpted from the commission's report.

JOBBER-CONTRACTOR RELATION

A decade ago the industry had risen out of the old sweatshop conditions in which much of the actual work had been done in tenement-house homes. Manufacturing had become concentrated in large "inside shops" under employers who were directly responsible both for manufacturing and for marketing the product. Since that time, however, there has been a gradual displacement of inside manufacturers by so-called jobbers. This has progressed to such a point that about three-fourths of the production now flows through the new jobbing-manufacturing system. This system has grown up partly as a device to escape labor responsibilities and partly as an adaptation to the new methods of retail buying.

An inside manufacturer creates styles, employs a permanent complement of workers, and seeks, so far as possible, to get advance orders from the retailers, placing his chief emphasis upon quality of production. The jobber . . . instead is an indirect manufacturer. He purchases his materials and then farms out the production to an elastic and shifting group of small submanufacturers who follow his instructions as to style. His emphasis is on mass production and on selling finished garments from the racks.

In determining the relationship between jobber, submanufacturer, and workers we should be concerned not so much with the form as with the substance. By whatever name he may call himself, the jobber controls working conditions; he controls employment, and that element of control imposes upon him the responsibility that he shall so conduct his business that proper working standards may be upheld instead of undermined, and that employment may be stabilized instead of demoralized.

The present method of doing business invites the splitting up of production units to a point which defies any real degree of supervision by the institutions in the industry and which makes impossible the maintenance of any satisfactory standards of employment.

We must appreciate that any remedy that is proposed must be reasonable, practicable and possible of being carried into effect without a disruption of the industry. Bearing this in mind the Commission recommends that there be such structural modifications in the existing jobbing submanufacturing system as would tend to regularize the flow of work into submanufacturing shops, raise the level of competition between submanufacturers, cause closer relations between jobbers and submanufacturers and stabilize working conditions in the shop.

With this in view, we recommend that the parties adopt a system of limitation of submanufacturers with whom a jobber may do business. At definite intervals every jobber shall, in accordance with a standard to be agreed upon between the parties, select and designate the submanufacturers he needs to handle his production, leaving him the necessary freedom in securing samples and in changing submanufacturers for cause shown; he shall not give work to other submanufacturers when his designated submanufacturers are not busy, and shall adhere, so far as practicable, to a policy of equitable distribution of work among the submanufacturers designated by him. The administration of such a system would, as cases arise, be subject to equitable interpretation through the impartial machinery.

A modern factory where brassieres are manufactured.

In the aftermath of the disastrous 1926 strike, ILGWU President Sigman returned to the task of dealing with the jobbers. The following is taken from *Justice*, November 4, 1927.

WHAT WE MUST DO
by Morris Sigman

While the union is willing to assume its share of responsibility and duty to see that our industry does not suffer from interrupted production, the situation is quite different in the camp of the employers. The submanufacturers and the contractors, of course, are under the thumb of the jobber and are not free agents. But the jobber who is and should be the boss in the industry rejects responsibility and obligations with regard to the workers. The jobber maintains that "he has nothing to do with labor because he does not hire it."

The removal of this abnormal condition is to be one of the main tasks of our [union] in the very near future. We must direct the situation so that the jobber is deprived of being able to use this alibi. If he does not hire the workers directly, they are employed by him, nevertheless. If the jobber is the boss in the industry, he must be made responsible for the labor conditions of his workers.

We have a contract with the Jobbers' Association, but this contract has no determining binding force behind it. There is not a proper machinery, a proper arrangement provided by this contract which would inform the union fully and accurately where the jobbers are sending their material to be made up into garments. The jobber still has a free hand to encourage more and more new shops in the trade and to create more and more competition in it.

It is this abnormal situation—the fact that the capital and productive power of the industry are concentrated in the hands of the jobber, while at the same time he refuses to be responsible for labor in the industry—which has created such a condition of chaos throughout the length and breadth of the cloak and dress trades. The so-called legitimate manufacturer who is still found in the industry is naturally driven, if he is to compete with the jobber, to act as the jobber does. This legitimate manufacturer, like the jobber, is trying to scatter his work among the various subcontracting shops and his "inside" workers meanwhile remain without work. When the union registers a complaint against him, he gives up his inside shop and becomes a full-fledged jobber.

What is then the result? The former workers of this manufacturer's inside shop are forced to go look for jobs in the subcontracting shops and work at lower wages. That is how the steady vicious circle of competition between worker and worker is set in motion, which demoralizes our members and breaks their spirit.

Frequently, after the inside workers lose their jobs, their former employer encourages them to open up a "corporation" shop and promises to give them work. In many cases these workers "fall" for the proposition and as a result we have a few more small shops in the industry and a little more chaos.

It seems to be clear, therefore, that the first and foremost duty of our union is to bring order into the industry. First of all, the fact must be recognized that it is the jobber who controls the wealth, the capital, in the trade and is therefore the person or group of persons to be made responsible for the industry.

Pricing and production problems were carefully scrutinized by two scholars. Under the direction of Walton Hamilton, of Yale University, Meiklejohn focused on the industry's technology in a study requested by President Roosevelt's Cabinet Committee on Price Policies. Sumner H. Slichter (1892–1959), of Harvard University, concentrated on labor-management innovations in Cleveland's garment industry in the mid-1920s. The Meiklejohn selection is from Hamilton's *Price and Price Policies,* 1938.

THE HAND AND THE MACHINE
by Helen Everett Meiklejohn

Since around 1850, when the sewing machine was first brought to market, there has been no "cataclysmic jerk forward" in technical processes. The cutting machines, by which many layers of cloth could be cut at one time, did much to increase output at a strategic point in the routine of production, but they were already in use when dresses began their factory career. It is astonishing that the 176,000,000 dresses in 1936 were made by processes in essentials the same as when the industry began.

The span from 1895 forward, the approximate life of the dress industry, has witnessed revolutionary changes in every one of our mass-production industries. The visitor to a steel plant, an automobile factory, a paper mill, a tool-making shop, a meat-packing establishment in 1895 would hardly recognize the physical reality of plant and

1. Handsewers attaching collars to coats.

2. Many layers of cloth are cut in single operation with electrically powered cutting machines.

3. Special and regular sewing machines are used to join garment parts.

4. Many parts are hand sewn by finishers.

5. Hoffman pressing machine raises a cloud of steam in pressing cloaks.

6. Sometimes hand irons are used for smaller, more delicate parts.

7. Highly standardized brassieres may be sewn by several machines operating in tandem.

process today. But the visitor of 1895 returning to a modern dress factory would today find his old friend the sewing machine—alone indispensable to the making of a dress—still there and easily recognized. It would, it is true, have undergone many improvements. The machine of 1895 may have been run by power, but it did not have the fineness of a machine today, which can make from 4 to 34 stitches per inch; nor did it have a speed ranging from 2,500 to 5,000 revolutions per minute. Our visitor would find in some shops additional machines for special processes—snap stitching, felling, blind stitching—but the underlying construction of these is the same as the sewing machine, and with their differences he could soon come to terms.

The dress industry is not the point where science has done its most spectacular work. Nor are the techniques of dressmaking the techniques of scientific method. The difference may be dramatized by a distinction between a pattern and a blueprint. The standards of accuracy in a machine shop require the fine precision of a micrometer, measuring to a thousandth of an inch. The cutting of a pattern or the sewing of a seam is in these terms mere wild approximation. It is safe to state that by the measurement of a micrometer no two dresses were ever alike.

Students of technology have noted the incidence of inventions falls where processes are reduced to typical mechanical improvements which can be emulated by the machine. In its simplest form the sewing machine itself might be interpreted as an imitation of the human hand placing one stitch after another. The machines that sew on snaps or buttons, make buttonholes, or baste a hem do it after a human fashion. But where is the machine that could know where to put a snap, how wide to make a hem, how large a buttonhole is required? It is at these points that workers must substitute for machines not yet invented and possibly never to be invented. It seems beyond human ingenuity to compass a machine which can deal with a wide variety of styles.

If all dresses were alike from year to year, we might expect that a machine could be devised which, with gauges set for different sizes, would know where to sew the buttons and how the neck should be finished. But at present the element of variation in design makes it difficult to foresee a time when a dress factory will be one great machine made up of interlocking mechanisms. Yet it would be folly to assert that the dress industry has reached the zenith of its technological development. A new concatenation of processes may be devised in which the old hand techniques will disappear forever. If it comes, job opportunities and production costs will likely be cut and the size of the industrial unit increased.

The drive toward mechanization is intercepted by other currents no less powerful. There is a strong consumer preference for handwork. Here we find the remnant of a battle which has been fought and lost on many another industrial front. The lure of craftsmanship still prevails in the field of dresses, reinforced by the practical fact that in case a dress is made over, hand sewing is the easier to take out and by the aesthetic fact that machine work is not yet able to compete in the invisibility of seam and hem, tuck and buttonhole.

But the technical progress within the industry must not be underestimated. The special machines devised to do various kinds of sewing are amazing in their cleverness. The Singer Sewing Machine Company, which supplies the dress trade with nearly 90 percent of its machines, produces more than 200 adapted to that trade alone. Some important machines of the trade, such as the cutting and blind-stitch machines, are not made by them, but by other companies. The variety of work done on these special machines is partially suggested by the following list: button sewing, buttonholes, snap sewing, seaming and hemming, zigzag stitching, hem stitching, picot edging, tucking, air ticking, cording, tacking, barring, shell stitching, scallop embroidering, edge stitching, ruffing and shirring, eyelet work, smocking, blind stitching, drop or moss stitching, and spiral braiding.

Not all these machines are found in any one shop, and the ratio of special to basic machines in shops of given sizes is quite unstandardized. Embroidery machines, for example, are seldom found in dress shops. Relatively few dresses are embroidered and some of the embroidery machines require special skill in operating. So if a dress requires embroidery it is commonly sent to an outside shop that specializes in the work. It is, however, hard to understand why certain other machines capable of more regular use have not been more widely adopted.

From *Union Policies and Industrial Management,* 1941.

INCENTIVES AND STANDARDS
by Sumner H. Slichter

Pursuant to the agreement of 1919, the union and the Manufacturers' Association engaged the engineering firm of Miller, Franklin, Basset and Company to study the industry and to propose a system of standards of production.

On June 23, 1920, the employers and the union agreed to adopt the plan which provided for setting a standard time on each job by time studies, and paying the workers at their regular hourly rates on the basis of the time value of each job. The standards were to be set and administered under the direction of a Bureau of Standards which would be maintained jointly by the manufacturers and the union and which would be responsible to the Board of Referees.

With the line of each manufacturer different, with many styles in each line, and with the lines changing several times a year, how could standards be set so as to provide some semblance of uniformity as between different shops and in the same shop over a period of time? This was made possible by basing standards upon "element times." Element times may be compared to bricks in houses; though the houses are not alike, they are composed of the same elements.

Setting standards required that the union and the manufacturers agree upon what was the proper speed of work and what was the proper method of work. As for the first, they agreed that standards should be based upon the average output of the average worker under prestandard conditions. As to the second, they agreed that the method of doing the work should be neither the best nor the poorest in use, but one which occupied a midway position.

When efficiency engineers undertake to set standard times on jobs in non-union plants, it is usually their custom to work out the best possible method and to make it the basis of the standard times. The union, however, was unwilling to consent to this procedure. For one thing, it would have been unfair to base standard times on ideal methods unless the manufacturers were prepared to train the workers in the best methods. The union could not be sure that the manufacturers were prepared to do this. More important, however, was the fact that under prestandard conditions the method of work was determined by the employees themselves.

In an industry as unstandardized as the manufacture of women's garments, where the product is changing and where subdivision of labor has not reduced operations to simple routine acts, freedom to plan the work affords pieceworkers an exceptional opportunity to increase their earnings by contriving a quicker way of doing the work than was assumed by whoever set the piece price. Had the engineers and the time-study men made a special effort to devise the best possible method of work, the employees would have been deprived of their traditional opportunity to increase their earnings by discovering shortcuts.

In other words, the union regarded the superior methods of work which some employees had discovered as the property of these employees and was unwilling for the employer to make the superior methods the standard methods without compensating the workers.

For example, in setting standards on pressing coats, 15,510 observations in 16 factories were taken to derive an average time for arranging the press cloth over areas of less than 110 square inches. In the operating department, the task of collecting the necessary data was formidable, and it was necessary to limit the work in order to save time and money. Hence the element times in the operating department were individual shop times and, in many instances, were based upon a very limited number of observations.

In selecting average methods of work, the shop rather than the market was the unit. This decision was largely dictated by practical considerations. To decide which method out of a great variety in use throughout the market was the average one would have been difficult in the extreme—in many cases impossible. This was particularly true in view of the fact that there were great differences in the organization of the work in the various shops. Some were sectionalized, others were not. Furthermore, there were great differences in shop customs and also differences in methods which were the result of differences in the quality and quantity of the goods manufactured.

Opposition to standards arose because they tended to disturb well-established earning differentials, particularly the spread between earnings of workers on the higher-priced garments and those of workers on the cheap garments. Under the bargaining system, managements had been more liberal in bargaining piece rates on the more expensive garments because a difference of 50 to 75 cents or even a dollar in the labor cost of an expensive garment made little difference to the manufacturer.

In the case of the cheaper garments, however, labor cost was of great importance, and manufacturers bargained tighter rates on these garments. Indeed, there had been some tendency for manufacturers to accept high rates on expensive garments in order to obtain low rates on cheap ones. No allowance was made for this customary liberality.

Nor did standards take account of differences in the run of work. Naturally the larger the lots in which garments came to employees and the longer an employee could work on a single number without changing, the faster he could produce. The cheaper garments came in larger lots than the expensive ones.

An adjustment could have been made for this by establishing different unavoidable delay allowances for the cheap and the expensive garments. This, however, was not done. All in all, therefore, standards were more unfavorable to the operators on expensive garments than on cheap ones.

The following six selections, spanning a generation, show the persistence of the problem of finding a satisfactory way for determining piece rates. The first selection is drawn from a pre-strike (1936) pamphlet entitled *Why This Strike?*, written by Hochman (1892–1970), ILGWU vice president and then general manager of the New York Dress Joint Board.

THE UNIT SYSTEM
by Julius Hochman

To eliminate still further any elements of doubt and speculation in the settlement of prices, we have devised the unit system. As worked out by the union, the unit system is a method of calculating the exact time it would take a worker to make a given dress.

In order to do this, the dress is split up into component parts. In spite of constant changes in styles, certain parts are common to all dresses at all times. These fundamental parts are called a "body." The time necessary to make the various possible body combinations has been studied. Another element in each dress, no matter the style, is the sleeve design. Some dresses have long sleeves; some have short sleeves; some have sleeves that are wide and open; some sleeves have cuffs; some are finished with piping or shirring. The time necessary to make all the various types of sleeves has been determined. The same thing is true of other "features" on a dress. There may be pointed seams, scalloped yokes, pleats and ruffles. There may be trimmings, such as bows, sashes, straps, etc.

All these parts have been separately studied, and their time determined and listed in a schedule. To find how long it takes to make a dress under the unit system, all that is necessary is to consult the schedule for the body time, and for each additional item. The time is then totaled up and we arrive at the time it would take to make that dress.

The next step in the system is to translate the units into terms of money. The wage clauses of the agreement, which fix the value of time for the workers, then establish the piece rate for the dress. Thus workers in all shops everywhere will receive the same rates for the same amount of labor.

Why do we consider this program basic and paramount? It is because any agreement without it means warfare every day in the year. And we want to spend our time working, not fighting. If we have to fight, we will fight one general strike, and frame an agreement that will give us conditions that will assure us enforcement, that will bring us peace.

The following statement by Willkie (1892–1944), 1940 Republican candidate for president of the United States was presented in behalf of the National Coat and Suit Industry Recovery Board to the Federal Trade Commission in December 1941.

MOST COMPETITIVE INDUSTRY
by Wendell L. Willkie

There is no concentration or combination in a single hand or hands, or in a single interest, of the ownership of several or numerous coat and suit enterprises, each enterprise being independently owned without connection financially or otherwise with other competing enterprises.

There are no "giants" in the industry capable of monopoly, restraint or suppression of competition, fixing of prices or use of the weapons of boycott or coercion, and none of such practices are, in fact, indulged in.

Virtually without exception, the enterprises in the coat and suit industry are either individual proprietorships, partnerships or closed corporations which are in substance partnerships, financed without resort to public large-scale financing, and consequently limited in capital to the restricted resources of the individual proprietor or proprietors.

The manufacturing processes are numerous and complex. From the initial step of designing to the final processes of cleaning and pressing of the garments, each phase of production is performed by workers who are specially trained and skilled at their respective crafts.

The products of the industry are sold to specialty shops, mail-order houses, chain stores, department stores, and other outlets. In order to increase and intensify their existing bargaining superiority over the members of the coat and suit industry, many of these buyers have consolidated their buying power into cooperative buying units, thereby concentrating the purchasing and bargaining power of many buyers upon a single seller. The average sale is small though the total quantity bought by each buyer is large. Garments are bought by specialists engaged solely for the purpose of purchasing the best values obtainable for their principals. The ready availability and accessibility of the sellers, by virtue of the geographic concentration of the salesrooms of the industry, facilitates comparison shopping by the buyers. The relative bargaining power of the buyer is superior to that of the seller.

Woolen fabrics constitute the principal raw material entering into the product. The woolen mills from which these are purchased are strong financially, are relatively few in number, and sell only a small percentage of the total volume of their product to the coat and suit industry. The relative bargaining power of the sources of supply of this principal raw material is superior to that of the buyers in the industry.

The industry is characterized by a highly irregular pattern of employment and sales. Consumer buying in concentrated periods, twice annually, is affected by weather and other fortuitous factors, which together with the constant demand for the newest styles compel the industry to be geared to peak rather than average production. Production based on long-term planning is impossible and long intervals of idleness are interspersed with periods of feverish and intense activity.

The industry is extremely hazardous. As a result of its hazardous character and intensive competition, the rate of business mortalities, through insolvency proceedings and enforced liquidations, is high. Profits are low. Plant equipment and machinery is inexpensive and extremely mobile, and very little capital is required to enter the business. Many new firms enter the industry each year and there is a constant flux of established firms leaving the industry and new firms entering the industry.

Style is the single item of greatest importance in the marketability of the product. It is the principal impelling factor which motivates the consumer and the retailer to make purchases. Thousands of styles are developed each season. Though all may conform to a current fashion trend each producer attempts to differentiate his product from those of his competitors. Styles change swiftly, obsolescence is rapid and the demand for new styles is constant. Within each style are thousands of variations of the nature and quality of the physical components of the garment, the fabrics, furs, trimmings, linings, buttons, interlinings and decorations. The quality of workmanship may vary from the entirely machine-made to the entirely hand-sewn garment with a multitude of combinations of partially hand–partially machine-made garments.

Every garment is in direct competition with every other garment in the same or approximately the same price level, in every aspect of its tangible, functional and aesthetic qualities. Policies governing production and price are the subjects of free and unrestricted choice of each manufacturer. Depending upon the particular garment, larger or smaller proportions of the cost of the garment will be spent for fabrics, furs, accessories or style and labor. Different garments selling for the same price will vary widely in the amount spent for materials and labor. When the prices of fabrics, furs or labor fluctuate, the manufacturer readjusts these components of his finished product by modifying them in such a manner as to permit their production at the prevailing markets.

The varieties of adjustment are infinite in number. He may use more or less expensive fabrics, or redesign his garments to use more or less yardage, or vary the quality of workmanship so as to use more or less labor per garment, or use cheaper or more expensive furs, trimmings or accessories. Each manufacturer strives to give and each retailer tries to secure the greatest values possible in style, quality and workmanship at the lowest price. Because of this competition, technological improvements and the unrestricted choices available to purchasers, the product of the industry constantly tends to improve and the prices tend to decrease to the ultimate benefit of the consumer.

To summarize: The manufacturing unit is small, mobile and inexpensive; competition is intensive; the industry is characterized by a highly irregular pattern of activity, marked by sharp fluctuations of employment; methods of production are variable and complex; as buyers, the relation of the industry to its source of supply is weak; as sellers, the bargaining power of its customers, individually, and collectively through cooperative buying offices, is great; the enterprise is hazardous and the returns are low. The elements of industrial chaos are present. The measures adopted to eliminate the social and economic waste incident thereto, and to achieve and preserve industrial decency, are more particularly hereinafter stated.

In 1933, collective agreements were entered into between respondent Union and respondent Employer Associations in the Metropolitan Area of New York, which incorporated in substance the recommendations of the Governor's Commission. These terms have been embodied in every collective agreement entered into between the parties from 1933 to the present. They provided for the jobber's responsibility for the wages paid and the hours worked in his contractor's premises, and they further provided that the jobber designate those contractors he actually required and that he divide his available work equitably among the contractors thus designated by him.

Provision was also made for the addition of new contractors if and when the contractors already designated by such jobber were fully engaged in the production of their garments. In case of a question as to the designation of additional contractors, the matter is resolved by the Impartial Chairman and Arbitrator appointed in the agreement. The jobber is required to pay to his contractor at least an amount sufficient to enable the contractor to pay to the workers the wages and earnings provided for in the agreement and, in addition, a reasonable payment to the contractor to cover his overhead. Competition among contractors is based upon efficiency of management, integrity and skill of operation and not upon the contractor's ability to depress wages.

The designation of contractors is not an end in itself. It is a method for stabilizing a chaotic industry. There is nothing in this method which in the remotest way tends to create a monopoly in the manufacture, production or sale of garments, or to fix prices of such garments or to limit their supply. No manufacturer or jobber is limited in the number of garments which he may manufacture or sell. The more they manufacture the better for the workers because the larger their earnings. All employers in the industry are entirely free to compete with each other for the market on the basis of the attractiveness of their styles, the quality of their product, the efficiency of their factory organizations and all other legitimate grounds of advantage.

> Did ILGWU contract provisions dealing with the jobber-contractor relationship come under the antitrust bans of the Taft-Hartley Act? An exchange on the floor of the Senate between Senator Robert A. Taft (1889–1953), a formulator of the act, and Irving M. Ives (1896–1962), the senator from New York, stressed the exception provided for the garment industry. From the *Congressional Record,* June 30, 1949.

UNIFIED AND INTEGRATED PRODUCTION

MR. IVES: The senator from New York has an important question. A question has arisen as to whether the secondary boycott provisions of the Taft-Hartley Act or of the substitute which is before us, and which has been offered by the distinguished senator from Ohio, were intended to apply to economic pressures exerted by a labor union against non-union employers in the ladies' garment industry who operate under a jobber-contractor system of production.

Let me put a typical case. A jobber is engaged in the manufacture of dresses. He buys piece goods. He employs designers to design the garments and perhaps cutters to cut the goods. But the dresses are not sewn and finished in his own shop. Instead the jobber sends out the cut goods, or sometimes the uncut goods, to contractors whose workers sew and complete the dresses according to the jobber's specifications. Then the contractor sends the finished dresses back to the jobber who sells them to the trade.

This is a typical example of jobber-contractor production. Governmental investigations have established, and the collective agreements in the industry have long recognized, that under this system the jobber is in economic reality the virtual employer of the workers in contractors' shops: that he must be responsible for their wages and labor standards, and indeed that the contractor is nothing more than the jobber's outside agent to obtain his required production. Of the 300,000 workers employed in the ladies' garment industry in the New York area alone, more than 80 percent of them are employed in contractors' shops.

Now, let us suppose the jobber is a non-union jobber or that he employs non-union contractors. Suppose, too, that the International Ladies' Garment Workers' Union, the union which functions in this industry, attempts to organize the jobber's workers or the contractor's workers or both groups of workers simultaneously. In this organizational drive the union may attempt to persuade the jobber's workers not to design or to cut goods to be manufactured in the shops of the non-union contractors, or the union may try to persuade the contractor's workers not to manufacture dresses for a non-union jobber.

It has been suggested that this might fall within the ban of the literal language of section 8(b)(4) and section 303 of the Taft-Hartley Act or of section 8(b)(4) and sections 16 and 17 of the Taft substitute. I am sure this was never the intention of the sponsors of the act or of the Congress. The jobber and his contractors are obviously engaged in a unified and integrated production effort, and they do not stand as neutrals with respect to one another in any labor dispute against the other. Rather, they are allies because they are engaged in a common enterprise. It seems plain to me that they are not to be deemed separate employers, but, rather, a single unified employer of all workers engaged in every phase of the manufacture of the garments, no matter on whose premises the workers are located. Economic pressure exerted against either jobber or contractor cannot be construed as secondary action against either, but must be deemed primary against both. The secondary boycott provisions of the act and of the Taft substitute therefore have not the slightest application.

Does the senator from Ohio agree that it was never the intention of Congress to have the secondary boycott provisions of the act apply to this situation?

MR. TAFT: Mr. President, the secondary boycott ban is merely intended to prevent a union from injuring a third person who is not involved in any way in the dispute or strike, and therefore should not suffer economic damage simply because of the action of a labor union. It is not intended to apply to a case where the third party is, in effect, in cahoots with or acting as a part of the primary employer.

On the basis of the facts stated by the senator from New York, I do not believe the law was intended to apply to the case he cites, where the secondary employer is so closely allied to the primary employer as to amount to an alter-ego situation or an employer relationship. It should not apply, and I think Judge Rifkind practically decided that in the so-called Project Engineering Company case.

I may say that one of the changes we are making in the law is to remove the ban on the secondary boycott in a case where there is a strike in one plant and then the work is transferred to another plant, because we feel that in that case the men who are striking should be able to picket the second plant in order that the men there may not work on the work on which the men in the first plant were refusing to work.

So not only do I think the law of the case is as I have indicated, and does not prohibit the particular action referred to in the facts cited by the senator in his question, which I have seen and have had the privilege of reading, but the spirit of the act is entirely contrary to applying it in that kind of a case.

MR. IVES: I thank the able senator from Ohio.

World War II brought significant changes in consumer demand, labor force, material supply, as well as garment design and production. The selection by Furnas, which appeared in the *Saturday Evening Post* on August 16, 1941, examines some of these changes on the eve of United States entry into the war.

THE PRICE LINE SHIFTS
by J. C. Furnas

This spring, with defense spending booming the dress trade, a melancholy New York contractor summed up what it's like on the lunatic fringe of this manic-depressive business:

"Last year I could get plenty of operators, but no work. This year I could get plenty of work, but operators? They all got jobs already. Business is good, I can't hire help. Business is bad, I can't get dresses to sew. So what?"

The employer's complaint was borne out by the union. President Dubinsky announced in early June that there would be an acute shortage of workers during the fall season.

It boils down to outsmarting the other fellow on style and price without outsmarting yourself on overhead. Without cost accounting and steady operation, that takes doing. The Seventh Avenuer pins his hopes on luck and haggling. He guesses as low as he dares—or as low as the union representative will permit—on what a new style will cost to make, and spends the next few weeks hoping fervently he was right. If right often enough, he suddenly gets rich on a turnover on invested capital that can reach 1,500 percent a year. If wrong too often, he becomes one of those thronging bankrupts.

One "runner" (a best-seller among dresses) has to pay for 10 styles that flop. Since the styles that buyers go for are the price of survival, style piracy is a scourge in the market, which is why this business is even goofier than show business a few blocks farther up Broadway.

For years, in what New York calls "the sticks," that calls itself the Middle West, unobtrusive factories had been supplying housewives with cotton dresses for housework. They were outright Mother Hubbards at first, as useful and about as handsome as plumber's dungarees, gradually coming to cost a little more, as fast-dyed cottons came in, and looking neat enough to wear to the store mornings.

Then and now, these companies dealt in dozens. Since wholesale prices ran from $2.75 to perhaps $10 a dozen, style meant little and manufacturing efficiency meant everything. Housedress firms always knew more than New York ever dreamed of about routing work efficiently, splitting operations among specialized workers, buying materials and planning lines months ahead, keeping down overhead by year-round operation.

Rayon produced the collision. Tinkering with cheaper rayons, housedress firms found they could turn out something definitely smart for very little, thanks to operating efficiency—and went on from there. Chain stores and mail-order houses found street-dress markets that "popular" 35th Street shops had always been shy of because they lacked volume. It is no accident that the dress pages of mail-order catalogs look so much smarter these days. And rayon was far more stably priced than silk, so they could safely buy materials far ahead, as they knew how.

By now, former housedress concerns are pushing into rayon street dresses wholesaling up to $80 a dozen, meaning at least $10.95 retail, right in the "better" market where Seventh Avenue has been taking its worst beating. While New York has stagnated, housedress sales have jumped ahead to a degree small on national totals, but, to observers on the corner of 38th [Street] and Broadway, already a cloud looking considerably bigger than a man's hand.

Clumsy and stumbly as New York looks from the outside, the feeling persists that, in any inter-area competition, the old fellow still has tremendous advantage in the number of expert workers, the prestige of the New York name and nearness of sources of trimmings and fabrics. After all, there is no law prohibiting the efficiency of Seventh Avenue. The fanciest shops in the market, with big payrolls, year-round operation and efficient work routing, not only hold their own, but expand and make money, even if they do stick to one-operator-to-a-dress methods.

On February 9, 1956, the *New York Times* described the traditional method for determining piece rates for garments made in New York City.

SETTLING PRICES
by Nan Robertson

As every man knows, women are funny. They hate to meet another woman wearing the same dress. This strange quirk is where fashion starts. Because of it the American garment industry grinds out 150,000 different styles a year, each as unique as a fingerprint.

Such wide variety has led to a system of "price settlements" on Seventh Avenue. No other industry, from autos to zithers, works on this system. Under it the labor cost of each new style is hammered out behind locked doors between manufacturers and the International Ladies' Garment Workers' Union.

A typical scene opens at the concern of Abe Schrader, 530 Seventh Avenue.

Abe Schrader does $6 million volume a year. He owns what is supposed to be one of the "hottest" (fastest-selling) lines in the dress industry.

When a dress comes out of the Schrader designing room he sets a wholesale price on it. He knows down to the last penny what the fabric and trimmings cost and what his overhead comes to. But he can only guess at the labor cost of making the garment.

The price settlement will not take place for at least a month, since the union's Price Settlement Bureau is unable to keep up with the constant flow of styles from Seventh Avenue. Meanwhile, store buyers want to place orders instantly for Schrader dresses.

It is now 10:00 A.M. on price-settlement day.

Enter the cast of characters in order of appearance:

Edward Kopp, management. He is Mr. Schrader's representative from the Affiliated Dress Manufacturers, a trade group. He says of the garment union: "We are friendly enemies."

Abe Feil, union. He is the "adjuster" from the ILGWU's Price Settlement Bureau, acting as spokesman for the factory representatives.

Max Korn, union, representing the factory of one contractor who will make some of the dresses under discussion.

Joseph Casella, union, representing the workers at another contracting shop.

Morris Tanenbaum, who looks like a grizzled Groucho Marx, is typical of many shop stewards. When he came to this country from Austria as a boy of 16, he started work in a garment sweatshop on the lower East Side for $1.25 a week.

He also remembers collective bargaining before 1936, when the present price-settlement system came in. In those days contractors stood in line at the manufacturer's back door, asking for work. It was a kind of auction sale in reverse. The contractor bargained first with the manufacturer and then with the workers, and whichever contractor offered the cheapest labor got the order to make the dresses.

The five men went into Mr. Schrader's office and shut the door, leaving Mr. Schrader outside. His representative, Mr. Kopp, was there as an onlooker only for the time being.

Eight dresses to be settled hung on a rack. Each of them consisted of about 23 parts to be priced. Mr. Feil took them down one by one, turning each inside out, picking at seams, counting pleats, buttons and zippers.

Mr. Feil knows when he starts analyzing a dress, that a shaped dart costs 2 cents to make and a waist seam is a nickel. So does Mr. Schrader. There will be no argument on these standardized parts, which make up 75 percent of the garment.

The rest of the items are "blind" ones that Mr. Feil has never seen before this season. Here is where style and bargaining begin, and the higher the style, the more blind items there will be.

For two hours Mr. Feil worked quietly over his dresses. Then Mr. Kopp was asked to leave while the union men decided on what price they would ask for each garment.

The four agreed quickly on most of the style numbers. On one complicated number, a copy of Dior's "Y-line," there was some discussion.

Finally all agreed. Mr. Schrader and Mr. Kopp were called in. Mr. Feil presented his price list to Mr. Schrader. Mr. Schrader submitted his to Mr. Feil. The bargaining went something like this:

MR. FEIL: "Number 1600—The labor cost should be $2.15."

MR. SCHRADER: "No sir. I make it $1.95."

MR. FEIL: "To sew in a zipper with shirring is hard."

MR. SCHRADER: "Why did you add 20 cents for shirring? Four stitches at 2½ cents a stitch doesn't come to 20 cents. I worked in a shop for 22 years and I ought to know."

MR. FEIL: "So what good does it do me?"

MR. KOPP: "So 1600, how much?"

No. 1600 was finally settled for $2.05.

Why does Mr. Schrader quibble for hours over such small change? He explained: "Every dime I dicker over, really represents 22 cents.

"I have to pay the 12 cents extra to cover each union machine operator's health, disability and state unemployment insurance. It also pays for her social security and for a 36 percent cost-of-living adjustment tacked onto her weekly wage.

"Just think," said Mr. Schrader, "I turn out 200,000 dresses a year. If it's a question of one thin dime, since the dime really costs me 22 cents on each dress, I can lose $44,000."

Yes, it's a complex business. It will remain so as long as women follow fashion, and refuse to look like peas in a pod.

Outside of New York, postwar changes in garment production and the spread of section work raised new problems in rate setting. The following excerpt is from an article by a professor, then at Pennsylvania State College, who for a time served as assistant director of the ILGWU Research Department. It appeared in the October 1954 issue of the *Southern Economic Journal.*

SECTION WORK
by Nathan Belfer

For many years the manufacture of women's garments in the New York market has been dominated by the so-called tailoring, or whole-garment, system. In this method of production a skilled operator sews the entire garment. One operator makes the outer shell of the garment, sews the parts of the lining together, and then attaches the lining to the body. In the newer section-work system, on the other hand, the sewing of the garment is broken down into many subdivisions with each operator performing only one small operation. Thus, one operator will work only on sleeves, another on collars, a third on cuffs, etc.

Under the whole-garment system the manufacturer or contractor can turn over the sewing of the garment to one individual worker and be assured that he will receive a satisfactorily completed garment. The demands on his managerial abilities are thus at a minimum. In fact, some firms have adopted section work and then decided to give it up because of the large amount of supervision required for its smooth and efficient operation.

The section-work system is, of course, an adaptation of mass-production assembly-line techniques, the success of which depends on a large output of a standardized product. Here we find the major deterrent to the use of the section-work system for the women's clothing industry is dominated by the style factor. No style stays on the production line very long, and the output of each is limited. Changing styles require flexibility in production techniques, and the whole-garment system provides the entrepreneur with more elasticity than the section-work system.

There have been cases of firms which installed section-work systems at great cost but had to discontinue them because frequent style change resulted in a small output for each style. Section work is superior if the manufacturer is assured of a long run on one style. Thus, its greatest success had been achieved in a field such as house-dresses where the style factor is at a minimum and long production runs of one style are possible. During World War II, when the traditional diversity of styles was restricted by the War Production Board to conserve textile fabrics and wartime influences confined styles to simple and severe lines to conform to the military spirit in the country, manufacturers were able to plan on long runs of a single style. Thus section-work systems were set up and operated successfully in a number of shops. When the war ended, however, style again became the dominant factor in the industry. Long production runs on a single style were no longer possible, and many firms, particularly in the dress section of the industry, gave up the section-work systems installed during the war.

Finally, section work substantially increases the process time involved in manufacturing. It is estimated that a section-work shop can deliver orders approximately three weeks after they have been received. A whole-garment shop, by contrast, can make deliveries in three to four days. Because the retailer of women's clothing is worried about the rapid obsolescence of his merchandise, he places his orders at the last possible moment to assure himself of the latest styles and presses the manufacturer for immediate delivery. In addition, a retail store places great emphasis on being the first to make the initial showing of a new style, so that a delay of even a week or two in delivery may destroy a large part of the value of a shipment. Thus, time is important in the industry. Section work may be more productive, but the jobber and manufacturer may want swift and flexible deliveries which can only be achieved by the whole-garment system. The small entrepreneur operating on the whole-garment system can survive because he provides the flexibility and elasticity which the industry requires.

In section work the development of sound piece rates raises many acute problems. Many section-work shops have operated on a week work basis and have thus avoided the problem of setting piece rates.

However, piece rates are favored in the industry as a spur to efficiency and the union has been increasingly faced with the problem of developing a sound piece-rate structure for section-work shops. The unit system of piece settlement cannot always be applied in section work.

The method of sectionalization varies widely from factory to factory. In section shops under agreement with the New York Dress Joint Board the number of sections varies from two to eighteen. Thus, a fixed rate for a specific occupational title has a different meaning in different shops. The operation of collar setting, for example, can be subsectionalized in a number of different ways. To develop a standard collar-setting rate which will be applicable on a market-wide basis is an exceedingly difficult task. The different degrees of sectionalization between shops makes it difficult to set market-wide piece rates, and at the same time secure equal earnings opportunities for all sections of the garment. The workers, of course, demand equal earnings opportunities if they believe that their skills are comparable. Section work piece-rate setting can thus create internal tensions and frictions for the union.

In negotiations to renew collective agreements covering key New York dress industry, union representatives (left to right: Vice Presidents Murray Gross, Frederick R. Siems, ILGWU President Sol C. Chaikin and Executive Vice President Wilbur Daniels) met with employer spokesmen until one hour before February 2, 1976, strike deadline.

The state of the garment industry in the United States at the start of the 1960s was surveyed by the British publication, the *Economist*, in its January 16, 1960, issue.

DRESSMAKER TO A CONTINENT

When six Russian economists came to the United States recently, an important item on their whirlwind tour was a visit to New York City's garment district. Here they saw for themselves that an industry composed of a large number of eagerly competing small firms has persisted into the twentieth century without showing any signs of "monopoly capitalism." There are many more Marxes than Smiths in the garment trade, but its philosophy comes from Adam, not from Karl.

The firms which make women's and children's clothes number in all about 16,000, most of them specializing in one particular line of business: in "unit-priced" dresses or in the cheaper "dozen-priced" dresses—producing 250 million a year altogether; in coats and suits—35 million a year—or in blouses—180 million a year; in sportswear, in underwear, or in knitwear. These small "shops" have on the average only 40 employees each and they survive partly because it takes relatively little capital to set up in business—anything from $15,000 upwards; partly because of the overwhelming importance in this industry of attractive new styles; and partly also because of the traditions of fierce individualism and mutual distrust established by the Jewish immigrants from eastern Europe who provided most of the original employers in the industry.

But even the garment trade is not altogether immune to the trend towards bigness. The total number of manufacturers has dropped sharply in the last decade—by 25 percent, according to one estimate. And the larger firms, with annual sales, say, of $5 million or more, are increasing their share of the market. But in contrast to most American industries, the trade has as yet no giants. A few leading firms may each have annual sales approaching $40 million, but this still represents well under 1 percent of the industry's total wholesale volume of about $6.5 billion a year. Because manufacturers are legion, few of them can hope to make their names known to the public, and retail shops sew their own labels into the clothes they sell. Thus advertising on a national scale by the original producers tends to be confined to foundation garments, to "swimwear" (where four or five firms dominate the market) and to a handful of producers of high-quality clothes.

The great hazard to the garment manufacturer is fashion; a firm is made or ruined by the success or failure of its designer to catch the eye of those all-important figures—the buyers for retail shops who are flocking into New York this month to lay in their spring and summer stocks. Styles are set at the top and filter down through lower and lower price ranges. The total volume of sales of clothing in any season can usually be predicted with some accuracy, but no individual manufacturer can tell in advance how well he himself will do. He complains, moreover, that he is squeezed between the large suppliers of cloth, who insist that he must take up the yardage he has ordered, and the retail buyers—organised for the most part in powerful groups—who cancel their orders right and left.

With meagre resources behind him, the small manufacturer can withstand neither a run of bad luck nor a recession in business. The casualty rate is therefore high; one in every five firms may disappear in a single year. But failure involves little financial loss, and often leads to a subsequent reorganisation in a new attempt to win the big prizes. The women's garment manufacturer likes to point to his low profits—between 1 and 2 percent of the value of sales. But in fact, with his own salary and expenses already allowed for, his rate of profit usually represents a return of 10 to 15 percent on invested capital. In general, garment manufacturers tend either to do nicely or to go out of business altogether.

As well as a diversity of manufacturers, there is also a high degree of vertical specialisation in the trade, with garments being moved backwards and forwards between firms, pushed on mobile dress racks round the crowded streets near New York's Pennsylvania Station. Often a manufacturer will do no actual sewing himself. He will design the clothes, buy the cloth, cut out the pieces (a hundred or two hundred layers at a time), assemble the parts of the garment into bundles and dispatch them to outside contractors for stitching. The garments are then usually returned to him for finishing, pressing and distributing to retailers. . . .

The congested heart of New York City has been the home of garment manufacturing ever since the second half of the last century when American women started to abandon home dressmaking for purchases off the peg. And while rival centres have grown up in other parts of the country, two out of every three manufacturers still have their headquarters in New York. But the tide continues to run against the city. Southern towns can offer employers lower wage rates and less unionisation. Sunny California is helped by the rising importance of sports clothes, for which the pavements of New York have no natural advantage. And high rents and traffic congestion are forcing many employers to consider less crowded locations outside the city. On the other hand, New York's position as the fashion capital of America has not been seriously challenged.

13. Old Battles, New Frontiers

Freed by production engineers from the restraints of style and whole-garment sewing skills, the 1930s saw the garment industry undergoing a major expansion trend out of the big urban centers to which it had previously been tied by its need for a steady supply of tailor-type sewers. While these central markets continued to flourish, an ever-expanding frontier held out the promise of a helpless, low-wage labor force to those employers seeking to increase profits by means of exploitation rather than through managerial know-how.

Where the union took root, wages were raised and hours were reduced even beyond the prescriptions of the Fair Labor Standards Act. One result was the development of regional differences in standards. Especially tempting to some employers were working conditions in the southeastern region. Even employers willing to tolerate unionization, as Ed Townsend reports, were rebuffed by traditionally antiunion communities who feared that the advent of the ILGWU would clear the way for other labor organizations. This, they were convinced, would eliminate their labor-cost advantage, which, together with tax rebates and other commitments, was their chief attraction for migrating northern firms. The particular form this resistance took in the city of Baxley, Georgia, is described by Morris P. Glushien.

But in a nation whose every region had been penetrated by radio and then by television, one in which the labor movement had fought for the passage of laws safeguarding the worker's right to organize, the appeal of the union could not be denied for long. Often the crucial battles were fought in the plant, as described by Justice Thurgood Marshall, or on the picket lines, as reported by *Newsweek*.

Although resistance to union efforts continued, progress was gradually being achieved. Discrimination on the basis of race, color, or other regional prejudices was countered through the simple union message that the life of *every* worker could be improved. The account by Alba B. Martin describes a major victory in this sphere in Little Rock, Arkansas.

Inevitably, an industry as portable as the sewing machine soon reached the limits of the shoreline. Work and wage conditions could be improved in Puerto Rico, Paul Douglas insisted, with no threat to the prosperity of that island commonwealth. During the 1950s a new force threatened the garment industry from across the ocean as Japan began flooding American stores with blouses selling for under $1, described in Gordon Walker's report.

In less than a generation American investors had taken the leap across the ocean, eventually competing with Japanese investors in Korea, as Fox Butterfield reports, in their search for a more defenseless labor force. Protected by import laws condoning the loss of American jobs to these new centers of exploitation, international profit hunters condemned thousands of American skilled workers, such as those portrayed by Bernadine Morris, to a fate of joblessness, with no gain for either the American consumer or the overseas garment worker.

At the three-quarter century mark, the ILGWU is once again fighting the sweatshop—this time a sweatshop beyond the reach of its organizers or the jurisdiction of the Fair Labor Standards Act. ILGWU President Sol C. Chaikin reports on the manner in which this fight is going forward.

Some employers moved out of the large northern centers in an attempt to locate low-wage labor in other sections of the country. The following five selections deal with the various types of organizing difficulties this move created for the union. The first is taken from the *Christian Science Monitor,* December 4, 1954.

THE ILGWU HEADS SOUTH
by Ed Townsend

A few weeks ago the International Ladies' Garment Workers' Union (AFL) announced that a New York garment manufacturer had agreed to pay the union an estimated $250,000, in monthly installments, during the next four years, covering the savings in labor costs derived from operating two plants in the South on a non-union basis.

The company, whose name has been withheld by ILGWU, has had a long, friendly relationship with the garment union headed by David Dubinsky, one of the nation's shrewdest—and often statesmanlike—labor leaders. When it decided to open plants below Mason and Dixon's line, it was prompted by considerations the union considered sound; it wasn't, in union terms, a "runaway" from higher northern labor costs.

Under the company's northern contracts with ILGWU, all work, no matter where done, has to be under union conditions. The company was perfectly willing to have its southern employees, about 300 in number, join ILGWU and to extend to them the wages and work conditions common in the North. However, ILGWU organizers were forced out of one southern plant town by threats of violence; other employers in the two communities, supported by public officials, made clear that they would consider any agreement with ILGWU, raising local pay and shortening work hours, "an unfriendly act" in the non-union area. The company placed its problem before Mr. Dubinsky. The $250,000 deal, turning four years' labor savings over to ILGWU, to use as it desires, was the result.

The garment workers' union, according to Mr. Dubinsky, plans to spend at least a part of the $250,000 in new efforts to organize the southern workers. If and when ILGWU succeeds in signing them up and the employer is able to sign a contract, the payments to ILGWU will stop; the company will pay the money out, instead, in higher wages and increased hour and welfare standards for its southern mill workers.

The ILGWU agreement caused considerable interest in labor and management circles. One employer commented in New York that it was "the sort of deal that just couldn't happen—but did." It's a good assumption, though, that it won't happen again. It resulted from special circumstances, backed by employer good faith in adhering to contract terms that might have been broken, if the employer had wished, by taking an ILGWU strike in the North while operating full blast, and perhaps, expanding, in the South.

About three months before, ILGWU made another, less publicized, move against operators of southern non-union garment manufacturers. Through Mr. Dubinsky, it issued an offer of a three-year "moratorium" on ILGWU organizing efforts to any employer willing to "raise the minimum wage in [his] shop to 15 cents an hour above the present or future government minimum," now 75 cents an hour. According to ILGWU, no employers accepted the offer, although it had expected "a handful of them [to] take the union at its word and step forward to take advantage of the unique offer."

The agreement with the New York garment manufacturer and the offer made to southern non-union mill operators in the summer are signs of concern in ILGWU—along with other unions—over "runaway" shops, those moving from tightly unionized communities to other areas with lower labor costs and little, if any, unionization.

There are a few signs, now and then, that the "runaway" trend to the South has slowed down; a few firms that moved to Dixie are heading back now, but so far they are exceptions. Bu although these signs are encouraging in labor's eyes, tharen't—yet—considered import nt. Unions like the ILGWU are still busy trying to work out solutions of their own to help stem the tide to unorganized areas.

It can get cold around Atlanta, Georgia, too as these Local 122 pickets, early in February 1965, showed.

> Hostility to unions appeared in a number of communities visited by ILGWU organizers. In Baxley, Georgia, town officials invoked an ordinance requiring solicitors to obtain a license. The ILGWU brought the case before the Supreme Court, which, in January 1958, sustained the union's position. The following selection is taken from the brief prepared by the ILGWU's general counsel.

THE BAXLEY, GEORGIA, CASE
by Morris P. Glushien

On February 19, 1954, Rose Staub and her companion Mamie Merritt were at a local restaurant in Baxley where they were sought out by the chief of police of the city of Baxley [and] questioned by him. Rose Staub told the chief of police that she was employed by the union, and she and Mamie Merritt both told him that they were in Baxley "going around talking to some of the women to organize the factory workers . . . to gain membership and gather members for it and hold meetings with them for that purpose." No permit had been issued to Rose Staub or Mamie Merritt, nor had they made application for a permit, as required by the ordinance. During their respective terms of office, no one has ever applied to either the chief of police or the clerk of the city council for a permit.

On the same day of the conversation with the chief of police, a meeting was held at the home of Mrs. Catherine Taylor, attended by her, Rose Staub, Mamie Merritt, and three others. Excepting Staub and Merritt, the other four at the meeting "all work in Hazlehurst" but "live in Baxley." According to Mrs. Taylor, Staub and Merritt had asked "that we hold a meeting at my house. They stated that the purpose of the meeting was for getting members for the union. They asked me to get others together." One of the four present stated that she "was interested in knowing what the union would mean to the workers." At the meeting, Staub and Merritt "just told us they wanted us to join the union, and said it would be a good thing for us to do—to join the union, and went on to tell us how this union would help us."

They also explained that the membership dues "would be sixty-four cents a week," but that dues were not payable until the plant was organized; no money was asked of the persons at the meeting. The cooperation of the four was invited "to get other girls from up there to join the union," and blank membership cards were offered for that purpose. Rose Staub explained that the objective sought was to "have enough cards signed to petition for an election . . . with the Labor Board." As none of the four was interested in joining the union, no membership cards were left with them.

On the same day that this meeting was held, a summons was issued by the chief of police commanding Rose Staub to "appear before the Police Court of said City [of Baxley] at 7 o'clock P.M. on the 22 day of February, 1954, to answer to the offense of Soliciting Members for an Organization Without a Permit & License." After trial, the mayor's court convicted Rose Staub of violation of the ordinance. She was sentenced to thirty days imprisonment in the city jail or a fine of three hundred dollars.

Mamie Merritt was tried together with Rose Staub, and she too was convicted and given the same sentence as Rose Staub for violating the ordinance. By agreement of counsel the disposition of the judgment of conviction of Mamie Merritt is to await and conform with the outcome of this appeal.

The ordinance conditions the solicitation of membership in a labor organization—and thus the exercise of the rights of speech, press, and assembly which is inseparable from it—upon securing a permit from the mayor and council of the city of Baxley who may grant or with-hold the permit in their discretion based on their consideration of "the character of the applicant, the nature of the business of the organization for which members are desired to be solicited, and its effects upon the general welfare of citizens of the city of Baxley." This constitutes previous restraint in its most vicious and primitive form.

The ordinance does not stop with censorship. It further provides that, if the person who would solicit members is a "salaried employee or officer of the organization," or receives "a fee of any sort from the obtaining of such members," he must, in addition to securing a permit, pay an annual tax of $2,000 plus "$500 for each member obtained." This annual flat tax is fixed in amount, unrelated to the scope of the activity, without basis either in present or potential revenue, and unapportioned in any way.

Its character as a flat license tax alone vitiates the levy imposed by the ordinance. But the tax is also prohibitive and discriminatory, and for these additional reasons cannot survive the First Amendment's guaranty against abridgement of the freedoms of speech, press, and peaceable assembly.

When a New York blouse firm moved to Brewton, Alabama, after a quarter century of peaceful relations with the ILGWU in New York, it arranged a contract with another organization before ILGWU organizers appeared on the scene. In time, workers seeking an ILGWU contract wore ILGWU buttons in the plant. The following selection is drawn from a brief, prepared by the solicitor general of the National Labor Relations Board in October 1966, defending the board's decision to uphold the ILGWU in the events described. The Supreme Court later sustained both the NLRB and the ILGWU. Marshall was appointed to the Supreme Court in 1967.

BATTLE OF THE UNION BUTTON
by Thurgood Marshall

On May 23, 1962, Fay Madden and Lynn Estes reported to work wearing ILG buttons. While several women employees held Madden, another employee removed the pin and threw it away. When Madden returned wearing another pin the employees again forcibly removed it, tearing Madden's dress in the process. Foreman Eskridge stood nearby watching the disturbance, but did nothing, and floorlady Gandy ran into the foreman's office and exclaimed "They've got the pin off her!" Gandy added that she "would stomp [Madden] in the floor!" and that she hoped "they would run her butt out!"

Plant manager Byrd then arrived, reprimanded Madden for wearing the button in the plant, and sent her home until the other women "cooled off." Later that morning, Byrd called Estes into his office and told him that he would be discharged if he wore an ILG pin in the plant again. Several hours later, Company Vice-President Rothenberg, speaking over the plant's public-address system, told the employees that "the International Ladies' Garment Workers' Union does not belong here and we will not tolerate any action which might create dissensions and disturbances in the plant. We are very gratified by the loyalty most of you have shown to the company. . . ."

Shortly after 1 P.M. that same day, a group of male employees forcibly ejected Estes from the plant for having worn an ILG pin. At the same time, a number of female employees, including Mary Braddick, forced ILG adherents Jones, West, Bell, and Chavers to leave the plant. Just before these evictions, floorlady Gandy told two other floorladies to come with her to foreman Williams' office, and during the struggling, Gandy watched from the office door with apparent glee.

The four evicted female employees complained to plant manager Byrd about their treatment. When West asked whether Byrd could make the plant workers behave so that the four could go back to work, Byrd replied, "No, I can't handle them . . . that's what you call a mob." Bell then asked whether she could return to work the following day, and Byrd answered that it would be at her own risk because he could not give her "any kind of protection in the plant." He told the group that they should stay at home for their own protection, and that, if they would call from time to time, he would advise them when to return. The four women left the plant and reported the incident to the local sheriff. On May 24, Byrd advised the group not to come to work for a few more days.

The next morning, May 25, the five evicted employees and Madden went to Byrd's office seeking to return to work. Byrd told them that they should lay off a few days longer as the women were still upset and he could offer them "no protection unless there is violence in the mill." Byrd assured four of the employees that they still had jobs, but he discharged Estes and Madden, the former allegedly for wearing an ILG pin on May 23 and the latter allegedly for failing to make her production quota.

On the morning of May 31, Chavers, Bell, Jones, and West reported for work at Byrd's office in accordance with his instructions. Byrd assigned Jones and Chavers to their old jobs but assigned West and Bell to operate sewing machines, so as to reduce their contact with other workers. He cautioned all four that he wanted no discussion of unions in the plant. Foreman Eskridge attempted to escort Jones and Chavers to their work stations, but a group of about 25 women forced them through the door leading into the lobby. Eskridge pulled open the door to Byrd's office and cried out, "Byrd, they are running [Jones] and [Chavers] out again, and Mary Alice Braddick started every darn bit of it." Byrd sent the four ILG supporters home, and the other employees returned to work. Mary Alice Braddick was not reprimanded; in June, she was promoted to floorlady.

On June 4, each of the four women employees wrote Byrd protesting that he had permitted the other employees to evict them from the plant; they also inquired when they could return to work and whether they would receive protection. Three weeks later, on June 25, Byrd replied that they had "intentionally and willfully provoked" the demonstrations against them and that, if they wished to work in the plant, they must "avoid the inciting of any further demonstrations." The four women returned to work on July 9, and there were no incidents on that day or the next.

On July 11, West heard a fellow employee tell floorlady Smith that "they were fixing to run us out again." Floorlady Smith walked off, and 15 or 20 employees removed West and the three other newly returned employees from their work stations. Floorladies Smith and Braddick watched the eviction but did nothing. Foreman Eskridge took Bell, Jones and Chavers to Byrd's office and told Byrd that they had not "done anything to cause the difficulty." Byrd replied, "I know they weren't causing any trouble," and asked the names of those who were in the offending group. Byrd sent the ILG supporters home, promising that he would call them when he thought it advisable for them to return to work. He did not thereafter recall any of them.

On August 3, four more employees came to work wearing ILG pins. Shortly thereafter, Byrd told them that wearing the pins could result in violence and that they must either take the pins off or go on layoff until sentiment in the plant had changed. The four employees left the plant rather than remove their pins, but returned to work on August 16, without the pins. On that date, they were evicted from the plant by a group of employees. During the eviction, floorladies Gandy, Smith, and Boddiford stood by watching and "snickering."

The evicted workers reported what had happened to Byrd, who told them that their presence in the plant was causing the disturbance and that "there wasn't anything he could do about it." He advised that, for their own protection, they stay home until the situation in the plant permitted their return. One of the four evictees called Byrd early in November and asked when she might return, but Byrd said he had no idea. Byrd did not call the others.

No employees were punished for taking part in the evictions, although the names of those responsible were given to Byrd by the ILG adherents, and by participating employees. Nor did Byrd interrogate the employees whose participation in the evictions was called to his attention.

The National Labor Relations Board concluded that the company, by failing to take reasonable measures to prevent that action, had "ratified and condoned the forcible ejection of the ILG supporters, and had thus in effect caused them to be laid off or discharged on account of their ILG activity, in violation of Section 8(a)(3) and (1) of the National Labor Relations Act."

Prominent among the situations that arose on the union's new frontiers were the Wentworth and the Kellwood drives by the ILGWU. The first of these, which occurred in Lake City, South Carolina, is described in the following account drawn from the October 21, 1968, issue of *Newsweek*.

THE COLOR LINE IS GREEN

In the drab Deep South textile town of Lake City, South Carolina, one day last week, two women strikers named Marianne Witherspoon and Mamie Wilkes were marching side by side on a picket line in front of the Wentworth Manufacturing Company, a firm which produces low-cost women's dresses. "Just look at this," snapped Marianne, handing Mamie a propaganda letter mailed to strikers by the stubborn management at Wentworth. "They just won't give up." "Yeah," Mamie chuckled, "they want to send all of us back to the cotton fields."

While strikes are nothing new in the industrial cities of the South, the color of the picket line at Wentworth is. For Marianne Witherspoon is black and Mamie Wilkes is white, and along with 490 other strikers at the Lake City plant and another Wentworth facility at nearby Florence, they are part of a newly integrated attack on anti-labor managements all over the South. The Negroes, of course, learned the value of militant solidarity in their battles for equal rights on the streets of Selma and Montgomery, Alabama, and they are leading the attack. Now white workers, whose own economic and social standing has been stagnant for years, are beginning to see the handwriting on the factory wall. As Sallie Nettles, one of the white strikers at Lake City, summed up: "We'll have to get together sooner or later. If we can work with 'em, we can strike with 'em. They stick together better than white people. That's why they've been getting ahead."

Just last week, a largely Negro local of the International Ladies' Garment Workers' Union (ILGWU) concluded a successful organizational strike at Laura Industries, Inc., a manufacturer of women's sportswear in Selma. Negroes are providing much of the support for a strike by a United Steel Workers local at Bush Hog, Inc., a machinery firm in Selma owned by Earl Goodwin, co-chairman of the Wallace for President finance committee. And at Memphis, where the Rev. Dr. Martin Luther King was murdered while leading a strike by sanitation workers, Negroes make up the majority of 1,300 workers striking for better wages and working conditions at city hospitals. But it is at Lake City and Florence that labor leaders see the most heartening demonstration of solidarity by black and white workers, who have come to realize that—in the final analysis—the only real color line is green.

At stake in the Wentworth strike is nothing less than the workers' jobs. Earlier this year, officials of the ILGWU learned that Wentworth not only was subcontracting work to non-union textile mills in Georgia but that it was building a new plant in job-hungry west Texas. When the company refused to grant the union a new contract guaranteeing jobs for the South Carolina workers after the non-union Texas plant opens, the union struck on August 29. All 330 workers at the all-Negro Florence plant walked out while 160 workers—half white and half black—walked out at Lake City. Another 315 white workers remained on the job.

From the start, opponents of the strike, both black and white, have tried everything they can think of to intimidate the strikers. In Florence, a group of Negro ward heelers offered a bribe to a Negro union officer if she would return to work. A white woman striker, whose husband is the chief of police in the nearby village of Olanta, was told by Olanta Mayor Marty Green that unless she went back to work, her husband would never get another police job in South Carolina. Tearfully, she told her fellow strikers she would have to scab. But perhaps the biggest ally of the Wentworth management is the spirit of the late Mother Cain, who enjoyed a reputation among local Negroes as a faith healer and prophetess before her recent death. "Sweet Mother Cain is watching you now," warned one of six mimeographed letters mailed Negro strikers, "Go back to work." Two of the letters contained grains of reddish-brown dirt said to be from Mother Cain's grave. According to local superstition, anyone who trifles with graveyard dirt will suffer. But in this case, the letter promised the dirt would bring good luck to anyone who returned to work.

The strikers—black and white—show no signs of backing down. A few weeks ago, a Negro minister was roundly booed at an integrated union meeting when he cautioned: "You gotta remember there gotta be biddies (baby chicks) before you have fried chicken. And you gotta have a company before you can have jobs. The union doesn't make any jobs." And the movement seems certain to grow. "Anywhere you have a large number of Negroes employed," says one union organizer, "you have a good chance of organizing the shop."

For more than a year there was no color line on the picket line at the huge Kellwood Corporation (Ottenheimer) plant in Little Rock, Arkansas. The following selection is taken from the decision of January 28, 1969, in which the National Labor Relations Trial Examiner found that a lack of good-faith bargaining by the company was a primary cause of the strike that began October 25, 1966.

THE KELLWOOD CASE
by Alba B. Martin

Nine days before the election, on January 3, 1966, the president of Kellwood Company, Fred W. Wenzel, talked to the Ottenheimer employees. He referred to union trouble hanging over the plant. He said, "I cannot say how long a strike at Ottenheimer's might last—for a week, a month, a year, or longer. But I can guarantee this—if the union gets in and there is a strike, Kellwood Company, all of Kellwood's facilities, and all of Kellwood's plants will stand behind Mr. Guthunz and will fully support him and Ottenheimer's during the strike."

Upon instructions from President Guthunz, the plant manager (Short) of Kellwood's loungewear plant in Little Rock, who had 230 employees under him, talked to about 200 of them in his office in groups of 4 to 6 at a time. He gave the same talk, based upon notes, about 30 or 40 times, beginning about November 3, 1965. Short credibly testified that he adhered closely to his notes because he knew that to deviate would be an unfair labor practice.

These carefully contrived expressions carried over to employees as they were obviously intended to carry. Thus two employees credibly testified that Short said the company would not sign a contract and would close the plant first. This is what they understood Short to say and what on the whole record I find the company wished them to understand.

During the campaign, according to uncontradicted credible testimony, minor supervisors interrogated employees concerning their own sympathy; tried to persuade an employee to remove a "vote yes" sign and wear a "vote no" sign; said that if you get the union in, you might be fired. In addition, several employees testified concerning the passing of anti-union petitions down the work lines during working hours while supervisors were on the line. One supervisor wrote on a petition "I would if I could" sign the anti-union petition. Another, Hendrickson, handed out anti-union leaflets to operators at work on the line.

One petition passing down a line said the employees should vote against the union because it would be impossible for 1,300 employees to find employment elsewhere. One witness testified that 25 to 30 employees signed an anti-union petition while a supervisor was on the line. A witness credibly testified that supervisor Turner had said President Guthunz had said he would not sign a contract and he meant it. Another witness testified Supervisor Bridges said the company lawyer said that to get the union in the employees would have to strike.

On January 3, 1966, Guthunz wrote the employees: "You already know you could lose your job in a union strike by being replaced with another worker. Can you afford to run the risks and dangers of a union strike?" He then asked employees to consider who was going to pay the rent, the groceries, pay the other bills, and where an employee could find another job, if he loses his job in a strike.

During the campaign, the company also mailed to employees a leaflet, and as to the future wrote this: "Ottenheimer Brothers will guarantee this: I, S. M. Guthunz, president of Ottenheimer Brothers Manufacturing Company, do hereby guarantee that if you do not have a union in our plant, you will not lose your job on account of a strike." (This was followed by the purported signature of Guthunz.)

During the campaign the company issued to employees and posted in the plant multicolor posters, some as large as 4 feet by 3 feet, carrying out the theme that unions and strikes go together.

The conclusion is inescapable that the company, in all of this, was seeking to show the employees the utter futility of their joining, supporting, and voting for the union; was seeking to convince the employees that Kellwood-Ottenheimer did not want the union and had no intent to sign a contract with the union; that it would not agree to the union's demands and that a strike was inevitable; and that an inevitable result of such a strike would be the loss of their jobs by the employees. I conclude that this was the state of mind, and the intention, with which Kellwood entered the bargaining negotiations.

Of particular note is that during the pre-election campaign, insofar as the record showed, there was no serious talk among employees or union organizers of striking the plant. In fact, referring to this period of time President Guthunz told employees on November 29, 1967, "The union told our employees there would be no strike, no trouble, and that there was nothing for them to worry about." Thus the company's propaganda was not in answer to any real threat of a strike, but was designed to frighten the employees away from the union and to defeat the union at the election. [On January 12, 1966, the union won the election by a vote of 666 to 564. Bargaining for a contract began.]

On July 18 Ottenheimer announced to its Lonoke employees that it was giving them a 10-cent wage increase effective August 1; and minutes later but not before, it offered the same increase to the union in

North (New York) or south (Lake City, South Carolina), alone or in groups, pickets patrolled at Wentworth shops in December 1968.

the negotiations at Little Rock. In making the offer to the union, Ottenheimer told the union that Kellwood was putting the 10-cent increase into effect at all its other plants (more than 30) on August 1, 1966.

The Lonoke plant is a part of the Ottenheimer Division under Guthunz and is about 25 miles from Little Rock. In announcing this wage increase to the Lonoke employees on July 18, plant manager McKibben of the Lonoke plant read a speech written by Guthunz on July 18 (and declaring in part:)

"Our company has always followed the policy of improving wages and working conditions whenever it was able to do so and it will continue to follow that policy in the future. No union can force us to do more than that. This increase should be proof that a union is not needed by a company like ours that treats its employees fairly and rewards them for their good work."

Although Guthunz had written this speech and was present with Kullman at the July 18 meeting with union representatives in Little Rock, which began at 4 P.M., neither of them initially mentioned the Lonoke wage increase or its impending announcement. Kullman made the company's 10-cent wage offer some 20 minutes after the session was under way with other topics, and stated that Kellwood was going to put a 10-cent raise into effect in all other plants effective August 1. Kullman stated that this decision had been made at a meeting of Kellwood officials in California. Within minutes thereafter and before the union representatives had expressed any or much reaction to the offer, the union representatives, Youngdahl and Siems, received a phone call from a union official telling them about McKibben's speech and the company's announcement of the raise to go into effect at Lonoke on August 1, 1966.

Siems returned from the telephone call and told Guthunz and Kullman in strong language that he thought Kellwood was bargaining in extremely bad faith to give a wage increase to other plants and then offer it to the union in negotiations. Siems, showing anger, expressed himself strongly and repeatedly to the effect that in the handling of this wage increase and offer, Kellwood was bargaining in bad faith with the union. For the first time, a bargaining session ended on this very unfriendly note.

The division presidents and President Wenzel in California were fully aware of the pending Little Rock negotiations and were briefed concerning them by Kellwood Company's employee relations direction, Keeline. No reason appears why Kellwood could not have offered the raise to the union on July 18 and thereafter, say on July 19, announced it to employees company-wide, thereby giving the union an opportunity to bargain concerning it for the Little Rock employees before announcing it company-wide. Under all the circumstances, it must be concluded that one of the reasons the company timed the announcement for July 18 instead of, say, July 19, was to maximize its adverse effect upon the union's bargaining power and bargaining position in the Little Rock negotiations.

No reason was offered for the 2-week delay between the announcement on July 18 and the effective date August 1. Under all the circumstances in this record, it must be concluded that at least one of the reasons for the delay was to maximize the adverse effect upon the union's bargaining power and bargaining position in the Little Rock negotiations. Thus, the delay allowed a 2-week period for Little Rock employees to contemplate the futility of their situation, to withdraw from the union, and to pressure the union to accept Kellwood's offer.

Kellwood could have simply told the Lonoke employees it was giving them the raise, without any reference to the union or the Little Rock employees. Instead, Guthunz went out of his way to tell the Lonoke employees, contrary to the admitted fact, that the union had nothing to do with their getting this raise. And instead, Guthunz emphasized that the employees did not need a union, did not need to pay union dues and fees, and would get the same rates of pay and benefits the Little Rock employees would get, a message Guthunz surely intended for the Little Rock employees as well as the Lonoke employees.

Kellwood's timing and language in announcing this increase to the Lonoke employees clearly tended to obstruct and inhibit the actual process of discussion of wages thereafter in the Little Rock negotiations. Its timing and language was clearly aimed at undercutting the authority and prestige of the bargaining representative at Little Rock and of creating the image of the employer as the protector of the employees rather than the union.

The timing and manner of this act changed the course of the union's bargaining thereafter and was one of the important factors that ultimately led to the strike. The timing of this increase and this McKibben speech written by President Guthunz, viewed in the light of the company's massive antiunion preelection campaign, revealed its true attitude towards the union and its rejection of the principle of collective bargaining, although it had gone through the motions of bargaining for some 4 months at some 20 meetings. Upon the preponderance of the evidence, I conclude that Kellwood's wage offer made to union representatives and employees on July 18 and 19 was made in bad faith and indicated it was bargaining in bad faith.

The ILGWU followed the industry to the farthest reaches of the nation. In Puerto Rico the cry arose among needle-trade employers that the union-supported drive to legislate higher minimum wages in the Commonwealth would erode the garment industry on the island. Douglas (1892–1976), a distinguished senator from Illinois, pointed out that, on the contrary, the move would replace homework with an established industry. From his letter to the *New York Times,* June 30, 1955.

MINIMUM WAGE IN PUERTO RICO
by Paul H. Douglas

On June 20 the *New York Times* published an article on Puerto Rico to the effect that the proposed minimum wage regulation for the island, contained in S. 2168, may cause great increased unemployment and curtail expansion of the Puerto Rican economy.

According to your report, 29,000 workers in the needle trades . . . are estimated as sure to lose their jobs. Let us look at these figures more closely.

In the home needle trades employment has declined from over 60,000 in 1950 to 29,000 in 1955. This is a decline of over 30,000 in five years. If present trends continue, homework will disappear in less than five years even if the industry should continue to operate at the 17½-cent-an-hour wage rate which prevailed during the period of the decline.

This decline in homework was partly compensated by an increase in factory employment. It is generally recognized that a growing and expanding economy is incompatible with the existence of sweatshop homework conditions. It is therefore false to blame minimum wage legislation for the unavoidable decline of the home needle industry.

The formula worked out to increase minimum wages in Puerto Rico has fully taken into consideration the complex and difficult situation of Puerto Rico. It provides for a special report by the Secretary of Labor to minimize unforeseeable hardships that may arise.

But the United States Senate does not only have a responsibility to facilitate industrialism in Puerto Rico. It has also a responsibility toward mainland industries. And some of these industries have had to compete with Puerto Rican firms under constantly increasing difficulties. In addition to the much-advertised tax exemptions there, the differential in average hourly earnings broadened from 98 cents in January 1950 to $1.31 in October 1954. The Senate proposal does not reduce this differential; it only tries to prevent an increase in this differential. It will, therefore, preserve the presently existing competitive advantage of Puerto Rico.

We have tried to understand and to adjust as fairly as we could these competing interests. We have good reason to believe that mainland and Puerto Rican industry can live with the Senate proposal.

In the mid-1950s the low-priced Japanese blouse invaded the American market. Foreshadowing things to come, the blouse, selling for under $1, was the product of a sweatshop operating on the far side of the globe. From the December 20, 1955, issue of the *Christian Science Monitor.*

MADE IN JAPAN
by Gordon Walker

OSAKA—Fumiko Tamashita, age 17 and just out of high school, is a worker in what is known as Japan's garment industry.

Like hundreds of other young girls in the smoky outskirts of Osaka, she races through a breakfast of cold rice and then takes a crowded tram to her "factory." It really isn't a factory; it is a poorly heated and poorly lighted shed in which 28 girls gather each day to sew, cut and pattern cotton blouses.

One might also say that there really isn't any garment industry, either. It is really only an adjunct to the textile-producing industry—a sort of cottage industry to which contracts are let out by the big spinning mills.

Unlike employees of the big textile mills with their labor standards laws, their company mess halls, and dormitories, the garment workers of Japan are in a different class. There are no such things as labor standards, no unions, no wage levels except very low ones, and no such thing as fringe benefits.

Fumiko gets an average wage—$9.25 a month for working six days a week at an average of 10 hours a day. She is a sewer in the establishment of a small enterpriser who manufactures cotton blouses on contract for one of the Big Ten textile manufacturers. When the blouses are finished, they are delivered to the textile firm which in turn processes them, packages them, and exports them.

Even with a liberal markup for local profit, the American importer gets the blouses at a ridiculously low cost, based upon the fact that Fumiko and others like her work for what amounts to slave-labor wages.

Women who work in the big textile mills make an average monthly wage of $34 for an eight-hour day. But in the subcontracted garment shops, a girl may make as low as $7 a month, and a maximum of $20. With thousands of young girls pouring out of the schools of Japan each year, the cottage-industry employer has little difficulty finding girls who are willing to lash themselves to his machines.

The problem which this poses, meanwhile, is only too obvious. American garment industry representatives are now protesting vigorously over what they consider to be Japanese "dumping." And they have a case. They are justifiably concerned over the fact that there are American importers who are willing and eager to accept Japanese blouses, manufactured under repressive labor conditions, and who in some cases put on American labels as a means of disguise for otherwise discriminating buyers.

The fact that the Japanese have voluntarily cut down on textile exports to the United States in recent weeks is not enough. And the claim, made here, that Japan is not dumping but merely engaging in free trade based upon an advantageous wage structure, is also unlikely to make for better international understanding.

What appears to be happening is that by pushing its garment exports to the United States, Japan is building up protectionist sentiments not only among American textile organizations, but over a much larger cross section of American industry.

It is too much to expect that the benevolence of Japanese garment manufacturers will result in Fumiko and her fellow workers receiving a substantial raise. That will come only through pressure from trade unions which so far have not penetrated into the dismal back streets of Osaka's industrial metropolis.

It is possible for the Japanese government to move in, as it has in other industries, and impose a series of controls. Government interference is not something which private manufacturers normally welcome. And yet in Japan today there appears to be little alternative. A refusal on the part of the Japanese to recognize the damage they are doing to their own export hrogram in the matter of large-scale garment sales abroad may result in injury to a wide range of other sales ranging from toys to cargo freighters.

A generation after Walker's dispatch from Osaka, apparel made in low-wage sweatshops came pouring into the United States from many parts of the world. The following dispatch from Seoul, Korea, appeared in the *New York Times* on August 17, 1974.

11 HRS/DAY—7 DAYS/WK
by Fox Butterfield

SEOUL—It is over 100 degrees in Shop 349 these summer days, and the 20 teenage girls who work in the crowded, airless loft in Seoul's Peace Market garment district get little relief from the one tiny fan.

The girls sew children's dresses for export to the United States; and they work 11 hours a day, 7 days a week, for $23 a month.

Under South Korea's labor law, the girls should not work more than 8 hours a day, 6 days a week. But the uniformed police and the plainclothes members of the South Korean Central Intelligence Agency stationed in the corridors outside Shop 349 do not seem to notice. . . .

Take the case of Park Dong Sook, an ebullient 22-year-old woman who has worked in a Seoul lingerie factory since she left her family's farm at the age of 16. (Park is not her real name, since if her company knew she had talked with newsmen she might lose her job. A dozen women in her factory have been fired without severance pay for trying to organize a union.)

Miss Park makes about $50 a month for working from 7 A.M. to 7 P.M. 6 days a week. But she is luckier than the women in her factory who work the 12-hour night shift for almost the same pay.

From her wages she pays $10 a month to live and eat in the factory dormitory, where she gets meals consisting of only rice, vegetables and soup. "Once a month the owner gives us meat as a treat," Miss Park said without rancor.

Two nights a week and on Sundays she can check out of the dorm to go downtown with her friends, but she hasn't seen a movie in over a year. "My money would run out if I did," she said.

Under the influence of an Urban Industrial Mission organizer, Miss Park took part in setting up a union in her factory this spring. But, she said: "We were very naive. We didn't realize that the owners finally consented to the union because the union leaders we picked are relatives of the owner's family."

The feebleness of South Korea's labor unions, in fact, has long been one of the workers' major problems. Under Korean labor law, unions are legal, and 620,000 of the 1.5 million factory workers belong to the nationwide Federation of Korean Trade Unions.

But union activity is hedged on all sides by legal restraints. To attract American and Japanese investment, for example, no union can be set up in a foreign-owned company without the management's consent. Collective bargaining is permitted in theory, but the government's Office of Labor Affairs has the right to impose a settlement. Strikes are banned.

According to union leaders, South Korean agents are stationed openly in every union office, and agents attend election meetings to dictate the results. Other union leaders are reportedly bought off by government bribes.

On the government's side, some officials do recognize the need to ameliorate the workers' conditions, since workers are such a valuable asset. But as the director of the Office of Labor Affairs, Choi Doo Yul, put it: "Because we are a developing country, we have to balance the welfare of the workers against the development of the nation." Mr. Choi, a stocky, square-jawed former head of the national police, added: "The question is where to make that balance."

Mr. Choi's critics concede that since he took over the labor office late last year, he has made some improvements. In one case, two Korean managers of an underwear factory were arrested last month for paying their 870 workers only $5 a month for 11 hours of work a day.

In another case Mr. Choi had the manager of a textile mill jailed for a week—even though he was a former military officer—because he had factory guards beat unconscious the head of the plant union for daring to address him in personal terms during a company party. The incident reflects the strong traditional class consciousness that still pervades relations between managers and labor in South Korea.

In the past few months, because of the government's concern over the effects of South Korea's inflation, Mr. Choi has even pressed some companies into wage hikes averaging 22 percent. But consumer prices have gone up close to 30 percent in the last year, foreign bankers here believe.

In addition to creating problems in the factories, South Korea's rapid industrialization has turned Seoul into a vast Asian Manchester. With a population of over six million sprawling endlessly over rugged granite hills, Seoul has now become the world's seventh-largest city.

By some estimates, about a million of these people live in slums, with little or no running water, with garbage rotting and with no guarantee that they won't be evicted for a new elevated highway or a factory.

Portraits of three ILGWU members, at a time when economic recession and rising imports were sharply affecting employment, were presented by the *New York Times* in its January 4, 1971, issue.

WITH THEIR HANDS
by Bernadine Morris

The gaiety is muted in many of the households of the city's quarter of a million garment workers as the new year dawns. How can there be good cheer when work is scarce?

"We have had hard times before," said Joseph Sussman, an old-time tailor who brought up three sons and is now seeing his grandchildren getting married, "but never has living been so high.

"When I began in 1906, I made $8 a week, but I paid $3 a month for my room and my landlady washed my clothes. Now, when I go to the union to see if there is work, the manager says to me, 'Sussman, shall I give it to you or to a man with little children?' and I say, 'Of course, give it to him, his need is greater.'"

Mr. Sussman, who worked only 13 weeks last year, checks in at his union twice a week. He usually walks from his Grand Street apartment on the Lower East Side to Seventh Avenue and 38th Street. It takes him an hour and a half. He's 80 years old, the oldest member of the United Cloak, Suit, Infants and Children's Coat Operators and Sample Makers, International Ladies' Garment Workers' Union, and he likes to be active.

"For me, it is not such a problem," he admits. "I have unemployment insurance, but the young people with little children—they are suffering."

Mr. Sussman was among the first of successive waves of immigrants who found solace and support in the garment trade. He was more fortunate than many of them, since he was already trained. He had been apprenticed to a tailor in Russia when he was 9 years old. Six years later, when he came to this country, he had no trouble finding a job.

"I arrived on Friday, by Sunday I was working," he recalled. His future wife was working in the same shop. Their courtship would begin three years later on a picket line.

His first job was on Spring Street. The garment center soon began moving uptown, but in the last ten years workshops have been appearing again on the East Side.

Wing Fong Chin works in one of them, on Elizabeth Street, along with some 50 other Chinese women. When Mrs. Chin started working fifteen years ago, there were only a few shops in the Chinatown area. Now there are 150.

Because she is a fast worker, she can make up to $45 a day, based on piecework. But her shop was closed last month because there was no work.

"After January, I will work again," Mrs. Chin said confidently. But she is worried; her son, Wilson, is studying engineering at New York University; her daughter, Winifred, will start college with the spring semester. Last week, her husband, Tung Pok Chin, closed his laundry in the Ridgewood section of Brooklyn "because the neighborhood was no good."

Mrs. Chin was able to go to work when the children were small "because my husband could watch them in the laundry." She had tried stringing beads at home—about the only occupation other than sewing open to Chinese women—but the pay was too poor.

So she went into a factory, learning first how to put zippers in, then how to make sleeves and collars. Today, she works on an entire garment, preferring skirts, for which she is paid 17 cents each, to dresses, for which she gets 50 cents.

"They are so simple, I can make 25 skirts in an hour," she explained. "I can only make about 4 dresses."

Last year Mrs. Chin earned $7,500, but this year it will be considerably less. "There is not always enough work," she explained.

When she started to work, before the union came in, she made $8 a day. (Of the 16,000 members of Local 23–25 of the Blouse, Skirt and Sportswear Workers Union, ILGWU, 10 percent are Chinese: it is the largest concentration of Chinese workers in the country.)

"At first, we worked from 8 in the morning to 8 at night," she recalled. "Now we only work eight hours a day; we have Blue Cross and unemployment insurance.

"Sewing is not the best job, but it is the only one for Chinese women. They can't stand American food. They don't speak English very much. They're afraid of the subway."

Mrs. Chin was an exception. Her father taught in an English school in Hong Kong and she could speak the language slightly. And living as she did in Brooklyn, near her husband's laundry, she always took the subway to work.

"But when the children were sick, I could stay home," she explained, adding that she was away from home so much "they almost forgot who I was."

Why do she and other Chinese women work?

"Living is so high, it is not enough for one member of the family to work," she said. "And some of them have no family at all."

Her job has other compensations: she used to make her children's clothes and she still makes her own clothes and slipcovers.

Sometimes Mrs. Chin recognizes the styles she has worked on in the stores. Once she saw a dress that she particularly liked in Goodwin's, a department store in her neighborhood. "It had my number on it, number 5," she said. "I bought it for my daughter." It cost her $7.99.

Ana Martinez, one of the estimated 17 percent of Latin American workers in the garment center, went to work 22 years ago, when her marriage broke up. She left her daughters with her mother in Puerto Rico and joined her sister in the Bronx. She found employment in a garment factory not far away. Eventually she found an apartment and was able to send for her children.

"I used to take work home and I didn't get paid very much, but I didn't have to travel and the school was close," she recalled. "I would pick up the girls and give them a cream cheese sandwich and they would nap on a pile of fabrics."

After 6 years she moved to Manhattan and got a better job. For 14 years she made duplicate samples for a factory that worked for Anne Fogarty and was earning about $8,000 a year. Her daughters grew up, finished high school and got married. She made their dresses for graduation, for proms and when they were bridesmaids.

"We never had to worry about what to wear, or about anybody showing up in the same dress," said her elder daughter, Ana Mojica, who is now the mother of four children. "I remember her sewing late into the night, even when she had to get up early and send us to school."

But two years ago her factory closed down and it was 10 weeks before Mrs. Martinez would find another job. She's been with the Richtone Dress Company—and has been laid off for three months of the year. The building she lived in was torn down, and she took $2,500 out of the bank to buy a cooperative apartment on Riverside Drive and 140th Street.

"Since I moved here in May, I haven't been able to put a penny in the bank," she said. "The maintenance on the apartment went up $20. I was living well on $150 a week a couple of years ago—I had money in the bank. Now I have to count my pennies.

"I used to have money to buy my own dresses in the stores. Now I have to make my own—I can't afford them otherwise. I haven't been to the movies in three years."

Because of her long years as a sample hand, Mrs. Martinez has to get used to piecework. But she's happy enough in her shop.

"My speed is picking up, and I can make good money when there is enough work," she said, holding out stubs of paychecks for $177, $193, $157. "It's such a friendly shop, like a family," she went on.

"There are Jewish people, Italians, only a few Spanish, and we all get along. When we order a container of coffee, three or four people

More than a quarter of a million ILGWU members across the United States demonstrated in their home cities and towns against the rising tide of apparel imports from countries with low-wage standards and the consequent loss of work, jobs, and pay. The national rally on November 16, 1972, was launched by ILGWU President Louis Stulberg at a Herald Square meeting in the heart of the New York shopping center. In smaller centers, such as Ste. Genevieve, Missouri, workers marched from shops to town square; in Jersey City, New Jersey, they rallied in business center.

share it. The only thing is, you don't see too many young people. They should teach the young girls, or there won't be anyone to do the work."

But Mr. Sussman is not so sure there will be any work to do.

"Even last year we worked overtime," he pointed out. "Now business is bad. The designers don't know what to make. The women are wearing trousers and that's killing everything. They're buying imports, which hurts us. And prices are too high for everything.

"I get $7 to make a coat. I've been making them a long time. I can do four, maybe five, in a day. Some people can only make two.

"None of the workers is getting rich. We don't make as much as a policeman, a fireman. Last year, my friend was the highest paid man in his shop. He made $8,000. This year the shop is out of business.

"Maybe in New York, there won't be a garment industry," he said, his blue eyes staring into the distance. "Maybe everything will be made in big factories in the South, where the rent is cheaper and the people work for less.

"For me, it has been a living. I never pawned anything. I never borrowed anything. I never bought anything on installment. I have a son, a doctor. My oldest son is a dentist and my middle son a businessman. I sent them all to college.

"In 1963, when I was married 50 years, I took my wife on a trip to Israel. I could afford it. I still feel I can work. I don't like to stay home. But today, there isn't enough work to go around."

The impact of increased volume of imports generally and the special problem created by Item 807 of the Tariff Schedule was analyzed by the president of the ILGWU in testimony given before the Subcommittee on Trade of the House Ways and Means Committee on March 25, 1976.

SWEATSHOP: ITEM 807 STYLE
by Sol C. Chaikin

Item 807 . . . stimulated the sending of cut fabrics out of the country, where they were made up into finished garments. It permitted a number of domestic garment firms to escape the payment of minimum wages and time and a half for overtime called for by the Fair Labor Standards Act, as well as the payment of wages and the maintenance of labor standards established in this country by custom, employer decision or collective bargaining. It also freed them from the payment of social security, unemployment insurance, workmen's compensation and other legally required contributions.

The lure of low wages, coupled with the incentive of lower duties provided by Item 807, was further magnified by inducements offered by foreign countries to firms that produced within their borders solely for export. These incentives do vary, of course, depending on the country. Income, sales and other taxes may be remitted in full or in part; customs duties may be waived on machinery and raw materials used in producing goods for export in full or in part, or else may be made payable in installments.

New plant construction may be partly subsidized through low-interest loans or otherwise partly financed by governmental agencies. Working capital and material may also be supplied and special credit terms arranged for the acquisition of the needed machinery and equipment. If monetary controls are in effect, special arrangements may be made for preferential treatment in obtaining foreign exchange and for taking profits out of the country. Accelerated depreciation may also be provided in some cases.

From 1965 on, the dollar value of imported apparel entering the United States under Item 807, whether made of knit and woven materials, or from rubberized fabrics, plastics and leather, grew steadily and excessively. In the 10-year period, 1965 through 1975, their dollar volume advanced by a hard-to-imagine 14,535 percent, while the dollar volume of all imported apparel (exclusive of Item 807 shipments) advanced only 286 percent and the dollar volume of domestic industry shipments went up only 46 percent.

Except for Canada, where the average hourly wage in the production of knit and woven apparel is 28 cents lower than in the United States, all the other areas where Item 807 work is carried on have one common characteristic—the payment of starvation wages when judged by standards to which we are accustomed in this country! Dollar for dollar, where fringe benefits exist, they are also significantly lower than what is found in the United States. Little wonder, therefore, that American garment workers shudder when the firms for which they work begin to send work to be completed abroad.

The use of foreign facilities to produce apparel out of fabrics cut in the United States is an out-and-out exportation of American jobs. On the average in an apparel plant, some 5 percent of workers perform operations in and around the cutting room and such operations as making buttonholes. The other 95 percent of the work force perform all other operations. Thus, when cut pieces are sent abroad to be completed there, the United States loses in effect 19 out of 20 jobs.

For every 100 women in a sample of ILGWU members, 64 had to support or partly support their children, husbands, parents or other relatives, in addition to supporting themselves. More married women than those who were single used their earnings for daily living, whether or not they were the sole earner in the family. Nearly one-third of the women supported at least one other person, one-fifth had two dependents and one-eighth supported three or more persons.

Workers in the industry have few alternative opportunities for employment. For the most part they are women with family ties which limit geographic mobility. . . . The industry itself is the largest employer of women, providing one out of every five manufacturing jobs available for women.

It thus performs a dual task. On the one hand, it provides the American people with a basic necessity. On the other hand, it is a source of jobs for a huge number of persons who would otherwise be jobless. This fully justifies every measure federal authorities can take to safeguard jobs in this industry.

Bear in mind also that the apparel industry is one of the most competitive in the United States. It "comes as close as any, in the manufacturing sector," in the opinion of a member of the Federal Trade Commission, "to the model of a competitively structured industry." More than in any other field of manufacture, it remains the mainstay of small business. To survive, each firm must compete vigorously for the available orders. Technology is relatively simple.

Profits per dollar of sales are among the lowest. It is relatively easy to start a new firm with only a modest capital investment. Smaller firms have a reasonable chance of success in competing with larger entities, since so much depends on the ingenuity of their principals in meeting market demand, in anticipating fashion developments and in providing the ultimate purchasers with good value.

Low-capital requirements, relatively simple technology, [and] ease of training new workers contribute to the industry's mobility. Some firms tend to move, unless checked, to escape higher labor standards or unionization of their employees. When relocation is planned, it is typically done in secrecy.

One can peruse in vain financial reports filed by companies with the Securities and Exchange Commission, annual reports to stockholders, or reports issued by credit agencies, and never discover that the particular company is utilizing out-of-the-country facilities as part of its production activity. The first clue typically comes when employment in a given plant begins to decline—only a subsequent investigation may reveal that production is being diverted to other plants, possibly a significant distance away, in a foreign country.

There are other reasons why Item 807 should be repealed. When an apparel company, for example, performs its so-called assembly operations abroad using fabric cut over here, it pays duty solely on the value added abroad. In 1974, the latest year for which the relevant data are available, duties levied on apparel entering the United

States under the provisions of Item 807 equalled 31 percent of what would have been collected under the rules which prevailed before 1963, i.e., before Item 807 was placed on the statute books.

The loss of revenue thus caused to the U.S. Treasury has to be made up by all taxpayers—you, and me, and all the others who pay taxes, including domestic firms who continue to produce garments in this country. All taxpayers, in effect, are forced to subsidize the export of American jobs under this unjustified provision of our tariff legislation!

The loss caused to the U.S. Treasury is likely to exceed what appears on the surface. It is recognized by the Customs Bureau that in most instances articles imported under Item 807 do not have a "price" in the standard meaning of this term. Much of the trade under Item 807 is between firms in this country and their affiliates or suppliers abroad. Goods are not transferred between them on the basis of value or price determined in the marketplace.

Foreign shippers of Item 807 goods and their domestic importers are not engaged in arm's-length transactions—in actuality, these are transactions between related persons. In these circumstances, it is extraordinarily difficult to determine what is the cost of production of the imported or similar goods and what are the usual general expenses and profit on sales of such merchandise produced in the exporting country when sold in the usual wholesale quantities packed and ready for shipment to the United States. Representations made to the Bureau of Customs by shippers and receivers of articles brought in under Item 807 often fail to make the full disclosures needed to make appropriate valuation of imported goods.

The elimination of Item 807 can be effectuated by Congress without the impairment of U.S. concessions, obtained in the process of trade negotiations. This is so, even though the result would be an increase in the amount of duty collected. This is the considered conclusion advanced by the Tariff Commission.

There is no question about it—Item 807 is a catalyst that induces apparel firms to run away to foreign shores. Additional stimulus is provided by excessively low wages compared to those in the United States and the subsidies offered by foreign governments. In our opinion, the interest of the United States would be served best, therefore, if Item 807 were stricken and we returned to the pre-1963 practice of dealing with American components incorporated in foreign-made articles abroad.

14. The Enduring Spirit

The founders of the ILGWU are gone. Huge housing developments, some of whose construction costs were financed with money drawn from reserves of the ILGWU Retirement Fund, have virtually replaced the slum ghetto where the sweatshop once flourished. An industry originally anchored to the seaport cities is now dispersed throughout the nation. The whirligig of fashion continues to create new challenges in the areas of production and pricing.

The union remains unfinished. New frontiers are waiting to be explored—shops to be organized, rates to be lifted, working conditions to be improved somewhere in the vast reaches of the garment industry.

The spirit of the founders of the ILGWU endures. Herbert H. Lehman bears witness to its existence, the *Justice* editorial salutes it, and Robert F. Wagner assesses its impact. Former ILGWU President Louis Stulberg links the past and the future in paying tribute to Brandeis. Pauline Newman urges a new generation of garment workers and leaders to keep the faith, and Judy Ackerman responds.

Some, as the portrait by Stein shows, must still pay the ultimate price of life itself and President Kennedy explains how the future must be purchased with idealism and sacrifice.

The present areas of ILGWU concern are outlined by Presidents George Meany and Chaikin, as well as in Damon Stetson's news feature and the Local 282 newsletter. That concern reaches out from the daily round of work in the shop to the enrichment of individual and family life in America. It extends to distant lands where men and women, denied the democratic lifestyle that makes a free trade union movement possible, mingle hope for change with a secret admiration of American workers.

At the celebration of the great 1910 cloakmakers' strike held in Carnegie Hall, in New York City, on September 17, 1960, Lehman, (1878-1963) a distinguished American who had served both as governor and senator of New York, and as head of the nation's first worldwide relief organization after World War II, reviewed the manner in which the ILGWU had grown.

PART OF THE AMERICAN STORY
by Herbert H. Lehman

To some if not most of you, the first collective-bargaining agreement in the history of the garment industry—the famous Protocol of Peace authored by the immortal Louis D. Brandeis—is no more than something you have read or heard about, something out of the dim and distant past. To me, the memory of that bitter strike of 1910 and of its victorious settlement is a memory almost as fresh as that of yesterday. I felt its impact. My sympathies marched in the wake of every stride taken on the picket line.

There were leaders of your union in those days and in the days that followed whom I came to know and to cherish as friends . . . men who have long since passed from among us, but whose memory lives on in the breasts of all who knew them. Their achievements form part of the bedrock of the ILGWU. I am thinking of such men as that brilliant leader and public figure Meyer London, whom you helped send to Congress in 1912, and that great lawyer, thinker and civic statesman, the late great Morris Hillquit.

In my judgment the ILGWU is a very great union. It has had a powerful impact on the entire trade union movement. It has had a mighty influence on America. It has a great tradition of service not only to its members, but to all workers and to all citizens and all peoples. It believes in service to the community; it has made itself an influential and integral part of every community in which its members have worked and lived.

The ILGWU is a sentimental union, and the practical expressions of its sentimentality, as in helping to renew and rehabilitate parts of the lower East Side, are deeply inspiring.

The story of the ILGWU is part of the story of America—the story of the transformation of an insurgent force—a force viewed a few decades ago as dangerously disruptive—into one of the basic balance wheels of our national economy and of our very system of democracy.

As a union, the ILGWU has been a major stabilizing force in a great industry. As a social force, the ILGWU has been one of the most restlessly progressive, liberal, and constantly forward-driving forces in America.

The ILGWU has been exploring the new frontiers of our community and national life for a long time. It has consistently been in the very vanguard of all the pioneer social movements of the past generation.

One of the things of which the ILGWU can be proudest is the fact that there always has been, in this great union, full and fruitful integration at all levels, involving all nationalities, colors and creeds. There has never been, as far as I know, any second-class membership status in the ILGWU. The ILGWU is an example of how people of different national origins, colors and creeds can work together in vibrant and constructive harmony . . . yes, in total and fraternal solidarity.

True to its principles, indeed to its very nature, the ILGWU has shown in a practical way how integration can work . . . not just integration of whites and Negroes, but integration of Poles, Italians, Puerto Ricans, Hungarians, Greeks, Cubans, Mexicans, Finns and Slovaks, Turks and lots more.

As far as the different religions are concerned, the ILG has been and is a true workshop of tolerance and brotherhood among Jews, Catholics and Protestants of every denomination. This is one of the special reasons for our special affection and regard for the ILGWU. It is one of the reasons for the greatness of the ILGWU.

As ILGWU members and officers join in march along Highway 80 from Selma to Montgomery, Alabama, after meeting with Martin Luther King, one of the fleet of ILGWU Mobile Health Centers speeds by to serve when civil rights marchers reach their destination (March 21, 1965).

In the 1960s few of the founding fathers of the ILGWU
were active. They had left an indelible mark on an industry, translating personal idealism into a better life for hundreds of thousands of garment workers and their families.
The following editorial appeared in *Justice,* the ILGWU
publication, on October 1, 1961.

LEDGER NO. 1

Only the cloakmakers knew him well but millions of garment workers,
knowingly or not, were the beneficiaries of his willingness to serve.
When he joined the ILGWU in 1902 the union's funds were nonexis-
tent, its membership was family-size, its strength was microscopic.

The shops in which he worked were dirty, dark firetraps. His
workday began in darkness and ended in darkness. Alone, he had
crossed a vast ocean, dreaming in the ship's steerage of freedom,
prosperity, sunshine in the Golden Land. When the reality of slum
and sweatshop confronted the dream, he held fast to the hopes and
the ideals he had brought from the Old World, strongly confident
that where freedom flourished, oppression and exploitation could not
long endure.

From the start, the union was for him the instrument of progress.
He was a charter member of his local. He was the chairman of his
shop. In the precious hours after the long day's work he met with
fellow members of his local's executive board, helping to plan its
campaigns, advising on strikes, debating strategy, combatting the
fears inspired by the bosses.

For 60 years, this was his life. His ILGWU membership started
when Theodore Roosevelt was president of the United States. It continued through six decades filled with growing social enlightenment,
two world wars, a major depression and the threat of a third war.
During all of this time he served as shop chairman, as chairman of his
local, as hall chairman in great strikes.

In him was no fear even though he was slender in stature. His
strength was made of pride in his union and his work, dignity in his
bearing and speech, determination in his resolve to act and a tena-
cious adherence to the ideals of brotherhood and cooperation he discovered in the resistance movement against Old World hunger,
prejudice and oppression.

He was expert at bolstering the waning spirits of a group of strikers.
No one knew better than he how to "stop the power," and when the
union committee walked into the unorganized shop in which he
worked as a young man, calling for the workers to rise from their

machines, it was he, in the moment of group indecision, who by being first on his feet, led the others out the door.

He was never big brass and the highest office he held in his union was that of business agent. In his later years, he returned to the shop, working at the machine but continuing as executive board member. When the time came, he left the shop and although he worked no more at the machine, he continued to spend many hours at his local union headquarters and was a welcomed, regular attendant at executive board meetings.

His kind grows rare. He was of that beginning breed in our union who put no limit on the time and the energy they gave to it, yet made no demands on it. Through all the storm and stress of building their union they never knew cynicism, managed to raise families, sent their children to college and took growing pride in the strikes and the collective bargaining and the hard-won contracts through which the workday and the workweek were shortened, standards were raised and the garment worker achieved democratic participation in the determination of work rates and conditions.

In his last years he was concerned with newcomers to the industry, with organization problems, with the educational work of his Local 23. His fellow cloakmakers, in six decades, were the pacesetters for the millions who in that time have been on the roster of the ILGWU. And in his cloak local he was a pacesetter. He died the other day at the age of 79. His name was Louis Gordon. His local ledger number was No. 1. His life was a thing of beauty.

During Democrats' Day at Sesser, Illinois, county fair in September, 1962, ex-President Harry S. Truman proudly tied the strings of ILGWU Union Label apron presented to him.

The impact of the ILGWU reached beyond the garment industry and the shop. At a ceremony held in February 1958, marking the presentation of the annual Murray-Green Labor Award to Dr. Jonas E. Salk, the mayor of New York provided a memorable example.

SON OF THE ILGWU
by Robert F. Wagner

Our immediate purpose is to do honor to a young man who has made a major contribution to the field of medical achievement. The union of organized labor and science which underlies his great accomplishment serves notice on the world that the welfare of the working man is also the welfare of the human race.

Back in 1933, when Jonas Salk was a junior at the College of the City of New York, Matt Woll and Dan Tobin set up a national committee to celebrate the birthday of Franklin D. Roosevelt and celebrate it in a fashion that would be socially useful.

All across the nation, under the leadership of this labor committee, scores of celebrations marking President Roosevelt's birthday were held. Half of the money realized at these events was given to the Warm Springs Foundation, an institution close to the heart of our late president. The remaining half was used, in each community, to help local sufferers of poliomyelitis.

Then in 1937, when Jonas Salk was still a student at New York University Medical School, out of the Warm Springs Foundation and this national labor committee, the National Foundation for Infantile Paralysis was founded. Tobin and Woll became joint labor chairmen for the first March of Dimes.

One of the hardest working, most devoted workers for the National Foundation and its March of Dimes has been George Meany. He directs the work of the labor services division of the foundation, and that division each year spends about $6 million to aid trade unionists and members of their families who are stricken by polio.

Today, the distinguished work of a devoted scientist, Dr. Jonas E. Salk, has brought us within sight of the conquest of this disease.

We in New York City are proud of Jonas Salk because we think of him as a product of our schools, of our educational system. He was born here, he attended our public schools, Townsend Harris High School, the College of the City of New York, and got his medical degree at New York University Medical School. In a way, Jonas Salk is also a product of the labor movement.

His father, Daniel Salk, was a member of Local 142 of the International Ladies' Garment Workers' Union; in fact, in the early days of the NRA, he helped to organize this neckwear local of the ILGWU.

I wonder if Jonas Salk would have been able to go through high school, on to college and through medical school to become the great doctor and great scientist he is if there had not been a garment workers' union to raise the wages, to win security, to raise the living standards of the family of Daniel Salk and the countless other families who are dependent on the garment industry. Had Daniel Salk, without the protection of a fine, clean union like the ILGWU, been forced to work under sweatshop wages, would his son, Jonas Salk, have been able to get a medical education? Perhaps—but it would certainly have been far more difficult.

For these many reasons it seems to me especially fitting that the labor movement, through its community services organization, is giving its Murray-Green Award to Dr. Jonas E. Salk for his outstanding accomplishments in the prevention of poliomyelitis.

A modern garment factory.

On March 6, 1969, ILGWU President Stulberg was in-
ducted as a Fellow of Brandeis University and a chair in law
and politics was established in his name. The following are
excerpts from his response to the citation read on this occasion.

THE ILGWU HERITAGE
by Louis Stulberg

I stand here tonight, the recipient of a great honor, only because of
what the trade union movement has been able to accomplish during
the years since Louis D. Brandeis came to New York to try to settle the
1910 strike. In little more than half a century the unions of this
country have changed the world in which working men and women
live and labor. In a very real sense, Brandeis and thz 1910 Protocol
announced the beginning of those changes.

Both proclaimed that workers ought to share in determining the
conditions of labor, that instruments of reason and bargaining had to
replace the use of force in the settlement of disputes and—far in
advance of the New Deal—that the health and well-being of the workers must be a concern of the community and the state.

Today, organized working men and women enjoy the conditions
and the benefits which were only dreams in 1910. The right to organize for bargaining purposes has been transformed from conspiracy to public policy. Law now sets the limits of the workday and
minimum pay; children of workers go to college and not to sweatshops. And a living wage must be decent and not just subsistent.
Workers endure illnesses with security and anticipate retirement with
confidence.

It is easy—and absolutely wrong—to say that such progress was
inevitable, that things get better by themselves. Only because trade
unions organized and demanded and insisted and fought for these
changes did they come about. The unions of this country were the
propelling force which in our time changed the conditions of the
workers' lives and the quality of American life in general.

The peculiar nature of our garment industry made us the crucible
for experiments in social innovation. In our industry, worker and boss
suffered the same physical plight of the shop. They confronted each
other daily and directly. They shared common immigrant, ethnic and
cultural origins, and therefore had no problems of absentee ownership or communications.

In the midst of strife, Brandeis perceived these assets. He articu-
lated an awareness of common industrial goals and needs. One result

has been that out of this most difficult and competitive industry of ours has come a great body of labor innovations and jurisprudence.

Here tonight we bear witness that beyond the interests of contending parties in our free society are the interests of the total community. Decent wages as well as financial solvency contribute to the strength of the community. We live in a time when conflict and confrontation shake our basic institutions. What an anguished need there is for some vast new Protocol to spread Brandeis's cure for irrationality in our society!

It is my fervent hope that the chair bearing my name, honoring my union, supported by the industry, saluting the garment workers in our shops, as well as the young people in this wonderful university, will provide opportunities for further progress.

The life of America and its workers is a thing of endless improvements. In the challenging days ahead let this chair become the instrument for further probing and applying the spirit of Brandeis's pioneer efforts—efforts first made in partnership with the workers and the employers of the ladies' garment industry more than half a century ago.

At the union's 1965 convention, ILGWU veteran Pauline Newman held out the torch to a younger generation. From *ILGWU Report and Record,* May 13, 1965.

WE HAVE KEPT THE FAITH
by Pauline Newman

I haven't much time to relate experiences over the years that I have been with the ILGWU. I will try, in a few moments, to leave just a few thoughts with you. I think it is rather important for you to know that out of the 65 years of the ILGWU's existence, I have been with it for 56. (Applause)

I am very grateful to the ILGWU for the opportunity it has given me to serve not only our own members but the labor movement as a whole. The ILGWU was my home, my school, my college, my university. I have learned a great deal because of my association withththe ILGWU, and the thing I am most proud of is that in all the 56 years, my record is unbroken of my loyalty, my devotion to the spirit and to the tradition of the ILGWU. (Applause)

I have not accumulated any fortune working for the ILGWU for 56 years. (Laughter) But I think I have accumulated a great deal of respect and affection of the ILGWU family, and that means more to me than anything else. (Applause)

I would like to tell the younger generation here—maybe they will take it back to the members of their locals—that my generation had the privilege, the great honor to fight and bleed in order to improve the conditions under which you work today. We worked 80 hours a week—I did anyway—in the Triangle Waist Company. You work 35. It took my generation to change conditions to those under which we work today. (Applause)

My generation has kept faith with the principles and the spirit of the ILGWU. I only hope and pray that you will do for the next generation what my generation did for yours. (Applause)

I have had the opportunity to serve the ILGWU in many capacities. I was the first woman organizer after the 1909 strike. I was legislative representative; I served the federal, state and local governments, because of my association with the ILGWU, and for this I am very grateful. (Applause)

We have kept faith with the people. I hope you will follow in our footsteps in your loyalty, in your devotion to the ILGWU. (Standing ovation)

Natividad Reyes proved her wish to be represented by the ILGWU in bargaining with her boss by marching for more than ten weeks in 1970 on an El Campo, Texas, picket line.

One week after Pauline Newman's remarks, at the final session of the convention, the delegate from Local 371 stirred the convention with a heartbreaking account that was, in effect, an answer to the veteran's challenge. From *ILGWU Report and Record,* May 20, 1965.

OUR UNION HAS KEPT FAITH WITH US
by Judy Ackerman

I would like to tell you something about our union in Andrews, South Carolina, about our battle with the Oneita Knitting Mills there. Oneita moved from Utica, New York, to South Carolina about 12 years ago. We organized the shop and were under contract for about 11 years. We thought we had good labor relations with the management until our contract came up for renewal in 1963.

We negotiated for five months in 1963 for a new contract without any results. And on July 10, 1963, we came out on strike. At that time 281 people came out and stayed out for seven months. We only lost a few who crossed our picket lines and went back to work.

A labor board hearing was held charging the company with refusal to bargain in good faith and unfair labor practices. So after the hearing we thought our best move was to offer to go back to work. But the company refused to take 34 people back.

The company appealed the decision of the trial examiner. But we won the appeal. So a second hearing was held on the 34 whom the company had refused to take back. We won this hearing also, and the company was ordered to take these people back with back pay.

Since this decision, the company has taken back 17 people. But I am one of the other 17 that are still left out. Negotiations began again in March of this year. To date, we have met six times and we are still not even close to any agreement. During all this time our members have voluntarily paid their dues and we are signing up some people who were hired during the strike.

I want everyone in this hall to know . . . that our union has kept faith with us and supported us to the fullest during the strike . . . and is still continuing its support. (The speaker was momentarily overcome by emotion.)

Even though we have not achieved our contract, we are determined to continue to fight until we do win it. Our battle will not be over until the 17 people are back to work and we have a decent contract. If it takes another strike . . . we are ready.

I would like to say, as a delegate in behalf of our local, that we appreciate the financial and moral support that we have all received.

We realize the tremendous amount of time, effort and expenses involved to fight our long battle, but we think it has been worth it. So I thank you, Mr. President, officers and members of the ILGWU. (Delegates rose and applauded.)

> Although the union's frontiers have been extended beyond the urban sweatshop to rural plant sites, the battle to improve the quality of life of garment workers continues; it has brought forth a new generation of heroes—and martyrs. On July 13, 1972, in Brownsville, Kentucky, the bitter sacrifice was again made. From *Justice,* July 15–August 1, 1972.

DEATH OF A CHAMPION
by Leon Stein

The news over the radio caught some in the kitchen fixing breakfast or washing the kids' faces or in their cars on the highway heading toward the struck plant for the change of shift in the strikers' watch.

The voice had said that Eugene Hampton, a Kellwood striker, had been shot to death in the early morning before sunrise while standing watch at the struck Kellwood Company plant in Brownsville, Kentucky.

Then phones throughout Edmonson County began to ring. Quickly, the word spread. They had killed Gano.

From all directions, cars began to fill the highway heading for Brownsville. In Cave City, Bowling Green, Park City and greater distances, Kellwood strikers—for one unbelieving moment—caught their breaths and then knew they had to go.

On the roads near the plant the cars jammed. They left their cars and walked the rest of the way, some carrying the children they couldn't leave at home.

They knew the place by his blood on the road. They gathered around in a huge semicircle on the road where Eugene Hampton—in high school they had called him Gano—had stood for the last time. They were silent at first, then the women weeping, the men grim, their lips tightly drawn.

Why Eugene Hampton? He was only 27—a quiet, thoughtful man. In sorrow, the crowd drew together, moving closer to the electric pole at the base of which he had fallen. Then, almost whispering, some began to remember. How he loved kids. He had three of his own. How he was respectful of women. He had married Anita Wheeler—his classmate. How serious he was at the cutting table spreading the fabric. How, during the strike, he volunteered to take the most difficult watch through the night.

How pleasant it was, the men remembered, having him in the bivouac during the long starlight hours of the night watch; the darkened plant in the distance; rock music in a faint echo from the transistor radios the Pinkerton detectives carried to keep themselves awake in the plant; the coke and beer cans in a circle around the small roadside campfire flickering where the men squatted; the good talk about the great times they had had in the days of their youth.

> That year, the kids at Park City High School went wild. In the first tryouts after the summer 1962 vacation, they knew they had the championship stuff. The coach knew it.
> There was this youngster, Gano . . . It was something about the way he carried the ball, about the way he received the passes. Most important, it was something he did for the team, playing the game clean, setting the pace, providing the spark of leadership in the huddles.

The strike at Kellwood began on June 21. It had taken less than a month for the majority of the 350 Kellwood workers in Brownsville to prove they wanted the International Ladies' Garment Workers' Union to represent them in bargaining with the company.

Soon after the rate cutting started, they had passed word on to the ILGWU that this time they needed help and this time they would welcome the union. They were tired of being pushed around, of having no say about their rates and of being moved from job to job so that they could never raise their earnings.

The ILGWU began an organizing campaign from its office in Bowling Green. By May 24 it was able to report that Kellwood workers were signing application cards in large numbers.

It had also called a meeting to set up an ILGWU organizing committee at Kellwood. Twenty-four Kellwood workers attended that first meeting. Courageously, 12 of them volunteered to form the organizing committee. First to volunteer was Eugene Hampton.

A week later, 68 more Kellwood workers had joined the committee. Forty ILGWU application cards were received at union headquarters through the mail in one day.

Then the union announced that a vast majority of Kellwood's 350 employees had signed ILGWU membership cards; that 21 more workers had joined the organizing committee, now totalling 89.

The union had asked to meet with the company. This was steadfastly refused. The company turned thumbs down on a check of ILGWU membership cards against its payroll, on a suggested election to be conducted by the American Arbitration Association or by the Kentucky State Department of Labor.

Kellwood workers met on June 20. The next day they struck the Brownsville plant. By the end of the week, the cutters walked out. At 3:30 P.M. on June 26, the company closed the plant.

In the spring of 1963 childhood ended. He was 18. Senior year had been a succession of triumphs. On the playing field he had done what he could do the best way he could do it. His body had responded with grace, speed, power, skill. He had played the game like the champion he was—clean, cooperative, patient, loyal to his teammates, enjoying their friendship. That's what counted—to win fair and square, to do your best, to carry the ball across.

He read the foreword in the school graduation annual Anita had helped write:

Eugene Hampton—champion.

"We, the Seniors of Park City High School
In order to always remember the School Year of 1962–63
Establish in our minds the wonderful days of work and
play
Ensure the memories of our classmates, friends and
teachers
Provide for the day when this will seem like a wonderful
dream. . . ."

There would be another game now, a bigger game, the game
of life itself. What were the rules?

"We, the class of 1963," he read, "dedicate our yearbook to
our country, the United States of America. This country
has given us more freedom and opportunity than people
of other lands will ever know. We hope we can use these
opportunities and make our country free for generations
to come."

Kellwood played the game according to its own rules. First of all,
there must be no union. The company, it announced, had an open-
door policy. Any worker having a complaint could come and talk it
over all alone with management. There was no need for the union. In
Brownsville, as in Little Rock, Arkansas, where it took 1,000 Kellwood
workers four years to convince the company it had to bargain with the
ILGWU by law, the company said it would deal fairly and squarely
despite its millions, despite its power to hire and fire, despite its
monopoly of jobs in Brownsville.

Secondly, Kellwood pleaded poverty. It was about to go broke. It
was losing money in Brownsville. Nevertheless, it was expanding and
improving its local offices. Nevertheless, it made a profit of
$5,943,916 in 1971, increased by 10.4 percent in the first quarter of
the new year. Nevertheless, Kellwood President Fred W. Wenzel, talking to financial experts in St. Louis last April, assured them that the
company, with some 50 plants employing about 17,000 in the South
and Southwest, expected record earnings in 1972, with over $300
million in sales to pass the $500 million mark by 1977.

All of this Eugene Hampton knew. He knew also of the company's
disdain for its employees, of the management man who had snapped
at the women that they smelled like horses' sweat, of the constant
shifting of workers from job to job so that earnings could never really
rise, of the rate cuts, of the low wages so that many of the women had
to apply for food stamps in order to get by with their families. Of the
management chief who had promised the women he would have the
factory hopping like an army camp before he was through with them.

On the day he received his diploma, Gano read again the words in the class yearbook:

"Determined were the Bears of 1962 to go all the way to a state championship. It is the first time in the school's history that Park City High School has won a state championship.

"Park City broke many records. Gano Hampton, one of the best quarterbacks this school has ever known, scored more touchdowns in one game than any other player in the conference when we walloped Gamaliel 81 to 9. In the Caverna game, deciding the conference title, our defense held the tough Caverna team to only 12 points as we clinched the Barren River Conference 39 to 13.

"The boys were under the expert leadership of Coach Aaron Turner who proved himself by being chosen 'coach of the year'. Mr. Turner, a fine leader of young men, teaches his team sportsmanship, alertness and the art of defense."

They sat at the base of the electric pole at the side of the road in the cone of light made by the single big bulb. The distant plant showed one rectangle of light in a lone window—the Pinkerton, probably asleep. By 2:30, they were playing poker with little talk. The beer and the coke had run out.

The car came at them slowly—a 1965 white Mustang convertible. One of the men remembered that the driver, without stopping, called out to them to follow him. Then he was at the end of the road disappearing into the turn toward the highway. He was back again in minutes, having used the highway to circle round.

Again he called to the men, moving on. They thought they recognized him as Harvey Gonterman from out Mammoth Cave way . . . Not one of them could remember a time when Harvey Gonterman worked on a job. They all remembered his wife. She supported the family, working at Kellwood, even during the week of the picketing.

Harvey brought his wife to the plant. He also enlisted his mother as a strikebreaker. He put them in his white Mustang convertible and drove them through the picket line, sometimes brushing the women with his fender to get through. He repeated the procedure at going-home time—taking his women through the line.

He was back a third time. By then the men had moved out of the circle of light to the darker side of the road. They remembered Harvey's reputation for carrying a gun. The car kept circling. The driver each time called to the men. They remained silent.

The fifth time the driver slowed the car and called insistently to the men through his open window on the passenger side. Eugene Hampton rose. He came round the front of the car, cutting through the parallel beams of light, now at the driver's open window1 He asked what was the problem.

The driver raised a .25 automatic pistol, rested it on his left arm near the elbow, turned, and fired through the open window. The bullet crashed into his chest. The impact whipped him around. The car took off like a rocket. He began to go down. The men were running toward him. His face was on the road. Then he was on his elbows trying to raise himself.

Three of them sprinted down the road. One leaped onto the porch of the first house and began to beat the door. The others kept running for another phone. To call a doctor. To call the police.

Those who stayed leaned over Eugene Hampton. Carefully, they tried to move him. He took his hand from his chest. "I've been hit hard," he whispered.

In the entrance corridor at Park City High, thzre is a display case filled with trophies, cups, autographed footballs and a jersey shirt. There is also a small picture of Gano and the text of remarks made by Coach Aaron Turner at a special event. It reads:

> "Gano Hampton's contribution to football throughout his high-school career includes quarterbacking Park City to its first undefeated football season and quarterback on the All-Conference Team.
> "He showed great poise in the Kentucky State Championship game, carrying the ball eleven consecutive times when the other backfield players were injured to break a tied ballgame in the closing seconds allowing the Bears to win the Kentucky Eight-Man State Championship.
> "Gano holds Park City School's scoring records for total points, 136, and individual game scoring of 38 points.
> "It is altogether fitting that Gano stands out as the greatest among Park City football players. I feel very humble in honoring Gano by retiring his jersey number 12, never to be worn by another Park City football player."

Early Saturday afternoon, two days after the shooting, Kellwood workers gathered for a roadside memorial meeting where Eugene Hampton fell. A thunderstorm had cooled the air, making all things green, greener, washing away the blood.

Union officers spoke. The 23rd Psalm was recited in unison. Then Aline Cummings of the Kellwood strike committee placed a single red rose to mark the spot and said:

"He gave his life. He wanted this union. He got more pay than the rest of us. But he was the first on the committee. If he were here now he would tell us to go on.

"He is here with us now in spirit. Wherever men and women walk a picket line from now on asking for fair play, for a fair share of the things of life for themselves and their families, for a little more human decency and respect, Gano Hampton will be there."

On a blazingly hot afternoon, May 19, 1962, the president of the United States dedicated the ILGWU Cooperative Houses in the Chelsea area of New York City. From *ILGWU Report and Record,* 1962.

UNFINISHED BUSINESS
by John F. Kennedy

We read frequently that one of the great problems that you face in organized labor is how to maintain the same fervor, the same spirit, the same zeal which motivated this and other unions in their early days of the great struggle to provide decent working conditions and pay for their members.

We still have great areas of effort which are left to this union in protecting the welfare of its members. But it is also important to emphasize—and there is also a great opportunity open to all unions across the country to participate in the strengthening of their country.

And that's what this union has done on this occasion as well as on so many others. The work available for organized labor in the United States today is just as important—in many ways more important than it was 25 years ago.

The unfinished business of our society still lies stretching before us, and this housing project demonstrates what labor with good, effective, progressive leadership, and the cities and the states and private groups and the federal government together in cooperation can do for this city and this country.

And that's why I think it most appropriate to come here today with your distinguished leaders and tell you that this union has done a good job, and to ask that other unions across the country imitate your example.

The unfinished business of this country is your business. And I can assure you after being in the presidency only 16 or 17 months that the progress of this country will depend in a great measure on the sense of public responsibility of members of organized labor.

If you want to have equal opportunity for all Americans, if we want to rebuild our cities, if we want to provide transit in and out of our cities, if we want to educate our children, if we want to have colleges and universities to which they can go, if we want to have medical schools to train our doctors, if we want to make this country as wonderful a place as it can be for the 300,000,000 who will live in this country within 40 years, then we have to do our task today. It is the task of every generation to build a road for the next generation.

This housing project, the efforts we're making in this city and state and in the national government, I believe can provide a better life for the people who come after us, if we meet our responsibilities.

There are those who say that the job is done, that the function of the federal government is not to govern, that all the things that had to be done were done in the 1930s and '40s and that now our task is merely to administer. I do not accept that view at all. Nor can any American who sees what we still have left to do.

So this is a great effort by you. This union deserves the heartiest commendations. I hope others will follow your example. And I come here today and ask you to continue to work as you have in the past, and as free labor organizations must do all over the world for the kind of progress upon which our ultimate security depends. We believe that there is much left to do. And I come here today and ask you to join us in doing it.

About 30 years ago a distinguished French marshal asked his gardener to plant a tree and the gardener said that the tree won't come to flower for 100 years. He said, in that case, plant it this afternoon. Well, that's the way I feel about all the tasks left undone in this country which will not be finished in our time. But we ought to do something about it this afternoon.

The following excerpt is from an address given on June 3, 1975, at the seventy-fifth anniversary dinner of the ILGWU by the president of the American Federation of Labor–Congress of Industrial Organizations.

MORE THAN A UNION
by George Meany

This union has been fortunate in the leadership that has been developed over the years in a tough industry, a leadership that never lost sight of the real big picture of the trade union movement. They always held to the great visions of what the labor movement was all about, and the dramatic changes it could make in the lives of millions of ordinary people. Louis Stulberg, like David Dubinsky before him, has embodied that kind of leadership, not only in the ILGWU but in the American labor movement as a whole.

Looking back over the years that it has been my privilege to observe the ILGWU in action, I realize that this institution is much more than a trade union. Oh, yes, it was vitally concerned with wages and work conditions for its membership, which were reflected in progressively better and better collective-bargaining agreements over the years.

The word "International" in the official title of your union has, for me, special significance. It indicates that the union embraces membership in Canada as well as the United States. But much more, it indicates the global philosophy of the ILGWU over the years, which philosophy could be best described, as it was described by the Philadelphia charter of the International Labor Organization, adopted in 1944, which stated very simply, "All human beings, irrespective of race, creed, or sex have the right to pursue both their material well-being and their spiritual development in conditions of freedom and dignity."

May I cite to you two outstanding examples of the global philosophy, where the ILGWU leadership demonstrated its concern for the plight of people in faraway places whose freedom was threatened by the forces of tyranny and despotism: In this city in April 1933, a gathering of liberal and labor representatives set up two instrumentalities to combat the forces that were crushing freedom in Nazi Germany. One of these organizations was the Non-Sectarian Anti-Nazi League, set up to promote a worldwide boycott of Nazi products. The other, the German Labor Chest, was to provide relief for German trade union officials who had gone into exile with the rise of Adolf Hitler.

One of the prime movers of these actions, who was present at that meeting, was the then president of the ILGWU, my good friend David Dubinsky. What was highly significant about this was that Dubinsky and those associated with him recognized the threat to human freedom that was inherent in the event taking place 6,000 miles away in Germany at a time, within 90 days after Hitler assumed power, when a lot of people were looking upon Hitler as some kind of political freak that would go away. Dubinsky, Bill Green, Matt Woll and a few more realized then the threat to our way of life and to our concept of freedom and dignity that was inherent in what was happening in Nazi Germany early in 1933.

And then, who can forget 1948, when a crucial election was held in Italy which could have resulted in Italy's going behind the Iron Curtain as a Soviet satellite? Well, I don't know about the CIA interfering in foreign elections, but I can confess that the AFL and Dubinsky and Luigi Antonini "interfered" in a foreign election in 1948, and I'm quite proud of the fact that they did. The courageous leadership of Dubinsky and Antonini played a major role in preventing at that time a complete takeover of Italy by the Communists.

I said at the beginning of my remarks that this union was built and made great by practical people with big ideas and, perhaps more important, high ideals about democracy, freedom and justice which were, in many cases, brought to this country by people who had to struggle for those ideas in the Old World. They came here looking, not just for bread, but also for justice.

Maybe that is why this union has been truly international in its outlook. Whether it was a fight against Fascism or a fight against Communism, the ILGWU was always in the forefront. This union never sat back and said "that's none of our business." If freedom was at stake, especially trade union freedom, anywhere in the world, it was the business of this union, and it is the business today of the entire trade union movement.

The great adventure which 11 workers in a small room embarked upon 75 years ago tonight is not yet over. Your legacy to all workers is a concept and a model of social unionism in the very best sense of the word. That for us is not a thing of the past, but that really is the wave of the future.

At the seventy-fifth anniversary dinner, leaders of government, community affairs, and organized labor saluted the garment workers. The following is from the feature written by the labor reporter of the *New York Times* and published on the anniversary day, June 3, 1975.

ILGWU DIAMOND ANNIVERSARY
by Damon Stetson

"As a union we've had a significance far beyond our numbers or our economic muscle," Sol C. Chaikin, the newly elected president of the International Ladies' Garment Workers' Union, said the other day as the union prepared to celebrate its seventy-fifth anniversary today.

"Our leaders—Benjamin Schlesinger, Morris Sigman, David Dubinsky, Louis Stulberg—have been men of integrity, determined trade unionists and men of social vision. Not only has the union won benefits and dignity for its members, but it has had a tremendous impact on the trade union movement . . . It has been a voice for social progress."

A group of retired members, schmoozing about the union at its Joint Coat and Suit Board headquarters on West 38th Street, spoke in more down-to-earth terms:

"I used to work in a shop that didn't even have a window—a real sweatshop," said Mabel Frazier, a Harlem resident who retired 12 years ago after years as a belt stitcher. "That was before I joined the union. After I joined, things began to improve. I got work in better shops with better conditions and my pay went up. The union's health center has meant so much to me, too, because I had a heart attack. But now I'm better and I'm getting a pension."

Amelia Cortez, who lives on Manhattan's West Side, came to New York from Puerto Rico in 1927 and has been a member of Local 40 for about 30 years, retiring in 1973.

"When I started as an operator," she said, "I made $30 a week. But when I retired I was making $155 a week. For me the union meant better pay and better conditions—also hospitalization benefits. And I used to go to Unity House (the union's resort in the Poconos) every year."

Abe Kawer, a gray-haired, 70-year-old immigrant from Warsaw who started as a $15-a-week errand boy and retired as a $200-a-week Bonnaz (embroidery) machine operator, chimed in: "We were the pioneers for the present generation of workers. They get the benefits we fought for."

The "ILG," as the union is known, now has 430,000 members, a level that has been relatively constant over the last two decades. New York City membership is 140,000—down from over 200,000 in the years before the industry began to disperse to other areas.

About 80 percent of the members are women, but the earlier predominance of Jewish and Italian workers has been diluted and the union now has large numbers of blacks, Spanish-speaking people, Greeks, Chinese, Yugoslavs and others.

In the Dubinsky years from 1932 to 1966, there were many firsts: The negotiation of a 35-hour, five-day work week; establishment of an employer-financed vacation fund; production of "Pins and Needles" on Broadway with a cast of garment workers from the shops; establishment of a union engineering department to assist employers; and negotiation of an employer-financed retirement fund for workers.

During Mr. Dubinsky's leadership, an International Labor Relations Department was created to support free trade unions abroad. A Political Department was organized to promote membership interest and participation in the nation's political life. A drug prescription plan was set up, making it possible for members to obtain drugs at relatively low cost. Since his retirement Mr. Dubinsky has directed an elaborate program to assist retired ILGWU members and to provide them with cultural opportunities.

Mr. Stulberg, in reviewing his nine years as president, cited such accomplishments as an increase of 65 percent in negotiated wage and cost-of-living adjustments; improvements in health care; development of a mail-order prescription program; a doubling of the death benefit; increases in the retirement benefit to the present level of $100 a month; and negotiation of a third week's vacation pay in labor agreements.

Now, as a new president, Mr. Chaikin, prepares to take over, there are new and difficult problems. The wages of ILGWU members, which once exceeded those of auto workers and steelworkers, are now lower, although Mr. Chaikin says they average $4.25 an hour. But the garment industry, with its many small units and a growing number of larger operations, is subject to severe competitive strains, he said.

"There is much non-union production also," Mr. Chaikin said. "And in the last five years there has been an ever-increasing influx of imports from countries with unconscionably low wages.

"I see the next five years as being almost crucial to the industry and the union. We have to seek help from Congress and the president to regulate the flow of imports with which we can't compete. We also have to bring the message of unionism to non-union areas. Then we can negotiate better agreements and also give employers respite from extraordinary (foreign and non-union) competition."

The present state and spirit of the ILGWU were analyzed by the president of the ILGWU on March 23, 1976, at the opening session of the World Congress of the International Textile, Garment and Leather Workers' Federation in Dublin, Ireland.

TRADITION AND CHALLENGE
by Sol C. Chaikin

Our members in the main produce women's and children's garments. Obviously, we have been significantly affected by our national recession, and other factors have served to worsen our circumstances. A significant increase in imports (the level of imports nearly doubled between 1966 and 1975) is responsible partly for the extraordinarily high level of unemployment and the tens of thousands of lost jobs and the hundreds of small companies which were forced into bankruptcy.

Added to this general problem was a unique and specific challenge which it was time for our union and industry to face. Until the last decade, employers in our industry would specialize as to product. For example, dresses, coat and suit manufacture, the production of skirts, blouses, sleepwear, etc. These product lines began to blur as a result of new merchandizing techniques, fashion demand, new manufacturing procedures, and the introduction of new machinery and a few technological developments. The jurisdictional basis for the settlement of labor contracts began to crumble, and this at the very time of economic recession served to compound our difficulties. Unemployment affected fully one-fifth of our experienced work force and encouraged resistance to our organizing efforts.

I took office as president-elect of our great union in June of last year. Together with our officers and active members we began to intensify our efforts, to restructure our union and, at the same time, to bring some rational system of collective bargaining to bear so that we could begin to accommodate ourselves to the new challenges posed by the shifting jurisdictional lines. We are in the midst of an attempt to diminish the differences of earnings between workers in the various branches in our industry, and hopefully within the next few years we will reach one national standard agreement in the outerwear field.

We have succeeded in breaking new ground in our most recent contract in the dress industry and we are preparing to negotiate with the balance of the major employers in the other areas where our union has jurisdiction.

We have established a particularly close relationship with the Amalgamated Clothing Workers of America and the Textile Workers

Union, both on the economic and legislative fronts. We are strengthening our organizing staffs and are determined to enlist under our banner many non-union workers who desperately need our representation.

We have promoted the identification and understanding of our union label as an effective weapon for the advancement of our union's goals and, hopefully, as a vehicle by which more union-made garments are sold. We have been the first trade union to bring a union label message to millions of Americans by using television.

Our union has always been actively concerned and involved in movements and ideas existing or emanating from your shores. For many decades our interest has been much more than just a sentimental expression of worker solidarity. Our relationships with and support of free democratic trade unionism in many countries of the world is part of the record.

In recent years, our concern has been expanded to include what we believe are major changes on the industrial scene. While business has always been "international" the acceleration of the multinational vehicle forcefully brings to our attention how the world continues to shrink every day. Business decisions, no less than political decisions, reached on international levels now affect the lives of people in all countries. Indeed, for some years now our own industries in America have begun to feel the pressures which these changes have brought. Our activities as trade unionists in each of the countries are now directly affected by decisions in the boardrooms of the multinational corporations.

Therefore, our involvement in international affairs is doubly important and indeed becomes mandatory if we should properly face up to the challenge of our role as trade unionists. Our concern and involvement in international affairs, however, remains primarily a political one. We are against violations of human rights and we are for the expansion of personal freedom and dignity. We oppose dictatorships of whatever color and of whatever type. We will wholeheartedly support the fight of workers for self-determination and aid the development of free democratic trade unions as the greatest bulwark for the preservation and progress of our humanistic civilization.

The founders of our great union were themselves refugees from oppression in their home countries. They came to America seeking freedom and opportunity and found instead exploitation and despair. The early garment workers, the early pioneers of our great organization, imbued our union with an extraordinary spirit.

Back in 1896, four years before the ILGWU was officially chartered by the American Federation of Labor, a union of workers making ladies' coats disbanded after an unsuccessful strike which ended in failure to maintain their organization. Their only asset was the receipt of some money from the sale of furniture and other items which they had in their office. When the time came for this handful of unionists to settle their affairs, instead of pocketing the money, they unanimously agreed to donate the funds to help the Cuban revolutionaries who were fighting against their Spanish oppressors.

Since then, in a hundred ways, in many countries, many thousands of individuals have been the beneficiaries of our interest in democracy, in trade unionism, liberty of conscience and political freedom.

This is our heritage and our tradition. It is in this spirit that we shall continue our work among the countries of the world and it is with this in mind that we pledge to you our very close cooperation in the days and years ahead.

> The union is people. It is also politics, collective bargaining, strikes, and economics. But first of all it is people—with worries, celebrations, births, deaths, and marriages. Deep in the heartland of America it is also the members of ILGWU Local 282 in Oshkosh, Wisconsin. Once a month Mary M. Schroeder puts together a cryptic chronicle that sets forth in a mimeographed newsletter the basic facts of life. The following is from "Sew and So," issued at the time the ILGWU marked its seventy-fifth anniversary.

SEW AND SO

Rose Schroeder has an anniversary May 20. She has worked 40 consecutive years with the C. A. Newburger Company . . . Laura Christensen and Roy Gabrielson were married April 26 . . . Pearl Seeley bought the first candy bar from the new machine; some bars are 15 cents and some 20 cents. Pearl bought her little 3-year-old grandson a purebred collie puppy for his birthday . . . Lucille Kuschel treated all the girls with homemade cookies she baked for her birthday, May 5. They were cherry winks. She sure is a good baker . . . Kathy Nichols' mother won a radio tape recorder from WOSH radio . . . The bowling team want to thank the union and Oscar and Burt for sponsoring the team. The team—Linda Koch, Gerry Warner, Hannelore Jarvenpaa, Vicki Haasl and Mary Bingen—had a total of 2435 at the AFL bowl in Watertown. They said they didn't do anything special, but had a good time at the tournament. After bowling they went to the Gobbler Supper Club in Johnson Creek. It was very plush, the food was delicious and reasonable. . . . Mary Bingen had a very busy but enjoyable vacation in Mexico. She visited Mexico City, Cuernavaca, Acapulco, Taxco, Toluca, Shrine of Guadalupe, saw a Mexican ballet. Also went to a bullfight. Very gory. Took a tour to the pyramids and went to an Indian market. Then had to go home and rest . . . Linda Ochawicz and Winnie Fritz were reinstated in the union in April. Carol Hillman became a new member . . . There will be a noon luncheon at Emmanuel United Church of Christ, Michigan Street at South Park Avenue. Price $2. They will serve ham logs, scallop potatoes, salad, vegetable, beverage, rolls and dessert. There will also be a bake and craft sale. Our retiree, Linda Hinz, was at the shop selling tickets Tuesday. In case you missed her or changed your mind about going, give Linda a call . . . Mrs. Elsie Bartelt, 85, a retired employee of C. A. Newburger and the mother-in-law of Sue Bartelt, office, passed away suddenly on April 21 . . . Eva's husband, Jim Hoeft, has been at Mercy Hospital for several weeks. He has had back surgery for slipped discs . . . Nancy Slye, one of our newer employees, will be married to Joel Whitty . . . Susan Baier, granddaughter of Georgine Yost, graduates from St. Mary's Menasha on June 9, and another granddaughter, Kathryn Schuster, from Green Bay West on June 5 . . . Karin Englemann, Anne's daughter, graduates from Oshkosh West on June 5. She was on the March of Dimes bike ride. Several of Anne's fellow workers sponsored Karin at so much a mile . . . Colleen Ziebell returned to work. She was out 7 weeks after her surgery, but she still doesn't feel too good . . . Debbie Zarling has been busy sewing. She made a suit, shirt and tie for her 4-year-old son, Jeffery, who will be ringbearer for the wedding of Debbie's brother, Jim Fournier, June

The largest rally of his campaign for the presidency of the United States drew close to a quarter of a million New Yorkers to the Seventh Avenue garment center on October 27, 1976, where Jimmy Carter was introduced along with his wife by ILGWU President Chaikin. (Photo by Adrian Manocchia, ILGWU)

21 to Linda Goodwin . . . Marjorie Ziegenhagen will attend the 50th reunion (class of 1925) at Elkhart Lake, June 28. There are only 3 left of Class 1924 and they will also attend. Marjorie attended school in Glenbeulah . . . Lenny Ott has 42 years with the C. A. Newburger Company. Anyone else with 40 years? . . . Della Footit and her husband drove to Fort Bragg, North Carolina, to visit her son, Harold (Champ) and daughter-in-law for two weeks' vacation . . . Helen Otto's mother was 99 years last week . . . Hannelore Jarvenpaa's sister is coming from Florida, June 23. She hasn't seen her for 15 years . . . Paula Brusius, 14-year-old granddaughter of Vi Brusius, is a finalist in the Miss Teenager for Nebraska. She is the daughter of Rev. and Mrs. Ronald Brusius . . . Our retiree Florence Abraham had a very enjoyable trip to the Grand Ole Opry in Nashville, Tennessee. She went with a group, chartered bus and stayed the first night at beautiful Galt House Hotel in Louisville, Kentucky. They did a lot of walking at Opryland, but in the afternoon it just poured and everyone was soaked before they got to the bus. Florence was brave; she went alone. She is 78 years old . . . Business Representative Don Kret sprained his ankle severely and was forced to use a cane several days. Brother Kret blames his new white shoes with the platform heels as the cause of the problem . . . Dorothy Trapp has moved closer to Oshkosh, about 4 miles out . . . Congratulations to Lee and Susan Soda who will celebrate their 10th wedding anniversary, June 19. Also to John and Gertie Bongert who were married 47 years June 6 . . . Carley Stiemert is driving a new car . . . New members in May—

Proud of their union, these ILGWU members strut up Fifth Avenue in New York in 1968 Labor Day parade.

Dorothy Praxl and Deborah Zarling . . . No union meeting in July or August.

A Short Course in Human Relations

The six most important words: "I admit I made a mistake."
The five most important words: "You did a good job."
The four most important words: "What is your opinion?"
The three most important words: "If you please."
The two most important words: "Thank you."
The least important word: "I."

From *Young at Heart Club News*,
published by Milwaukee ILGWU retirees.

Index

363